30-

OLD TEXTBOOKS

Left: Wooden Hornbook, over 300 years old—no J or U.

Right: "St. Pauls 1729" engraved on back of this pewter Hornbook.

ii

OLD
TEXTBOOKS

SPELLING, GRAMMAR, READING, ARITHMETIC, GEOGRAPHY, AMERICAN HISTORY, CIVIL GOVERNMENT, PHYSIOLOGY, PENMANSHIP, ART, MUSIC—AS TAUGHT IN THE COMMON SCHOOLS FROM COLONIAL DAYS TO 1900.

JOHN A. NIETZ

EMERITUS PROFESSOR OF EDUCATION
UNIVERSITY OF PITTSBURGH

UNIVERSITY OF PITTSBURGH PRESS

Library of Congress Catalog Card Number: 60-13851

© 1961, University of Pittsburgh Press

Printed in the United States of America

By American Book–Stratford Press, Inc.

PREFACE

Soon after the writer began teaching graduate courses in the history of education he realized that to determine what was really taught in the schools of the past one would have to know what was in the textbooks used in the past. So he became interested in collecting old textbooks. Inevitably it would be difficult to get textbooks from many countries, so he tried to gather as complete a collection as reasonably possible of texts published in America. However, he also collected many European books which found their way to America or were reprinted here.

This collection now contains more than 8,000 volumes published before 1900. Roughly it contains about 340 spellers, 850 readers, 400 grammars, 325 geographies, 250 American histories, 170 social science books, 120 physiologies, and fewer in other elementary school subjects. The remainder are rare professional books, and old secondary school textbooks.

During the years more than thirty doctoral dissertations at the University of Pittsburgh have been devoted to an analysis of old textbooks in various fields. In every instance the writers of these used not only the relevant texts in the Nietz Collection, but also those in other appropriate libraries, such as the Library of Congress, the Plimpton and the Smith Collections at Columbia

University, the New York City Public Library, the Harvard Library, the Antiquarian Society Library at Worcester, Massachusetts, and many others. Thus the findings in these studies in the several fields reflect the nature of the content of old American school textbooks. Ample use has been made of the findings of these studies in the writing of this book. Use has also been made of studies known to the writer made elsewhere.

Obviously every one who can read has studied some textbooks. If at all interested in them such persons may also want to know how these compare with the textbooks of other periods. Thus most literate persons may find it both interesting and profitable to read about the textbooks of the past and how they have changed from time to time.

A more technical and professional use may be made of this book by all interested in the history of education. If not used as a basic textbook for a course, it surely may be most profitably used as a supplementary reference book by all students studying the history of education.

Every American, which we mean to apply to those living in that part of the Americas now known as the United States, ought to understand something about the past struggles and development of our evolving civilization. Those who greatly helped mold the beginnings and the continuing development of our American civilization were the products of the schools of the past. The study of the textbooks in those schools certainly greatly influenced their thinking and ideals. Thus an understanding of the textbooks of the past should throw considerable light upon the evolution of our culture and civilization. Certainly the McGuffey *Readers* did much to mold the character of the culture and ideals of the Middle West for more than a half century.

* * * * *

The writer is keenly aware that in dealing with thousands of textbooks of the past it is easy to commit errors of statement. Such errors may relate to the dates of their first publication, whether or not the nature and characteristics of certain textbooks were the first to have them and whether or not particular books were the first to appear in a certain field. For example, what

Reader first contained pictures or first contained colored pictures; or whose was the first American textbook in spelling, reading, geography, arithmetic, grammar, history, civil government, physiology, penmanship, music, and art? The writer merely claims that he has attempted to be as accurate in his statements as research known to him warrants.

The writer acknowledges his debt to many persons and libraries. He is grateful to his colleagues and library staff at the University of Pittsburgh for their encouragement and cooperation in the development of the collection and in the pursuance of the many studies involving the textbooks; to the thousands of students in his history of education classes who manifested interest in the old textbooks, and in many cases contributed old books to the collection; to the many other librarians who generously aided the students carrying on researches of the old textbooks; to the editors of professional journals who published articles relating to old textbook studies; and to news reporters who helped publicize the collection, which in turn resulted in obtaining additional books. He is also grateful to his wife, Florence, and to a number of colleagues for having read certain chapters in manuscript form and made helpful suggestions. Acknowledgment is made of the help and cooperation of Mr. Thomas Jarrett, University Photographer, who prepared the pictures appearing in the book, and to Mrs. Agnes Starrett, Editor of the University of Pittsburgh Press, for her constant encouragement and editorial assistance.

JOHN A. NIETZ

Pittsburgh, Pa.
November 1, 1960

CONTENTS

CHAPTER 1

OLD TEXTBOOKS—
A HISTORY OF EDUCATION

A N analysis of the school textbooks used in the past reveals a truer history of what was taught in the earliest schools than does a study of past educational theories alone. This is particularly true for the early American schools. The teachers in the early days of our country were so meagerly trained and educated that they depended strongly on the textbooks for what to teach and how to teach. Most authorities agree that in the United States the old textbooks in use in any particular school largely constituted the school's course of study. And so an analysis of old American school textbooks reflects the evolution of the American school curriculum and the teaching and learning methods.

My study attempts to show only the development of the so-called "Common School" subjects. The Common School was the term applied to the schools first established at various dates in the different states of the Union for all children—the schools now known as the Elementary Schools. A full chapter is devoted to each of the following: spelling, reading, grammar, arithmetic, geography, American history, civics, and physiology; and the final chapter is on penmanship, art, and music. The author hopes that his second book will present the evolution of the important secondary school textbooks.

I have made a serious attempt to present as true a picture as reasonably possible of the changing nature of American "Common School" textbooks published before 1900. Two reasons may be given for selecting the terminal date: (1) Most persons reading this book will be more or less versant with the more recent textbooks; and (2) the scientific influence on American education began about 1900, causing the textbooks to change markedly after that date.

CHANGING CHARACTERISTICS

Size. In most subject fields, the older the textbooks the smaller they were, particularly those used in the elementary level. This is objectively shown for the texts in several fields in Table I.

TABLE I

A COMPARISON IN THE SIZE OF OLD AND RECENT
TEXTBOOKS IN SEVERAL FIELDS.

Field	Period	Books	Average Pages
Geography:			
Old	1784-1895	134	211
Recent:			
Ele.	Since 1895	24	253
Jr. H.S.	Since 1895	54	309
American History:			
Old	1795-1885	54	295
Recent	Since 1885	28	639
Civics:			
Old	1789-1889	70	210
Recent	Since 1889	33	566
Physiology:			
Old	19th Century	62	242
Recent	1900-1940	19	286

The older books not only contained fewer pages, but commonly the pages were much smaller. For example, the pages of many of the earliest editions of the *New England Primer* were 3¼ by 4½ inches in size. The pages of the *Elements of Geography* (1796) by Jedidiah Morse were 3 by 4¾ inches. Nearly all very early geography textbooks were small and contained only a few folded maps, if any at all. However, by the 1880's geographies became very large, even larger than they are at present and contained large maps.

Bindings and Paper. In general, the bindings of the books intended for elementary children were very different from those for secondary school youth. For example, most editions of the *New England Primer* were bound either in rather limp paper covers or with very thin wooden boards covered with paper. On the other hand, most Latin and Greek grammars were bound in leather. A few were bound with homespun linen over stiff board covers. In many the leather covered very thin wooden boards.

Most of the earliest spellers were bound either in stiff paper cardboard with leather spines or in full leather. The later spellers were commonly bound in stiff paper cardboard covers and cloth spines. Leather bound books on the elementary level were rare after 1800. However, the texts for the upper grades and secondary schools often continued to appear bound in leather until about 1850.

Nearly all old textbooks were printed on rag paper. Thus the paper in texts over 400 years old is commonly still in rather good condition. More recent texts commonly are printed on less durable pulp paper which ultimately disintegrates. Thus further textbooks collectors may find textbooks difficult to preserve.

Print and Pictures. In general, old textbooks were printed in much smaller type than the later ones. Two of the oldest readers written in America were by Noah Webster and Caleb Bingham. Webster's book was printed with 9 point type and Bingham's with 8 point. McGuffey's *Primer* (1849), as well as most other primers of that period, was printed with 12 point type. Commonly, recent primers are printed with 18 or 24 point type. Incidentally, the first edition of Webster's *Compendious Dictionary* (1806) was printed with 3 point type. It is evident that printers in those early days knew little of visual hygiene.

Very few textbooks before the 1830's contained pictures, other than the pictures illustrating the letters of the alphabet, as was done in the *New England Primer* and some early spellers. Then

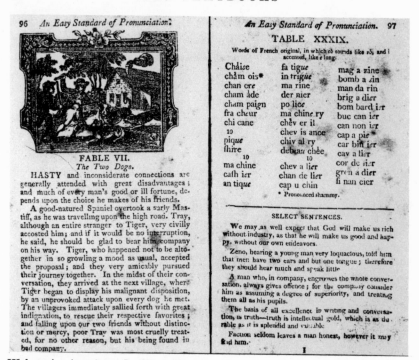

Webster's *American Spelling Book,* 1809, shows how reading and spelling were a unit.

in the 1830's, when the textbooks in several fields began to appear in series, usually only the lower ones would contain pictures. One author was a marked exception; namely, Peter Parley (S. G. Goodrich). He wrote textbooks in a number of fields in the 1830's and 40's, and nearly all of them contained many pictures. Some authors, particularly in history and geography, included a considerable number of horror pictures. Beginning in the 1850's the physiology textbooks began to have more pictures than was true in other fields. Calvin Cutter's *Physiology* in 1852 contained more than 150 engravings. Other physiologies soon followed a similar practice. Some even included colored pictures much earlier than was true in other fields, particularly showing the blood vessels and other physical characteristics. Colored pictures did not appear commonly in readers or in other textbooks until the 1890's.

Directions for Teaching. Since the early American teachers were very poorly prepared for teaching, it was rather common for textbook authors to include teaching suggestions in their books. It must be kept in mind that the earliest popular pedagogical textbook, *Lectures on Schoolkeeping,* by Samuel Read Hall, was not published until 1829; and that the first public normal school, at Lexington, Massachusetts, did not open until 1839. So many early textbooks contained rather extensive and detailed directions for teaching the subject or using the text. In some instances these reflected peculiar whims of the authors.

The directions were presented in several ways or places. Most commonly they appeared in the preface, the introduction, or in a section addressed "To the Teacher." In some instances, and particularly in arithmetic books, the helps were presented in the back of the book. In some arithmetic books approaches for the solution of the problems even appeared in the back.

Where the skills were to be taught by a particular system, such as in penmanship, art, and music, many pages of detailed teaching instructions were common. In fact, in art and penmanship entire teachers' manuals of instructions were common. In music these instructions were usually very detailed and technical. Even in a geography textbook by Cummins in 1818, fourteen and one-half pages were devoted to teaching suggestions.

Learning and Teaching Aids in Textbooks. There have been marked changes in the practice of including learning and teaching aids in textbooks. With time there has been a steady increase in their inclusion. Table II shows how many textbooks in certain subject fields included them. Unfortunately it would require a too extensive and complex table to show how the earliest textbooks differed from the later ones in this regard. However, a detailed analysis of the studies from which this table is constructed would show that the earliest books rather commonly would contain only either a preface or an introduction or both, and sometimes a table of contents and an appendix. Early grammars and geographies rarely contained even a table of contents. Indexes and references were not too common until the latter half of the nineteenth century. Except for the very earliest

TABLE II[1]

NUMBER OF OLD TEXTBOOKS CONTAINING CERTAIN
LISTED LEARNING AND TEACHING AIDS.

Aids	76 Grmrs. Before 1850	49 Geog. 1784-1845	97 Geog. 1840-1890	54 Am. Hist. 1795-1885	87 Jr. H.S. Am. Hist. 1886-1954	70 Civics 1793-1890	62 Physiology 1800-1900	Per Cent
Preface	71	41	84	47	53	66	59	85.8
Introduction	21	22	37	26	28	18	23	35.3
Table of Contents	27	20	48	44	86	57	61	69.3
Questions	32	36	90	36	77	44	52	74.1
Notes		26	61	19		32	52	57.2
Summaries		10	3	10	47		15	21.2
Illustrations	2	17	81	38		4	57	49.6
Tables		33	63	15	74	16	23	59.6
Maps		31	80	22	87			76.6
References		11	16	10	72	12	26	35.1
Index	6	5	11	17	83	47	38	41.8
Glossary		6	34	4		6	31	24.4
Appendix	29	16	48	29	86	51	25	57.4
Pictures		21	88	39	86		57	83.4

[1] The authors of the studies used in this table will be referred to in detail in the appropriate subsequent chapters.

books, some sort of visual aid—an illustration, picture, table, chart, graph, or map—was rather commonly included, although often only a few. The use of colored pictures was rare until just before 1900. Notes and glossaries never became common. The use of questions was not universal, but the practice was somewhat constant throughout in all fields. Not only did the later textbooks include more learning aids, but these aids improved in form and usefulness.

SOME PECULIARITIES

Printers and Publishers. The earliest American textbooks were not printed by one particular publishing house, as is common today. The absence of early copyright laws, railroads, good roads, and efficient mail service, prevented large scale publishing by particular firms. Thus the earliest books were produced by local printing shops. In the early colonial period the Boston area printed most textbooks. Later, possibly partly due to Franklin's influence, Philadelphia led in book production. Eventually New York City took the lead.

Before copyright laws became effective, local printing shops were not only the printers of books, but also the sellers of them. Any printer could secure a copy of a popular book and reprint it for local sale. In many cases more than one local printer would reprint the same book in the same town. For example, the 36 different copies of Lindlay Murray's *Readers* of different dates and titles in the writer's collection were printed by 22 different printing shops, nine of them in Philadelphia. To prevent this practice Noah Webster attempted to get the federal government to pass an early copyright law. Since he failed in this, he succeeded in getting a number of states to enact such laws. Thus he was able to collect royalties from the local printers in the states reprinting his books. These royalties aided his family to live while he was writing his dictionary. It was not until after the development of railroads that large publishing houses developed which were to sell and deliver books over the nation.

Advertisements in Textbooks. Even before 1800 a number of textbooks began to contain advertisements listing textbooks in other subject fields for sale by the same printer. In the beginning only a few printers did this. For example, in the different editions of the Murray *Readers* only a few of the printers included advertisements. But beginning in the 1830's this practice became more common, and for several decades after 1850 most of them did.

The 1853 edition of Murray's *English Exercises* printed by a Philadelphia firm contained 25 pages listing textbooks for sale, together with signed recommendations for them. In 1872 Martindale's *Human Anatomy, Physiology, and Hygiene* included 14 pages of advertisements. This practice lessened after 1880.

Testimonials and Recommendations. Even more common than the practice of including advertisements in textbooks, the earliest ones contained recommendations for the text in which they appeared. Usually these were written by very prominent persons. For example, Nicolas Pike, before he published his *Arithmetic* in 1788, secured recommendations from four college presidents and from Benjamin West to be printed in the book. Daboll's *Arithmetic* (1802) included recommendations by Noah Webster, John Adams, and several others.

The prize example of including numerous endorsements was in John Jenkins' *The Art of Writing* in 1813. It contained endorsements by 220 persons and recommendations by 109. However, it should be stated that the signatures of many of these appeared in groups. Many were signatures of very famous Americans. For Pittsburghers it may be interesting to know that one of the editions of Joseph Stockton's *Western Calculator,* which was first printed in Pittsburgh in 1819, contained 25 individually prepared recommendations in the back of the book. Among them were Western Pennsylvania's most prominent persons of that day, chiefly ministers, lawyers, and teachers. Sanders' *Spelling Book* (1838) contained recommendations or endorsements by 55 persons.

Interestingly, as the practice of including advertisements in textbooks increased during the middle of the nineteenth century, the practice of including recommendations and endorsements decreased. No doubt, this was true because of the development of large publishing firms. In most cases the advertisements would include a description of the purposes and merits of their books, making separate recommendations less essential.

Great Variation in Content. The content of old textbooks in most fields during any particular time varied more than is common today. Evidently the chief reason was the absence of the existence of professional societies or organizations, such as the American Historical Society, American Mathematical Society, and so on, which now more or less help determine the content of the textbooks in the respective subject fields. Before the organization of these societies each author could largely determine what his text would include and what omit. So individual whims and interests of the authors greatly determined the nature of the textbooks. In other words, the authors could be more independent.

Long Titles of Textbooks. A large fraction of America's earliest textbooks had very long titles. These titles often involved both the purpose and a description of the book. One marked example of this practice was Noah Webster's Reader. Its full title was,

An American Selection of Lessons in Reading and Speaking Calculated to Improve the Minds and Refine the Taste of Youth. And Also to Instruct Them in the Geography, History, and Politics of the United States. To Which Are Prefixed, Rules in Elocution, and Directions for Expressing the Principal Passions of the Mind. Being the Third Part of the Grammatical Institute of the English Language.

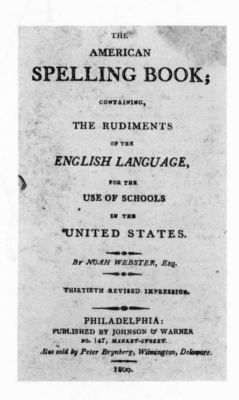

THE
AMERICAN
SPELLING BOOK;

CONTAINING,

THE RUDIMENTS

OF THE

ENGLISH LANGUAGE,

FOR THE

USE OF SCHOOLS

IN THE

UNITED STATES.

By NOAH WEBSTER, Esq.

THIRTIETH REVISED IMPRESSION.

PHILADELPHIA:
PUBLISHED BY JOHNSON & WARNER
NO. 147, MARKET-STREET.
Also sold by Peter Brynberg, Wilmington, Delaware.

1809.

Title Page of Noah Webster Blueback *Speller,* revision of original 1783 edition—millions were used.

CHAPTER 2

———————◦∞◦———————

SPELLERS

OMNIBUS TEXTBOOKS

THE books from which the colonial children in America learned to spell were very different from spellers of today. In fact, when the earliest American schools were opened in Massachusetts and Connecticut, there were no regular spelling books. Apparently, whatever words the children learned to spell in school were from the *New England Primer*. An examination of more than a dozen different editions of the *Primer* reveals that nearly all of them contained word lists to be spelled. One of the most popular editions began with the alphabet; followed by 180 syllables, as ab, ac, ad; ba, ca, da; etc. These were followed by a list of 84 words of one syllable such as age, all, ape, are; 48 words of two syllables, as absent, abhor, apron; 24 words of three syllables, as abusing, amending, argument; 21 words of four syllables, as a-bi-li-ty, af-fec-ti-on; 14 words of five syllables, as a-bo-mi-na-ble, ad-mi-ra-ti-on; and 12 words of six syllables, as a-bo-mi-na-ti-on, gra-ti-fi-ca-ti-on. Peculiar syllabication of the longer words may be noted.

The next spelling books were those brought by the colonists from England. These, too, were not entirely devoted to spelling. One of the earliest, if not the earliest, was Thomas Dilworth's *Spelling Book, or New Guide*, published in England in 1740. It

American printing of Dilworth's text, first published in England, 1740.

included grammar, English substantives, etc., in addition to spelling. This book was later revised and published by Dilworth under the title of *A New Guide to the English Tongue*, which became very popular in England, Ireland, and the English colonies. Later it was reprinted by numerous printers in America and gained wide circulation. It consists of five parts, and really meant to constitute the entire elementary school curriculum. Much of its content was a correlation or mixture of reading material, *spelling*, grammar, and religious content. Of the 146 pages in a fine edition printed in Carlisle, Pennsylvania, in 1801, 41 pages were definitely spelling, and many other pages were a mixture of reading and spelling.

In 1767 Daniel Fenning published the *Universal Spelling Book* in London. It was reprinted in Boston in 1767, and in New

York in 1787. However, it never attained the popularity of the Dilworth books.

George Fox, founder of the Quakers, in 1769 published in England a book entitled, *Instructions for Right Spelling and Plain Directions for Reading and Writing True English*. This like the others was an omnibus book dealing with different aspects of English. No doubt, some copies of this book were brought to America by the Quakers.

Of the spellers first published in England, the one that had most usage in America, next to Dilworth's, was written in 1780 by William Perry, a lecturer in the Academy of Edinburgh. To counteract the influence of Dilworth's *A New Guide to the English Tongue*, Perry entitled his speller, *The Only Sure Guide to The English Tongue, or New Pronouncing Spelling Book*. It was more specifically a spelling book than was Dilworth's. The famous colonial printer, Isaiah Thomas, reprinted several editions of this speller in Worcester, Massachusetts. The sixth edition contained 91 pages of words, carefully syllabified and marked for pronunciation. These matters received marked attention in Perry's *Speller*, since he was also the author of *The Royal Standard English Dictionary*, which was also first published in England. The sixth edition contained 17 pages of "Moral Tales and Fables"; 39 pages of grammar; and 33 pages of appendix material, consisting of miscellaneous contents; plus a rather extensive list of words with definitions diacritically marked.

Kneeland's *Instructor*, 1762, spelling and reading taught together.

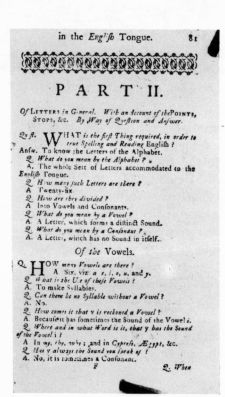

The last specific speller to be mentioned among the English authors is one by Lindley Murray. In fact, Murray was born and educated in America, but after a rather successful business career moved to England in 1784. There after teaching for some time, he became one of the most successful textbook writers in both England and United States. His English readers and grammars were the most widely used in the United States during our early national period. After writing the grammar and readers, he published the *English Spelling Book with Reading Lessons* in 1804. It was meant to be used by beginners and to precede his *English Reader*. Although it was reprinted in New York in 1823, it never became popular here.

Apparently there were other books published in England containing spelling lessons, but not reaching much circulation in America. Evidence of this appears in the oldest speller printed in America in the writer's collection. It is, *The Youth's Instructor in the English Tongue: or, The Art of Spelling Improved*. It was printed in Boston by D. and J. Kneeland in 1762 for M. Dennis. A statement on the title page states that it was "Collected from Dixon, Bailey, Owen, Strong, and Watts." Evidently the books of the five authors mentioned were used from which the contents of this book were collected. Like books heretofore discussed, it was more than a speller. Part I of 80 pages was a mixture of spelling and moral lessons in reading. The syllabication of many of the words seems strange to us today, for example, spi-ri-tu-a-li-ty and ple-ni-po-ten-ti-a-ry. Part II of 23 pages was in catechetical form dealing mainly with matters of orthography, grammar, and religion. For example: "Q. How do you pronounce the Consonant c? A. Sometimes hard like k, sometimes soft like s." Part III of 46 pages covered "Rules in Arithmetic, with Forms of Bills, Bonds, Releases," etc. However, 22 of the 46 pages dealt with the Bible and other religious content.

The earliest speller printed in America seems to have been written by Stephen Daye. He was the first to set up a printing press in America, and in 1639 published the first book printed here, *The Freeman's Oath*. The Dunster Mss. in Harvard Library list the books printed by Daye. Between *Capital Lawes* (1642) and Winthrope *Declaration* (1645) there is listed *A Spelling Book*.

So about in 1643 the first American book in spelling was published. The lack of the existence of known copies of it indicates that its influence must have been small.

Thus it can be seen that the children of the American colonies largely learned spelling either from books originally written in England or from books mainly copied from them, even though they were printed here. Too, none of these books were solely spellers. Usually they were a mixture of spelling, reading, grammar, religion, and even arithmetic. In other words, they could be characterized as books of *correlated or integrated English.*

WEBSTER'S BLUE-BACKED SPELLERS

Noah Webster (1754-1843) was America's first prolific textbook writer. In all, he was a teacher, lawyer, popular lecturer, lobbyist, and lexicographer. As an author he wrote a grammar, and American history, readers, two dictionaries, and numerous patriotic and civic materials, in addition to the spellers.

In referring to the reason for writing his first so-called speller, Webster wrote, "I kept a classical school at Goshen, N.Y. (in 1782). The country was impoverished, intercourse with Great Britain was interrupted, and school books were scarce and hardly attainable, . . ." In addition to the desire to meet a need, he possessed an even greater urge; namely, to write textbooks that would be American rather than English. He was a great American patriot. He believed that America should proclaim a Declaration of Independence culturally and academically as well as politically.

Originally he planned to entitle his first book, *The American Instructor*, which was to be similar to its English predecessors, a combination of speller, reader, and grammar, but with American word lists and illustrations rather than British. However, on the advice of Dr. Ezra Stiles, President of Yale, he adopted a more classical title. Since Webster planned to write several textbooks, a general title was given the series, with a specific subtitle for each book. The title became, *A Grammatical Institute of The English Language, Comprising an Easy, Concise, and*

Systematic Method of Education, Designed for The Use of English Schools in America. Part I Containing a New and Accurate Standard of Pronunciation. Part II became an English *Grammar*, and Part III *An American Selection of Lessons in Reading and Speaking.* Part I has commonly been accepted to be the speller, although that word does not appear in the title, which had also been true of some of its English predecessors. It was first published in Hartford in 1783.

Since there was no federal copyright law when he planned this series, and even before the speller was completed, Webster began to tour the states to secure state copyright laws to protect his forthcoming publications. Eventually he succeeded in getting such protection in most of the populous states. The royalties he thus obtained helped maintain him and his family while he was writing his dictionaries, which were published in 1806 and 1828.

It may be noted that the subtitle of Part I apparently did not stress spelling, but rather pronunciation, although it has been commonly mentioned in the history of education as a *Speller.* In the main, Webster's 1783 edition was strongly patterned after the two English books fairly popular in America; namely, Dilworth's and Fenning's. However, certain internal changes were made. First, Dilworth's lists of English place names and abbreviations were replaced by American names. Next, much of Dilworth's religious content was replaced by precepts of The Poor Richard (Franklin's) type. Thirdly, Webster changed the syllabication of many words in harmony with the developing American ways of pronouncing words. The suffixes of words ending with ti-on, si-on, and ci-on were changed to be pronounced as one syllable rather than two. Also, such words as clu-ster, ha-bit, etc., were changed to clus-ter and hab-it.

Soon Webster became aware that the long classical title of his books was not well accepted, so in 1787 he changed the title of Part I (the *Speller*) to *The American Spelling Book.* In spite of the Dilworth and Perry followers, this edition became very popular. One edition published in Philadelphia in 1809 is the "Thirtieth Revised Impression," and a footnote mentions that over 3,000,000 copies had already been sold. The 1816 edition is the "Nintieth Revised Impression." These editions include 168 pages of content. The first 150 pages consist mainly of spelling with brief moral reading selections interspersed. These editions end with "A Moral Catechism" of questions and answers on such matters as humility, mercy, peace-making, purity of heart, anger, revenge, justice, generosity, gratitude, and truth. "The Moral Catechism" evidently was included as a substitute for the Puritan "Catechism" of the *New England Primer*. Webster believed that only non-sectarian teaching should be given in a country not having a state religion.

In 1829 a new revised edition appeared as *The Elementary Spelling Book; being an Improvement on The American Spelling Book*. There were several urgent reasons for making this change. The two earlier *Spellers* were largely the total primary school curriculum, consisting of spelling, reading, elements of grammar, and moral lessons. By the late 1820's separate textbooks in these basic fields had appeared. So it became logical for so-called spellers to be only spellers. This was true of the new 1829 edition. All except a few pages consist of spelling words and their use in sentences. A second reason was because his large *American Dictionary* was published in 1828. So the rules governing the spelling, syllabication, and pronunciation needed revision to be in full accord with the Dictionary. The purpose was to render "its orthography more simple, regular, and uniform, and by removing difficulties arising from anomalies."

The Elementary Spelling Book became the most popular speller in the United States. As late as the 1866 edition, the outside cover included the statement, "more than 1,000,000 copies of this work are sold annually." In fact, it was still being published at the end of the nineteenth century. It is claimed that approximately 100,000,000 copies of the Webster *Spellers* were sold.

But why did *The Elementary Spelling Book* remain so popular? Of course, by 1829 the Webster name bore great prestige. In addition, however, it was well prepared. The lessons were numbered and were presented in logical sequence. For example, after several pages of syllables using the different vowel sounds, the spelling words sequentially appear according to length and vowel sounds, and often with the words used in sentences. In sequence, first appear words of three letters with the short sound of the vowels, then words of four letters and long vowel sounds. These are followed by words of two syllables beginning with short vowels and changing to long vowels. Thus a logical sequence follows throughout the book, ending with words of many letters, syllables, and sounds. However, the arrangement is more logical and psychological, and the principle of future word usage is greatly ignored. For example, there are such words as, ar mig er ous, o le ag in ous, ne o ter ic, and so cin i an ism.

Although the Webster *Spellers* have been popularly referred to as "Blue-Backed," yet that description was not universally true. The color of the books was determined by the printers. The twenty-five different copies in the writer's collection were printed by seventeen different printers. Most of these have blue covers, but some are brown, gray, green, and even leather covered.

OTHER EARLY SPELLERS

Soon after Webster's first *Speller* was printed, a virtual epidemic of spellers appeared. In addition to the 1762 American text, heretofore discussed, several others were published before 1800, and many more soon after. Caleb Bingham, a school master in Boston, wrote *The Child's Companion, being an Easy and Concise Reading and Spelling Book in 1792.* Like its predecessors, it too contained numerous reading selections, and some grammar. This book later was reprinted in numerous editions.

In 1795 *The New, American Spelling-Book* by John Peirce was published in Philadelphia. Apparently this book was fairly well received, since its 1808 printing was the Sixth Revised Edition. It consisted of three parts: Part I contained tables of common words, Part II dealt with the meanings of words as well as their spelling, and Part III was "A Practical English Grammar."

In 1798 a book was printed for Mathew Carey in Philadelphia entitled *The Columbian Spelling Book, or an Easy or Alluring-Guide to Spelling and Reading.* The long title aimed to describe both the purpose and the content of the book. To illustrate some of the moral stories several pictures were presented. This was not commonly true of the earlier spellers. In 1799 Caleb Alexander's *The Young Ladies' and Gentlemen's Spelling Book* appeared. It also contained reading, fables, and moral sentences.

Immediately after 1800 new spellers appeared in frequent succession. *The Definition Spelling Book* by Abner Kneeland was published in 1802. Later editions added the word *American* to the title. This book was really a cross between a speller and a dictionary. According to the title page, "The words are not only rationally divided into syllables, accurately accented, the various sounds of vowels represented by figures, and their parts of speech properly distinguished, but the definition or signification affixed to each word." The lists of words were somewhat classified according to their characteristics.

In 1803 Fiske's *The New England Spelling-book* was printed in Brookfield, Massachusetts. In addition to spelling and moral lessons, it contained the U.S. Constitution, Declaration of Independence, and Washington's Farewell Address.

Fiske's book was followed by several different spellers written by A. Picket. *The Union Spelling-Book* printed in New York in 1805 was already the third edition. The first 112 pages contained nearly 3,000 spelling words and reading lessons. The remaining 44 pages contained numbers, punctuation rules, abbreviations, and more than 300 words with their meanings. A second one was *The Juvenile Spelling-Book*. This one in turn was followed by a much larger and more advanced book entitled, *The Juvenile Expositor, or Sequel to the Common Spelling-Book*. The first 198 pages were a composite of words, reading, and dictionary of word meanings. The next 157 pages constituted an abridgment of Murray's *English Grammar*. All of these books appeared in several editions. The pronunciation rules followed those of Walker's *Dictionary*. Incidentally, later in life Fiske went west and helped found The Western Literary Institute and College of Professional Teachers in Cincinnati. This organization did much to advance and improve education in the Ohio Valley.

In 1809 *The United States Spelling-Book* was published in Pittsburgh. Its authorship was by "Sundry Experienced Teachers." It has been said that this was the first textbook to be both

THE
UNITED STATES'
SPELLING BOOK,

WITH APPROPRIATE

READING LESSONS:

BEING AN EASY STANDARD

FOR SPELLING, READING AND PRONOUNCING THE
ENGLISH LANGUAGE,

ACCORDING TO THE RULES ESTABLISHED BY JOHN
WALKER, IN HIS CRITICAL AND PRO-
NOUNCING DICTIONARY.

BY SUNDRY EXPERIENCED TEACHERS.

Where now the thorn or tangled thicket grows,
The wilderness shall blossom as the rose.——*Humphreys.*

NINETEENTH EDITION.

PITTSBURGH,

PRINTED AND PUBLISHED BY CRAMER AND SPEAR,
AT THE FRANKLIN HEAD BOOKSTORE,
WOOD STREET.

1821.

Probably first textbook published west of the Alleghenies, 1809.

written and printed west of the Allegheny Mountains. Its contents apparently constituted the total elementary school curriculum for the children of the west, for it included spelling words, reading, lists of words with their meaning, lists of geographical places with an explanation of their locations, lists of proper and Bible names, arithmetic numbers and figures, grammar, and a chronological table of important historical events. This speller went through many reprintings. The 1821 book was the Nineteenth Edition. The title page states that it follows "the rules established by John Walker, in his critical and pronouncing Dictionary." As one examines many of the early spellers it becomes evident that there was keen and even bitter rivalry between those authors who followed the rules of Walker *versus* those of Webster.

In 1812 *An Introduction to Spelling and Reading* by Abner Alden was published. This book was similar to many others, although a little larger, and provided the different kinds of exercises for the "learning of the English language." It followed the dictionaries of Walker and Sheridan. The 1819 printing was the Eighth Edition.

An Improved Spelling Book; or Youth's Literary Guide by Joshua Bradley was published in Windsor, Vermont, in 1815. This book was different from many others in several respects. First, Bradley frankly acknowledged that the "extracts have been taken from Webster, Wood, Picket, Alden, Bingham, Flint, Murray, Hubbard, Fordyce, Walker, the *American Gentleman's Pronouncing Dictionary*, Dr. Johnson, Dr. Morse, and Dr. Blair." It should be noted that not all of the mentioned persons were authors of spellers. A second different feature was that all of the content, other than the spelling words, was presented in catechetical form. Pages 65 to 180 inclusive dealt with many matters, as grammar, punctuation, and "A Short System of Polite Learning," which dealt largely with matters of geography and rhetorical writing. All these matters were treated in question-and-answer form.

For example: *Tutor*—How many kinds of seeds are there?

Pupil—About twenty thousand.

— — — — —

Tutor—Is our language copious?
Pupil—Few languages are more copious than ours.

CHANGES IN SPELLERS

Until just before 1820 nearly all the so-called spellers were more or less similar, in that they were virtually correlated English books. Nearly always the greater part of the book would be a mixture of spelling with reading lessons. Then most of them would include in the latter part of the book matters of grammar, punctuation, and rhetoric. In addition, often numbers, geographical terms, and even historical events would be added in the end of the books.

Then rather suddenly a change took place, and spellers became more fully only spelling books. This no doubt was true because separate textbooks appeared in reading, geography, and grammar. In other words, the so-called speller no longer constituted the major part of the common school curriculum. A few of the old kind continued to appear.

One of the first to be virtually only a speller was *The Pronouncing Spelling Book* by J. A. Cummins in 1819. About 85 per cent of the pages were spelling. Too, pictures accompanied the few reading lessons it contained. The pronunciation of the words was directed by diacritical marks and other symbols. For
$$f \quad \bar{e} \, k$$
example: hī-ē-rō-glȳph-i-căl. The pronunciations were based on Walker's *Dictionary*. Nearly all early spellers ended with long and uncommon words, which likely would never be used by the children after they left school. Words were not selected on the basis of children's needs.

The very next year (1820) the *New American Spelling Book* by Stephen Byerly appeared. It was a revision of the *Pennsylvania Spelling Book*, which had appeared in 1815 and was written by an "Association of Teachers." Apparently Byerly had assisted in writing the earlier book. To overcome the localism of the title of the earlier book, Byerly substituted the word *Ameri-*

128	*Words of Five Syllables,*	*Variously accented.*	129

sŭp-plē-mĕnt'ă-rў	tўp-ō-grăƒ͟h'ĭ-ĕ̆al	ĭ-măğ-ĭn-ā'tͪŏn	mē-tĕmp-sў-ĕ̆hō'sĭs
sўs-tē-măt''ĭ-ĕ̆al	văl-ē-dĭ̆e͛'tĕ̆r-ў	ĭn-âŭ-gū-rā'tͪŏn	nē-gō-ĭ̆ͪĭ-ā'tͪŏn
tặ̆-ĭ-tŭr'nĭ-tў	vēr-să-tĭl'ĭ-tў	ĭn-dĭs-pō-ṣ̌ĭ-tĭ̆'ŏn	pặ̆-pĭl-ĭ̆ō-nā'ĕ̆eoŭs
tâŭ-tō-lŏğ'ĭ-ĕ̆al	ŭn-ă-vŏĭd'ă-blₑ	ĭn-fặt-ᵞū-ā'tͪŏn	ƒ͟hặr-mă-ĕ̆ō-poē'ĭ̄ā
tĕs-tĭ-mō'nĭ-ăl	ᵞū-nĭ-fôr'mĭ-tў	ĭn-tēr-rō-gā'tͪŏn	prē-ĕ̆ĭp-ĭ-tā'tͪŏn
t͟hē-ō-lō'ğĭ-ăn	ᵛū-nĭ-vēr'sĭ-tў	ĭn-vĕs-tĭ-gā'tͪŏn	prō-nŭn-ĕ̆ͪĭ-ā'tͪŏn
t͟hē-ō-lŏğ'ĭ-ĕ̆al	vŏl-ă-tĭl'ĭ-tў	jŭs-tĭ-fĭ-ĕ̆ā'tͪŏn	prŏs-ō-pō-poē'ĭ̄ā
trĭg-ō-nŏm'ē-trў	vŏl-ū-bĭl'ĭ-tў	mặt͟h-ē-mă-tĭ-ĕ̆ĭ'ăn	q̇uặl-ĭ-fĭ-ĕ̆ā'tͪŏn

ăb-brē-vĭ-ā'tͪŏn	ăs-săs-sĭ-nā'tͪŏn	rĕ̆ĕ-ᵉŏm-mĕn-dā'tͪŏn	sŭb-tĭl-ĭ-zā'tͪŏn
ăĕ̆-ᵉă-dē-mĭ-ĕ̆ĭ'ăn	ăs-sō-ᵉĕĭ-ā'tͪŏn	rē-ğĕn-ēr-ā'tͪŏn	sū-pēr-ĭn-tĕnd'ĕnĕ̆e
ăĕ̆-ĕ̆ĕnt-ᵞū-ā'tͪŏn	ĕ̆h͟ăr-ăĕ̆-tē-rĭs'tĭ̆ĕ̆	rē-ĭt-ᵉēr-ā'tͪŏn	sŭp-pŏṣ̌-ĭ-tĭ-tĭ̆'oŭs
ăl-lĭt-ēr-ā'tͪŏn	ĕ̆ĭĕ̆-ă-trĭ-zā'tͪŏn	rē-sŭs-ĕ̆ĭ-tā'tͪŏn	tēr-ğĭ-vēr-sā'tͪŏn
ă-măn-ū-ĕn'sĭs	ĕ̆ĭr-ĕ̆ŭm-lō-ĕ̆ū'tͪŏn	rē-vēr-bĕr-ā'tͪŏn	trăns-fĭg-ū-rā'tͪŏn
ăn-ĭ-măd-vēr'sĭ̆ŏn	ĕ̆ĭv-ĭ-lĭ-zā'tͪŏn	sănĕ̆-tĭ-fĭ-ĕ̆ā'tͪŏn	vēr-sĭ-fĭ-ĕ̆ā'tͪŏn
ăn-nĭ-hĭ-lā'tͪŏn	ĕ̆ŏm-mĭ̄s-ēr-ā'tͪŏn	sō-lĭĕ̆-ĭ-tā'tͪŏn	vĭv-ĭ-fĭ-ĕ̆ā'tͪŏn
ăr-tĭĕ̆-ū-lā'tͪŏn	ĕ̆ŏr-rŏb-ō-rā'tͪŏn	stēr-ē-ō-grăƒ͟h'ĭ̆ĕ̆	vō-ĕ̆ĭf-ēr-ā'tͪŏn

ĕ̆rўs-tăl-lĭ-zā'tͪŏn	ē-măn-ĕ̆ĭ-pā'tͪŏn	ĕ̆ŏn-ĕ̆ĭl'ĭ-ă-tŏr-ў	ĭn-tēr-rŏg''ă-tŏr-ў
dē-nūn-ĕ̆ͪĭ-ā'tͪŏn	ĕn-t͟hū-ᶻͪ͟ĭ-ăs'tĭ̆ĕ̆	ē-jăĕ̆'ū-lā-tŏr-ў	ĭr-rē-ĕ̆ŏv'ēr-ă-blₑ
dₑ-sịd-ē-rā'tŭm	ĕp-ĭ-ĕ̆ū-rē'ăn	prō-pĭ-tͪĭ-ă-tŏr-ў	ĭr-rē-mē'dĭ̆-ă-blₑ
dĭ-ăƒ͟h-ō-rĕt'ĭ̆ĕ̆	ĕᵉх-ăğ-ğē-rā'tͪŏn	rē-vēr'bĕr-ă-tŏr-ў	sū-pēr-nū'mēr-ăr-ў
ĕĕ̆-ĕ̆lĕ-ᶻ ĭ-ăs'tĭ̆ĕ̆	ĕх-pŏst-ᵛū-lā'tͪŏn	t͟hrŏn-ō-lŏğ'ĭ-ĕ̆al-lў	t͟hē-ō-rĕt'ĭ-ĕ̆al-lў
ĕd-ĭ-fĭ-ĕ̆ā'tͪŏn	ğē-ŏm-ē-trĭ-ĕ̆ĭ'ăn	ĕ̆ĭr-ĕ̆ŭm-lŏĕ̆'ū-tō-rў	ăd-mĭ-rā-bĭl''ĭ-tў
ē-jăĕ̆-ū-lā'tͪŏn	ğĕs-tĭĕ̆-ū-lā'tͪŏn	ēle-ē-mŏᶻ'ў-năr-ў	ăn-tē-mē-rĭ'dĭ̆-ăn
ē-lū-ĕ̆ĭ-dā'tͪŏn	hĭ-ē-rō-glўƒ͟h'ĭ̆ĕ̆	ĭn-dē-fặt''ĭ-gă-blₑ	ăn-tĭ-mō-năr'ĕ̆hĭ-ĕ̆aĮ

Cummins' *Pronouncing* speller, 1823.

can, and embellished the title page with a symbol of the American
Eagle. This was solely a speller with only a few partial pages of
reading.

In 1823 *The Critical Pronouncing Spelling-Book* by Hezekiah
Burhans was published. It was more solely a speller than any that
had yet appeared. The keys to the pronunciation of the words
were similar, but simpler, than in Cummins' text.

Cobb's Spellers. Although many of the spellers heretofore mentioned appeared in more than one printing, yet none gave
Webster's books serious competition until Lyman Cobb's *Spellers*

were published. The Nietz Collection contains twenty different printings or editions of Cobb's *Spellers*. Lyman Cobb (1800-1864) was born and reared in Massachusetts, but most of his educational career was spent in New York State.

His first *Speller* was published about 1821, and it had many faults. In 1825 Cobb's *Spelling Book* appeared as a revised edition. This edition went through many reprintings. In The Preface of the 1825 edition he daringly analyzes the faults of Webster's *American Speller*. The two basic criticisms were that Webster had departed too much from Walker's "principles of Orthography and Orthoepy, which are universally acknowledged to be superiour to any other extant"; and that many matters in Webster's *Speller* were inconsistent with those in his *Dictionary*.

The book began by presenting twelve pages of the "Rudiments of the English Language" in catechetical form. These dealt mainly with letter sounds, of vowels and consonants, diphthongs, combinations, and syllables. Then the remainder of the book, with the exception of a few pages, dealt solely with spelling and matters of pronunciation together with just a few reading lessons mixed in. It contained no pictures. In this regard Cobb stated in his Preface that "it appears to be evident that they are of no advantage." In regard to the paucity of reading lessons, he remarked that "The Author is highly pleased that our schools are furnished with reading books adapted to the capacities of scholars of every age."

The last 40 pages presented words under rather specialized classification according to spelling, pronunciation, or meaning. Page 19 to page 128 presented lists of words by chapters according to their sound and number of syllables. A casual examination of the longest words indicate that they were not as uncommon or as difficult as those in many other spellers of that period. Chapter LVIII presented ten pages of words of the same pronunciation, but of different spelling and definition. For example: "Ail, to pain, to trouble, Ale, a kind of beer." Chapter LIX presented the written and phonetic spelling of words. For example: ewe and you, does and duz. Chapter LX presented words with proper and vulgar pronunciations, such as boil and bile, point and pinte. In the Appendix are many words that were spelled variantly in

Walker's *Dictionaries* as printed in different American cities, and words that were spelled variantly in Webster's *Speller* and his *Dictionary*.

In 1833 Cobb's *Expositor, or Sequel to the Spelling Book*, "containing about 1200 of the most common words of the language" was published. It virtually was a small dictionary of 216 pages.

In 1842 Cobb's *New Spelling Book* appeared. It was a thorough revision of his 1825 *Spelling Book*. In the Preface he stated that the "objects of a Spelling Book should be to aid the pupil in learning to spell, pronounce, and read with ease, accuracy, and precision." In regard to the selection of the words he stated that the *Speller* should "contain most of the common and useful words of the language, properly classed, divided, pronounced, and accepted." Here he recognizes a modern guiding principle in the selection of words for a speller. However, no statement was made as to how he determined which words were common and useful. He divided this book into six parts, as follows: Part I, easy words; Part II, various and peculiar sounds of single vowels and diphthongs; Part III, various and peculiar sounds of consonants; Part IV, verbal distinctions; Part V, lists of proper names; and Part VI, rudiments of the language in catechetical form. Too, Cobb apparently changed his mind regarding the use of pictures, for this book contained over thirty pictures. It retained considerable popularity until after 1850.

Less popular spellers. In 1828 B. D. Emerson's *The National Spelling Book and Pronouncing Tutor* was published. Like most spellers up to that time, except Webster's, its rules of orthography and pronounciation were based on Walker's principles. It eventually appeared in several editions.

The next speller to give Webster and Cobb considerable competition was written by Edward Hazen, entitled, *The Speller and Definer; or Class Book, No. 2* in 1829. It was "designed to answer the purposes of a spelling book, and to supersede the necessity of the use of a dictionary as a class-book." Hazen further stated that it was published "with the avowed object of banishing the Spelling-Book from the schools and the Dictionary also, so far

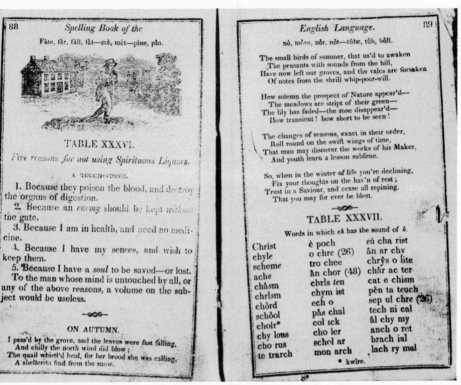

Marshall's speller, 1831, taught morals.

as the latter was used as a class-book to be committed to memory." He apparently was critical of too much stress on memoriter learning. He also wrote the *Symbolical Primer*. Editions of his *Speller* appeared as late as 1856.

In 1830 Samuel Worcester, author of an early graded series of readers, published *A Second Book for Reading and Spelling*, and *A Third Book for Reading and Spelling*. In these two books he attempted specifically to correlate reading and spelling. While this had actually been done in many earlier spellers, yet it had not been so definitely done before. In 1831 he published a *Sequel to The Spelling Book*. This really was a small dictionary, except the words did not appear in a single alphabetical list. Rather they appeared alphabetically under certain headings, as Nouns dealing with animal life, or Verbs, etc.

A number of other spellers were published in the 1820's and early 1830's, which apparently failed to receive wide acceptance. Among them were Israel Alger's revision of Perry's *Speller* (1825); Elihu Marshall's *A Spelling Book of the English Language* (1831), which even contained a set of rules for temperance; Peter Parley's (S. G. Goodrich) *Spelling Book* (1834), which contained many pictures; L. W. Leonard's *The North American Spelling Book* (1835); Samuel Gummere's *The Scholar's Progressive and Etymological Spelling Book* (1836); Bentley's *The Pictorial Spelling Book* (1839); Bumstead's *Spelling and Thinking Combined* (1841); Fowle's *The Common School Speller* (1842); William Russell's *Spelling Book* (1844); Tower's *The Gradual Speller and Complete Enunciator* (1845); James McElligott's *The Young Analyzer, Spelling Book, and Dictionary* (1845); William Swan's *The Spelling Book* (1848); and Ticknor's *Columbian Spelling Book* (1849).

It may be interesting to note that some of the above titles describe the nature and claims of the books. Apparently authors were trying to gain attention and adoptions for their books by doing things differently from other authors. However, getting textbook adoptions is different than attracting readers through unusual titled articles in periodicals or newspapers.

Two other spellers will be mentioned here before going to other later and more popular books. These two were published by religious agencies. The first one was *The Sunday-School Spelling-Book* published by the Episcopal Sunday and Adult-School Society of Philadelphia in 1822. The title page further stated that it was "Compiled with a view as well to teach Children to Spell and Read, as to Contribute to Their Moral and Religious Instruction." It was similar to other much earlier spellers with a religious catechism added.

The other one was *The Union Spelling Book* published by the American Sunday-School Union in 1838, which was an improved edition of the earlier *Union Speller* (1827?). These spellers were exceptions to the tendency for spellers to be rather solely spelling books after the appearance of Cummins' book in 1819. Rather they were like the earlier books containing the various basic elements of learning. The reason for the nature of their content, however, is quite clear. They were for use in Sunday schools, which would meet only once per week instead of daily. These early Sunday schools were usually non-sectarian or inter-denominational, and would meet nearly all day on Sunday. Too, they were most numerous in the states not yet having public schools. In fact, when the American Sunday School Union was formed in 1824 public schools existed only in New England and in New York State. Thus the Sunday schools aimed to provide the elements of a basic education, particularly for the poor, on Sunday. This *Speller* even included several songs with the musical notes, and a map of the western world.

OTHER SPELLERS BEFORE 1850

One of the most prolific spelling book authors was Salem Town (1779-1864). He said that when principal of Granville Academy

20	PARLEY'S SPELLING BOOK.		
WORDS OF FOUR LETTERS.			
Back	jack	pack	sack
band	hand	land	sand
bank	hank	rank	tank
bard	card	hard	yard
beat	feat	meat	seat
bell	dell	sell	tell
bend	lend	mend	send
best	lest	pest	rest
bide	hide	ride	side
bill	fill	hill	kill
bind	find	hind	mind
bite	kite	mite	rite
boat	coat	doat	goat
bold	cold	hold	gold
book	cook	look	took

PARLEY'S SPELLING BOOK.			21
born	corn	horn	morn
both	doth	loth	moth
bows	cows	rows	vows
bray	dray	fray	gray
buck	duck	luck	suck
buff	cuff	muff	puff
bump	hump	lump	rump
bust	dust	must	rust
cake	lake	make	rake
camp	damp	lamp	ramp
cane	dane	lane	mane
cape	gape	rape	tape
cell	fell	well	yell
cold	fold	sold	told
crow	grow	prow	trow
cull	dull	hull	lull

The man has a hat.
The man has a stick.
The man walks.
The man has two feet.
What has the man got in his right hand?
What does the man wear in his hand?

This hen has an egg.
The hen walks.
The hen is on the hay.
The hen has two feet.
Does the hen sing?
Do not throw stones at the hen.
Do not scare her.

Peter Parley speller, 1834, one of the first illustrated.

Union Spelling Book for Sunday School beginners in reading.

from 1807 till 1822 he observed that the scholars had difficulty "in tracing Latin and Greek derivatives to the radical words." So he began collecting and defining "*prefixes and suffixes*, as the modifiers of the significant import of radical words." This work resulted in Town's *Analysis of Words* in 1835. This book gained wide usage. The next year his *Spelling and Defining Book; Being an Introduction to Town's Analysis* appeared. The 1840 printing of this book was the Eighty-Third Edition. This *Speller* was a rather conventional speller with some attention given to analysis of the more common prefixes and suffixes. These two books were followed by his *Speller and Definer* in 1847; the *Progressive Speller* by Town and Holbrook in 1859; and Town's *New Speller and Definer* in 1863, which continued in print as late as 1890.

Two other spellers, later to attain considerable popularity, were published in 1838. One was *The Eclectic Progressive Spelling Book* by A. H. McGuffey, brother of the famous William McGuffey, the original author of the famous Readers. Except for a few pages it was completely a speller. Instead of following the pronunciation principles of Walker, which were followed by most authors of spellers up to that time, McGuffey followed those of Webster, as most later authors did.

McGuffey's *Speller* contained only a few pictures and a few very brief reading lessons, but its peculiar feature was the system used for the pronunciation of the vowels in words with aid of Arabic numerals. The "Table of Vowel Sounds" stated that "A" has four sounds, as follows: $\overset{1}{\text{fate}}$, $\overset{2}{\text{far}}$, $\overset{3}{\text{fall}}$, and $\overset{4}{\text{fat}}$; "E" two sounds, as $\overset{1}{\text{me}}$, $\overset{2}{\text{met}}$; "I" two sounds, as $\overset{1}{\text{pine}}$, $\overset{2}{\text{pin}}$; "O" four sounds, as $\overset{1}{\text{no}}$, $\overset{2}{\text{move}}$, $\overset{3}{\text{not}}$, $\overset{4}{\text{good}}$; and "U" three sounds, as $\overset{1}{\text{tube}}$, $\overset{2}{\text{tub}}$, $\overset{3}{\text{full}}$. Then in the body of the book the words were presented in lists of similar vowel sounds and number of syllables. For example:

4	2	4	2
nav	i	ga	ble
prac	ti	ca	ble
hab	it	a	ble
lap	id	a	ry
ac	cu	ra	cy

Otherwise this *Speller* was similar to contemporary spellers.

In 1846 it was slightly revised by lengthening some of the reading selections with accompanying pictures, and introducing "as many *primitive* words as the space would allow, and then, in subsequent lessons, illustrating by examples and rules the formation of the more important *derivatives*." It was copyrighted again in 1865 with only a few minor changes.

In 1879 a major revision of the McGuffey *Speller* was made by W. B. Watkins, D.D., whom the publishers employed. The numeral system indicating vowel sounds was dropped in favor

...STIONS TO TEACHERS.

...method of distinguishing vowel sounds ...es placed at the top of the column has ...en adopted in this book, it is important that the pupil should be *perfectly familiar* with the several sounds which the figures indicate. To facilitate the acquisition of this familiarity, the table of sounds has been placed at the head of each page. But it is recommended that the pupil be so practised, as to enable him to tell, without hesitation, what figures should be placed over any word which the teacher may pronounce; and this before he is permitted to advance far in the Speller.

As the object of a Spelling Book is to aid the pupil in learning to spell, pronounce and read with accuracy and precision, the author has thought fit to add an appendix, containing some of the most obvious and important principles of orthoepy, to which the attention of the teacher is particularly directed.

The Speller seems to be the proper book to contain such exercises; as the foundation of all the mumbling and indistinctness which characterize the reading of children, is laid whilst learning to spell, and in his first efforts is to read.

[Eclectic School Ser...

THE

ECLECTIC

PROGRESSIVE SPELLING BOOK,

ON AN IMPROVED PLAN:

SHOWING THE EXACT SOUND OF EACH SYLLABLE,

ACCORDING TO THE MOST APPROVED

PRINCIPLES OF

ENGLISH ORTHOEPY.

DESIGNED TO PRECEDE

THE ECLECTIC READERS.

BY A. H. McGUFFEY.

CINCINNATI:
PUBLISHED BY TRUMAN & SMITH.

1838.
[PRICE 19 CENTS.]

McGuffey's *Speller,* 1838, price 19 cents, to precede the Readers.

of the use of diacritical marks. The number of reading selections was decreased, and many more difficult words introduced, particularly some derived from foreign languages. One needs to raise the question why the children should be expected to learn to spell so many rare words when they would never or rarely use them in later life. For example such words as: chĕ vaux̆ de frïsé (she vō' de frēz') (p. 135). This edition continued to be republished even after 1900. The covers of all the McGuffey *Spellers* were colored in different shades of brown, in contrast to the many other spellers that were blue in imitation of Webster's.

Charles Sanders' *Spelling Book* was the third speller to be published in 1838. It soon provided both Webster and McGuffey considerable competition. It, like the McGuffey *Speller*, followed the principles of Webster rather than Johnson or Walker. It, too, used Arabic numerals above the vowels to indicate their sounds. The book began with ten pages of questions and answers concerning the rules and principles of orthography. Then the remainder of the book was nearly entirely a speller. Even though in The Preface he stated, "A Spelling Book should not only comprise a system of instruction, embracing the subjects of orthography and pronunciation, but should also teach the signification and use of words," actually less attention was given to the *meaning* of words, except just a few pages at the end, than was true of many other earlier spellers. This edition went through several reprintings.

In 1854 Sanders' *New Speller, Definer and Analyzer* appeared as a revised edition. He claimed:

It employs almost every possible expedient for the development of their *meanings* also: comparing and contrasting them one with

136   ECLECTIC SERIES.   SPELLING-BOOK.   137

Lesson 233.

Words of irregular Pronunciation.

bus'i ness (biz'nes)	rŏq'ue laurẹ (rŏk'e lŏr)
colo nel (kûr'nel)	sāe'ri fīçẹ (sāk'ri fīz)
hau tẹûr' (hō tûr')	çhẹf-d'œuvrẹ' (shä dōōvr')
½dell'ium (dĕl'yum)	es eri toirẹ' (es krī twôr')
eui räss' (kwe räs')	bellẹs-let'trẹs (bel let'ter)
gauçhẹ rie' (gōsh rē')	rẽs tau räụt' (rēs to räng')
trọụs seau' (trōō sō')	mĭgñ on ettẹ' (min yon ĕt')
gûn'walẹ (gŭn'nel)	fueli'si ä (fōōk'si ä)
däli'lia (däl'yä)	re veïi'lẹ (re väl'yä)
soi reẹ' (swä rä')	păp e tẹrīẹ' (păp a trē')
săp'phīrẹ (săf'ir)	sur veïi'lançẹ (-väl'yans)
eôg'ñae (kŏn'yak)	Plĕ'ia dĕs (plē'ya dēz)

Lesson 234.

Words of irregular Pronunciation.

nes'ciençẹ (nesh'ens)	re çhér çhé' (rūh shèr shä')
ba regẹ' (ba räzh')	sō brī quẹt' (sō bre kä')
dïph'thong (dĭf-)	ạ̈ïd'-de-camp (äd'de kŏng)
sŏl'dier (sŏl'jer)	mag ğïo're (mad jō'ra)
fôrt'ûnẹ (fôrt'yun)	mädẹ moi sellẹ' (-mwạ zĕl')
neph'ew (nĕf'yu)	flẹụr-de-līṣ' (flụr de lē')
let'tuçẹ (let'tis)	dĕb au çhēe' (dĕb o shē')
eụ trée' (ŏng trä')	rēṣ er vôïr' (rēz er vwôr')
re gīmẹ' (rä zhēm')	ṣfis tĕdd'fŏd (is tĕth'fŏd)
seru toirẹ' (skru twôr')	prō té gé' (prō tā zhä')
phy ṣiqụẹ' (fe zĕk')	de nouẹ'menṭ (-nōō'mong)

Lesson 235.

Words of irregular Pronunciation.

erī tiqụẹ' (krī tĕk')	eụ eôrẹ' (ŏng kŏr')
peụ çhanṭ' (pŏng shŏng')	sé ançẹ' (sä ōns')
çhïg'ñoụ (shĕn'yŏng)	mor çeau' (mor sō')
çha lẹt' (sha lā')	daụ ṣẹûsẹ' (dŏng zûrz')
é lăn' (ā lăng')	sang-froid' (sŏng frwä')
mĕm'oir (mĕm'wor)	qụ̈i vivẹ' (kē vēv')
moụ sïeụr' (mo sēr')	faux päṣ' (fō pä')
blanc-mangẹ' (blo-mŏnj')	bŏụ tŏụ (bŏng tŏng)
a mendẹ' (a mŏngd')	bŏụ'mŏṭ (bŏng'mō)
çeụ tïmẹ' (sŏn tēm')	mil liẹr' (mi lyä')
biv'ọụăe (bīv'wăk)	sä vaụṭ' (sä vŏng')

McGuffey's *Eclectic Spelling Book*—few words for daily use.

another, unfolding their significations by formal definitions, and everywhere rendering prominent those distinctions which are likely to escape the notice of youth.

An examination of this book reveals that his claims were much more fully fulfilled than in his earlier edition. Diacritical marks were used as guides to pronunciation.

This book was followed by Sanders' *The Primary Spelling Book* in 1858. Here he tries to do for spelling what has already been done in other subject fields by *grading* the books. This book used much larger type, including many pictures, and listed simpler and fewer words. He suggested that it be used as an introduction to the 1854 edition. It, too, presents the meanings of many words, particularly of words "alike, or nearly alike, in sound, but unlike in meaning." For example, ale and ail, air and heir, and so on.

In 1886 Sanders' *Test-Speller* appeared. In The Preface he states that it will be "suitable for the higher classes in Schools and Teachers' Institutes." It contains about 5,000 words, including "all those about which people are most apt to differ, or to be at a loss." For example, it contains numerous lists of words as strange as the following:

ap′ pan age – – – lands for the younger son of a prince
ba liz′ – – – a sea-mark
sych no car′ pous – – – bearing frequent crops
pa ron′ y mous – – – of like sound

When one sees many of these unusually unfamiliar words, one may wonder why an author should expect anyone ever to learn to spell them. In fact this can be said about many words in most of the old spellers.

A *New Spelling Book* compiled by John Comly was published in 1842. This was a revision and enlargement of a previous smaller, and not too popular, speller by the same author. It went through several reprintings for more than a decade. The first 110 pages were spelling with a few brief reading selections. Then there were 63 pages of words with their meanings. Lastly, it contained several pages of arithmetical tables.

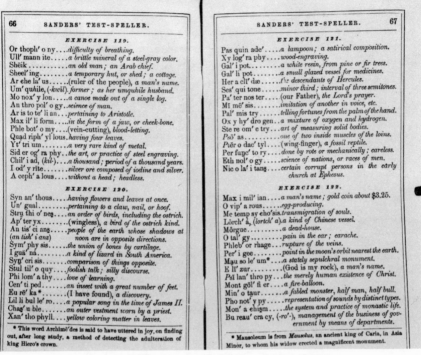

A test speller, not graded for maturity, 1866.

Also in 1842 Albert D. Wright's *Elements of The English Language; or, Analytical Orthography* was published. While this was not a regular speller, it dealt with the rules of pronunciation and derivation of words, as well as their meaning. So in a sense, it was a supplementary speller. It continued to be reprinted until the 1870's.

Another author whose speller first appeared in the 1840's was R. M' K. Ormsby. It was *The American Definition Spelling Book* of 1844. It was similar to a number of other spellers during that period, being really a combination of speller and dictionary. However, the words were arranged in lists phonetically rather than alphabetically. In 1857 Ormsby's *Vermont Speller; or Progressive Lessons in The English Language* appeared. It was a little smaller than his earlier book, and went through several reprintings.

The last author before 1850 to be mentioned here is James Lynd, although he did not write a regular speller. In 1847 he published *The First Book of Etymology*. It continued to be reprinted as late as the 1870's. It was similar to, but larger than, Town's *Analysis of Words* (1835). Both writers presented the words in lists according to their prefixes or suffixes, together with their definitions. Apparently, considerable attention was given to the composition of words during that period of American educational history. Although only a few books arranged all the words in this manner, yet many other regular spellers had similar but fewer lists of words thus arranged usually near the end of the book.

SPELLERS, 1850-1900

The spellers of no author written after 1850 attained the popularity or continued to be republished over as long a span of time as was true of the spellers written by Webster, McGuffey, Sanders, and Cobb. In fact, the spellers of Webster and McGuffey continued to have considerable popularity throughout the second half of the nineteenth century. Possibly one reason why their circulation continued was because the later editions were published by strong book publishing houses, which could promote their sale, rather than merely being printed by local printers in different cities as was the common practice earlier. Improved mail and transportation facilities made it possible for the printing and publishing practices of textbooks to be changed.

As was true before 1850, many different spellers were published between 1850 and 1900. The writer's collection contains spellers written by nearly seventy-five different authors during this period. Most of these were published only in one or two editions. A considerable number of them appeared in three or more editions. Only a few attained wide acceptance. The purpose now is to describe briefly the more popular ones, and then merely mention those which appeared only in several editions or printings.

One of the first authors after 1850, whose books gained considerable circulation, at least regionally, was Lucius Osgood. His

Progressive Speller was first published in Pittsburgh in 1856. Later editions were also published in Philadelphia and New York. He claimed to have arranged the lessons simply, but systematically. He classified the words "with reference to the vowel sounds in the accented syllable and the initial letter." The sounds of the vowels were indicated by numerals, similar to the system previously used by McGuffey. The latter part of the book contained a mixture of different kinds of lessons, as dictation exercises, abbreviations, Latin phrases, French and Italian words, proper names, and derivatives.

In 1873 Osgood published two new spellers in graded form; namely, the *American Primary Speller*, and the *American Advanced Speller*. Both of these were considerably different from his earlier *Speller*. Although graded textbooks had already appeared in other fields, they had not yet become common in spellers. The *Primary Speller* had several interesting features. The type was larger than in most spellers, the lessons were shorter, many more pictures were included, the words were much more elementary, and the vowel sounds were indicated by diacritical marks rather than by numerals. The *Advanced Speller*, as its title would indicate, contained more difficult words, longer lessons, and fewer pictures. Numerals were used to indicate vowel sounds. The latter part of the book contained many miscellaneous types of lessons similar to those used in Osgood's *Progressive Speller*, but more difficult. Both were published in Pittsburgh and New York.

Another one first published in 1856 was Epes Sargent's *The Standard Speller*. One unique feature of this book was the manner in listing the words. Other spellers arranged them in columns; Sargent presented them in rows or lines. For example, a line of page 72 is as follows: a-e' ri-al, al-lu' vi-al, col-lo' qui-al, di-lu' vi-al. It appeared in a number of editions. In 1873 his *A School Manual of English Etymology* was published. It was very similar to other books of like title.

In 1857 J. E. Worcester published the *Pronouncing Spelling-Book*. In the Preface the author admits that there were already many spelling books "of different degrees of excellence," but justified the publication of this one as particularly suitable to be used in connection with the Worcester *Dictionaries,* which were giving Webster's *Dictionaries* stiff competition. He used a very detailed system of diacritical marks to indicate pronunciations. This *Speller* was republished many times for twenty years.

Also in 1857 *The National Pronouncing Speller* by R. G. Parker and J. M. Watson was published. This was the first one of three written by them. These spellers had wide circulation for more than thirty years. The title of the first one, as was true of many spellers written during this period, indicated that the emphasis was not merely on learning to spell the words, but also on correct *oral* enunciation and pronunciation. It should be kept in mind that readers written during this period also emphasized *oral* reading or elocution. Interestingly, this book combined characteristics in regard to which there were differing practices; namely, the procedure in presenting the words, and the method of indicating the sounds of letters. In the first part of the book the words are arranged in columns, as had been the common practice. Then in about two-thirds of the book the words are presented in rows or lines, as was done by Worcester in his book published the same year. Then in regard to the letter sounds, the vowel sounds were indicated by numerals, as had been done by McGuffey, but diacritical marks were used for consonants. For example, sta tis tic'al, le git' i ma cy, ad vis' a ble. Like many other spellers the end of the book contained a number of miscellaneous lessons.

In 1859 the same authors published the *National Elementary Speller.* This they said was to accompany their *National Series of Readers.* In about two-thirds of the book the words were arranged in columns and one-third in lines. Otherwise it was similar to their earlier one, except that it was smaller and more elementary.

These two books were followed in 1875 by the *Complete Speller* written by Watson alone, which was very different than the others. In the Preface he stated:

The Exercises must be both ORAL *and* WRITTEN, the lessons

and Methods strictly educational, and in conformity with the Laws
of Mental Association.

Diacritical marks were used to indicate the sounds of both vowels
and consonants. Then a new feature was introduced. Part Second
is entitled "Popular Words," which part constitutes one-half of
the book. The words related to topics "embrace *Man*, and the
Animal, *Vegetable*, and *Mineral Kingdoms*." Here an attempt
is made to relate the words to the world and the aspects of life.
Apparently these features helped to popularize the book, for it
went through frequent and numerous editions.

Following 1857 many new spellers appeared in rather rapid
succession, but none really became popular until Swinton's was
first published in 1871. The writer's collection contains spellers
by sixteen different authors appearing between 1857 and 1871.
However, a few of these did go through several editions. In 1858
Wm. W. Smith's *The Speller's Manual* was published. This was
a small book containing a "collection of words usually misspelled." All the words appeared alphabetically together with
their definitions and roots.

In 1863 Marcius Willson published his *Primary Speller*, and
in 1864 the *Larger Speller*. Thus like Osgood, he graded his
spellers. The latter went through several editions, one as late as
1892. These *Spellers* contained no unusual features. He used
diacritical marks to indicate sounds.

In 1865 Albert N. Raub published *The Normal Speller*, which
was about two-thirds a speller and one-third an orthography. It
contained 10,000 words. Raub used numerals to show the sounds
of vowels and diacritical marks for consonants. He particularly
emphasized the rules of spelling. The next year he published
The Normal Primary Speller to precede the other. Like other
primary spellers, it contained many pictures, larger type, and
simpler word lists. Then in 1881 his *Tests in Spelling and Pronunciation* appeared. It really was a small dictionary of what
he considered to be the more important words for spelling, but
today many of these would be thought to be unimportant.

Beginning in 1867 A. C. Webb began publishing a Model
Word-Book Series, composed of *The Model Etymology*, *The*

Model Definer, and *A Manual of Etymology*. These appeared in various editions even as late as the 1880's.

In the late 1860's Wm. R. Creery, superintendent of schools of Baltimore, published *The Primary School Spelling Book*, which in 1869 was followed by a more advanced one entitled, *The Grammar-School Spelling-Book*. Part IV of the latter was entirely Etymology.

In 1869 N. P. Henderson published two books that were identical, but with different titles; namely, *Test Words in Spelling*, and *Test Words in English Orthography*. Both seem to have been widely used until the late 1880's, even without revision. They contained about 2,000 words with definitions, plus sixteen pages in fine print of modern geographical names diacritically marked. Most other similar books arranged the defined words alphabetically, but Henderson mixed their arrangement. For example, the very first word was vi-cis' si-tude. Apparently he believed the alphabetical listing would be too similar to a dictionary.

The writer whose spellers went through more editions than any written after 1850 was William Swinton. The writer's collection has seventeen, all of different date or title. Swinton (1833-92) was really a journalist by profession. During the Civil War, as a reporter for the *New York Times*, he was so critical in reporting from the fronts about the conduct of some of the battles that eventually the government deprived him of the privileges of a war correspondent. Later he wrote some outstanding war histories. This work led to an appointment as a professor of English at the University of California. There he proved insubordinate to the president. He returned to the East to devote full time to textbook writing. Soon he wrote textbooks in the fields of spelling, American history, world history, grammar, composition, and geography.

The first (1871), entitled *Word Analysis*, was "a graded classbook of English derivative words, with practical exercises in spelling, analyzing, defining, synonyms, and the use of words." It really was a combination text in etymology and spelling. It soon appeared in many editions.

The next year (1872) the *Word Book of English Spelling, Oral and Written* appeared. The writer has nine of different dates. The emphasis on written as well as oral spelling was then rather new. The book was designed to precede the *Word Analysis*. Some of the points of superiority claimed by the author were short lessons, a careful division of lessons into written and oral spelling, division of lessons into monthly and yearly sections, systematic review lessons, short lessons of the names of common objects and activities of life, and uses of the principle of associ- ation of ideas by classifying words with reference to leading ideas.

In 1873 Swinton published the *Word Primer*, which was a beginner's book in oral and written spelling. It was intended for use after a child had gone through some reading primer. It was characterized by very short lessons, the grouping of words according to leading ideas, selection of common words that can be understood by young children, and the division of the book into specific "Monthly and Yearly Sections." The last feature was very new in the specific grading of teaching material.

Finally, in 1879 Swinton published a major revision of his first book, entitling it the *New Word-Analysis*. He retained the old approach, but added considerable new *matter*. Much emphasis was on the structure of words and their derivations, particularly those from the Latin and Greek. Part V dealt with "Miscellaneous Derivatives." The divisions of this section then dealt with "Words Derived from The Names of Persons"; "Words Derived from The Names of Places"; and "Etymology of Words Used in The Principal School Studies," listing terms in the fields of geogra- phy, grammar, and arithmetic. Truly Swinton was a terrifically prolific textbook writer.

Calvin Patterson's *Common School Speller* was published in 1874. He claimed that it contained "only those words in general use and which every pupil should know how to spell." Then he said that the pupil "must not only be able to spell orally, but to write the English language without mistakes." The book was divided into seven parts according to the type of words presented. Thirteen tables of arithmetic were presented on the inside of the covers. This book appeared in a number of editions.

In 1875 Patterson published the *Speller and Analyzer*. It virtually was a combination of speller, etymology, and dictionary. Then as late as 1897 he published *The American Word Book*. It contained graded lessons in spelling, defining, punctuation, and dictation. The word lists were commonly interspersed with quotations from famous writers.

In 1877 Josiah Gilbert published *A Graded Spelling-Book*. In 1884 the same author published *School Studies in Words*, which went through several editions. He aimed "to combine in one manual some simple exercises in spelling and language." He particularly stressed dictation exercises and work in sentence building.

H. F. Harrington wrote *A Graded Spelling-Book* in 1880 in two parts. The two parts meant that it was suitable both for primary and grammar schools. He said that a speller "must be illustrative of the natural laws of intellectual progress." These words should not appear according to the number of syllables, but in the order in which they would help the child advance in knowledge. Since the usefulness of being able to spell is limited largely to the connection with what one writes, so it is the eye rather than the ear that needs most training. This book continued publication until the late 1890's. Interestingly, nineteen tables of arithmetic appeared printed on the inside of the covers.

The Modern Spelling-Book by J. N. Hunt and H. I. Gourley appeared in 1883. Peculiarly, the six copies in the writer's collection were published by five different publishing houses, four printed in 1883 and two in 1896. This cooperative arrangement among these companies, no doubt, increased its circulation. The authors refer to a developing opposition to the use of separate spelling books in school. So they claim to have carefully selected the words from modern readers. Thus a correlation of spellers and readers was attempted. Special features included drills in grammatical forms of words, topical lessons on different subjects, word building and word analysis exercises, and the origin of words. Then in 1904 Hunt alone published *The Progressive Course in Spelling* in Two Parts. Each part was to be for three years or three grades. These parts could be purchased either as separate books or as one complete book.

Word Lessons: A Complete Speller by Alonzo Reed was published in 1884 and reprinted in 1894 and 1897. He, like Hunt and Gourley, also referred to the growing opposition to the specific use of spellers. He then mentioned that the unusual words of the "old-time speller," and the common words rarely misspelled should be dropped from spellers. The book was designed to teach correct spelling and pronunciation of the words most commonly current in literature, and as most likely to be misspelled. Too, it hoped to awaken new interest in the study of synonyms and word analysis. It was to serve the higher primary, intermediate, and grammar grades. Much script type appeared throughout the book, so that the child could see how words look in written form.

The spelling books heretofore discussed went through three or more editions or printings. The following spellers published between 1850 and 1900 apparently proved less popular, but did appear in at least two editions: Daniel Leach's *The Complete Speller* in 1856; J. W. Westlake's *Three Thousand Practice Words* in 1874; Lewis Monroe's *The Practical Speller* in 1875; Richard French's *Study of Words* in 1877; E. A. Sheldon's *The Graded Speller* in 1877 (Also his *Word Studies* in 1886); *Seventy Lessons in Spelling* by Williams and Rodgers in 1885; *Seventy Lessons in Spelling* by A. S. Osborn and J. E. King in 1885; and Martin G. Benedict's *The Advanced Speller* in 1898.

The last book to be discussed was *The Rational Speller*, Part I (first three grades), and Part II (next three grades) written by J. M. Rice in 1898. In the late 1890's Rice conducted a careful study involving nearly all of the large cities of the country regarding the actual spelling proficiency of more than 33,000 pupils. Then the results were analyzed and summarized in an article entitled "The Futility of The Spelling Grind," which appeared in *The Forum* for April and June, 1897. These articles have been credited as having given an impetus to the measurement movement in the U.S.

The characteristic features Rice claimed for his *Speller* were "careful grading of the work in accordance with the natural growth of the child's comprehension," the precedence given to common words, the small number of words in relation to the ground covered, and ample provision made for thorough drill by means of frequent reviews between the children and the teacher.

It should be noted that only spellers first published before 1900 have been dealt with in this chapter. The spellers in the writer's collection were written by more than one hundred and twenty five different authors, but only one-third of them have been discussed here. The books by two-thirds of the authors failed to get wide usage.

SUMMARY

The earliest spellers commonly used in America were written in England. Then they were either brought here by the colonist or reprinted and sold here. Most of the earliest spellers written in America, except Webster's, were modeled after the English. Most of the authors, except Webster, until the late 1830's, used English dictionaries, such as Walker and Johnson, for their bases of syllabication and pronunciation. Thus the English influence on our learning and culture continued long after our political independence.

The first author of spellers to depart from the strong English influence was Noah Webster. Being an ardent American patriot, he believed that our independence should become more or less total. So in his spellers he set up rules and principles for the syllabication and pronunciation according to the ways in which Americans were actually pronouncing words. His spellers remained popular for a century. The first important spellers to follow the principles of Webster rather than Walker were the McGuffey and Sanders *Spellers.*

Another important characteristic of the earliest spellers was that they contained not only spelling, but also reading lessons, grammar, and often arithmetic and geography. In other words, their content constituted the entire primary school curriculum. It was not until approximately 1825 that spellers began to appear which were largely only spellers. By 1820 separate textbooks in the fields of reading, grammar, geography, and arithmetic appeared.

From the beginning spellers would commonly include a list of words defined, usually near the back of the book. Soon, too, they would include lists showing the roots and derivatives of words. Later these two features would often be combined. In fact, for about fifty years, during the middle of the nineteenth century, many textbooks even bore the title of *Etymology*. These books commonly would be a combination of speller and dictionary.

It was not until the late 1850's that spellers appeared in graded series, and then only in two books, the primary book for the lower grades and the advanced for the upper grades. Textbooks in several other fields had commonly appeared in series beginning in the 1830's.

The evolution of the methods of presentation need to be noted. The earliest spellers usually indicated the pronunciation of words by the use of diacritical marks and syllabication. McGuffey, and a number of others, for several decades, used Arabic numerals above the vowels to signify the sound. Later some used numerals to signify the sounds of the vowels, but diacritical marks for consonants, such as the sound of the "c" or "g." After the 1870's most spellers used diacritical marks only.

Most early spellers apparently expected all spelling teaching to be oral only—with great emphasis on pronunciation. Beginning in the early 1870's a number of spellers suggested that the teaching be both oral and written. One writer suggested that since most use for spelling is in writing, the eye rather than the ear should be more fully trained.

In regard to the words, their selection and arrangement were usually logical rather than psychological. With only a few exceptions, none of the early authors mentioned that the words of most common use only were selected. Cobb in 1825 did mention it. After 1875 frequent claims were made regarding the selection of the most useful words, and also that they were presented according to their difficulty in learning. Reed even said that words rarely misspelled were omitted, so that emphasis could be placed on teaching the more difficult ones. It is evident that American spelling textbooks have gone through many evolutionary changes.

Although no attempt has been made to analyze spellers published after 1900, yet a few comments about spellers since then should be made in general. After J. M. Rice's study of spelling practices, other studies soon followed, particularly to determine the most commonly used words. Such studies were made by L. P. Ayres, W. N. Anderson, W. A. Cook and M. V. O'Shea, Ernest Horn, J. D. Houser, E. J. Ashbaugh, and Edward Thorndike. The best known study was made by Thorndike. In 1921 he published *The Teachers Word Book*, which contained an alphabetical list of the most frequently occurring 10,000 words as determined from a count of 625,000 words of children's literature; about 3,000,000 from the Bible and English Classics; 300,000 from textbooks; 50,000 more or less technical words from books on cooking, sewing, farming, and trades; 90,000 from newspapers; and 500,000 from correspondence. In 1932 Thorndike published a 20,000 basic word list, and in 1944 a 30,000 basic word list. In 1926 Horn and Ashbaugh published a *Speller* based on the most frequently used words derived from a study of 5,100,000 words of ordinary writing. Since then most spelling textbooks use only the three or four thousand most frequently used words of these studies as the spelling words to be learned. In fact it is claimed that if a child learns to spell the 2,800 words most frequently used by adults, he will have learned about 97 per cent of the words needed in most common types of adult writing. Truly the teaching of spelling in the American schools has gone through many changes.

CHAPTER 3

----------·-(◌◌◌)·----------

READERS

INTRODUCTION

L ONG before reading textbooks appeared the children of the
American colonies learned to read from a hornbook, a so-
called speller, or a primer. The so-called hornbook was really
not a book, but a thin board generally shaped like a paddle on
which was pasted a printed page and covered with a thin sheet
of transparent horn for protection. Some of the hornbooks contained only the alphabet, while others included some syllables,
and even the Lord's Prayer. These were commonly used in the
dame schools from which the children would at least learn the
alphabet as a first step toward learning to read. [See Frontis-
piece]

Mention was made in the chapter about Spellers that the early
spellers usually contained reading and grammar material in
addition to spelling. The earliest spellers used by the colonists
were brought here from England, or reprinted here. The most
popular of these was Dilworth's *New Guide to the English
Tongue.* The writer's oldest edition of Dilworth contains 146
pages. About 56 pages of this book were devoted to reading
selections, many of which were selected fables. The next most
popular speller was Perry's *Only Sure Guide to the English
Tongue.* Nearly one-half of the book was devoted to reading

THE

NEW-ENGLAND

PRIMER

IMPROVED

For the more eafy attaining the true reading of Englifh.

TO WHICH IS ADDED

The Affembly of Divines, and Mr. COTTON's *Catechifm.*

BOSTON:

Printed by EDWARD DRAPER, *at* his Printing-Office, in *Newbury-Street, and *Sold* by JOHN BOYLE in *Marlborough-Street.*   1777.

New England Primer—primary curriculum, Colonial New England, 1777.

lessons, many of these, too, were fables—stories to teach manners.

In the oldest American printed speller, *The Youth's Instructor in the English Tongue: or, the Art of Spelling Improved*, published in 1762, roughly, one-half of the pages were reading selections, many of which were religious in nature. By far the most popular early American spellers with readings were those by Webster. The earlier editions contained considerable reading material, but not as much as most other early spellers, possibly because he also was the author of a reader. In general, the early American spellers contain less reading than those brought from England. However, there is one marked exception to this; namely, *The Union Spelling Book*. Instead of the reading lessons being mixed in with the spelling, as was most common in other spellers, the spelling words appear in connection with the reading selections. Thus it is more fully a reader than a speller.

The other chief source of reading material for the children of the colonial period was the so-called primers. The earliest primers, also, were first produced in England. Since England did not provide for mass education during that period, these primers were either published by or for religious and charitable agencies, which tried to provide some learning for the poor in charity schools. Many such primers were published and copies of them were brought here by some of the colonists.

Fortunately, Benjamin Harris, an English printer, who had experience dealing with primers in England, came early to America. Before coming here he had published in 1679 *The Protestant Tutor*. Being an ardent non-conformist in religion he had printed a number of tracts which were offensive to the English government; consequently, he was arrested, tried, and put in a pillory, and required to serve two years in jail. Later he came to Boston, where in 1686 he set up a book and "Coffee, Tee and Chucaletto" shop. Soon thereafter he prepared *The New England Primer*, modelled after some of the British primers.

How the alphabet was taught, *New England Primer*.

FEar thou the Lord and prize him more
Than shining Gold and richer Oar:
For when thy Worldly Treasure's past,
The Fear of God will ever last.

Good Children must
Fear God all Day,   Love Christ alway,
Parents obey,   In secret pray,
No falfe Thing fay,   Mind little play,
By no fin ftray,   Make no delay,
In doing Good.

Learn thefe four Lines by Heart,
Have Communion with few,
Be intimate with ONE,
Deal juftly with all.
Speak Evil of none.

AGUR's Prayer.
REmove far from me vanities and lies;
give me neither poverty nor riches;
feed me with food convenient for me; left I
be full and deny thee, and fay, who is the
Lord? or left I be poor and steal, and take
the name of my God in vain.

MR. JOHN ROGERS, Minifter of the Gospel in London, was the first Martyr in Queen Mary's Reign, and was burnt at Smithfield, February the Fourteenth, 1554. His Wife, with nine small Children & one at her Breaft, following him to the Stake, with which sorrowful Sight he was not in the leaft daunted, but with wonderful Patience died courageously for the Gofpel of JESUS CHRIST.

18 PROGRESSIVE SERIES.

LESSON III.

2 4 2 1 2 1 1 3 1
o, a, u; i, i, o; e, a, o.

sir (sur)²	whip²	o'ver¹
fence²	strike²	on'ly
an'y	do'ing³	close
serve⁴	be cause'³	goes
smack⁴	un less'²	slow

THE BOY THAT BEAT HIS HORSE.

Man. Stop! stop, my lad; tell me why you whip your horse so.

Boy. I do not know, I am sure, sir.

19 OSGOOD'S SECOND READER.

Man. Does he want to stand still?

Boy. No, sir.

Man. Does he go too slow then?

Boy. No, sir.

Man. Does he want to jump over the fence, or to lie down on the grass?

Boy. Oh no, sir.

Man. Then, pray, what do you beat him for, my lad?

Boy. I do not know, I am sure, unless it is because I like to hear my whip smack.

Man. Well, I like to hear my cane smack; so I will lay it on your back.

Boy. Oh no, sir; pray do not. Pray do not, sir.

Man. But why not?

Boy. Why, it would hurt me; and I do not know that I have done any thing wrong, for which you should whip me.

Man. And does it not hurt your horse, when you beat him?

Boy. Yes, sir; but not much, I think.

Man. And yet you beat him, though he has not done wrong.

Boy. Yes, but he is only a horse; and then he is my horse, and I may do what I please with my own horse.

Man. No, no, my lad, you must not use any thing ill, though it may be your own, and though it may be only a horse.

Now if I were to beat you well with my cane, it would serve you just right; for you have done

B. Teaching morals through persuasion, Osgood's *Second Reader.*

No existing copy of the first edition seems to be extant. Newman's *News of the Stars*, in 1690 contained an advertisement of a second and enlarged edition of *The New England Primer*. Since no copyright laws were in effect, printers in nearly every American town began to reprint it, including, changing, adding, or omitting what they saw fit, and then selling it locally. The title would even be changed, such as *The New York Primer, The American Primer*, or *The Columbian Primer*. With a change of government in England, Harris later returned there. The *New England Primer* certainly was the most widely used textbook in the colonial period, and even had considerable usage after 1800. It has been estimated that ultimately about three million copies were sold.

Although the editions of the various printers were not fully alike, their similarity was quite marked. Most of them were $3\frac{1}{4}$ by $4\frac{1}{2}$ inches in size, yet some were 4 by 6 or $4\frac{1}{2}$ by $5\frac{1}{2}$ inches. Many of the earlier editions contained 88 pages, but some of the later ones were printed in finer print and contained fewer pages and less content. After several pages containing the alphabet, syllables such as, ab, ac, eb, ec, if, ic, ob, oc, ub, uc, and short lists of words of one, two, three, four, five, and six syllables, the alphabet was presented in verse with accompanying wood-cut pictures. To learn the letter "A" the verse was "In Adams fall, We sinned all." The writer has examined more than a dozen different editions of the *New England Primer* and found that most of them contained the alphabet in verse; however, not in all were the verses alike. For example, for "E" one was, "Elijah hid, By Ravens fed"; another was, "The Eagles flight, Is out of sight." For "O" one was, "The Royal Oak it was the Tree, That sav'd His Royal majestie"; another was, "Young Obadias, David, Josias, All were pious."

The remainder of the content was nearly all religious in nature, such as questions on Bible facts, Bible verses alphabetically arranged, several prayers, The Creed, Bible names, and the Shorter Catechism of 107 questions and answers. Some of the older editions also contained "Spiritual Milk for American Babes" by John Cotton. Many also included a wood cut of the burning of "John Rogers, minister of the gospel in London, (who) was the

first martyr in Queen Mary's reign." This certainly was a rather
morbid picture for a primer. Regardless of what one may say
concerning the shortcomings of the *New England Primer* as an
appropriate beginning reading text, yet it constituted the basic
elementary curriculum for the mass of children in colonial New
England, and to a lesser extent in some other colonies. Apparently only few children, other than the boys who attended
Latin Grammar schools, remained in school long enough to study
the *Psalter* in addition to the *New England Primer*.

CONTENT

A number of studies have been made dealing with development of
the content of American readers. One of the earlier studies was
made by Reeder.[1] In the beginning chapters he merely describes
the evolution of the horn-book, some spellers, the more popular
primers, and a few of the most popular advanced readers. In the
latter part he discusses the evolution of the methods and approaches of teaching reading.

Vail[2] wrote a descriptive development of the McGuffey Readers.
Since Vail was a member of the publishing firm, this book deals
more with the business aspects of publishing these readers than
with an analysis of their content. Later Minnich[3] dealt more
fully with the evolution of the nature of the content of these
readers.

One of the most comprehensive studies was made by Robinson.[4]
One may question how thoroughly he could have analyzed the
content of 1,370 readers. However, he should be given credit for
attempting to classify the nature of the content under many
topics, and classifying them according to prose and poetry. As
a base for beginning the treatment of the content in readers, his

---

[1] R. R. Reeder, *The Historical Development of School Readers and Methods
of Teaching Reading.* N.Y.: Columbia University Press, 1900.

[2] Henry H. Vail, *A History of the McGuffey Readers.* Cleveland: Burrows
Brothers, 1911.

[3] H. C. Minnich, *William Holmes McGuffey and Readers.* N.Y.: American
Book Company, 1936.

[4] R. R. Robinson, *Two Centuries of Change in the Content of School Readers.*
Nashville: George Peabody College for Teachers, 1930.

summary table is here reproduced. An examination of the so-called topics of this table will soon reveal that some actually dealt with the nature of the topics concerned, while others dealt with the form in which the content was presented. For example, the essay, oratory, folklore, and fairy stories indicate the form of presentation rather than the thoughts involved in the content. Nevertheless, the data of the table certainly roughly reveal the changes in the content of readers during two centuries.

TABLE III[1]

PERCENTAGE DISTRIBUTION OF READING CONTENT SUMMARIZED FROM THE STUDY OF 1,370 READERS BY PERIODS.

Criteria		Before 1775	1775 to 1825	1825 to 1875	1875 to 1915	1915 to 1926
Animals and Birds	Prose		1	16	15	18
	Poetry		2	2	2	2
Adventure	Prose			2	3	4
	Poetry			1	1	3.5
Boys and Girls	Prose		2	3	18.5	10.5
	Poetry			1	2	1
Nature Study	Prose		2	8	8	3
	Poetry		2	1	3	3
Essay	Prose		8	5	3	2
	Poetry					
Thrift	Prose			.5	2	5
	Poetry					
Oratory	Prose			7.5	1	1	.5
	Poetry					
Geography	Prose			4	2	1	1.5
	Poetry					
Religion	Prose	70	18	5	1	1
	Poetry	15	4	2.5	.5	.5
Myth	Prose				2	3
	Poetry				1	.5
Folklore	Prose				3	5
	Poetry				1	.5
Fairy Stories	Prose			.5	6	9
	Poetry				1	.5
Fables	Prose		1	2	4	7
	Poetry				1	1

TABLE III (*continued*)

Criteria		Before 1775	1775 to 1825	1825 to 1875	1875 to 1915	1915 to 1926
Biography	Prose		3	2	3	2
	Poetry					
Patriotism	Prose		1	1	1	2
	Poetry			2	1	1
Morals and Conduct	Prose	6	20	20	5	3.5
	Poetry	2	8	3	2	1
History	Prose		2	3	3	2
	Poetry			1	1	.5
Legend	Prose			1	1	1
	Poetry					.5
Science	Prose					
	Poetry					
Spelling	Prose		10	6		
	Poetry					
Principles of Government	Prose		1	3		
	Poetry					
Other Forms	Prose	7	2	3	3	6
	Poetry		1	2	2	3
TOTAL PER CENT	Prose	83	83	85.5	81.5	81.5
	Poetry	17	17	14.5	18.5	18.5
No. Readers Scored		4	85	481	588	212

1Robinson's Table VI.

Religion and morals. All studies of the content of readers agree that the books during the colonial period most fully stressed religion, and in most instances were sectarian in nature. In New England, where the Puritans held a monopolistic control of governmental matters, the Calvinistic religious principles were taught even in the public schools. In the other colonies, where parochial schools were more common, the various religious groups taught their respective religious principles from their own primers. These primers usually contained a sectarian catechism.

Following our independence from England and the adoption of our constitution, which theoretically separated church and state, the teaching of sectarian religion began to be questioned.

Therefore, according to Robinson's data, the percentage of religious content dropped from 92 per cent during the colonial period to 22 per cent during the next fifty years. The religious content that did remain in was more or less non-sectarian in nature. Tingelstad[5] found that the leading readers between 1830 and 1840 averaged 16.7 per cent religious content. However, the famous McGuffey readers retained considerable religious content much later than most other readers. For example, Hughes[6] found that nearly 30 per cent of the lessons in the *Fourth Reader* (1837 and 1844) were religious. The *Fifth* and *Sixth Readers* contained less, but considerably more than other readers, particularly in the poetic selections. All the studies show that little religious content remained in the readers after 1850.

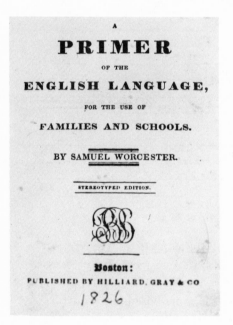

A

PRIMER

OF THE

ENGLISH LANGUAGE,

FOR THE USE OF

FAMILIES AND SCHOOLS.

BY SAMUEL WORCESTER.

STEREOTYPED EDITION.

Boston:
PUBLISHED BY HILLIARD, GRAY & CO

1826

Title Page of one of the earliest graded primers.

Warren's[7] study dealt with the nature of the religious content in detail. He found that the concepts dealt mainly with God, man in his religious relations, Christ, immortality, and the Bible. Such attributes of God, as good, invisible, omniscient, and wise, were mentioned. God was frequently referred to as the Creator of nature, the universe, and of man, especially mentioned between 1830 and 1860. God's providential rela-

5 Oscar A. Tingelstad, "The Religious Element in American School Readers." (Unpublished Master's Thesis, University of Chicago, 1913.)

6 Raymond G. Hughes, "An Analysis of the Fourth, Fifth, and Sixth Mc-Guffey Readers." (Unpublished doctor's dissertation, University of Pittsburgh, 1943.)

7 Harold C. Warren, "Changing Conceptions in the Religious Elements in Early American School Readers." (Unpublished doctor's dissertation, University of Pittsburgh, 1951.)

tions to his creatures were expressed in lessons dealing with afflictions, discouragements, human experiences, historical events, and nature. In the McGuffey *Readers* appear references that "The heavens declare the glory of God," "The hand that made us is divine," and "We should praise our Creator as the sky lark does; but also that God's judgment is seen in the thunder cloud, war, and plagues." Disappointments are even pictured as blessings in disguise.

In dealing with the nature and duties of man, readers are referred to repentance, sin, and punishment. Mistreatment of birds and animals, blasphemy, bad companions, hypocrisy, intemperance, lying, and stealing, were to be avoided. Then even more frequently lessons appear exalting the positive virtues of man, such as caring for animals and birds, performing acts of charity,

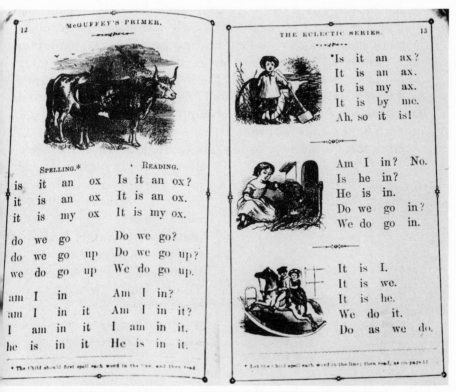

McGuffey's *Primer,* coordination of spelling and reading.

cheerfulness, contentment, courage, diligence, forgiveness, love of neighbors, peace loving, tolerance, bearing social responsibility, and practicing the Golden Rule.

A surprising number of references that relate directly or indirectly to immortality continued to appear in readers, particularly until about 1860. Lessons contained such concepts as the endless life, only goodness there (in heaven), reunion, the soul's immortality, virtues rewarded, supreme society, and treasures laid up.

The references to Christ did not appear nearly so frequently as the above mentioned concepts. The prevailing nature of the religion reflected in the books was more in harmony with the spirit and stories of the Old Testament than the New. In this regard Warren states, "Much more palatable for children's taste in reading than theological considerations is the relationship of Jesus to our way of life and our daily interests." Thus the thoughts relating to Christ dealt mostly with his exampleship in exhibiting virtues and wisdom, bearing responsibility, suffering, and then dying for us. Very few of these ideas appeared after 1850. Likewise the references to the Bible were not very frequent, and then mainly between 1820 and 1845. The Bible was referred to as the Book of God, source of happiness and inspiration, and important as a basis for life.

Even though the more or less purely religious concepts largely disappeared in readers shortly after 1850, references to morals and conduct continued much longer. However, the individualistic rather than social virtues were emphasized throughout. Warren says, "With similar tenacity, successive and contemporary writers, through repeated editions and revisions, con-

First English reader written in America, Noah Webster, 1785.

tinued to present certain familiar stories and specific teachings. This seems to have had much to do with sustaining the religious tone of the books long after the technically religious elements had disappeared." In other words, the authors and compilers of readers were loath to abandon totally the dual purpose of teaching children to read and inspiring them to live noble lives. For example, the Lord's Prayer in verse appeared in a number of readers including the popular McGuffey and Sanders series, as follows:

> Our Father in heaven,
> We hallow thy name!
> May thy kingdom holy,
> On earth be the same!
> O, give to us daily
> Our portion of bread!
> It is from thy bounty
> That all must be fed.
> Forgive our transgressions,
> And teach us to know
> That humble compassion,
> That pardons each foe.
> Keep us from temptation,
> From weakness and sin,
> And thine be the glory,
> Forever — Amen!

Myth, Folklore, Fairy Story, and Fable. Commonly myths, folklore, fairy stories, and fables dealt with morals and ways of conduct. Thus when these four types of lessons are grouped together they constitute the most frequent appearing topic after 1875, according to Robinson's study. During the 1875-1915 period nearly one-fifth and during 1915-1926 period more than one-fourth of the lessons were classified under these types. This would indicate that before the 1875-1915 period the teaching of religious and moral concepts was attempted more or less through the direct method or approach, while after that date they were more largely taught by means of stories and the different forms of literature. The latter approach was more in harmony with Pestalozzian and Herbartian principles of teaching.

Animals, Birds, and Nature Study. Another type of content

which became more and more popular by the middle of the last
century was that dealing with animals, birds, and nature study.
Robinson found that more than one-fourth of the lessons after
1825 dealt with them. Evidently the attention given to animals
and birds was the beginning of what is now known in the elementary schools as nature study. Both Pestalozzianism and the
Oswego Object Lesson movement contributed greatly to this
attention. In fact, Sheldon in his *Lessons on Objects* (1863)
listed many other forms of biological life besides animals and
birds. Certainly, any teacher carrying out Sheldon's suggestions
would have been teaching nature study.

Boys and Girls. After 1875 an increased number of lessons dealt
with boys and girls. During the 1875-1915 period 18.5 per cent and during the 1915-1926 period 10.5 per cent related to boys and girls. This certainly was in harmony with the growing psychological attention given to the nature, interests, and the study of the child.

T H E

Young GENTLEMAN and LADY'S

M O N I T O R,

A N D

Englifh Teacher's ASSISTANT;

B E I N G

A COLLECTION of SELECT PIECES
from our beft MODERN WRITERS:

CALCULATED TO

Eradicate Vulgar Prejudices and Rufticity of Manners; Improve the Underftanding; Rectify the Will; Purify the
Paffions; Direct the Minds of Youth to the Purfuit of proper
Objects; and to facilitate their Reading, Writing, and
Speaking the Englifh Language, with Elegance and Propriety.
Particularly adapted for the Ufe of our eminent Schools and A-
cademies, as well as private Perfons, who have not an Opportunity of perufing the Works of thofe celebrated Authors,
from whence this Collection is made.

D I V I D E D   I N T O

Small Portions for the Eafe of Reading in Claffes. To which
is added, The Elements of Gefture.

The N I N T H   E D I T I O N.

By J. H A M I L T O N M O O R E,
Author of the Practical Navigator, and Seaman's
New Daily Affiftant.

H U D S O N:
Printed by A S H B E L S T O D D A R D,
M,DCCXCV.
1795

Aims and purposes beyond learning to read: morals, manners, self-
control, literature, 1795.

Literature. The most thorough treatment of the development of the literary content
of American readers was made
by Davis.[8] His study clearly
reveals that the compilers of

---

[8] Vincent Davis, "The Literature of Advanced School Readers in the U.S.:
1785-1900." (Unpublished doctor's dissertation, University of Chicago, 1934.)

school readers recognized the value of literature as an important feature of textbook content. He states, "This resumé shows that the compilers have regarded literature as a powerful agent for the teaching of political, social, moral, and religious lessons." He refers to such prefatory statements found in readers, as "masterpieces of style," "literary masterpieces," and "the best in English and American literature."

The percentage of the literary content in the readers varied somewhat from decade to decade, and among authors. Certain objectives affected the amount of literary content. For example, the readers that emphasized the didactic did not include as much good literature as those aiming to present mainly selections of superior literary value. The readers from 1860 to 1900 consistently included a higher percentage of excellent literature than

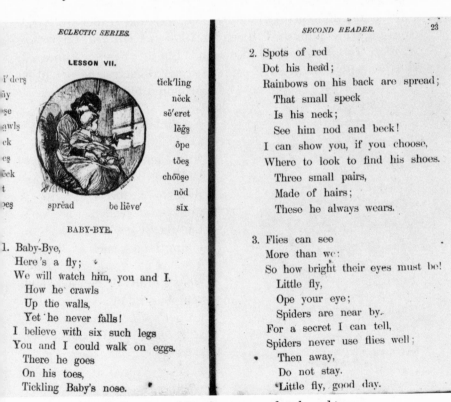

ECLECTIC SERIES.

LESSON VII.

i'dерs
äy
se
awls
ck
es
ěck
t
эеѕ

tĭck'ling
něck
sē'eret
lĕg̣s
ōpe
tōes
chōōṣe
nŏd
six

spread   be lieve'

BABY-BYE.

1. Baby-Bye,
Here's a fly;
We will watch him, you and I.
How he crawls
Up the walls,
Yet he never falls!
I believe with six such legs
You and I could walk on eggs.
There he goes
On his toes,
Tickling Baby's nose.

SECOND READER. 23

2. Spots of red
Dot his head;
Rainbows on his back are spread;
That small speck
Is his neck;
See him nod and beck!
I can show you, if you choose,
Where to look to find his shoes.
Three small pairs,
Made of hairs;
These he always wears.

3. Flies can see
More than we:
So how bright their eyes must be!
Little fly,
Ope your eye;
Spiders are near by.
For a secret I can tell,
Spiders never use flies well;
Then away,
Do not stay.
Little fly, good day.

McGuffey *Second Reader,* improved style and type.

the readers of the first half of the nineteenth century. Prefatory statements in the readers after 1860 definitely indicated that the authors aimed to emphasize literature rather than history or science. However, there was at least one curbing influence in the later readers; namely, as the authors became more conscious of the interests and needs of children, the selections chosen for that purpose often lacked literary quality. Naturally this would apply more fully to the lower rather than the advanced readers. The McGuffey *Readers* particularly contained many selections of superior literary value.

Toward the end of the last century several authors even indicated by the titles of their readers that the literary element would be stressed. In 1897 *Stepping Stones to Literature—A Reader for Sixth Grades* by Sarah Arnold and C. B. Gilbert was published. In 1898 *Lights to Literature*, a first reader, by Avis Purdue and Florence LaVictoire, and a second reader by Sarah Sprague were published. Then in 1900 the *Graded Literature Readers* by Harry P. Judson and Ida C. Bender appeared. It is evident that literary content received increasing attention around 1900.

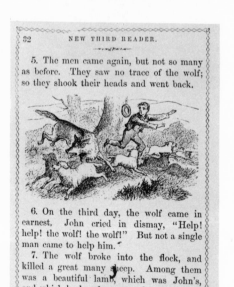

32 NEW THIRD READER.

5. The men came again, but not so many as before. They saw no trace of the wolf; so they shook their heads and went back.

6. On the third day, the wolf came in earnest, John cried in dismay, "Help! help! the wolf! the wolf!" But not a single man came to help him.

7. The wolf broke into the flock, and killed a great many sheep. Among them was a beautiful lamb, which was John's, and which he loved very much.

8. The truth itself is not believed, From one who often has deceived.

EXERCISES.—Relate the story of the wolf. Why did not the men come the third time? What did John lose? What may we learn from this story?

Special Readers. A considerable number of readers bore titles indicating either a special type of content or an appeal to a special group. A number of readers were written particularly for girls or young ladies, such as Bailey's *The Young Ladies Class Book* (1831). Several were religious in purpose, such as Collier's *The Evangelical Instructor* (1811), and Emerson's *The Evangelical Primer*

McGuffey *Third*, 1857, better literary content.

(1811). In 1822 Blake's *The Historical Reader* was published, which later reappeared in numerous editions. Other specially titled books were: *The Etymological Reader* (1872) by Epes Sargent and Amasa May; Carpenter's *Geographical Readers* (A Series) beginning in 1899; Judson's *The Young American— A Civic Reader* (1897); and Wilson's *Nature Study in Elementary Schools: Second Reader* (1898).

Speakers. Nearly all readers until just before 1900 emphasized the mastery of effective oral reading or elocution. While this emphasis was more or less common for reading at all levels; it was often the prime objective in the advanced readers. Not only was this true in the upper books of a series, but many special advanced readers were published for this purpose. This was persistently true from the appearance of some of the earliest readers and up to the end of the nineteenth century. Their titles usually contained one or more of the following definitive terms: Speaker, orator, rhetorical guide or manual, elocution or elocutionary, vocal culture, dialogues, or dramatic. The writer's collection contains approximately seventy-five books that may be classified as elocutionary or rhetorical readers or speakers. A number of them appeared in numerous editions.

It is quite clear why speaking and oratory became popular in our early national history. In the first place, the democratic political development of our country required the election of persons to public office. So public speaking on the part of the candidates and their friends became common. Thus effective public

Town and Holbrook, 1856, teaching the vowel sounds.

THE PROGRESSIVE FIRST READER.			11
THE ELEMENTARY SOUNDS.			
VOCAL ELEMENTS.			
*A*pe	*a*le	*a*ge	*r*ace
ā	*a*im	*a*te	*b*ake
*A*rm	*a*nt	*a*rc	*c*art
ä	*a*sk	*a*sp	*p*ath
*A*wl	*la*w	*a*ll	*b*ald
a	*a*we	*ja*w	*ta*ll
*A*x	*na*g	*ma*t	*tra*p
a	*va*n	*la*d	*s*ack
*Ea'*gle	*ea*t	*pe*a	*fee*t
ē	*se*e	*ke*y	*lea*f
*E*gg	*fe*n	*be*d	*re*st
e	*ve*x	*ne*t	*dec*k

speaking became important. Likewise, in the field of religion, evangelists held revival and camp meetings, demanding effective oral appeals. Thus to prepare the youth for future effective participation in activities requiring public speaking, the authors of textbooks prepared readers suitable for the development of effective oral delivery. Some were special books to serve this purpose solely, others did so more particularly in the upper readers of a series.

As early as 1785, H. Gaine's *The Art of Speaking* was printed in New York. In the same year the first English reader written by an American appeared; namely, Noah Webster's *American Selection of Lessons in Reading and Speaking*. The very beginning of this book dealt with rules and examples for "Reading and Speaking." In 1797 *The Orator's Assistant; Being a Selection of Dialogues* by Alexander Thomas was published. It contained many famous literary dialogues, such as the one by Brutus and Cassius, and one by Cato, Lucius, and Sempronius. In 1799 Caleb Bingham's *Columbian Orator* was published. A prefatory comment stated that the selections were "calculated particularly for Dialogue and Declamation." The first 23 pages dealt with "General Instructions for Speaking." Then the reading selections were preceded by the following statement: "Practical Pieces for Speaking; consisting of Orations, Addresses, Exhortations from the Pulpit, Pleadings at the Bar, Sublime Descriptions, Debates, Declamations, Grave and Humorous Dialogues, Poetry, etc." Editions of this book continued to appear for at least four decades.

The next popular text of this type was William Scott's *Lessons in Elocution* (1814), or "A Selection of Pieces, in Prose and Verse, for the Improvement of Youth in Reading and Speaking." The "Elements of Gesture" were illustrated by four plates. Part II presented the following types of lessons: Eloquence of the Senate, Eloquence of the Bar, Speeches on Various Subjects, Dramatic Pieces: Dialogues, Speeches, and Soliloquies.

The most popular one of all was Ebenezer Porter's *The Rhetorical Reader*, first published in 1831. It still appeared in the 1860's. The first 70 pages defined and discussed reading, articulation, inflection, accent, emphasis, modulation, and gesture. Then

60 pages were devoted to technical exercises pertaining to the above. Lastly, there were 170 pages of literary selections for oral exercises. Most of the latter were by recognized literary authors.

In 1843 Parley Pippin published *The Orator's Ladder* in three parts. The title page included a picture showing ten ladders each of ten steps reaching above the clouds toward the sky with a different sized learner on each ladder. The symbolism of the picture was to carry "the learner quite above the level of the common plan of learning to read." Similar special books for "speakers" continued until 1900, but only a few became popular.

Beginning in the 1840's special books for "speakers" were largely replaced by readers appearing in series, usually in series of five or six. Then commonly the fifth, or the sixth, or both, would contain the word "speaker" or "rhetorical" in the title. One of the first of these was Alexander (not William) McGuffey's *Rhetorical Guide or Fifth Reader* in 1844. The first 60 pages of this dealt with the principles of elocution. Next appeared Richard Parker's *Exercises in Rhetorical Reading* in 1849. Epes Sargent's *The Standard Speaker* was published in 1852. The Sanders Series, which provided keen competition for the Mc-Guffey Series, included the *Rhetorical, or Union Fifth Reader*, and the *Rhetorical, or Union Sixth Reader*. In 1854 Salem Town's *Fifth or Elocutionary Reader* appeared. In 1874 Hillard and Sprague's *The Franklin Sixth Reader and Speaker* was published. One appearing in a popular series of readers was William Swinton's *Fifth Reader and Speaker* in 1883. All of these fifth and sixth readers appeared in numerous editions.

Osgood, 1855, teaching phonics and elocution.

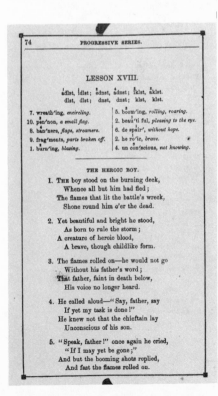

74   PROGRESSIVE SERIES.

LESSON XVIII.

ădlst, ĭdlst; ĕdnst, ădnst; ĭklst, ăklst.
dlst, dlst; dnst, dnst; klst, klst.

7. wreath'ing, *encircling.*
10. pæn'non, *a small flag.*
8. ban'ners, *flags, streamers.*
9. frag'ments, *parts broken off.*
1. burn'ing, *blazing.*

5. boom'ing, *rolling, roaring.*
2. beau'ti ful, *pleasing to the eye.*
6. de spair', *without hope.*
2. he ro'ic, *brave.*
4. un con'scious, *not knowing.*

THE HEROIC BOY.

1. THE boy stood on the burning deck,
   Whence all but him had fled;
The flames that lit the battle's wreck,
Shone round him o'er the dead.

2. Yet beautiful and bright he stood,
   As born to rule the storm;
A creature of heroic blood,
   A brave, though childlike form.

3. The flames rolled on—he would not go
   Without his father's word;
That father, faint in death below,
   His voice no longer heard.

4. He called aloud—"Say, father, say
   If yet my task is done!"
He knew not that the chieftain lay
   Unconscious of his son.

5. "Speak, father!" once again he cried,
   "If I may yet be gone;"
And but the booming shots replied,
   And fast the flames rolled on.

From the foregoing data it is clear that oral rather than silent reading was deemed more important until nearly 1900.

Summary of Content. A thorough examination of the table shows that readers varied greatly in the attention given the various topics, in any particular period, and that also ,there was great variation relating to particular topics in the different periods. Some topics were never given more than 5 per cent of the space in any period.

MOST POPULAR AMERICAN READERS

Noah Webster (1754-1843). Webster wrote the first American written reader in 1785; he had also written the first popular American speller. It was the "Third Part of a Grammatical Institute of the English Language"; the First Part having been the *Speller,* and the Second Part the *Grammar.* The title of the reader was *An American Selection of Lessons in Reading and Speaking.* Its contents consisted of: Rules for Reading and Speaking, Lessons in Reading, Lessons in Speaking, Dialogues, Poetry, and Appendix. The lessons in reading were largely moral in character, such as "Honesty Rewarded," and "Character of a Young Lady." The lessons in speaking and the dialogues were largely historical and patriotic in nature, such as "Oration on the Boston Massacre," and "Brutus and

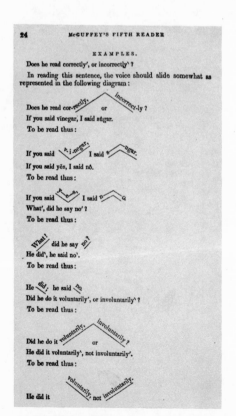

McGuffey, 1844, another method of teaching elocution.

Cassius." This reader was printed in several cities and by 1789 had appeared as the sixth edition. In 1790 Webster wrote *The Little Readers Assistant*, which apparently did not become as popular as the *Selection*. In 1802 he published the *Elements of Knowledge*, Vol. I, which contained a "Historical and Geographical Account of the United States; for the Use of Schools." This book apparently served the joint purpose of being a reader, history, and geography. Such correlation was rather usual in those early days before separate and distinct books in the different subject fields were common. This book appeared in numerous editions. Although Webster wrote three readers, they did not constitute a graded series.

Caleb Bingham (1757-1819). Bingham was the second American author whose readers became popular. In 1794 his *The American Preceptor* was published. This was followed in 1797 by *The Columbian Orator*. Both books appeared in many editions, even after 1850. Why did they become so popular? Evidently because they fulfilled the two primary aims of the teaching of reading then; namely, the teaching of morals, and of elocution or speaking. The chief purpose of the *Preceptor* was to teach moral precepts. In the preface he stated in part:

Convinced of the impropriety of instilling false notions into the minds of the children, he has not given place to romantic fiction. Although moral essays have not been neglected; yet pleasing and interesting stories, exemplifying moral virtues, were judged best cal-

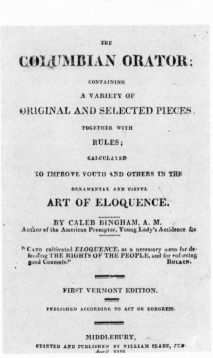

THE

COLUMBIAN ORATOR:

CONTAINING

A VARIETY OF

ORIGINAL AND SELECTED PIECES.

TOGETHER WITH

RULES;

CALCULATED

TO IMPROVE YOUTH AND OTHERS IN THE

ORNAMENTAL AND USEFUL

ART OF ELOQUENCE.

BY CALEB BINGHAM, A. M.

Author of the American Preceptor, Young Lady's Accidence, &c

" CATO cultivated *ELOQUENCE*, as a necessary mean for defending THE RIGHTS OF THE PEOPLE, and for enforcing good Counsels." ROLLIN.

FIRST VERMONT EDITION.

PUBLISHED ACCORDING TO ACT OF CONGRESS.

MIDDLEBURY,

PRINTED AND PUBLISHED BY WILLIAM SLADE, JUN.
April 1816

Caleb Bingham, 1816, elocution with a political aim—defense of democracy.

culated to engage the attention and improve the heart. Tales of love have not gained admission. . . . neither a word . . . would "raise a blush on the cheek of modesty."

The following were some of the lesson titles: "On the Duty of School Boys," "Character of Fidelia," "Filial Duty and Affection," and a rather morbid title, "The Child Trained up for the Gallows." The book contained 100 lessons.

The Columbian Orator was "calculated to improve youth and others in the ornamental and useful Art of Eloquence." On the title page Rollin was quoted as saying, "Cato cultivated Eloquence, as a necessary mean for defending the Rights of the People, and for enforcing good counsels." The book contained 84 oratorical exercises, most of which were extracts of famous speeches by such famous men as Washington, Cato, Milton, Buonaparte, Cassius, Pitt, Fox, and others. *The Columbian Orator* continued in publication even much longer than the *Preceptor*. These books did not constitute a graded series. Evidently they were used in the upper grades of schools and in academies.

Lindley Murray (1745-1826). Early readers which became even more popular in America than those of Webster and Bingham were written in England by Murray, who was born, reared, and educated in America. The writer's collection contains 36 copies each bearing a different title, date, or printer. The first one was published in 1799. It was *The English Reader*, "or Pieces in Prose and Poetry, selected from the best writers, designed to assist young persons to read with Propriety and Effect, to improve their language and sentiments; and to inculcate some of the most important Principles of Piety and Virtue." Since this book was written in England, where Latin and Greek readers were still in common academic use, he called this *The English Reader*. Although in the sub-title Murray referred to its purposes as teaching effective *oral* reading and virtue, he evidently aimed at much broader purposes for the teaching of reading. An examination of the table of contents shows that he conceived of the reading selections as being literature, classifying them under prose and poetry, and further presenting them as representing different types of literature. The prose pieces were classified in the different chapters, as narrative, didactic, argumentative, descriptive, pathetic, dialogues, public speeches, and promiscuous pieces. The chapters of poetry were: Select sentences, narrative, didactic, descriptive, and promiscuous pieces.

In 1800 the *Sequel to the English Reader* and in 1801 the *Introduction to the English Reader* were published. The stated purposes and the plan of presenting the lessons of these two books were about the same as in *The English Reader*. In a sense these three books were to constitute a series. In the preface of the *Introduction* Murray stated that "it has been his aim to form a compilation, which would properly conduct the young learner from the Spelling-book to the English 'Reader.' " It must be kept in mind that at that time, before regular reading primers were common, most children learned to read from the simple reading lessons in the spellers. Thus the *Introduction* was to be used between a speller and *The English Reader*, and these to be followed by the *Sequel*. All three presented the reading selections in chapters under the above mentioned types of literature. The only differences, according to Murray, were in the length and difficulty of the reading material. None of these books made any use of learning aids, such as questions, pictures, or word lists.

Apparently printers all over the United States felt free to reprint these books for their own profit. The 36 above mentioned copies were published by 22 different printers. Among these the latest one appeared in 1848. The wide appearances of these readers is ample evidence that the Murray books were widely used in the schools of the United States during the first half of the nineteenth century.

John Pierpont (1785-1866). Many readers were published between the first appearance of the Murray *Readers* and those by Pierpont, but none gained wide acceptance, except Scott's *Lessons in Elocution*, which has been discussed elsewhere. Like several other early authors, he first wrote his most advanced book, *The American First Class Book; or, Exercises in Reading and Recitation*, in 1823. He succeeded in having the School Committee of Boston adopt this book to replace Scott's *Lessons*. It was a large book of 480 pages. Unlike most advanced readers, no rules for elocution were included. In organization he rather closely followed Murray. Part First. Lessons in Prose. In order the following appeared: Narrative, Descriptive, Didactick, Pathetick, Dramatick, Humorous, and Miscellaneous Pieces, and with some for Recitation. In Part Second the poetic pieces in the same order were presented.

In 1827 Pierpont compiled *The National Reader*. It was adopted in Boston to replace Murray's *English Reader*. It was 200 pages smaller than his *Class Book*, and thus could precede the latter. The lessons in it were not classified. In the meantime, Pierpont apparently began to think of a series, so in 1828 he prepared the *Introduction to the Reader*. By 1835 it reached its sixteenth edition. In 1830 there followed *The Young Reader* to precede the *Introduction*, and soon thereafter *The Little Learner*. Thus five books constituted Pierpont's series of readers. The idea of a series apparently was an afterthought, for they were prepared in the exact reverse order to the sequence in which other later series were compiled. It may also be noted that they were not called First, Second, etc., or No. 1, No. 2. Nevertheless his readers went through numerous editions.

Lyman Cobb (1800-1864). Cobb apparently was the first author to conceive a really graded series of readers, and to begin with the lowest reader. In 1830 he published the *Juvenile Reader, No. 1*. On the title page a statement said that it contained "interesting, moral, and instructive Reading Lessons, composed of easy

COBB'S
JUVENILE READER,
No. 1;
CONTAINING
INTERESTING, MORAL, AND INSTRUCTIVE
READING LESSONS,
COMPOSED OF EASY WORDS OF
ONE AND TWO SYLLABLES.
DESIGNED
FOR THE USE OF SMALL CHILDREN,
IN
FAMILIES AND SCHOOLS.

BY LYMAN COBB,
AUTHOR OF THE SPELLING-BOOK, EXPOSITOR, SCHOOL DICTIONARY, JUVENILE
READERS, SEQUEL, EXPLANATORY ARITHMETICA, NOS. 1 & 2, NORTH
AMERICAN READER, AND CIPHERING-BOOK, NOS. 1 & 2.

ITHACA, N. Y.:
ANDRUS, WOODRUFF, & GAUNTLETT.

Cobb, *Juvenile Reader*, 1830, earliest well-graded series.

words of one and two syllables." It was a simple book of 72 pages with five pictures. The next year the *Juvenile Reader, No. 2* was published. It used words of one, two, and three syllables. It contained 144 pages and six pictures. In the reading lessons the paragraphs were numbered. Also in 1831 the *Juvenile Reader, No. 3* appeared. It contained 212 pages, and words with a greater number of syllables, but no pictures. In 1832 he wrote a larger book entitled, *Sequel to the Juvenile Readers.*

Beginning in 1842 he revised several of these books. The second one was changed to *New Juvenile Reader, No. II*, and the reading content was greatly reduced, but each reading lesson was preceded with a list of its key words together with their meaning and pronunciation. In 1843 the *Sequel* was changed to the *New Sequel, or Fourth Reading Book.* It also interspersed the reading lessons with word lists. A note before the first lesson stated, "This Spelling Lesson contains all the words of Reading Lesson I, which were not in any Reading Lesson, contained in Juvenile Reader, Nos. I, II, or III." The first word appeared as follows:

4 4 1 1
"A bil i t y (a bil le te), *n. capacity, skill; power; means.*"
He also wrote the *North American Reader*, which evidently was meant to be a fifth reader. It is evident that Cobb made a definite contribution in the development of serially graded readers.

Samuel Worcester. As early as 1826 Worcester published *A Primer of the English Language.* It is not certain whether at that time he meant this to be the beginning of a series, for his later books did not appear for several years. In some respects it imitated the *New England Primer* by illustrating the letters of the alphabet with pictures. He then went further by using visual aids with lessons. For example, Lesson III, in part, follows:

> A nice Fan.
> This is a nice Fan.

Some spelling lists interspersed the reading lessons. It had a limp paper backed cover.

In 1830 *A Second Book for Reading and Spelling* was published, soon followed by *A Third Book. A Fourth Book of Lessons for Reading* was published in 1834. The attention to spelling was diminished, but each lesson was preceded by a rule of something involved in the lesson and then each was followed by errors and questions. Then ten years later *An Introduction to the Third Book for Reading and Spelling* appeared. It contained 264 pages, and each lesson was preceded by "errors to be avoided" and followed by questions about the content of the lessons. While several of the Worcester *Readers* were published in several editions, they did not become popular.

One interesting incident may be added here. When William McGuffey first wrote his *Third Reader* in 1837 he used several selections from a Worcester book. In turn Worcester sued McGuffey and his publisher. It was settled out of court, and McGuffey immediately revised his book.

B. D. Emerson. In 1833 Emerson, a principal of a grammar school in Boston, prepared *The First-Class Reader.* The same year *The Second-Class Reader* was published. Then in 1834 *The Third-Class Reader* appeared. Peculiarly, *The First-Class Reader* was the advanced book for upper grades, *The Second-Class Reader* was "designed for the use of the middle class of schools," and *The Third-Class Reader* "for the use of the younger classes." He may have been influenced by the practice in which the Boston Latin Grammar School numbered its grades or "forms" in reverse order. These books were published in several editions.

William Holmes McGuffey (1800-1873). The best known textbooks ever written in our country were the McGuffey *Readers,* even out-distancing the *New England Primer* and Noah Webster's blue-backed *Speller* in sale. Many factors helped make them famous. In addition to their good original authorship there should be mentioned the vision and energy of the publishers, the geographical location of the publishing company, the careful revisions, and the nature and demand of the times when they appeared.

McGuffey was born in a log cabin in southwestern Pennsylvania, and when still very young his family moved to near Youngstown, Ohio. Apparently he learned the rudiments of elementary education from his mother, and together with his sister Jane received some training in a private school operated by a Reverend Wick in Youngstown. Later he attended Greersburg (later called Darlington) Academy in Pennsylvania near the Ohio line, where he lived in the principal's home earning his way by doing chores. In 1819 he entered Washington and Jefferson College in Pennsylvania. He accepted a teaching position at Miami University, Oxford, Ohio, even before receiving his degree at Washington and Jefferson.

After spending ten years teaching at Miami he accepted the presidency of the reorganized Cincinnati College. However, the financial panic ruined its success. Then in 1839 he became presi-

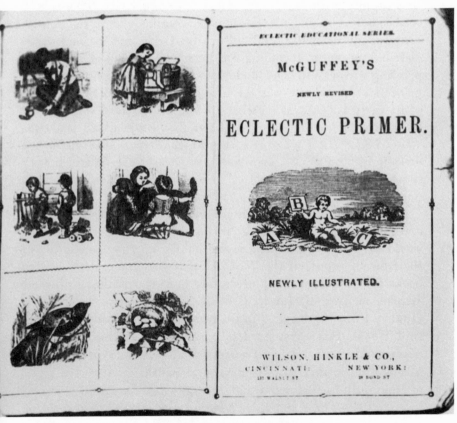

An early McGuffey *Primer*.

dent of Ohio University, at Athens, Ohio. There, likewise, he met difficulties in financing the operation of the school. Evidently his talents were those of a scholar rather than of an administrator. After four rather unhappy years there he accepted a professorship in languages at Woodward College, Cincinnati. Then in 1845 he went to Charlottesville as professor of political economy and moral philosophy at the University of Virginia. There he remained until his death in 1873. While there he distinguished himself as a great scholar, lecturer, teacher, and advocate of a state public school system, which was established before his death, with a former student as its first superintendent.

But how and when did the McGuffey *Readers* come to be? During McGuffey's stay in Ohio the Ohio Valley was developing very rapidly, with Cincinnati as its center of activity. There many activities were taking place—industrially, financially, religiously, socially, educationally, and culturally. It became the mid-west's distribution center, including the distribution of books. Numerous printing presses and book binderies were set up. Among the larger printers or publishers was the firm of Truman and Smith. Most of its early books were merely reprints of standard works likely to have a sale in the mid-west. Their first copyrighted book was *The Child's Bible* (1834). Also in that year they published Joseph Ray's *Eclectic Arithmetic*, which was the first of a very successful series of arithmetics, and also Lowell Mason's famous *Sacred Harp*.

In the meantime, W. B. Smith of the firm, a man of vision and energy, envisioned the publication of a series of readers which would be properly adapted to the habits, energy, and ideals of the frontier people of the West. He felt that the eastern written books failed to meet their needs. He first approached Catherine Beecher, a sister of Harriet Beecher Stowe, to write the *Readers*. However, she was engaged in founding and developing the Hartford Female Seminary. Next he approached McGuffey, who already had been working on a series of readers. So on April 28, 1836, he made a contract with Truman and Smith for a graded series of four readers. The *First* and *Second* were already in preparation, and the *Third* and *Fourth* were to be completed in eighteen months. The terms of the contract called for a 10 per cent royalty on all books until the sum should reach $1,000, after which the *Readers* would become the absolute property of the publishers. Later William McGuffey was paid to write the *Sixth Reader*, and his brother Alexander was paid for writing the *Fifth*. Beyond that the McGuffeys received little or no compensation for these famous *Readers*, except a few voluntary gifts from the publishers. Mr. Louis Dillman, president of the American Book Company in 1920, estimated that seven million copies were sold during 1836-1850, forty million during 1850-1870, sixty million during 1870-1890, and fifteen million during the 1890-1920 period. Many copies have been sold since. In all, well over 122,000,000 copies have been sold.

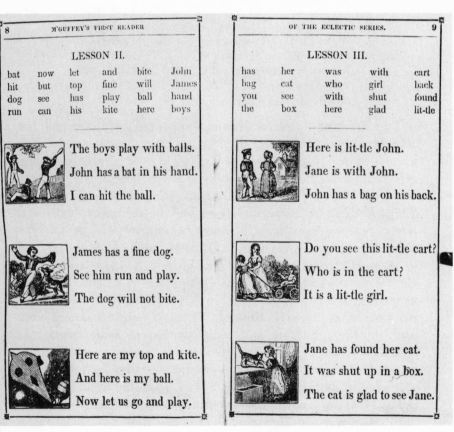

McGuffey, *First Reader,* appealing to the child.

A word should be said about the publishers. **Truman** did not agree with Smith regarding the future success of textbooks. After some differences, it is said that Smith came to the shop early one morning and made two piles of their books. On one he placed all the miscellaneous books, including the *Child's Bible*, the *Sacred Harp*, and the firm's cash; and on the other pile he put the half dozen small textbooks, including the four McGuffey *Readers*. When Truman came he was given the choice of the piles. As expected he took the first pile. Thus W. B. Smith became the sole publisher of the *Readers*. As a consequence the following firms have been the parent publishers of the McGuffey *Readers*:

Truman and Smith	1834-1841
W. B. Smith	1841-1852
W. B. Smith & Company	1852-1863
Sargent, Wilson & Hinkle	1863-1868
Wilson, Hinkle & Company	1868-1877
Van Antwerp, Bragg & Company	1877-1890
American Book Company	1890-

The *First* and *Second Readers* appeared in 1836, and the *Third* and *Fourth Readers* in 1837. In 1838, Truman and Smith were sued for infringement of copyright, for allegedly having copied material from Worcester's *Second*, *Third*, and *Fourth Readers*. The case was settled out of court, and the *Second* and *Third Readers* were immediately revised by McGuffey. Numerous later revisions were made in order to improve the books. The *First Reader* was revised in 1841, 1844, and 1848; the *Second* in 1838, 1841, and 1844; the *Third* in 1838, 1843, and 1848; the *Fourth* in 1844 and 1848. The *Fifth Reader*, written by Alexander McGuffey, was published in 1844. In 1853 all five readers reappeared as "Newly Revised." In 1857 some changes were made in the gradation and redistribution of some lesson materials, and the *Sixth* and *High School Reader* were first published. In 1879 all six readers were rather radically revised and appeared in uniform binding in brown. Then finally in 1901 and in 1920 they were recopyrighted with only slight changes.

Interestingly the McGuffeys had very little to do with the revisions. For them, the publishers must be given considerable

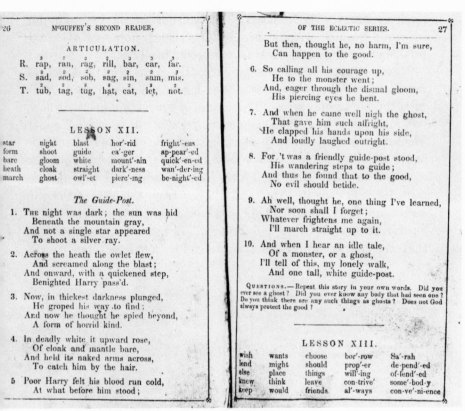

McGuffey, *Second Reader,* vowel sounds and finer print.

credit in employing very competent help. Whether outside help was employed to avoid giving the McGuffeys heavy royalties, as has been suggested, is not certain. The first one employed by Smith was Dr. Timothy S. Pinneo, who later became the author of a popular series of *Grammars* published by Smith. Some of the minor revisions were made by members of the publishing staff, especially by Obed J. Wilson. Of all the revisions, the one made in 1878-1879 was both the most radical and most popular; for sixty million copies of this edition were later sold. The persons employed to make this revision were Robert W. Stevenson of Columbus and Miss Amanda Funnelle of Terre Haute for the first three readers; and Edwin C. Hewett of Bloomington, Illinois, and Thomas W. Harvey of Ohio for the upper three readers. Harvey later became the author of a very popular series of grammars published by the same company. Also, the publishers secured criticisms from selected teachers.

Next, attention must be given to the appealing features of the *Readers*. One feature was the use of the word "Eclectic" with the books and series. This is not a very familiar word now, but must have been then. It means "choice, or selective." Since McGuffey was a scholarly man, he took great pains to include in the *Readers* largely *choice* lesson materials. For example, the cover of an early *Eclectic Third Reader* mentioned that it contained "Selections in Prose and Poetry from the Best American and English Writers." The *Fourth* said that it contained "Elegant Extracts in Prose and Poetry." It has often been claimed that the literary pieces in the McGuffey *Readers* often consti-

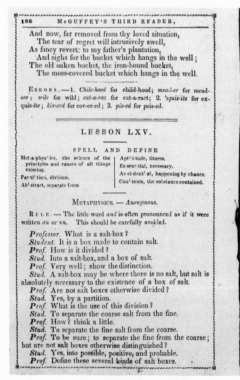

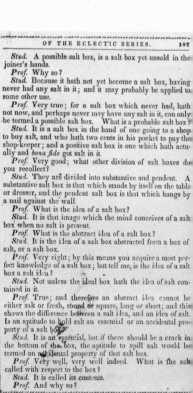

186 McGUFFEY'S THIRD READER,

And now, far removed from thy loved situation,
The tear of regret will intrusively swell,
As fancy reverts to my father's plantation,
And sighs for the bucket which hangs in the well;
The old oaken bucket, the iron-bound bucket,
The moss-covered bucket which hangs in the well.

ERRORS.—1. *Chile-hood* for child-hood; *mead-er* for meadow; *wile* for wild; *cat-a-rac* for cat-a-ract; 2. *'squis-ite* for exquis-ite; *kiv-crd* for cov-er-ed; 3. *pis-ed* for pois-ed.

LESSON LXV.

SPELL AND DEFINE

Met-a-phys'-ics, the science of the principles and causes of all things existing.
Par-ti'tion, division.
Ab'stract, separate from

Apt'-i-tude, fitness.
Es-sen'-tial, necessary.
Ac-ci-dent'-al, happening by chance.
Con'-tents, the substance contained.

METAPHYSICS. — *Anonymous.*

RULE. — The little word *and* is often pronounced as if it were written *an* or *un*. This should be carefully avoided.

Professor. What is a salt-box?
Student. It is a box made to contain salt.
Prof. How is it divided?
Stud. Into a salt-box, and a box of salt.
Prof. Very well; show the distinction.
Stud. A salt-box may be where there is no salt, but salt is absolutely necessary to the existence of a box of salt.
Prof. Are not salt boxes otherwise divided?
Stud. Yes, by a partition.
Prof. What is the use of this division?
Stud. To separate the coarse salt from the fine.
Prof. How? think a little.
Stud. To separate the fine salt from the coarse.
Prof. To be sure; to separate the fine from the coarse; but are not salt boxes otherwise distinguished?
Stud. Yes, into possible, positive, and probable.
Prof. Define these several kinds of salt boxes.

OF THE ECLECTIC SERIES. 187

Stud. A possible salt box, is a salt box yet unsold in the joiner's hands.
Prof. Why so?
Stud. Because it hath not yet become a salt box, having never had any salt in it; and it may probably be applied to some other use.
Prof. Very true; for a salt box which never had, hath not now, and perhaps never may have any salt in it, can only be termed a possible salt box. What is a probable salt box?
Stud. It is a salt box in the hand of one going to a shop to buy salt, and who hath two cents in his pocket to pay the shop-keeper; and a positive salt box is one which hath actually and *bona fide* got salt in it.
Prof. Very good; what other division of salt boxes do you recollect?
Stud. They are divided into substantive and pendent. A substantive salt box is that which stands by itself on the table or dresser, and the pendent salt box is that which hangs by a nail against the wall.
Prof. What is the idea of a salt box?
Stud. It is that image which the mind conceives of a salt box when no salt is present.
Prof. What is the abstract idea of a salt box?
Stud. It is the idea of a salt box abstracted from a box of salt, or a salt box.
Prof. Very right; by this means you acquire a most perfect knowledge of a salt box; but tell me, is the idea of a salt box a salt idea?
Stud. Not unless the ideal box hath the idea of salt contained in it.
Prof. True; and therefore an abstract idea cannot be either salt or fresh, round or square, long or short; and this shows the difference between a salt idea, and an idea of salt. Is an aptitude to hold salt an essential or an accidental property of a salt box?
Stud. It is an essential, but if there should be a crack in the bottom of the box, the aptitude to spill salt would be termed an accidental property of that salt box.
Prof. Very well, very well indeed. What is the salt called with respect to the box?
Stud. It is called its contents.
Prof. And why so?

McGuffey, *Third Reader,* longer words, titles, pronunciation.

tuted the only real literature many of its readers ever read. However, there were two drawbacks to including largely only choice literary pieces. One was that too often the vocabulary in these selections was ill adapted to the age level of the children using the books. The application of the Yoakam Readability Formula to an early edition of the *Second Reader* revealed that its vocabulary was at the eighth grade reading level. The second drawback was that often the choice literary selections contained concepts too difficult for a full understanding by children. For example, the 1843 edition of the *Third Reader* contained a selection entitled "Metaphysics." Hughes found that all of the different editions of the McGuffey *Fourth, Fifth,* and *Sixth Readers* contained a total of 1,067 separate titles. Of these, 247 appeared in readers of more than one level, and 607 appeared only once. The fact that 607 appeared only once, and that more than 23 per cent appeared in readers of more than one level is proof that experience with the use of the early readers revealed poor grading of the selections. Five of the fifteen most frequently repeated titles appeared in readers of all three levels. Thus by trial and error the gradation improved in the later editions. It may be added, however, that these two drawbacks were not common only to the McGuffey *Readers,* but to other readers as well, during the period covered. It is the impression of the writer, who has examined hundreds of old readers, that McGuffey's were less guilty than most other readers in this respect.

The positive merits of the McGuffey *Readers* greatly outweighed their weaknesses, especially when compared with their competitors. One feature was the systematic way the pupils were guided in the process of learning to read. The older way was to learn to spell first and then to read. The McGuffey *First Readers* began with words used in sentences, and usually the content of the sentences was related to accompanying pictures. The *Third Readers* early included "Plain Rules for Reading." The 1843 edition even included lessons in enunciation. At that time oral reading was strongly emphasized. The 1844 edition of the *Fourth* began with 26 pages dealing with such matters as articulation, tones, inflections, and emphasis. The first edition of the *Fifth* (1844) devoted 48 pages to an "Analysis of the

Principles of Elocution," which ended with a list of "character" keys to denote the different qualities of elocution. Then the lessons were interspersed with these "characters" to assist the students in effective oral reading. For example ($\diagup$) denoted rising inflection, and ($\diagdown$) falling inflection. Later editions contained even more helps. The 1857 edition of the *Fourth* defined the key words before each lesson and asked questions or suggested exercises after the lesson.

Another feature of the McGuffey lower *Readers* was the use of short sentences and brief lessons. The first edition of the *Second Reader* (1836) had 85 lessons in 164 pages of content. Furthermore, the paragraphs were usually short and were numbered. The later revised editions had even shorter sentences and paragraphs.

A third feature that was more or less characteristic of the *Readers* in all their editions was the human interest appeal. For example, a lesson entitled "The Three Cakes" as used in some contemporary readers was called "Three Boys and Three Cakes" by McGuffey; "The Little Boats" was changed to "The Little Sailor Boys"; and "The Guide Post" to "Harry and the Guide Post."

Closely related to the human appeal was the way in which morals were taught in the McGuffey *Readers*. Such moral qualities as honesty, truth and truthfulness, obedience, temperance, kindness to humans and animals, thrift, work, and patriotism were largely taught by means of actual human and situational stories. Note the following titles taken from the 1853 edition of the *Third Reader:* "Harry and the Dog," "Perseverance," "The Song of the Dying Swan," "The Noblest Revenge," "The Goodness of God," "The Generous Russian Peasant," "Try, Try Again," "We Are Seven," and "Touch Not—Taste Not—Handle Not."

It has been recognized by students of history that the lessons in the McGuffey *Readers* did much to set the standards of morality and of the social life in the pioneering west for more than half a century. Many of the truths and poetic expressions memorized from these *Readers* were quoted by parents, preachers, and others to counteract acts of intemperance, vulgarity, laziness,

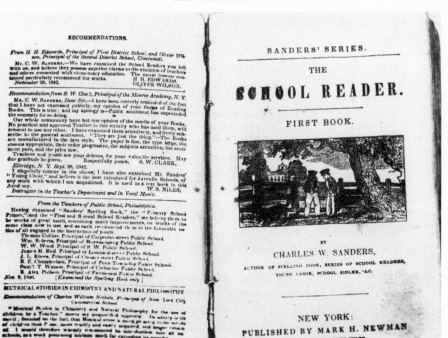

Note teachers' recommendations for use.

brutality, dishonesty, and lawlessness, which were altogether too common among frontier people.

Even the pictures upheld the standards. The earliest editions of the *Primer*, and *First* and *Second Readers* contained pictures. The *Third Reader* had only a few until the 1857 edition, which contained many. The same was true of the *Fourth*. The *Fifth* and *Sixth* contained no pictures until the 1879 edition, and then only a few.

Many distinguished Americans who were reared west of the Appalachians, where the McGuffey *Readers* held dominant sway, have acknowledged the deep debt they owe to the lessons learned from these *Readers*. Among them may be mentioned Henry Ford, Senator Borah, Senator Beveridge, William McKinley, Lew Wallace, James Whitcomb Riley, Mark Twain, Rutherford Hayes, Robert LaFollette, and thousands of others. The National Education Association, in its 1873 national convention, passed the following memorial resolution to a great teacher and colleague:

> Resolved, 1. That in the death of William H. McGuffey, late Professor of Moral Philosophy in the University of Virginia, this Association feels that they have lost one of the greatest lights of the profession whose life was a lesson full of instruction, an example and model to American teachers.
>
> 2. That his labors in the cause of education extending over a period of half a century, in the several offices of teacher of common schools, college professor and college president, and as author of textbooks; his influence upon his pupils and community; his care for the public interests of education; his lofty devotion to duty; his conscientious Christian character—*all these* have made him one of the noblest ornaments of our profession in this age, and entitle him to the grateful remembrance of this Association and of the teachers of America.

S. G. Goodrich (1793-1860). Goodrich, whose early writings appeared under the pen name of Peter Parley, wrote textbooks in many fields. Nearly all of these books contained many pictures, certainly many more than there were in most other textbooks during their time. In 1839 *The Comprehensive Readers*, a series of four, were printed in Louisville. Most of his other books were printed in the East. One may wonder why he had these printed in the West. It may be that he hoped to cash in on the growing demand for textbooks on the frontier, as W. B. Smith hoped to do with the McGuffey *Readers*. The *First* and *Second Readers* contained many pictures and simple lessons to appeal to children. The *Third* contained no pictures and in general was unattractive. The lessons were followed by questions regarding words, pronunciation, and the content. The *Fourth* was much more technical in nature. It began with eight pages of rules for oral reading, followed by fifteen pages dealing with prefixes and roots. No questions, pictures, or exercises accompanied the lessons. The *First* and *Second* were revised in 1846, and a *Fifth* and *Sixth* were added in 1857, which were edited by Noble Butler. Goodrich's *Readers* never became as popular as his history and geography books.

Charles W. Sanders (1805-1889). In the 1840's, and even later, the Sanders' *School Readers* were the most popular readers in the East. In 1840 he published the *Primer*, and the *First* and *Second School Readers*; in 1841 the *Third*; and in 1842 the *Fourth*. In 1848 the *Fifth* appeared, and in 1862 the *Sixth*. In addition to the *School Readers* he published a series of the so-called *Union Readers* in the 1860's, with the *Fifth* and *Sixth* bearing the additional term of *Rhetorical*. Also, in 1855 he had prepared a special reader for use in the "Higher Female Seminaries" entitled *Young Ladies Reader*. Most of these *Readers* were revised and recopyrighted a number of times. For example, the *First* was copyrighted in 1840, 1853, and 1861; the *Second* in 1840, 1853, and 1860; the *Third* in 1841, 1855, and 1860; the *Fourth* in 1842, 1854, 1855, and 1863.

Sanders' *Primer* and *First Reader* from the beginning had many pictures, large type, and were pleasant to read. He stated that the first fifty pages of the *First Reader* contained monosyllables and the dissyllables were gradually introduced. The first edition of the *Second* had only two pictures, but the later editions contained many. Most of the lessons were preceded by key word lists. In the 1861 edition these words were even defined. He aimed, not to present classical literary pieces, which he considered too difficult for children, but to present lessons which would be meaningful, carefully graded, interesting, and of high moral value. Numerous lessons in the *First Reader* dealt with animals. In the *Second* were lessons dealing with animals, fish, birds, and even insects. The first three lessons in the *Third* were, "The Boy Rebuked by his Dog," "The Swallow and

Sanders, 1840, keen competition for McGuffey—oriented to whole curriculum and to life.

the Red Breast," and "The Sun-flower." The lessons in the *Fourth* dealt with a great variety of subjects, but very few of an abstract nature. These readers represented a marked contrast to the readers previously in common use in the East, which contained many lessons of an abstract and a theological nature.

The *School Reader, Fifth Book,* was very different from the first four readers. The first 58 pages dealt with "Rhetorical Principles" treating such topics as, articulation, emphasis, inflection, modulation, expression, personation, rhetorical pause, and poetical elocution. Part Second consisted largely of selections, both prose and poetry, taken from famous writings. Explanatory notes preceded many of the selections. The *School Readers* series contained no sixth.

In 1861 Sanders began publishing the *Union Readers.* In the preface of *Number One* he stated: "The increasing demand for greater variety of exercises in reading, both in style and matter, has led to the preparation of Sanders' Union Series." Every lesson in *Number One* was illustrated by a picture. In *Number Two* each lesson was preceded by a list of defined key words, and about one-half of the lessons contained a picture. *Number Three* was similar except the word lists and lessons were longer, and

thirteen pages were devoted to principles of elocution. The *Union Fourth Reader* devoted 38 pages to elocution and contained no pictures. The aims were to "leave the best moral impression" and to "furnish the best possible exercises for practice in Rhetorical reading." The *Union Fifth* was similar in make-up, but presented lessons of a more highly recognized literary quality. This series,

An elocution reader, 1843—note *The Orator's Ladder* in picture.

unlike the *School* series, included a *Rhetorical, or Union Sixth Reader*. Sanders stated: "Viewed in the light of its *primary* purpose, without reference to collateral aims, the present work is simply a comprehensive course of reading." Throughout, the authors of the selections were identified.

In the preface of the *Young Ladies' Reader*, Sanders quoted the Younger Pliny as follows:

As in life, so in one's studies, the most beautiful and the most humane is, I think, so to blend the grave and the gay, that the one may not settle down in melancholy, nor the other in levity.

He then proceeded to say that he aimed to do this in all his *Readers*, but "more studiously" in this one. A few of the lesson topics follow: "The Sense of Beauty," "I Love to Live, and Live to Love," "The Wants of Man," "Domestic Life," "The Virtuous Woman," "The Lovers Leap," "Pride," "The Talking Lady," "Moral Beauty," "The Broken Hearted," "The Needle."

Sanders was a prolific and successful textbook writer. In addition to the two series of readers, he was also the author of popular spelling books. It has been estimated that about 13,000,000 of his books were sold.

David B. Tower. Although all early readers seemed to have greatly stressed exercises relating to oral reading, no author so fully stressed the importance of letter sounds and their combinations as did Tower. Today such exercises are called *phonics*. He published *The Gradual Reader, First Step; or, Exercises in Articulation* in 1841. Later this book became the third reader in a series. In some introductory remarks he stated, "In using the 'Exercises,' no regard should be paid to the *meaning* of the examples. Let the whole attention be given to articulating the Elementary Sounds and their Combinations distinctly and properly, and to pronouncing the words correctly." The first 46 pages he devoted wholly to phonic exercises dealing with such letter combinations, as bd, bld, bst, dzh, dldst, dths, glst, kndst, ksth, lpst, and so on. These he followed by 142 pages of reading lessons.

In 1845 Tower began his series of readers by publishing *The*

Gradual Primer, or Primary School Enunciator. It was a rather attractive book with fairly large type and many pictures, but extreme attention was given to letter sounds. The next year the *Introduction to the Gradual Reader* appeared as a second reader. Soon, together with Cornelius Walker, he wrote the *Sequel to the Gradual Reader* as a fourth. The emphasis on phonics was not as strong in this book as in the *Gradual Reader* (The Third).

The fifth and sixth books in the series were written by the same two men but bore the title, *North American First Class Reader; the Fifth Book* in 1846, and the *Sixth Book* in 1848. In these readers the emphasis changed from letters and letter combinations to elocution. In the *Fifth* 64 pages dealt with principles of elocution. The subsections were entitled Remarks on Inflection, Stress, Tremulous Movement of the Voice, Emphasis, Pause, and Circumflex. The subsections in the *Sixth* dealt with

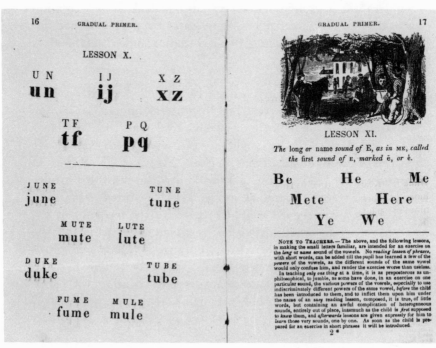

Tower's, *Gradual Primer,* 1845—note instructions to teacher.

Pitch, Monotone, Quantity, Rate, Semitone, Aspirated Function of the Voice, Force, Feebleness of Voice, Suppressed Force, and Transition. In both of these readers most of the reading selections were identified as to authorship, and represented rather high literary quality. These *Readers* apparently attained considerable circulation for more than a decade.

William D. Swan. In 1844 a series of readers by Swan appeared. The regular series consisted of *The Primary School Reader, Parts I, II,* and *III.* This series was intended for use in the primary schools. These were followed by *The Grammar School Reader.* The regular series was then concluded with *The District School Reader; or, Exercises in Reading and Speaking.* These books either must have been considered good or Swan and his publishers must have been good salesmen, for they were adopted for use in at least twenty of the largest cities of Massachusetts, including Boston. The lessons in these books, as was true of the books by Sanders and McGuffey, dealt with many topics, particularly with animals and stories involving a moral quality.

In contrast to most primary readers of that period, Swan did not favor pictures. He criticized the use of "cuts" to illustrate words and sentences by calling their use an "absurdity." On the other hand, he was strong for the use of phonics. Even in the *Part First* (really the *First Reader*) the lessons were "arranged upon the plan of teaching the *powers* of letters, as well as their names. The attention is to be directed to *one* sound in each lesson." Thus he really began to stress elocution in the lowest reader. For example, the first lesson in *Part Second* revealed his scheme, as follows:

LESSON I

Exercises on the Sounds of bl, br, bz, and dr.

blame	brave	jobs	dream
bleak	break	mobs	drive
blow	breeze	robs	drove

I will not blame the boys.
They did not mean to break my cup.
I can see the webs on the wall.
See me drive my new hoop.

The District School Reader began by devoting 52 pages to Principles of Elocution. Swan went even into more detail here than many of the so-called *Speakers*. He injected short reading pieces to be used for practice regarding the principles. In dealing with emphasis, he listed three degrees with practice examples, as follows:

Single Emphasis
Study not so much *to show* knowledge as *to acquire* it.

Double Emphasis
To *err* is *human;* to *forgive, divine.*

Treble Emphasis
Had you rather Caesar were living, and die all slaves,
Than that Caesar were *dead,* to *live* all *freemen.*

In dealing with Tones of Voice he listed extracts illustrating the following qualities: cheerfulness, mirth, joy, pity, hope, hatred, anger, revenge, reproach, fear, grief, remorse, despair, surprise, and malice. No aids for the pupil or teacher were connected with the lessons.

In 1848 Swan published a supplementary reader entitled, *The Instructive Reader; or A Course of Reading in Natural History, Science and Literature.* In defense, he said, "Many children are compelled, from various causes, to leave school before completing, or hardly commencing, a regular course of instruction upon these subjects." Nearly all of the lessons dealt with some aspect of science. This book was intended for the upper grades. In 1850 he published *The Introduction to the Instructive Reader.* It was designed for the primary and intermediate grades. Only about half of the lessons dealt with science. Thus Swan was one of the first authors to publish supplementary readers.

Salem Town (1779-1864). Town, like several others, was the author of very popular spellers as well as readers. He published his *First Reader* in 1844. Quite different from most first readers, which commonly began with the alphabet, or syllables, or easy words, and often a picture, this one opened with a lesson entitled, "The Lost Purse," which covered three and one-half pages. Many of the later lessons were interspersed with spelling words and some pictures. The *Second Reader, or Progressive Lessons* appeared later. It opened with a table of numbers and a table of elementary sounds. The first lesson was short, and was accompanied with a picture and a list of words. Later in the book the words to be spelled were also defined. The *Third Reader* opened with 48 pages devoted to rules and exercises related to effective oral reading. It had no pictures, but the lessons contained defined words to be spelled and were followed by questions pertaining to the lesson. In other words, the lessons were not only to be read well orally but also understood for meaning.

The *Fourth Reader* (1847) opened with 66 pages dealing with rules for oral reading, interspersed with illustrative reading exercises. The authorship of the regular reading selections was commonly identified. The last of the series was entitled *Fifth or Elocutionary Reader*. More than half of this book consisted of elocutionary principles extensively applied to reading lessons. Even regular lessons in the latter half of the book had parenthetical notes referring to particular rules. For example, Lesson XLVIII, "The Right of Free Discussion" by Webster, contained the following note: [See Rule 3, p. 168, and Rule 12, p. 193]. In 1850 Town wrote the *Grammar School Reader* which was not a part of a regular series, but which appeared in several editions.

In 1856 an entirely new series of readers appeared under the joint authorship of Salem Town and Nelson M. Holbrook. Apparently these were largely prepared by Holbrook, for the copyright was taken out in his name. Town's name was apparently used for its likely sales value, because his earlier readers were well-known. These new readers were entitled *Progressive Readers*. The *First Progressive Reader* was entirely new. It was attractively printed, and contained many pictures. It even attempted to illustrate letter sounds by means of pictures. For example, ā with a picture of an ape, ä with an arm, a with an awl, ă with an ax, and so on. The *Second* was enlarged, and defined the words appearing at the beginning of each lesson. The *Third* devoted more space to rules and exercises for good reading than the earlier *Third*, and also introduced some pictures. The arrangement of the *Fourth* was changed considerably. The rules and the exercises were separated, not interspersed; and the regular lessons had defined word lists at the beginning and thought provoking questions at the end of each lesson. The first part of the *Fifth* remained largely unchanged, but some of the regular reading selections were changed. In other words, the *Progressive Readers* largely constituted a new set of readers except the *Fifth*.

Henry Mandeville. In 1846 he wrote *A Course of Reading.* This book was intended for the upper grades and was very different from most upper readers of the period. It was divided into three parts. The first contained a description of the letters of the alphabet and their various sounds, of syllables, and of words as parts of speech. Short reading selections showing their uses were interspersed. The second part dealt with a classification and description of sentences or formulas of thought, with detailed instructions as to how they should be orally read. In other words,

22   PICTORIAL PRIMER.

LESSON XXVIII.

John	fond	lamb	fast
drum	play	soft	does
beats	wolf	wool	fife
goat	lives	wild	rake
kid	woods	deer	cake

John has a new drum.
How he beats his drum!

See the goat and her kid.
The kid is fond of play.

Here is a big wolf.
He lives in the woods.

Ann has a pet lamb.
The lamb has soft wool.

Here is the wild deer.
How fast he does run.

PICTORIAL PRIMER.   23

LESSON XXIX.

boys	rides	with	hoops
girls	cart	their	swing
one	some	guns	jump
flies	ball	swords	rope
kite	train	roll	dolls

THE PLAY GROUND.

See the boys and girls at play.
One boy flies his kite, and one
  rides in his cart.
Some play at ball; some train
  with their guns and swords.
The girls roll their hoops, or
  ride in the swing.
Some jump the rope, and some
  play with their dolls.

Blue Pictorial Primer, 1846—note emphasis on outdoor play.

the principles of elocution were taught by means of reading selections illustrating them. The third part was a sequel to the second part. It contained longer selections involving the previously taught principles. Before writing this book Mandeville had been a minister, and at the time of writing was a professor of Moral Science and Belles-Lettres at Hamilton College. The fact that he was not engaged in public school work likely explains why the book was a departure from common practice. Nevertheless the book went through several editions.

In the late 1840's Mandeville began publishing a complete graded series of five readers. The *Primary* and *Second Reader* opened with the alphabet and short lists of words in script, because he believed that the children should learn to read both print and script. Throughout, he correlated spelling and reading. The readers also contained many pictures. The *Third Reader* was much more advanced and difficult than the *Second*. He devoted the first 22 pages to detailed instructions and exercises for effective oral reading. Some of these certainly were too technical for a third reader. He used such terms as, "Exercise on the Bend and Perfect Close," "Upward Slide," "A Combination of the Bend, Close, and Slide," "Exercises on Compellatives in Connection with the Closes and Slides," "Emphatic Sweeps," and "Exercises on Pitch, Force, and Rate." Then 130 lessons were presented on the remaining 178 pages. No pictures appeared in this book. The *Fifth Reader* was composed of extracts of both prose and poetry by well known writers or stories about significant events. The literary selections were usually followed by a brief biography of the author. The topics of the lessons were very miscellaneous in character.

Richard G. Parker (1798-1869) *and J. Madison Watson* (1827-1900). Parker first gained his reputation as a textbook writer in the fields of English composition and natural philosophy. His *Progressive Exercises in English Composition* was first published in 1832 and was reprinted as late as 1879, and his *School Compendium in Natural and Experimental Philosophy* in 1837 and as late as 1871. Watson had also done some writing. In 1855 these two authors joined their efforts in a series of *National*

Readers. The lowest one was the *National First Reader, or Word Builder.* They claimed that the word-method united all the advantages of the old method by "first commencing with the alphabet, and the new and preferable one, which begins with entire words." The *Primer* was restricted to 1,500 monosyllables, none of which contained more than five letters. Most of the short lessons were illustrated with pictures. The *First* had a few longer words in the latter part of the book. The *Second* introduced specific exercises in articulation, which usually was not done so early in other series of readers. Interestingly a *Third* was written by Parker alone in 1851 and contained no rules for reading. Then in 1857 the two authors rewrote it, and included 30 pages of rules and exercises before the regular reading lessons. It was again revised in 1866.

The *Fourth* was also written alone by Parker in 1851, and without elocutionary rules, which was contrary to common practice in fourth readers of that period. In 1857 the two revised it and included 34 pages of principles of elocution. The Table of Oral Elements listed Tonics, Subtonics, and Atonics. Then Cognates received treatment. No word lists or questions accompanied the regular lessons. In 1866 it was again revised. The *National Sixth Reader* aimed to be a "complete and sufficient work for advanced classes in Reading, Elocution, and English and American Literature." It included many extensive biographical and explanatory notes in connection with recognized literary selections. Most of these selections were extracts from well known writers. This book was also revised several times. The *National Readers* went through many revisions and reprintings and had considerable circulation for at least two decades.

Even before the *National Readers* were written Parker had published *Exercises in Rhetorical Reading.* This was a rather technical and advanced book and likely was used mainly in academies. It had several reprintings.

As Parker had written some of the readers alone, so also had Watson. In 1858 he wrote the *National School Primer, or Primary Word-Builder.* In 1868 he published a series of readers: namely, the *Independent Series.* It consisted of six readers. For example, the *Fourth* devoted 15 pages to orthoepy and 14 pages to expression. It included several pictures. Few fourth readers then had pictures. The *Fifth* and *Sixth* were similar to the *Fourth* only larger. This series also went through several reprintings.

Epes Sargent (1813-1880). Sargent, like several other authors of readers, began by writing the most advanced one first. Thus in 1852 he published *The Standard Speaker*, which was designed for "schools, academies, lyceums, colleges." After dealing with the principles of elocution, he presented and classified the reading selections, as moral and didactic, martial and popular, senatorial, forensic and judicial, political and occasional, narrative and lyrical, scriptural and devotional, rhetorical and dramatic, and comic and satirical. Later he wrote an *Intermediate* and a *Primary Standard Speaker*. All these received several printings.

Next, in 1854, he published *The First Class Standard Reader*. This apparently was intended to be a sequel advanced reader to the *Speakers*. The next year he made this a *Fifth Reader*, and prepared a graded series by writing *The First Standard Reader*, the *Second*, the *Third*, and the *Fourth*. The *First* and *Second* were profusely illustrated with pictures. He mentioned that his chief endeavor was "to graduate the exercises carefully to the taste and comprehension of those for whom the work is designed; and this without falling below a just literary standard."

In 1871 a series of five *New American Readers* under the joint authorship of Epes Sargent and Amasa May was published. Apparently Sargent's name was retained for prestige, but May did the work. These were very attractive both from the standpoint of the print and the profuse use of pictures. Even the *Fourth* and *Fifth* had pictures, which was unusual for upper readers. They claimed that the series was carefully graded, handsomely illustrated, clearly printed, strongly bound, and that they combined "all the advantages of the word method, the Phonic System, the A B C Method, and Object-Teaching." These comments clearly indicate that the authors were very conscious of different methods of teaching reading. Finally, in 1872, these authors wrote the *Etymological Reader*. The peculiar feature of this book was that it presented long lists of prefixes, suffixes, Saxon roots, Latin roots, and Greek roots together with their meanings. Then at the end of the regular reading selections there appeared "Select Etymologies" dealing with the most difficult words of the lessons.

G. S. Hillard (1808-1879). Hillard, like Sargent and several others, wrote an advanced reader first. In 1855 he wrote *A First Class Reader*, with "biographical and critical notices of the authors." Contrary to many other advanced readers, he claimed this to be "exclusively a reading book. Pieces suitable for declamation have been inserted only incidentally and occasionally." In fact it was really an anthology of literary pieces rather than a Speaker. The next year *A Second Class Reader* appeared. However, it was a smaller and simpler book than the *First*. In 1857 appeared the *Third Class Reader*, and in 1858 the *Third Primary Reader*. These readers were really numbered in reverse. The higher numbered books were the lower. The *Third Primary* greatly emphasized enunciation.

Apparently Hillard's emphasis upon literary silent reading rather than on the rhetorical was too revolutionary for the period; so in 1863 he published the *Fifth Reader* to replace the *Second Class Reader*. In it he devoted 60 pages to letter sound exercises and elocution. The regular reading lessons were preceded by brief biographical sketches of the authors, and followed with key words defined. The *Sixth Reader* replaced the *First Class Reader*. "An Introductory Treatise on Elocution" by Professor Mark Bailey was included. The reading selections were classified under Didactic, Narrative and Descriptive, Humorous and Pathetic, Declamatory, and Dramatic. Rather long biographical notes preceded the lessons. These two books appeared in many editions.

Ultimately Hillard must have realized that the demand for books stressing elocutionary reading was still strong, so he prepared an entirely new series along these lines and called them the *Franklin Series*. It began with the *Franklin Primer or First Reader*, and ended with the *Franklin Sixth Reader and Speaker*. In several of these he even included pictures of persons speaking orally, showing the varied positions or gestures of the hand, head, and feet for different expressions of feelings and emphases. In other words, the emphasis in the last series was nearly opposite to the first. His experiment with literary silent reading did not succeed.

Lucius Osgood. In 1855 Osgood began publishing the *Progressive Series* of readers, which began with the *Primer* and ended with the *Fifth* in 1858. These constituted the most popular series of textbooks ever published in Pittsburgh. After building up a basic vocabulary in the *Primer*, the lessons in the *First Reader* began by adding new words to those already learned. Each lesson was preceded by a picture and the new words which had not been learned. These words were to be pronounced and spelled, and no doubt, their meanings given by the teacher.

The *Second Reader* began with tables of letter sounds and their markings. Arabic numerals were placed above the vowels to indicate their sounds, as had been done in the McGuffey *Speller*. Again lessons were preceded by marked word lists, and some had pictures. The *Third Reader* began with twelve pages devoted to "Elementary Principles" (of elocution). It contained combinations of vocals, subvocals, and aspirates, as

$$\overset{1}{\text{bla}}, \overset{2}{\text{bro}}; \overset{1}{\text{glo}}, \overset{1}{\text{gru}}.$$

Then rather long marked word lists preceded the reading lessons. Beginning on page 45 the words were also defined. Most lessons were followed by questions concerning the facts or thoughts involved. Many of the lessons attempted to teach morals.

Osgood's *Primer,* first of most popular series printed in Pittsburgh, 1855-1858, and later.

In the *Fourth Reader* Osgood went all out in stressing elocutionary reading. The first 140 pages dealt with matters of articulation, accent, emphasis, inflection, and modulation, interspersed
with reading exercises involving them. These were followed by
244 pages of reading selections. The selections were preceded
by a list of words to be spelled and defined, and were followed
by many questions concerning their content. One half of the
lessons were either poetry or dialogues. The *Fifth Reader* had
48 pages dealing with elocution, not as many as in the *Fourth*,
but the treatment was much more technical. Most of the regular
lessons were presented without word lists and without questions
following them. More of the lessons were extracts from classical
writings.

By 1870 Osgood evidently learned that there were certain
objections to his *Progressive Readers*, so he wrote the new *American Series*. The *Primer* and *First Reader* were published in 1870,
the *Second* and *Third* in 1871, the *Fourth* and *Fifth* in 1872, and
the *Sixth* in 1873. These represented considerable improvement
over the *Progressive Series*. The lower readers were very attractive, with larger print and profuse use of interesting pictures.
Furthermore, the first three changed from the numeral markings
of vowels to the use of diacritical marks.

The *Fourth Reader* was published in two forms, one using the
numeral marking of vowels and containing only 224 pages, the
other using diacritical marks and containing 258 pages with
thirteen additional lessons. Likewise, the *Fifth* was printed in
two forms, one containing 109 lessons, the other, 225. The smaller
one contained many pictures; the larger had none. The *Sixth*
appeared only in one form of 512 pages. It contained a number
of pictures, which was uncommon for sixth readers. Apparently
these readers were more widely used in the western Pennsylvania
area than either the McGuffey or Sanders' *Readers*.

Lewis B. Monroe (1825-1879). Beginning in 1871 Monroe prepared a full graded series of six readers, and in 1877 a primer.
The lower readers were printed in rather large type and profusely illustrated with pictures, mostly of children and animals.
The upper readers had a few pictures. Monroe had been con-

nected with several types of schools in New England and ultimately taught elocution in Boston University. The latter experience would naturally make him stress the sounds of letters and their combinations. So beginning with the *Primer* he presented words, often illustrated, according to the sounds of the vowels in them. For example, the first lesson in the *Primer* included a note to the teacher that the words contained the sounds of m, n, and short a. In the *First Reader* the notes about the letter sounds appeared at the bottom of the page. The *Second* and *Third Readers* did not play up the letter sounds so fully. However, the *Fourth Reader* used 15 pages to present pictures showing facial positions when pronouncing the different letter sounds. The first one is a crosscut picture of a head showing the windpipe, vocal cords, pharynx, soft palate, tongue, teeth, and lips. The later pictures appeared in pairs of a crosscut and a facial expression in pronouncing the various sounds. These were the first pictures of this type in any popular readers up to that time. The *Fifth Reader* used 31 introductory pages to deal with articulation and gesturing. A number of pictures illustrated different kinds of gestures. However, none of the lower five readers used the term *elocution,* but the *Sixth Reader* devoted 46 pages to "Practical Elocution." The terms in connection with elocution were not as difficult and technical, however, as was true of many earlier upper readers.

Interestingly, in his "Hints to Teachers" Monroe warned against beginning "by teaching the alphabet." The children should be taught "the letters only as fast as they make use of them." The way to acquire the language is through the ear. In none of the readers did he stress reading merely to get ideas from the printed page, but rather to get the ideas of the words in the sentences so that they could be effectively read orally with the proper tone of voice, articulation, stress, and gesturing.

Most of the books in the Monroe Series were revised and enlarged at least once and all of them went through several printings. Apparently they were widely used during 1870's and 1880's.

William T. Harris (1835-1908), *Andrew J. Rickoff, and Mark*

Bailey. These three men were the authors of the well-known *Appleton School Readers*. The *First* and *Third* were first published in 1877 and the other three in 1878. No doubt, one very evident reason for the immediate success of these *Readers* was their authorship. All three men were well-known educators at the time. Bailey was an Instructor of Elocution at Yale, and Rickoff was Superintendent of Instruction at Cleveland. At the time of the publication of these books Harris was the very successful Superintendent of Schools of St. Louis (1867-1880).

Harris became even more famous during the following years. Several biographies have been written about him. While he was an educational administrator he became very much interested in philosophy. In 1867 he founded the *Journal of Speculative Philosophy*. After leaving St. Louis he helped found the Concord (Mass.) School of Philosophy and Literature. In 1889 he was appointed United States Commissioner of Education, which position he filled with distinction for seventeen years. One book about him is called *Yankee Teacher; The Life of William T. Harris*. Counting all of the separate titles of his writings, books, articles, various annual and other reports, etc., the total reached 479. He was one of the outstanding educators of America in his time.

These *Readers* were very well planned and attractively printed. In the Preface of the *First Reader* it was suggested, "The teacher using this book can teach by any method which he may prefer; but the experience of many years has convinced us that a judicious combination of the word and phonic methods is the best." It contained very interesting and instructive pictures in connection with the "beautiful and child-life reading lessons."

The *Second Reader* con-

LESSON II.

Words and Phrases to be learned by Sight only.

rat   black

the rat

the black rat my cat

my black cat

Appleton, 1878, sight reading.

tinued the plan of the *First*, but added a table of vowel and consonant sounds. Of course the lessons were longer. Word lists diacritically marked preceded the lessons, and many pictures were included. The *Third* continued the plan of the others with lessons, "How We Read," placed at intervals through the book. This was Professor Bailey's way of introducing elocution.

Originally there were only five readers in the series, but apparently the *Fourth* was found to be too difficult to follow immediately after the *Third*, so the *Introductory Fourth Reader* was prepared. In the *Fourth* the "domain of literature proper" was introduced from standard writers representing "English undefiled" in their best style. "Preparatory Notes" were appended to the lessons to aid both teacher and pupil. The elocutionary work of the *Third* was continued in the *Fourth*.

The *Fifth* (and last) presented extracts from the world's greatest writers. The authors of the readers claimed it to be "a textbook of *belles-lettres*, as well as of reading and spelling." The "Preparatory Notes" were more advanced, and the lessons in elocution fuller. Literary history and criticism were woven into the lessons so as to evoke thought and inquiry in the minds of pupils. Like in the *Third* and the *Fourth* a collection of "Unusual and Difficult Words" was presented at the end of the book.

These *Readers* apparently had wide circulation for at least ten years, for most of them had new annual printings for many of these years. For example, the writer's collection contains seven *Fourth Readers* each bearing a different date of printing, even though the content was unchanged. The later editions of the first four books contained advertising in the back of the books. In fact, the changes in the advertising were the only pages that were different in the earliest editions of 1877 and 1878 and the editions printed as late as 1889.

William Swinton (1833-1892). Swinton, whose contributions as the author of textbooks in the fields of spelling and grammar are discussed in this book, was also the author of a series of readers. In 1882-1883 he wrote the *Primer*, and five readers. Then in 1885 he wrote the *Sixth or Classic English Reader*, and in 1886 an *Advanced Fourth Reader*. He wrote these readers at a time when authors were apparently very sensitive about methods of teaching reading. He, like several other authors of that period, tried to combine several methods. In the Preface of the *Primer* he mentioned that the "word method is used alone where it serves best, the phonic method is used alone where it serves best, and at a later stage the two are combined." Pictures were used in all except the *Sixth Reader*. Script was considerably used in the *Primer*, and in the *First* and *Second Readers*. He justified this by saying that most teachers commonly teach words and sentences by writing them on the blackboard. In the *First Reader* words were diacritically marked and a picture preceded each lesson. On page 109 the colors are taught by means of colored rectangles. This was one of the earliest examples of the actual use of color in a textbook. The *Second Reader* began with several lessons dealing with the sounds of vowels and consonants. Otherwise it was merely an advance over the *First*.

In the *Third Reader* a new feature was introduced. Since at the top of the title page of all the readers there appeared a heading entitled, "The Reader the Focus of Language-Training," so in the *Third* he injected practice exercises correlating reading and language lessons. These were partly oral and partly written. Some sort of language lesson preceded each reading lesson. The *Third* ended with five pages devoted to word-analysis of the principal English derivatives of the words of the book. The *Fourth* was similar to the *Third*, but considerably larger and contained more selections written by well-known writers.

The *Fifth Reader* was two-thirds a reader and one-third a speaker. Most fifth readers written before this were generally solely speakers. Swinton apparently believed that getting thought from the printed page was more important than mere elocution. His emphasis on connecting language study

Learning words three ways, by print, script, and picture.

with reading continued. At the end of the book 18 pages were devoted to an analysis of Latin derivatives.

The *Sixth or English Classic Reader* was different than the others. In it the emphasis was on literature. He presented brief biographies and then several selections of ten British and ten American famous authors: Shakespeare, Milton, Addison, Pope, Franklin, Burke, Scott, Webster, Irving, Byron, Bryant, Macaulay, Emerson, Longfellow, Whittier, Poe, Holmes, Tennyson, Thackeray, and Lowell. A glossary was included at the end of the book.

Although Swinton's *Readers* were attractive, and unusual in several respects, they were not reprinted as often as several other series. It may be that the new features were too different and revolutionary to receive common acceptance.

Ellen M. Cyr. She was one of a few women who authored a successful series of readers before 1900, the end date for this work. In 1891 she published *The Children's Primer*. She aimed to have children learn to throw "expression into sentences." So she attempted to provide a functional vocabulary of simple words. *Action* pictures accompanied the lessons. The pictures in the beginning often occupied more than half the page. The print was large. A list of the words used in the *Primer* appeared at the end of the book. The *First Reader*, published in 1892, in a slightly advanced manner, continued the same approach, with the word list at the end much longer.

Book Two consisted largely of many short stories, simple, and in touch with daily life. For example, the first five stories were: "Jessie and the Gander," "Playing with the Sand," "One Little Duck," "Something to Guess," and "Charlie and the Cars." The end word list was longer. In *Book Three* she introduced considerable poetry. In justification, she said, "If 'Heaven lies about us in our infancy,' the realm of poetry cannot be far distant." In this volume she presented numerous poems of Whittier and Lowell. Pictures of these authors and of their homes illustrated the poems. Twelve pages of words used in the book were listed at the end.

The plan of *Book Four* was similar to *Book Three*, but the poems were by Emily Dickinson, Holmes, and Bryant. Prose lessons by Louisa M. Alcott, Felicia Hemans, Abby Diaz, Harriet Beecher Stowe, Celia Thaxter, Fanny Fern, Lucy Larcom, and Elizabeth S. Phelps also appeared. It will be noted that Ellen Cyr included the writings of many women. In contrast, in the *Fifth Reader*, written much later (1899), the authors of nearly all the selections were men. Among them were Wordsworth, Thoreau, Poe, Coleridge, Emerson, Goldsmith, Macaulay, Tennyson, Burns, Cervantes, Carlyle, Kipling, Scott, Milton, Shakespeare, and Johnson. Pictures of many of these writers illustrated the extracts of their writings.

In *Book Six* (1898) the practice of presenting extracts from the great writers of literature continued. Strangely, *Book Six* is 200 pages smaller than the *Fifth*. In 1899 *Book Seven* and *Book Eight* were published. They followed the pattern of *Book Six*, both in small size and in the type of literary selections. Incidentally, Miss Cyr's series was the first discussed in this work to have eight readers.

In summary of Miss Cyr's books, it can be said that in several ways they were different. She began treatment of famous writers lower in the series; she included the writings of more women; after *Book Two* she leaned toward the pure literary rather than lessons on nature study, games, life activities, and so on; and she paid little attention to elocution. Her books went through numerous printings.

James Baldwin. In 1897 a series of readers by Baldwin was published. The series took two forms of combination; namely, readers for *First Year, Second Year, Third Year, Fourth and Fifth Years Combined*, and *Sixth and Seventh Years Combined*, and separately books for *Sixth Year, Seventh Year*, and *Eighth Year*. Apparently the combined readers were to be used in rural schools, where it was the common practice to combine grades.

The *First Year* book was the first one of all the series discussed to contain many colored pictures. Likewise it was one of the first to begin with the sentence method. For example, the first lesson had a picture of a ball, beside which was the sentence, "This is a ball," both in script and Roman lettering. It was attractively printed.

Pictures or portraits appeared in all the readers. However, in contrast to Miss Cyr's readers, lessons dealing with birds and animal life were common. Of course, the upper readers, as in most series, contained mostly extracts of well-known writers. No treatment of elocution was included.

LESS POPULAR READERS

The writer's collection contains readers written by 179 different authors. The readers of only 23 of these have been discussed at any length. The readers of many other authors also went through two or more editions. In this section mere mention will be made of some of these.

Other Early Readers. Among the readers that were more or less popular before it was common for them to appear in series were the following: Daniel Adams' *The Understanding Reader; or Knowledge before Oratory, Being a New Selection of Lessons* (1803); John Walker's *Elements of Elocution* (1810); T. W. Strong's *The Common Reader* (1818); Joshua Leavitt's *Easy Lessons in Reading* (1823); Samuel Putnam's *The Analytical Reader* (1826); Mrs. Barbauld and Edgeworth's *American Popular Lessons* (1829); and Moses Severance's *American Manual or English Reader* (1830). Most of these were written primarily for training upper classes in elocution. All of these went through several printings.

The Less Popular Series of Readers. One of the earliest graded series written in the United States was the *New York Reader* (1817), which appeared as *No. 1, No. 2,* and *No. 3.* Beginning in 1831 Oliver Angel wrote *The Union* reading series as *No. I, No. II, No. III, No. IV, No. V,* and *No. VI.* In the 1840's William Russell wrote several readers for the lower grades entitled, *The Primary Reader, Introduction to the Primary Reader,* and *Sequel to the Primary Reader.* Beginning in 1857 E. A. Sheldon began publishing readers under different titles which continued to appear for more than twenty years. In the 1860's Richard Edwards wrote the *Analytical Reader* series in six forms. In 1870 Noble Butler began publishing readers later known as the *Butler Series*. Later in the 1870's Sadlier's five *Excelsior Readers* were printed both in New York and Montreal. Beginning in 1878 Albert N. Raub published a series of five *Normal Readers*. In 1882 H. I. Gourley and J. N. Hunt published a series of *Modern Readers*. Charles Barnes wrote the *New National Readers* in 1883. In 1886 Loomis J. Campbell wrote a series of five *New Franklin Readers*. In 1888 the *Harper's Readers*, and also the *Normal Course in Reading* series by Emma Todd and William Powell appeared. In 1889 the *Synthetic Readers* by Mrs. Rebecca S. Pollard were published. All these series appeared in more than one printing.

CHARACTERISTICS OF AMERICAN READERS

Titles. A rather large fraction of the authors of American readers used some descriptive or definitive term in connection with the titles. Some of the terms were used by several series, such as *National* or *Progressive*. The following list represents some of the definitive terms: Monitorial, Understanding, Standard, American, American Educational, Child's, Progressive, Select, Historical, Phonetic, Scholar's, National, Popular, English, Orator, Preceptor, Pictorial, Grammatical, Excelsior, Illustrated, Geographical, Comprehensive, Juvenile, North American, Evangelical, Analytical, Questional, First Class, Exhibition Speaker, Common-School, Modern, Art-Literature, Classical, Graded-School, Ladies', Dramatic, Anglo-Saxon, Child's Guide, Eclectic, Wide-Awake, Young Gentleman's, Cathedral, Synthetic, Rhetorical, Normal, Practical, New School, Etymological, Modern, District School, Introductory, Gradual, Rational, Independent, Model, Explanatory, and Elegant.

Readers in Series. The idea of producing readers in a graded series was slow in developing. Although both Webster and Bingham rather early wrote more than one reader, neither of them graded their books. In a sense, the Murray *Readers* ultimately were graded. Apparently, however, he did not have grading in mind when he first wrote the *English Reader* in 1799. He later wrote a *Sequel*, which was more difficult, and an *Introduction* as an easier one. All were too difficult for the lower grades. The two earliest series really were the *New York Reader, No. 1, No. 2*, and *No. 3;* and Cobb's *Juvenile Reader, No. 1, No. 2*, and *No. 3* in 1830. Later he wrote a *Sequel* as a fourth reader. Several other famous series began with only four readers; namely, those by Worcester, McGuffey, and Goodrich. To the latter two, higher books were later added.

It is really puzzling why so many series consisted of five readers. Among them were those written by Swan, Tower, Mandeville, Sargent, Harris, and Osgood (*Progressive* series). Although all schools were not well graded at that time, particularly the rural schools, certainly some cities had eight elementary grades. So a plausible explanation may be that each of the first four readers would be used in two grades. During the first the pupils would be introduced to the contents of the reader and during the second year would virtually commit much of it. Thus the first four readers would be studied for eight years. Then the fifth reader, usually an elocutionary reader, was used in the academies and high schools or as a supplementary reader in the upper grades.

On the other hand, even more series contained six readers. Among these were those written by Goodrich, Sanders, Tower (later), Parker, Hillard, Osgood (*American* series), Monroe, Swinton, and eventually McGuffey.

No series contained eight until in the 1890's, when the Cyr and the Baldwin books appeared.

Oral Emphasis. Beginning with Webster's first book and until the 1890's most readers were written with the aim to develop effective oral reading. In many instances the emphasis would begin in the form of phonics in the lower readers by providing exercises on letter and syllable sounds. This was particularly true in books by Tower, Swan, and Monroe. Then commonly in the third or fourth reader the books would begin with rules and principles of elocution. Many fifth and sixth readers devoted from 40 to 60 pages to such rules and exercises. One of the first authors to pay attention *also* to get meaning from the printed page was Town in his *Third Reader* (1848). The lessons in this book were followed by questions regarding the information or thoughts involved. Later the readers by Hillard, Swinton, Cyr, and Baldwin did likewise. In fact, the Cyr and the Baldwin *Readers* in the 1890's omitted serious treatment of the principles of elocution.

Literary Readers. As soon as readers began to appear in series the upper readers commonly contained literary extracts from famous authors. The upper readers by McGuffey were famous for this. Since only a small fraction of the pupils would attend an academy or a high school, the chief means for most pupils to learn at least a little about the great writers of the past was through the upper readers. As early as 1856 Mandeville in his *Fifth Reader* included brief biographies about the authors of many of the selections. Thus the pupils were really studying literature. Other authors to follow this practice, some even presenting photographs of them, were Parker and Watson, Hillard, Swinton, and Cyr.

Script. Mandeville and Swinton presented the alphabet and some of the earlier lessons in the lower readers both in script and Roman type. Since most teachers used the blackboard freely it was thought wise to have the children learn to read script from the beginning.

Pictures. Except for the very earliest readers, it was common to use pictures in the first and second readers. It was not until after 1850 that the fourth and even later the fifth and sixth readers contained pictures. Only Baldwin (1897) used colored pictures, and then only in the *First Year Reader.*

Sensitivity to Methods. In general, the compilers of readers for a long time were not very conscious or sensitive to how reading should be taught, except their emphasis on teaching elocution. Without doubt, the publication of graded series of readers naturally made compilers more conscious of approaches in teaching, especially in compiling the primary readers. Possibly, Tower's emphasis on phonics in 1841 in his *Gradual Reader* caused other authors to consider the merits and demerits of the different methods. This was reflected in the preface of Sargent's *First Standard Reader* (1855), when he endeavored "to graduate the exercises" to the taste and comprehension of the children. Subsequently, statements in the prefaces of the readers by Harris, Swinton, Baldwin, and others, all reflected the keen attention given to the most effective methods of teaching reading. It may well be added that these discussions continue to the present.

CHAPTER 4

GRAMMARS

Apparently English grammar was taught in very few colonial schools before 1750. In the colonial period the word "English" needed to be used in connection with grammar, for both in England and in early colonial America the word "grammar" was most commonly associated with the study of Latin and Greek. It was in America, where soon the vernacular received greater emphasis, that the study of English grammar was to receive marked attention.

According to Lyman's[1] scholarly study very few public schools in America taught English grammar before 1775. However, it was taught in a considerable number of private schools earlier. According to a newspaper advertisement a William Waterman taught the "Rudiments of Grammar" in the Wassamacaw School in South Carolina in 1734. In 1743 Charles Fortesque announced the teaching of "English in a grammatical manner" in Chester, Pennsylvania. After 1750 many private schools began teaching grammar. This was not so true in New England as in the middle colonies. Lyman could find only six references before 1775 to

---

[1] Rollo L. Lyman, *English Grammar in The American Schools Before 1850*, U.S. Bureau of Education Bulletin No. 12 (Washington: Government Printing Office), 1921.

schools in all New England as teaching English grammar. On the other hand, at least thirty-nine schools in New York, New Jersey, and Pennsylvania were doing so. In fact, there were at least eight schools in Philadelphia alone teaching it before 1760. No doubt, the emphasis given it by Benjamin Franklin in his Academy, beginning in 1750, greatly hastened this development.

A word should be said about the nature of those early schools. Only in New England were public schools found in the colonial period. The mass of the children attended only the Reading and Writing school, where the emphasis was to learn to read, so that all could read the Bible, religious books, and the laws. A few of the abler boys attended the Latin grammar schools. There seemed no need for English grammar for the masses. In the other colonies there were no public schools, and so many private schools arose. Since the maintenance of private schools greatly depended upon the tuition of the students, necessarily the schools would teach the subjects most useful to the students. English grammar soon began to be considered a useful subject. In other words, the need was felt to write "grammatically," as well as to read. The private schools, however, were generally more secondary in nature than elementary, though very few were strictly graded. Not only did English grammar become popular in secondary schools, but also in certain colleges. No doubt, the reason grammar was given in the colleges was to make up for the language deficiencies of the students who had not attended a Latin grammar school.

Consideration must be given the materials for the study of English grammar in America. As was true of the textbooks in other fields, the earliest were brought from England, and then soon some were reprinted here. There were no copyright laws then to prevent this practice. Lyman lists evidence that at least twelve grammatical texts first written or published in England were brought or reprinted here before 1784, when Webster's *Grammar* was first published. Even others may have been brought over. Advertisements in various colonial newspapers announced sale of "Spelling Books by the dozen," "English Grammars," etc.

The earliest mentioned by Lyman was James Greenwood's *An Essay Towards a Practical English Grammar* published in

London in 1711. A later edition was brought here. However, at least one copy of the older book was brought here, for the writer has a copy of it. This was Humphry Hody's *The Royal Grammar Reformed into a More Easie Method, for the Better Understanding of the English:* and *More Speedy Attainment of the Latin Tongue,* published in London in 1694. The first part of the book is English grammar, and later in the book there is a chapter entitled "Prosodia," which also deals with an aspect of grammar.

At least three other grammars not mentioned by Lyman were brought here. The earliest one was *A Short Introduction to Grammar* by S. Buckley and J. Osburn, printed in London in 1733. Apparently copies of it were brought here, for the writer has two different editions of it, used here. The other two not mentioned were even reprinted here; namely, James Buchanan's *A Regular English Syntax* printed in Philadelphia in 1780, and Thomas Sheridan's *A Rhetorical Grammar of the English Grammar,* Philadelphia, 1783. Both of these books were larger than most early grammars.

The second one listed by Lyman was Thomas Dilworth's *New Guide to the English Tongue* in 1740. This gained the widest usage in America of all the English published books during the colonial period. This was reprinted in America in 1747, and thereafter reprinted by many different American printers. Likely a reason why it became so popular was because it was a combination of speller, reader, grammar, and literature. Thus it served the purposes of several textbooks. Of the three American re-

A
RHETORICAL GRAMMAR
OF THE
ENGLISH LANGUAGE,
Calculated folely for the Purpofes of Teaching
PROPRIETY OF PRONUNCIATION,
AND
JUSTNESS OF DELIVERY,
IN THAT TONGUE,
BY THE
ORGANS OF SPEECH.

By *THOMAS SHERIDAN*, A. M.
Author of the LECTURES on ELOCUTION.

This AMERICAN EDITION is publifhed under the Infpection of
ARCHIBALD GAMBLE, A. M. Profeffor of Englifh
and Oratory, in the Univerfity of Pennfylvania.

PHILADELPHIA:
Printed and Sold by ROBERT BELL, in *Third
Street,* and FRANCIS BAILEY, in *Market Street.*
M,DCC,LXXXIII.
1783

Grammar and Elocution combined, 1783, Sheridan, University of Pennsylvania.

printed copies in the writer's collection, the oldest copy devoted 40 pages to grammar, the next oldest 20 pages, and the latest no grammar, even though the table of contents listed grammar as part of the book.

A third book listed was written by James Harris in 1751, entitled, *Hermes, or a Philosophical Inquiry Concerning Grammar*, which was reprinted in Philadelphia, reaching its seventh edition in 1825.

The first one to be more strictly only a grammar was Robert Lowth's *A Short Introduction to English Grammar* in 1758. This text was used at Harvard for several decades. Lowth's rules were later copied by other authors. Another English book used here was *The British Grammar*, anonymous, London, 1760. Two more were printed in London in 1763; namely, Ash's *Grammatical Institutes*, and Fisher's *Practical New Grammar*, which reached its twenty-eighth edition here by 1795.

The grammar originally written in England to attain widest usage and to exert most influence here was Lindley Murray's *English Grammar*, first published in York, England in 1795. Murray was born and edu-

cated in America but later moved to England, where he wrote his popular texts in the fields of spelling, reading, and grammar. An *Abridgement of Murray's English Grammar* was printed in Philadelphia in 1797 containing 108 pages. In all, the Nietz Collection contains twenty-four different Murray *Grammars* published by sixteen different American printers dating from 1797 to 1870. Too, these vary greatly in size. The smallest book,

ABRIDGEMENT
of
MURRAY's
ÉNGLISH GRAMMAR.
WITH AN
APPENDIX,
Containing
EXERCISES IN ORTHOGRAPHY, IN PARSING, IN SYNTAX, AND IN PUNCTUATION.
Designed for the
YOUNGER CLASSES OF LEARNERS.

BY LINDLEY MURRAY.

FROM THE THIRTIETH ENGLISH EDITION, CORRECTED BY THE AUTHOR.

PHILADELPHIA:
PUBLISHED BY JOHNSON & WARNER.
WILLIAM GREEN, PRINTER.
1797

Most popular grammar in the United States, 1797.

containing 72 pages was printed in Boston in 1816, and the largest was printed in New York in 1819, containing 376 pages of grammar (Vol. I) ; 298 pages served as a "Key to the Exercises" (Vol. II), and appeared as one book bound in fine leather. The smallest books were usually entitled *Abridgements*. The others usually contained from 250 to 325 pages. Apparently each printer decided what to include and what to omit. The "Table of Contents" of most of them was somewhat as follows:

Part I—Orthography	Part II—Etymology
Chapter 1. Of letters	(This part contained nine chapters)
Chapter 2. Of syllables	Part III—Syntax
Chapter 3. Of words	Part IV—Prosody

APPENDIX

Rules and observations for promoting perspicuity and accuracy in writing

Part I—Perspicuity and accuracy of expression, with respect to single words and phrases.

Part II—Perspicuity and accuracy of expression, with respect to the construction of sentences.

Further references will be made concerning the influence of Murray's grammars when dealing with the American written grammars. Murray has been referred to as the "father of English Grammar."

CONTENT OF AMERICAN GRAMMARS

There is a common belief that grammars have changed very little through the years. It is true that they have changed less than the textbooks in most other subject fields, but there have been changes. A detailed analysis of the 76 most commonly used American grammars before 1850 was made by Huston.[2] Several of the earliest popular grammars were actually written in

---

2 Jon Huston, "An Analysis of English Grammar Textbooks Used in American Schools Before 1850." (Unpublished doctoral dissertation, University of Pittsburgh, 1954).

England, but republished in America. Naturally thus they would also greatly influence the earliest American written grammars as to content and approach. Of these the one that had widest and longest usage here was Lindley Murray's *English Grammar*, which set a pattern for American grammars. It was divided into four parts, plus an appendix, as follows: Part I, Orthography; Part II, Etymology; Part III, Syntax; Part IV, Prosody; and Appendix, Perspicuity. Thereafter many authors of grammars included these same four parts, so that their inclusion became somewhat traditional. However, a number of authors courageously departed from this traditional practice. Table IV, which is based on Huston's findings, shows how many of the 76 grammars contained each of the four parts by periods, and the average per cent of space devoted to each. It should be noted that one-third of the books failed to include orthography and prosody, but that more than 80 per cent contained separate parts for etymology and syntax. Others combined etymology and syntax.

Orthography. Murray said, "Orthography teaches the nature and powers of letters, and the just method of spelling words." Goold Brown said, "Orthography treats of letters, syllables, separate words, and spelling." Since words are composed of letters, and sentences composed of words, most authors apparently thought it logical to begin with the treatment of letters, which is orthography. However, one-third of the books omitted it, and only one-eighth of the average space dealt with it.

Etymology. Murray said that etymology "treats of the different sorts of words, their various modifications, and their derivation." Brown said that it "treats of the different parts of speech, and their classes and modifications." These definitions show that what we today commonly call grammar was etymology. However, the parts of speech included in many of the early grammars were not termed the same as the eight now commonly recognized; namely, noun, pronoun, adjective, verb, adverb, preposition, interjection, and conjunction. Murray mentioned the article instead of the adjective, and the substantive instead of the noun. Too, many used the participle as a part of speech.

Table IV

Number of Grammar Books Including Orthography, Etymology, Syntax, Prosody, Combined Etymology and Syntax, and Appendixed Material During Certain Periods Before 1850.

Periods	Total Number of Books	Books with Orthography	Books with Etymology	Books with Syntax	Books Combining Etymology and Syntax	Books with Prosody	Books with Appendixed Material
1745-1790	10	7	9	6	2	3	5
1791-1820	18	12	16	16	2	11	12
1821-1850	48	30	38	39	10	35	22
TOTAL	76	49	63	61	14	49	39
Average % of Space Devoted to Each		12.2%	32.2%	25.1%	12.3%	7.0%	10.0%

Since etymology dealt with the classification of words, the bulk
of its content related to the parts of speech and parsing. With
each part of speech were its various modifications and subdivisions. The process of pointing out these modifications or sub-
classes was parsing. Harvey said that "parsing consists (1) in
naming the part of speech; (2) in telling its properties; (3) in
pointing out its relation to other words; (4) in giving the rule
for its construction." For example, when applied to a noun it
would analyze whether it was proper or common; singular or
plural; masculine, feminine, or neuter; and nominative, possessive, or objective case. Similar analyses would be applied to
words of other parts of speech. Some texts made much of parsing,
such as Barrett's *Principles of Language*, others gave it little or
no attention.

Syntax. Brown defined it as follows: "Syntax treats of the relation, agreement, government, and arrangement, of words in
sentences." In other words, it dealt with functions and relations
of words in sentences. A fully consistent grammar would not deal
separately with etymology and syntax. Huston found that fourteen of the grammars did combine the treatment of etymology and
syntax. They then were considered the progressive and non-
traditional textbooks. Among the authors who did this before
1850 were Webster, Cobb, Ingersoll, Kirkham, Smith, Greene,
Hazen, and Weld. Their books will later be described. Only three
of the 76 grammars failed to deal with syntax, either as such or
in combination with etymology. One of these was Dilworth's *New
Guide to the English Tongue*, which was a combination of speller,
reader, and grammar. The average number of rules of syntax per
book in all the 76 grammars was 21.

Prosody. Brown defined it as the treatment of "punctuation, utterance, figures, and versification." Murray presented it under
two parts: pronunciation, "comprising accent, quality, emphasis,
pause, and tone"; and the laws of versification. Kirkham agreed
with Murray. Only two-thirds of the books dealt with this branch
of grammar, and most of them merely briefly. Only 7 per cent
of the space in all the books related to prosody. It may be noted

that Brown included punctuation under prosody, but most authors
dealt with punctuation either separately or with syntax.

EARLIEST AMERICAN GRAMMARS

Following the detailed analysis of the contents of American
grammars, it should be meaningful next to consider just whose
grammars were most popular and something of their general
characteristics by periods.

The first grammar written in America was by Hugh Jones in
1724, but was sent to England for printing. The first one to be
both written and printed here was by Samuel Johnson, the first
president of King's College, now Columbia University, in 1765;
it consisted only of 36 pages. Two other American grammars
appeared before Webster's; namely, Thomas Byerley's *A Plain
and Easy Introduction to English Grammar*, 1773; and Abel
Curtis's *A Compend of English Grammar: Being an Attempt to
Point Out the Fundamental Principles of the English Language*,
1779, containing 48 pages.

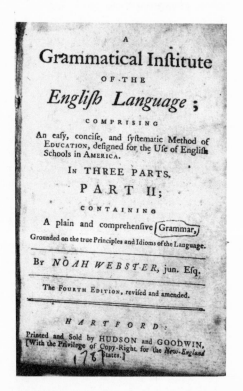

Noah Webster's was the
first grammar written here to
receive considerable acceptance. It was published in 1784
as Part II of *A Grammatical
Institute of the English Language*, the *Speller* was Part I.
By 1787 a fourth edition appeared. The definitive parts
of this grammer were in catechetical form. For example:

What is Grammar?
Grammar is the art of communicating thoughts by words
with propriety and dispatch.

Webster's *Grammar*, Part II of
Grammatical Institute; Speller
was Part I.

What is the use of English Grammar?
To teach the true principles and idioms of the English language.

Apparently Webster borrowed many of the definitions from British grammars, especially from Lowth's. In 1831 he published a radically revised edition entitled, *An Improved Grammar of the English Language*. It, too, appeared in several editions. The catechetical form of presentation was abandoned. Webster's *Grammars* were not as systematically organized as those by Murray.

Another early American grammar was *The Young Lady's Accidence* written by Caleb Bingham in 1785. The following couplet appeared on the title page:

> Delightful task! To rear the tender thought,
> To teach the young idea how to shoot, —

The first edition was printed in 1797, and the twentieth in 1815. These books contained only 60 pages. It is claimed that a hundred thousand copies of them were sold. Although very small, they dealt with all of the more important aspects of grammar, but very simply and briefly. Although written primarily for girls, the grammar was used by all children in Boston public schools, and no doubt elsewhere.

After Webster's *Grammar* was first published in 1784, the number of grammar textbooks to appear in America increased rapidly. According to Lyman's study the appearance of these textbooks was distributed by decades as follows: 1760-1770, 1; 1771-1780, 5; 1781-1790, 9; 1791-1800, 18; 1801-1810, 14; 1811-1820, 41; 1821-1830, 84; 1831-1840, 63; and 1841-1850, 66.

AMERICAN GRAMMARS: 1820-1840

The foregoing data show that more grammar textbooks were first published in the 1820's than in any decade for a century. Too, three of these became very popular, and more than a half dozen others appeared in more than two editions; while none of the 1830 books became popular. The three authors whose grammars of those decades to become most popular were Goold Brown, Samuel Kirkham, and Roswell Smith. The books of these three men virtually replaced the use of Webster's grammars and greatly reduced the use of Murray's.

Goold Brown (1791-1857). His parents were Quakers. At first he engaged in mercantile work, which he found repugnant. Then he became a teacher in John Griscom's well-known school in New York. Later he was the principal of a private academy in New York City. It was then that he began to write the textbooks that became so popular.

In 1823 Brown published both the *Institutes of English Grammar* and the *First Lines of English Grammar*. The latter was "A Brief Abstract of the Author's Larger Work Designed for Young Learners." In a sense these two books constituted a graded series even before grading textbooks was common. Both texts continued to appear, with some revisions, for more than fifty years after the death of the author. Evidence indicates that the *First Lines* became popular in common schools (elementary), while the *Institutes* gained very wide usage in academies. For example, in 1850, in New York State, Murray's *Grammar* was used in one, Kirkham's in 15, and Brown's in 72 academies.

But why did the *Institutes of English Grammar* become so popular? An examination of it soon reveals certain characteristics or merits of the book. First, it was well and clearly organized. Part I dealt with Orthography; Part II,

2   ENGLISH GRAMMAR.

The letters in the English alphabet, are twenty-six; *A a, B b, C c, D d, E e, F f, G g, H h, I i, J j, K k, L l, M m, N n, O o, P p, Q q, R r, S s, T t, U u, V v, W w, X x, Y y, Z z.*
The letters are divided into *vowels* and *consonants.*
A *vowel* is a letter which forms a perfect sound, when uttered alone.
A *consonant* is a letter which cannot be perfectly uttered without a vowel.
The vowels are *a, e, i, o, u,* and sometimes *w,* and *y.* All the other letters are consonants.
W and *y* are consonants when they precede a vowel in the same syllable; as in *wine, twine, youth:* in other situations, they are vowels.
The consonants are divided into *mutes,* and *semi-vowels.*
A *mute* is a consonant which cannot be sounded at all without a vowel. The mutes are *b, d, k, p, q, t,* and *c* and *g* hard.
A *semi-vowel* is a consonant which can be imperfectly sounded without a vowel. The semi-vowels are *f, h, j, l, m, n, r, s, v, x, z,* and *c* and *g* soft. Of these *l, m, n,* and *r,* are termed *liquids,* on account of the fluency of their sounds.
In the English language, the Roman characters are generally employed; sometimes, the Italic; and occasionally, the old English. The letters have severally two forms, by which they are distinguished as *capitals* and *small letters.* The small letters constitute the body of every work. Capitals are used for the sake of eminence and distinction.

RULES FOR THE USE OF CAPITALS

RULE I.

The titles of books, and the heads of their principal divisions, should be printed in capitals. When books are merely mentioned, the principal words in their titles begin with capitals, and the other letters are small; as, "Pope's Essay on Man."

Brown, *Institutes of the English Language,* 1823—how orthography was taught.

Etymology; Part III, Syntax; and Part IV, Prosody. Then each part was clearly sub-divided into sections. For example, there was Prosody of Punctuation, of Utterance, and of Versification. Secondly, there was clarity. The definitions, rules, examples, and questions were very clearly and simply stated. For example, the very first sentence in the body of the book states: "Grammar is the art of speaking and writing the English language correctly." Thirdly, following the definitions were many examples and exercises. Lastly, the printing was well and attractively done, and most of the earlier editions were bound in fine leather.

There may be several reasons why Brown's books were so well written. In the preface of the *Institutes* he stated, "For his own information, he has carefully perused more than fifty English grammars, and has sought, . . . The analogies of speech, in the structure of several languages." Too, his teaching experience provided him pedagogical insights regarding the presentation of the material. After Brown's death the publishing company employed Henry Kiddle to revise the *Institutes*, and thus its sale continued for many decades.

Another contribution made by Goold Brown was to publish *The Grammar of Grammars* in 1851, which appeared in several editions. It contained 1,102 pages. It was one of the most exhaustive treatments of English grammar ever written. It began by listing alphabetically the names of the authors of 463 grammars which had been published by 1850. Then after an analytical introduction of grammar, 750 pages were devoted to detailed analyses of the four parts of grammar; namely, orthography, etymology, syntax, and prosody. The remainder of the book presented a "Key to the Oral Exercises" of the foregoing four parts. Thus it can be said that Goold Brown made a definite contribution to the development of textbooks as well as to the teaching of English grammar in the United States.

Kirkham. In the same year (1823) that Brown's *Institutes* was first published, another grammar was published, which too became very popular: Samuel Kirkham's *A Compendium of English Grammar*. It was a small book of 84 pages, and apparently adapted well for use in the common schools. In 1825 Kirkham

A COMPENDIUM OF ENGLISH GRAMMAR, BY SAMUEL KIRKHAM;

DESIGNED, NOT TO BE STUDIED, BUT TO BE SPREAD BEFORE THE LEARNER IN PARSING, PREVIOUS TO HIS HAVING THE DEFINITIONS AND RULES COMMITTED TO MEMORY.

ETYMOLOGY.

NOUNS.

A NOUN is the name of any person, place, or thing.

A common noun is the name of a sort or species of things.

A proper noun is the name of an individual.

The masculine gender denotes the male sex.

The feminine gender denotes the female sex.

The neuter gender denotes things which have neither sex.

The first person denotes the speaker.

The second person denotes the person or thing which is spoken to.

The third person denotes the person or thing which is spoken of.

The singular number implies but one.

The plural number implies more than one.

The nominative case denotes the actor or subject of the verb.

The possessive case denotes the owner or possessor of something.

The objective case expresses the object of an action of a relation.

VERBS.

A VERB is a word which signifies to be, to do, or to suffer.

ARTICLES.

An ARTICLE is a word prefixed to nouns to limit their signification.

ADJECTIVES.

An ADJECTIVE is a word added to a noun to express its quality or kind.

PARTICIPLES.

A PARTICIPLE is a word derived from a verb, and partakes of the nature of a verb, and also of an adjective.

ADVERBS.

An ADVERB is a word used to modify the sense of a verb, a participle, an adjective, or another adverb.

PREPOSITIONS.

A PREPOSITION is a word which serves to connect words, and show the relation between them.

PRONOUNS.

A PRONOUN is a word used instead of a noun.

PRONOUNS are those which de-

persons of the nouns for which they stand.

RELATIVE PRONOUNS are a kind of adjective which point out nouns by some distinction.

The distributive adjective pronouns are those which denote the persons or things that make up a number, each taken separately and singly.

The demonstrative are those which precisely point out the subject to which they relate.

The indefinite are those which point out their subject in an indefinite or general manner.

ADJECTIVE PRONOUNS are such as relate, in general, to some word or phrase going before, which is called the antecedent.

CONJUNCTIONS.

A CONJUNCTION is a part of speech that is used to connect sentences, joining more simple sentences into compound ones. It sometimes connects only words.

A copulative conjunction serves to connect and continue a sentence by joining on a member, which expresses an addition, a supposition, a cause, &c.

A disjunctive conjunction serves to connect continue a sentence by joining on a member, which expresses opposition of meaning.

INTERJECTIONS.

An INTERJECTION is a word used to express some sudden emotion of the speaker.

RULES OF SYNTAX.

RULE 1. The article a or an agrees with nouns in the singular number only.

RULE 2. The definite article the belongs to nouns in the singular or plural number.

RULE 3. The nominative case governs the verb.

RULE 4. The verb must agree with its nominative in number and person.

RULE 5. Every verb, when it is not in the infinitive mood, must have a nominative, expressed or understood.

RULE 6. A noun or pronoun placed before a participle, and being independent of

the rest of the sentence, is in the nominative case absolute.

RULE 18. Adjectives belong to, and qualify nouns, expressed or understood.

RULE 7. Two or more nouns, or nouns and pronouns, signifying the same thing, are put, by apposition, in the same case.

RULE 8. Two or more nouns, or nouns and pronouns, in the singular number, connected by copulative conjunctions, must have verbs, nouns, and pronouns, agreeing with them in the plural number.

RULE 9. Two or more nouns, or nouns and pronouns, in the singular number, connected by disjunctive conjunctions, must have verbs, nouns, and pronouns, agreeing with them in the singular.

RULE 10. A collective noun, or noun of multitude, conveying the idea of a plurality, may have a verb or pronoun agreeing with it in the plural.

RULE 13. Personal pronouns must agree with the nouns for which they stand, in gender and number.

RULE 14. Relative pronouns agree with their antecedents in gender, person, and number.

RULE 15. The relative is the nominative case to the verb, when no nominative comes between it and the verb.

RULE 23. Prepositions govern the objective case.

RULE 33. Conjunctions connect nouns and pronouns in the same case.

34   THEORY OF THE ENGLISH LANGUAGE.

SECT. II.—OF THE NOUN.

A NOUN is the name of any person, place, or thing; and may be known by its taking an article before it, or making sense of itself; as, a house, the sun, modesty, industry, chastity.

Order for Parsing the Noun.

A noun, and why? proper or common, or why? gender, person, number, case, and why?

A noun is said to be proper when it is appropriated to an individual; as London, George, Thames. It is said to be common when it stands for kinds containing many sorts, or for sorts containing many individuals under them; as animal, man, tree, &c.

Gender is the consideration of nouns with regard to sex. There are three genders, the masculine, feminine, and neuter.

The masculine gender denotes animals of the male kind; as, a man, a horse, &c. The feminine denotes an animal of the female kind; as, a woman, &c.; and the neuter denotes objects which are neither male nor female; as, a house, a field.

Of the *animal* world, { All *males* are *masculine*, and all *females* are *feminine*. } Form the *neuter*.

And all the objects of the *vegeta-{ ble* and *inanimate* kingdom, }

By a figure of speech called personification, by which life and action are attributed to inanimate objects, many neuter nouns, especially by the poets, are converted into those objects which are of a *masculine* or *warlike* nature, are put in the *masculine*; while the *receiver*, and objects assimilated with the *feminine*, on account of *music, beauty, benevolence,* or *goodness*, are made *feminine*.

Sun, the *giver* of light, is *masculine*; *Moon, receiver,* is *feminine; time* is always *masculine*, being described in

---

PRACTICE—GRAMMATICAL ANALYSIS.   35

How-oft the laughing brow of joy,
A sick'ning heart conceals:
And through the cloister's deep recess   25
Invading sorrow steals.

In vain, through beauty, fortune, wit,
The fugitive we trace:
It dwells not in the faithless smile
That brightens Clodia's face.   30

Perhaps the joy to these [persons] deny'd,
The heart in friendship finds.
Ah! dear delusion, gay conceit,
Of visionary minds!

How'er our varying tudious rove,   35
Yet all [persons] agree in one [notion which is]
To place its being in some state,

At distance from our-own, [state],
O blind [persons] to each indulgent aim
Of power supremely wise,   40
Who fancy happiness in aught [which]
The hand of Heav'n denies. [which]
Vain is alike the joy [which] we seek,
And vain what we possess
Unless harmonious reason times   45
The passions into peace.

To tempered wishes, just desires,

Barrett, 1836—note the parsing procedure.

enlarged the book and changed its title to *English Grammar in Familiar Lectures Accompanied by a Compendium*. In 1829 he enlarged it again (to 228 pages), with the title unchanged. Kirkham's *Grammar* was considerably more popular for more than a decade than Brown's *Institutes*. For example, in 1840 Kirkham's was used in 61 New York academies, and Brown's was used in 40. However, in 1850 Kirkham's was used only in 15, but Brown's in 72. Kirkham's book was even more popular in the common schools. In 1838 his book was used in the schools of 427 towns in New York, but Brown's in only sixty. Due largely, no doubt, to its smaller size Kirkham's book was better adapted to the elementary level, while Brown's larger book of roughly 300 pages later became more often used in academies. Too, Kirkham's popularity largely ceased in the 1840's, but Brown's continued somewhat throughout the nineteenth century.

The organization of Kirkham's book was considerably different from Brown's. It was presented in the form of lectures rather than parts. In a sense the material was in two parts rather than the four which was common in most grammars. Orthography came first, as was usual. Then etymology and syntax were combined, and prosody was omitted entirely. This simplification evidently aided the grammar's beginning popularity, particularly at the elementary level. However, later a reaction set in against this over-simplification. The 1829 edition had one feature which the present writer has not seen in any other earlier grammar; namely, a large folded page, 12 x 15 inches, six columns, containing a compen-

FIRST

LESSONS IN LANGUAGE,

OR

ELEMENTS OF ENGLISH GRAMMAR.

LANGUAGE.

Do all nations use the same language? They do not.
What language do the people of France use? The French.
What language do the people of England use? The English.
What language do we use? The English.
What is the use of language? To express thought.
How is thought expressed in words? By combining them.
How many words are necessary to express an idea or thought? There must be two, at least.
If I say, "*boys John*," do I express an idea? No.

Tower and Tweed, 1853—note the inductive approach.

dium of all important definitions and rules of grammar. There were 60 definitions of grammar, and 35 rules of syntax. This page was folded opposite the title page.

Smith. The third author whose grammars became popular was Roswell C. Smith. His first one was the *Intellectual and Practical Grammar, in a Series of Inductive Questions.* Although the copyright date was 1830, it contained a recommendation dated 1829. As indicated by the sub-title, this book followed the inductive rather than the deductive approach. In the preface the author quotes Barnard's *Journal of Education* (No. 38, p. 97) in defense as follows:

> Pestalozzi endeavored, in the first place, to ascertain, by questions adapted to the tender age of the pupil, whether any idea existed in the mind upon the subject to which he wished to direct his attention; *and from any one clear idea, of which he found the child in possession, he led him on, by a series of questions, to the acquirement of such other ideas as were most intimately connected with that primary conception.*

In other words, instead of having the child first commit to memory the definitions and rules, and then apply them, Smith attempted to develop an understanding of the rules and definitions by means of leading questions. In all, this book contained 122 pages, 41 lessons, and 30 rules. It went through several editions.

In 1832 Smith published his *English Grammar on the Productive System.* Without much further change this book

Smith's *Grammar,* inductive in approach.

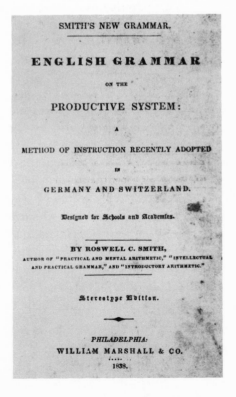

SMITH'S NEW GRAMMAR.

ENGLISH GRAMMAR

ON THE

PRODUCTIVE SYSTEM:

A

METHOD OF INSTRUCTION RECENTLY ADOPTED

IN

GERMANY AND SWITZERLAND.

Designed for Schools and Academies.

BY ROSWELL C. SMITH,

AUTHOR OF "PRACTICAL AND MENTAL ARITHMETIC," "INTELLECTUAL AND PRACTICAL GRAMMAR," AND "INTRODUCTORY ARITHMETIC."

Stereotype Edition.

PHILADELPHIA:
WILLIAM MARSHALL & CO.

1838.

was printed in numerous editions until the 1860's. It was a thorough revision of the *Practical Grammar*, particularly in regard to the presentation of the material. For example, it began as follows:

I. Of the Noun

Q. What is a name?
Q. What is the name of the town in which you live?
Q. What does the word *noun* mean?
Answer. The word *noun* means *name*.

Thus he dealt with number, gender, proper and common nouns, person, case, articles, adjectives, pronouns, verbs, tense, mood, prepositions, conjunctions, and interjections. The plan really was an inductive catechetical approach. Beginning on page 41 the remainder of the book dealt with all these matters in a positive form much like other grammars. In all, the book contained 192 pages. In 1840 Smith's *Grammar* was next to Kirkham's in popularity in New York academies, but greatly declined in use by 1850. In New England towns it was by far the most popular grammar in 1840. Like Kirkham's Smith's *Grammar* did not remain popular over as extended a period as did Brown's.

Less Popular Grammars. Many other grammars in addition to those of Brown, Kirkham, and Smith first appeared in the 1820's, but apparently were not so widely accepted. However, a number did appear in several editions. In 1821 *A Self-Explaining Grammar* by Enos Cobb was published. This was a rather small grammar which abandoned the old Four Part organization then common. It followed a rather simple functional approach. However, its departure from the formal type of organization must have been too radical for common acceptance.

Also in 1821 Charles M. Ingersoll published his *Conversations on English Grammar*, which appeared in a number of editions. This was a rather large book, which was presented in three sections or parts: Conversation, which in part was in question and answer form; Additional Remarks, which consisted of material amplifying the earlier section; and Punctuation, which dealt with definitions and rules, together with their application to punctuation.

John Comly, whose *Speller* was very popular, published in 1826 an *English Grammar, Made Easy to the Teacher and Pupil.* This small book was divided into a treatment of orthography, etymology, syntax, and punctuation. He aimed "to abridge and arrange the definitions and rules necessary to be committed to memory, as not to burden the pupil."

In 1826 Rufus Nutting published *A Practical Grammar of the English Language,* which appeared in numerous reprintings before it was revised and enlarged in 1840. It at first consisted of four parts: Etymology, Syntax, Punctuation, and Prosody. The definitions and rules were tersely and clearly stated. The revised edition was considerably different. In Part I the simple elements were presented inductively. Then in Part II orthography, etymology, and syntax were presented much like other grammars. In Part III exercises involving various aspects of grammar were given. Somewhat like Kirkham's *Grammar* a folded chart, with printing on both sides, was included presenting a "Synoptical View" of the aspects of grammar.

In 1828 John Frost published the *Elements of English Grammar: With Progressive Exercises in Parsing.* It was a small book, which he claimed to be an improvement of Lowth's and Murray's *Grammars.* He claimed that the definitions were simplified, the rules of syntax "given in clear and intelligible language," and the exercises "digested according to their syntactical form."

Apparently no grammar that was first published in the 1830's became very popular. Several, however, went through more than one edition. First may be mentioned L. F. Hamlin's *English Grammar in Lectures.* The material was presented in 13 Lectures, as follows: I, Of Orthography; II, Of Etymology; III, Of the Article; IV, Of the Adjective; V, Of the Pronoun; VI, Of the Verb; VII, Of the Adverb; VIII, Of the Preposition; IX, Of the Conjunction; X, Of the Interjection; XI, Of Syntax; XII, Of Criticism; and XIII, Of Prosody, Of Punctuation. It may be noted that this organization was considerably different than in most grammars.

The second one was *The Principles of Language* by Solomon Barrett, first published in 1836. This book was unique in several respects. The first twelve pages dealt with the theory of the principles of language, and with syllogistic reasoning applied to grammatical matters. The first contents page began as follows:

Universal Grammar is a science which treats of	
Persons, Places, and Things,	i.e. nouns and pronouns.
With their Qualities,	i.e. art., adj., and part.
Existing and Acting,	i.e. verbs, neu., and act.
Either Jointly or Severally	i.e. sing., plur., and conj.
With the Manner of such	i.e. adverbs, adverbial
existence and action	phrases, and prep.

Then eleven pages presented the chief definitions and rules of grammar. More than thirty pages were devoted to detailed parsing of each word of numerous poetic selections. For example:

> art a8 ncf3s adv v r n ind pr 3s
> "The midnight moon serenely smiles"

The latter part of the book dealt at length with the theory and practice of language and syntax. Later Barrett published *The Principles of Grammar*, which appeared in several editions, even in the 1860's.

GRAMMARS OF THE 1840'S

The 1840's, like the 1820's, constituted a fruitful period for the publication of grammars. At least seven authors published grammars then which gained rather wide acceptance.

Bullions. The first of these authors was Peter Bullions. Although he had published a grammar in the 1830's, it really was a virtual reprint of William Lennie's *The Principles of English Grammar*, published first in Edinburgh, Scotland. In 1844 Bullions published his *Practical Lessons in English Grammar*, which appeared in several revised forms later, one of which was a smaller book for "Beginners." The 1853 edition, considerably enlarged, was entitled *An Analytical and Practical Grammar*. In 1857 he published the *Progressive Exercises in Analysis and Parsing*, and in 1862 the *Common School Grammar*, which was to serve as an introduction for the *Analytical and Practical Grammar*. It is evident that Bullions, possibly more than any grammar author up to that time, attempted to revise his books frequently, apparently in response to the criticisms of his competitors. Goold Brown was a severe critic of other grammars during that period. Nevertheless during the late 1840's, and throughout the 1850's, Bullions' books were next to Brown's in popular usage in the academies of New York, and also used in many common schools.

An examination of Bullions' *Grammars* indicates that he consciously attempted to pattern after the grammars of Lennie and of Murray rather than those of Brown. He indicated, in his preface, that the chief criticism of Murray's books was that the unabridged were too large and the abridged too small. Bullions' earlier books were of average size. Later he wrote smaller books as introductions for his larger works. In other words, he published grammars in series. In organization he followed the traditional pattern of four parts: Orthography, Etymology, Syntax, and Prosody. Too, he gave considerable attention to parsing. As noted above, he eventually published a separate book of parsing exercises. Bullions also wrote a number of Greek and Latin grammars, which, no doubt, somewhat influenced the structure of his English grammars.

Greene. The second author of note during the 1840's was Samuel S. Greene. In 1846 he published *A Treatise of the Structure of the English Language*, which aimed at an "analysis and classification of sentences and their component parts." This book clearly indicated a change in the approach to teaching grammar, from the emphasis on memory, as favored by Murray and Brown, to that of analysis. The organization of the book departed radically from the traditional form. Chapter I dealt with the "Elements of the First Class," really words and their parts of speech. Chapter II dealt with "Elements of the Second Class—Phrases." Chapters III, IV, and V dealt with sentences as the "Third Class." Then in the appendix the traditional divisions of orthography, etymology, syntax, prosody, and punctuation were presented briefly.

In 1848 Greene published his *First Lessons in Grammar*, which was to serve as an introduction to the *Treatise*. It dealt with the derivation and composition of words, parts of speech, inflection, simple sentences, complex sentences, compound sentences, and prosody. In 1858 he published *The Elements of English Grammar*. Apparently he realized that the earlier books represented a too radical departure from the traditional for ready acceptance, so he retreated somewhat in this book by trying to combine the newer approach with the older. For example, the sub-title stated that it was "so arranged as to combine the analytical and synthetical methods: with an introduction for beginners, and various exercises, oral and written, for the formation, analysis, transformation, classification, and correction of sentences." Then in 1856 his *An Introduction to the Study of English Grammar* appeared. Its purpose was to be introductory to the *Elements*. In 1860 he published *A Grammar of the English Language*, a somewhat larger book than the *Elements*. In its preface he suggested the serial order in which his grammars may be used, as follows:

I   *Introduction.*
II   *The Grammar of the English Language.*
III   *The Analysis of Sentences.*

From the foregoing it is evident that Greene, like Roswell Smith earlier, attempted to abandon the old deductive and memorization approach of teaching grammar. However, he soon sensed that changes must come gradually, so his later books represented a compromise in methods. Evidently this compromise resulted in greater acceptance of his books, for they still had a wide usage as late as the 1870's.

Weld. A third author of the 1840's whose books appeared in numerous editions was Allen H. Weld. His first book was published in 1846, entitled *English Grammar*, "illustrated by exercises in composition, analyzing, and parsing." In the preface he acknowledged his debt to Webster, Murray, etc., and to Latin and Greek grammars. This meant that he followed more fully the traditional pattern both in method (deductive) and in content by presenting it in the four conventional parts. In 1847 he published a small book entitled, *Parsing Book*. Apparently this was to accompany some regular grammar book. Its popularity is attested by the fact that its 1853 edition was the fiftieth. In 1859 both of these books appeared in revised editions with the word *Progressive* attached. He claimed to have removed certain difficulties and clarified certain parts. Too, they were somewhat larger. His books met decreasing usage in the early 1860's.

Wells. The fourth successful writer of this period was W. H. Wells. He published *A Grammar of the English Language* in 1846. The 1866 edition stated that it was the 260,000th. The later revised editions were somewhat enlarged. In the preface he stated that he possessed more than 300 treatises on English grammar, and then he listed more than 125 grammars that he had consulted in the preparation of his book. The text was organized into the four traditional parts. He claimed that "grammar is too often taught as if it were merely the art of *parsing*. It is hoped that instructors will find the present work adapted to teach 'the art of speaking and writing.'" So before presenting the regular grammar material his book devoted the first 24 pages to oral work, upon the suggestion of Henry Barnard, then the head of the schools in Rhode Island. Too, the grammar was presented very plainly so that it could be more easily understood.

Tower. The fifth author, whose grammar appeared in 1846, was David B. Tower. His first was the *Gradual Lessons in Grammar; or, Guide to the Construction of the English Language.* Previously, in 1841, he had published *The Gradual Reader.* The title indicated the nature of his ap-

Wells, 1858—note the definitions of four parts of grammar.

ENGLISH GRAMMAR.

§ 18. GRAMMAR is the science which treats of the principles of language.

English Grammar teaches the art of speaking and writing the English Language correctly.

§ 19. Grammar is divided into four parts ; — *Orthography, Etymology, Syntax,* and *Prosody.*

Orthography treats of letters, and the proper method of combining them to form syllables and words.

Etymology treats of the classification of words, their derivation, and their various modifications.

Syntax treats of the construction of sentences, according to the established laws of speech.

Prosody treats of accent, quantity, and the laws of versification.

PART I.

ORTHOGRAPHY.

§ 20. ORTHOGRAPHY treats of letters, and the proper method of combining them to form syllables and words.

LETTERS.

§ 21. A *letter* is a mark or character used to represent an elementary sound of the human voice.

The word *letter*, like many other terms used in orthography, is often applied to the sound represented, as well as the written character.

The letters of a language, taken collectively, are called its *Alpha-*

What is grammar ? What does English grammar teach ? How is grammar divided ? Of what does Orthography treat ? Etymology ? Syntax ? Prosody ? What is a letter ? *What are the letters of a language called ?*

2

proach and the purpose of grammar. In 1853 together with B. F. Tweed he published the *First Lessons in Language; or Elements of English Grammar*. This was a small book and very different from the earlier one. Its parts were language; analysis, or parsing; sentences, simple and compound; and rules. The material was nearly all in question or inductive form. Since this book was so different in approach from the *Gradual Lessons*, it was necessary for him to prepare a new advanced book to follow the *Elements*. So in 1859 he published the *Common School Grammar*. However, it was not in question form. All of these books went through several editions.

Clark. The sixth author to be mentioned in this period was S. W. Clark. In 1847 he published *A Practical Grammar*, and also a *Diagram System*. In 1870 the latter was incorporated into *The Normal Grammar: Analytic and Synthetic*. In 1851 the *Analysis of the English Language* appeared. He also wrote a *First Lesson in English Grammar* for beginners as an introduction to the *Practical Grammar*.

In the preface of his first book he said that in his teaching experience in an academy he had consulted many grammars and then prepared manuscript materials from which he taught his own classes. After seven years of such experimentation he published the *Practical Grammar*. It is at least partly inductive, and uses both the analytic and synthetic approaches. Too, Clark introduced many diagrams and included many exercises throughout the book. This book of 218 pages was

DIAGRAMS. 13

and connecting both; as 15 connecting 12 and 16—21 connecting 3 and 22.

7. A word used only to connect, is placed between the two words connected; as 10 between 7 and 11; and a word used to introduce a sentence, is placed above the predicate of the sentence, and attached to it by a line; as 0 above 2.

8. A word relating back to another word, is attached to the antecedent by a line; as 6 attached to 1, and x to 22.

Explanation of the preceding Diagram.

0—Introduces a sentence,	- - - - -	Rule 7.
Principal parts. { 1—Subject,	- - - - -	" 2.
2—Predicate of 1,	- - - -	" 3.
3—Object of 2.	- - - - -	" 4.
4 and 5 individually, and 6 to 19 inclusive, collectively, qualify or define 1,	- -	" 5.
6—Subject of 7 and 11, and relates to 1, -		" 2 and 8.
7—Predicate of 6,	- - - - - - -	" 3.
8 and 9—Modify 7,	- - - - - - -	" 5.
10—Connects 7 and 11,	- - - - - -	" 7.
11—Predicate of 6,	- - - - - - -	" 3.
12—Object of 11,	- - - - - - -	" 4.
13,14, (15, 16, 17, 18, 19)—Qualify or define 12,		" 5.
20 and (21, 22, 23, 24)—Qualify or define 3,		" 5.
21—Shows a relation of 3 and 22,	- - -	" 6.
22—Object of 21,	- - - - - - -	" 4.
23, 24, (25, 26, x)—Qualify or define 22, -		" 5.
25—Subject of 26	- - - - - - -	" 2.
26—Predicate of 25,	- - - - - -	" 3.
x—Object (understood) of 26 and relating to 22,	- - - - - - - - -	" 4 and 8.

Clark, 1847—note the system of diagramming.

enlarged to 305 pages and recopyrighted in 1855, and again in 1864. These books had wide usage during the decades of the 1850's, '60's, and '70's.

Pinneo. The last and seventh popular author whose first grammar appeared in the 1840's was T. S. Pinneo. His first, in 1849, was the *Primary Grammar of the English Language.* This was a book of 110 pages written particularly for beginners. Except in the recapitulation at the end of the book, the traditional four parts of orthography, etymology, syntax, and prosody were not even mentioned. It dealt simply with the various parts of speech and their properties. It contained a mixture of questions, statements or rules, and exercises. It contained 204 numbered sections and 106 exercises. This book was revised and enlarged in 1854.

Pinneo's second book, in 1850, was the *Analytical Grammar.* Its approach was similar to the *Primary Grammar,* except that it was nearly twice as large and much more analytical in its treatment of the parts of speech. It, too, gave only meager attention to the traditional four parts of grammar.

His third book, in 1852, was the *English Teacher.* It paid much less attention to formal grammar, but aimed to teach "the structure of sentences by analysis and synthesis." This departure from formal grammar probably was more radical than was true of any popular grammar of that period. However, this book did not appear in as many editions as his other two grammars.

All these books were printed in Cincinnati by the same firm that published the famous McGuffey *Readers* and the Ray's *Arithmetics,* and like them they had wide circulation in the mid-west.

A number of other grammar textbooks first appeared in the 1840's, but none in numerous editions. However, Noble Butler published two grammars in Louisville in 1845, which appeared in several editions. These were: *Introductory Lessons in English Grammar,* and *A Practical Grammar of the English Language.*

GRAMMARS, 1850-1900

In discussing the grammars of the second half of the eighteenth century, it must be kept in mind that most of the many popular *revisions* grammars that were first published in the 1840's continued to be revised and republished in the 1850's, and even in the 1860's and 1870's. So it could be expected that not many new popular grammars would be published in the 1850's, or even in the 1860's. That was exactly what happened. The books first published in the 1850's of only two authors attained considerable circulation —those of Covell and of Burtt.

Covell. In 1852 L. T. Covell wrote *A Digest of English Grammar, Synthetical and Analytical.* However, it is more than a digest, for it contained 219 pages of context. Incidentally, this book contained 22 extra pages of advertising of other books for sale by the publishers. Although the book used the then modern terms of synthetical and analytical in the title, its organization reverted to the four traditional divisions of grammar. Nevertheless it must have had considerable circulation, for it was republished in numerous editions for at least two decades. In 1853 Covell wrote a *Primary Grammar* of 120 pages as introductory to the *Digest.*

Burtt. The second author to publish a grammar in the 1850's was Andrew Burtt. In 1859 the *Elements of English Grammar, Synthetic and Analytical* appeared. In 1874 a revised and enlarged edition of this book was published. In 1868 his *Practical Grammar of the English Language, Synthetic and Analytic* appeared as a larger book. It, too, used the four traditional divisions. However, the emphases of these divisions differed considerably. For example, in the *Elements* only 80 pages were devoted to syntax; in the *Practical,* 116 pages. The latter appeared in several editions for a decade. Then in 1873 Burtt wrote *A Primary Grammar* to precede the *Practical.*

Kerl. In 1861 a *Comprehensive Grammar of the English Language* by Simon Kerl appeared. It was somewhat larger than most grammars of that period. Too, it was organized very differently from the grammars of Covell and Burtt. As Kerl stated in the preface, "It is built up, in Part First, by a regular synthesis, from the Alphabet to Analysis; in Part Second, from

Pronunciation to Versification; and closes with a thorough and well-authorized section on Punctuation, as teaching the finish to the whole." In the latter part of the book there is a treatment of "Rhetorical Devices." Throughout, definitions or rules are always preceded by a question and followed by examples.

Apparently certain objections arose to the arrangements of the *Comprehensive Grammar*, for in 1865 Kerl's *Common-School Grammar* was published. It was divided into six parts, as follows: Part I, An Outline for Beginners; Part II, Words Uncombined; Part III, Words Grammatically Combined; Part IV, Words Logically Combined; Part V, Words Improperly Combined; and Part VI, Ornament and Finish. Too, the material was presented in a less complicated manner. Evidently this book was more successful, for it appeared in many editions for about two decades. Both books certainly represented radical departures from the traditional presentations of grammar.

Also in 1865 Kerl wrote the *First Lessons in English Grammar*. As the title implied, this was a smaller and simpler book. Its parts were: Part I, Definitions; Part II, Inflections; and Part III, Constructions. In 1870 Kerl's fourth grammar was published, *A Shorter Course in English Grammar*. Evidently he keenly wanted to overcome the criticisms of his previous grammars, for in the preface he frankly discussed the problems in writing a grammar. He said, "Great care has been taken, and no inconsiderable expense has been incurred, to ascertain the views of the ablest teachers, and to modify the work accordingly." He then claimed that this was "different from any thing of the kind," and yet he "carefully avoided oddity, for innovation is not necessarily improvement." The book was divided as follows: Oral Course, and Text Course Words, Sentences, and False Syntax.

The foregoing facts about these grammars certainly revealed that Kerl, like Roswell Smith in 1829, attempted to change and vitalize the teaching of grammar by departing from the traditional organization and procedure commonly followed in grammar books.

Quackenbos. G. P. Quackenbos, like Noah Webster, Peter Parley

(S. G. Goodrich), Comstock, and a few others, was a prolific textbook writer. His textbooks in the fields of English composition, American history, and natural philosophy (physics), gained wide circulation. Eventually, in 1862, he wrote *An English Grammar*. He presented the material in the form of short lessons. In all, the book contained 101 lessons. Although the material did not appear under the four traditional parts, the contents of the lessons appeared largely in the same order of the traditional organization. However, the approach was not fully deductive, for the "definitions are approached by means of preliminary illustrations, which make their abstract language intelligible while it is in process of learning." Thus the emphasis was on developing an understanding rather than mere memory. This book appeared in numerous editions for at least a decade.

Hart. Also in 1862 *A Grammar of the English Language* by John S. Hart was published. In the same year it was "introduced as a class book into the Grammar Schools of the (Philadelphia) District." It followed the traditional organization and was smaller than many other grammars. The definitions and rules were very plainly presented, and apparently were to be memorized. In 1874 he revised, enlarged, and changed this book. Part III presented the following: Sentences, Syntax and Analysis; Punctuation; Figures; and Versification. It included more analytical exercises.

Also, in 1874 he wrote the *Language Lessons for Beginners*. This was a very small book of 79 pages, merely dealing briefly with the various parts of speech. In 1878 he published *An Elementary Grammar*, apparently to replace the smaller *Language Lessons*. The three parts dealt briefly with orthography, etymology, and syntax. Hart also wrote books on literature and composition. His *Manual* of Composition and Rhetoric, first published in 1870, appeared in many editions for more than two decades. It was much more popular than any of his grammars.

Harvey. In 1868 the same publishing company that published the McGuffey *Readers* and the Ray's *Arithmetics*, which would help the sale of any textbook, produced *A Practical Grammar* by Thomas W. Harvey. The title page stated that it was for "use of schools of every grade." This, like many grammars, presented the content in the four traditional parts. Apparently its chief appeal was its concreteness. For example, definitions were always followed by illustrations, as follows: "A *verb* is a word which expresses being, action, or state; as, I *am;* George *writes;* The house *stands.*" In 1878 this book was somewhat revised with a section on Diagrams added. In 1900 Harvey radically revised it and changed the title to *A New English Grammar.* Too, he changed its organization as follows: Part I, Elements of Syntax and Etymology; Part II, Elements of Orthography; Part III, Etymology; Part IV, Complex Syntax; Part V, Punctuation and Capitals; Part VI, Prosody; and then a section on Diagrams. Its concreteness was retained, with more questions and work exercises added. His books had a big sale in the midwest. Harvey also wrote *An Elementary Grammar,* in 1869, which apparently did not attain the popularity of the above mentioned books.

Hadley. In 1871 Hiram Hadley wrote *Lessons in Language.* This book was very different from even the elementary grammars written theretofore. It was largely inductive in approach and attempted to teach grammatical matters without using the regular grammatical terminology. Too, it included many pictures about which many questions were asked, such as the objects shown, action represented, and other character-

Hadley, *Lessons in Language,* 1871—note the inductive approach to composition.

LESSONS IN LANGUAGE. 59

LESSON LI.

A PICTURE.

1. Name all the objects you see in the picture. Put these names in one statement, and write the statement on your slates.
2. In what position do you see the boy? Write.
3. Where is the dog? Write.
4. What has the boy in his hand? Write.
5. Does he look angry? Write.
6. Do you think he is going to strike the dog? Why?
7. What is the cow doing? Write.
8. Does she look as though she had been hurt?
9. Do you suppose the dog has been harming her in any way? Write.
10. Do you think the cow had hurt him? Write.

istics involved. Then in 1876 and 1878 it was markedly revised and appeared in two volumes, as Part I and Part II, both bearing the old title, *Lessons in Language*. Part I again included many pictures, and omitted the use of technical terms, but instead referred to Action-words, Modifying-words, Quality-words, etc. On the other hand, Part II omitted pictures, and began to use such grammatical terms as nouns, verbs, etc.

Swinton. The author whose grammars had the greatest circulation during the second half of the nineteenth century was William Swinton. He, like several other authors, was also the writer of popular textbooks in other fields. He wrote books in the fields of literature, composition, reading, and spelling. In the latter two fields his books were widely used. He was unusually prolific in producing textbooks in rapid succession. His first speller appeared in 1871, grammar in 1872, composition in 1874, literature in 1880, and readers in 1882. And in most of these fields he wrote more than one textbook.

His first grammar was *A Progressive Grammar* in 1872. Courageously he stated that, "In this textbook, of the four medieval 'branches' of grammar, two have been lopped off —*to wit*, Orthography and Prosody." However, this book was also divided into four parts, but two were not the traditional. The parts were: Etymology, Syntax, Analysis and Construction, and English Composition. Like Harvey's *Grammar*, it contained many examples and exercises.

Harvey, *Practical Grammar,* 1868 —popular for many decades in the Midwest.

In 1873 he wrote the *Language Lessons* as an introduction to his *Grammar*. The emphasis in the *Lessons* was on language and composition. Much of the work was presented inductively so as to lead to an understanding of sentence structure. Then in 1874 he wrote the *Language Primer* to precede even the *Lessons*. Thus a graded series of three books resulted. This, too, was largely inductive. In 1877 he revised and enlarged the *Lessons*, and entitled it the *New Language Lessons*, with the sub-title of *An Elementary Grammar and Composition*.

Also in 1877 he wrote *A Grammar*. This was to replace his first, *A Progressive Grammar*. When he first wrote the latter he intended it to be his only grammar. When he began a series this new advanced grammar became one of the series. It was divided into three sections: Etymology, Syntax, and Analysis. In contrast to the *Primer* and the *Lessons*, it was more like other grammar textbooks, and was largely deductive in approach. A statement on the title page claimed it to be "for advanced grammar grades, and for high schools, academies, etc." It was published in two forms or editions, one solely a grammar of 256 pages, and the other with *A School Manual of English Composition* of 113 pages added as a supplement. One of the outstanding characteristics of these books was their emphasis on composition, rather than a mere understanding of technical grammar. Finally, in 1880 he wrote *An Elementary Grammar and Composition*. In summary, apparently Swinton's English books took the grammar market by storm. These books appeared in many editions for more than a decade. However, their use did not continue as long as many other grammars.

Reed and Kellogg. The last really popular grammars written during this period were those by Alonzo Reed and Brainerd Kellogg. They, like several authors, also wrote texts in spelling, rhetoric, and literature. Their *Work on English Grammar and Composition* was published in 1877. This book, like Swinton's, stressed language and composition rather than technical grammar. The authors were critical of the disciplinary value of traditional grammar in saying:

The worth of grammar as mental gymnastics or as linguistic philosophy or as both cannot and will not much longer justify for a place
in our common and our graded schools—it must bear on its branches
more obvious and more *serviceable* fruit, or the tree will be hewn
down and cast out of the way.

Its study should become a "tributary to the Arṭ of Expression."
Their approach was to deal with the function of language before its technical analysis. Their grammar was divided into the
following four parts: The Sentence and the Parts of Speech, 120
pages; Parts of Speech Sub-divided, 34 pages; Modifications
of the Parts of Speech, 80 pages; and Composition, 34 pages.
These parts were radically different from the traditional four
of Murray and his many disciples. The book was slightly revised
and enlarged in 1885, 1896, and 1909. The last edition was
entitled *Higher Lessons in English*, but the titles of the four
parts remained the same in all of the editions.

In 1878 the same authors wrote *An Elementary English Grammar* to precede the *Work on English Grammar*. In this introductory book they also stressed the study of language rather
than technical grammar. Concerning other grammars they critically stated:

> The greater number bewilder the pupil with prolix discussions, and
> vex him with obscure definitions, and numberless rules with their
> suicidal exceptions. They load his memory, with technicalities and
> appall him with authorities, and dull his understanding with endless
> routine parsing and analysis. With them Grammar is a science, or it
> is nothing.

The book contained 100 lessons and 164 pages. It was recopyrighted in 1889 with 34 pages added in the back, mostly consisting of "Notes for Teachers." In 1898 Reed alone wrote even a
simpler book entitled, *Introductory Language Work*. All of
these books appeared in numerous editions for at least three
decades.

Hyde. Mention should be made concerning a woman author of
this period. In 1887 there appeared the *Practical Lessons in
the Use of English, First Book*, by Mary F. Hyde. It contained

two parts with many pictures. The next year came the *Second Book* with *Supplement*. It contained Parts III and IV. The *Supplement* provided 202 pages of review lessons, in all 419 pages. In 1893 Miss Hyde wrote the *Advanced Lessons in English*, designed primarily for pupils who had completed the *Practical Lessons* series. It was divided in four parts: Kinds of Words—The Parts of Speech; Classes and Forms of Words; Relations of Words—Syntax; and Structure and Analysis of Sentences. However, it was much smaller than the Second Book. These books appeared in several editions.

Others. The grammars of a number of other authors gained limited popularity during the last two decades of the nineteenth century. William D. Whitney's *Essentials of English Grammar* was published in 1877, and later appeared in several editions. *Lessons in English* by Sara E. Lockwood was published in 1888, and her *An English Grammar* in 1892. *Lessons in Language* by Horace S. Tarbell was published in 1890, and then revised with the assistance of Martha Tarbell in 1900.

METHODS AND APPROACHES

Most of the early American grammars followed their English predecessors in organizing into large parts, commonly four, and then often dividing the parts into sections, chapters, or lessons. Several books were originally used in manuscript form in the classroom and then later published. These were then organized in the form of lectures or lessons. It can be concluded that the organization of the grammars was much more varied than the content.

More important than the major divisions of the organization was the more detailed arrangement and presentation of the learning content. Here there was much variation. Most of the early grammars used the deductive approach. In these the definitions and rules were first presented, apparently to be memorized, then followed by exercises in which they were applied. However, certain authors, beginning in the 1820's, used the inductive or modified approaches. In 1821 Ingersoll's *Conversations on*

English Grammar was published. Then followed a more popular grammar by Smith in 1830 entitled, *Intellectual and Practical Grammar, in a Series of Inductive Questions.* This, and other books by Smith, created a considerable stir in grammar teaching. This approach was favored by the famous Henry Barnard. Later one of Nutting's books also used the inductive approach. These books were severely criticized by Goold Brown, who in later life assumed the position of critic extraordinary, in his *Grammar of English Grammars,* in the following terms:

> The vain pretensions of several modern simplifiers, contrivers of machines, charts, tables, diagrams, vincula, pictures, dialogues, familiar lectures, ocular analysis, tabular compendiums, inductive exercises, productive systems, intellectual methods, and various new theories, for the purpose of teaching grammar, may serve to deceive the ignorant, to amuse the visionary, and to excite the admiration of the credulous; but none of these things has any favorable relation to that improvement which may justly be boasted as having taken place within the memory of the present generation . . . but no contrivance can ever relieve the pupil from the necessity of committing them (definitions and rules) thoroughly to memory. (p. 107)

Then Brown became more personal, in pointing his criticism against the above mentioned grammar by Smith, saying, "It is a work which certainly will be *'productive'* of no good to anybody but the author and his publishers." In spite of Brown's criticism many later grammars used the inductive approach.

During the 1850's another approach developed; namely, the analytical. In fact, in 1849 Peter Bullions published *An Analytical and Practical Grammar of the English Language.* Soon thereafter the popular grammars written by Clark, Pinneo, and Covell used the word analytical in the titles, and those of Greene and of Burtt followed this approach. Kerl and a few others used what may be termed the developmental approach. Then in the 1870's the emphasis was on correct composition and rhetoric, both oral and written. The popular books by Swinton and also those by Reed and Kellogg emphasized the functional approach of English grammar. The books of the latter authors continued in use until well after 1900. Although the writer has not attempted to analyze grammars after 1900, Lyman has characterized the period of 1891-1920 as the "elimination period or the incidental study period, the chief tendency of which is the gradual subordination of formal grammar to its proper place as incidental to the study of composition and literature."

The approaches of teaching grammar have varied and changed from time to time between 1750 and 1900, and at no time did all the leading grammars follow the same procedure.

CHAPTER 5

ARITHMETICS

THE EARLIEST

RECOGNITION of elements of arithmetic seem to be as old as recorded history of man. Ancient Egyptians, Babylonians, Hindus, Greeks, and Romans all have made contributions to the development of arithmetic. With the growth of fields of learning arithmetic became recognized as one of the seven Liberal Arts. Arithmetic is one of the oldest of school subjects.

Possibly the first treatise on arithmetic in English was written and published in England in 1537, and entitled, *An Introduction for to: Lerne to Reckon with the Pen and with the Counters after the True Cast of Arsmetyke or Awgrym.* Likely the first popular English arithmetic was Recorde's *Arithmetick: or, The Grounde of Arts* in 1542. Other very early English arithmetics which evidently influenced early American texts were Edmund Wingate's *Arithmetique Made Easie* (1629); William Mather's *The Young Man's Companion: or, Arithmetick Made Easy;* John Ward's *The Young Mathematician's Guide. Being a Plain and Easie Introduction to the Mathematicks* (1706), of which Part I and part of Part V dealt with arithmetic; John Hill's *Arithmetick, Both in Theory and Practice* (1712); and others, some of which later were reprinted in America to be discussed subsequently.

THE

Young Man's

COMPANION

In Four Parts.

Part I. Containing Directions for Spelling, Reading & Writing *True English.*
Part II. Arithmetick made easie, and the Rules thereof Explained and made familiar to the Capacity of those that desire to learn in a little time.
Part III. The Method of Writing Letters upon most Subjects whether Trade, Traffick or otherwise.
Part IV. Contains a choice Collection of Acquittances, Bills, Bonds, Wills, Indentures, Deeds of Sale, Deeds of Gift, Letters of Attorney, Assignments, Lease and Releases Counter-Securities, Bills of Exchange, with many other useful Presidents, Profitable both for Old and Young to learn and know.

The second Edition corrected & Enlarged,

The whole Adorn'd with Variety of other Matters, as will appear by the Contents,

Printed and Sold by William and Andrew Bradford, at the Bible in New-York, 1710.

First English Work to Include Arithmetic (Bradford, 1705)

HODDER's
ARITHMETICK:
OR, THAT
Necessary ART
Made most Easy.

Being explained in a way familiar to the Capacity of any that desire to learn it in a little Time.

By JAMES HODDER, Writing-Master.

The Five and Twentieth Edition, Revised, Augmented, and above a Thousand Faults Amended, by HENRY MOSE, *late Servant and Successor to the Author.*

BOSTON: Printed by J. Franklin, for B. Phillips, N. Buttolph, B. Eliot, D. Henchman, G. Phillips, J. Eliot, and E. Negus, Booksellers in Boston, and Sold at their Shops 1719.

Left - First Separate
English Arithmetic
(Hodder, 1719)

Right - First Arithmetic
by a Native American
(Greenwood, 1729)

ARITHMETICK
Vulgar and *Decimal* ;

WITH THE

APPLICATION
THEREOF TO
A VARIETY of CASES

IN

Trade, and *Commerce.*

BOSTON: N.E.
Printed by S. Kneeland and T. Green, for T. Hancock at the Sign of the Bible and Three Crowns in Annstreet. MDCCXXIX.

The Title Pages of Three Historic Arithmetics Published in America
(from Karpinski, Bibliography of Mathematical Works)

Title pages of three historic arithmetics published in America: first English series to include arithmetic, Bradford 1705; first separate English arithmetic, Hodder 1719; first American arithmetic, Greenwood 1729.

THE
SCHOOLMASTER'S
ASSISTANT,
BEING A
COMPENDIUM OF ARITHMETIC, ‑
BOTH
PRACTICAL AND THEORETICAL.

In Five Parts.

CONTAINING,

I. Arithmetic in whole Numbers, wherein all the common Rules, having each
of them a sufficient Number of Questions, with their answers, are methodi-
cally and briefly handled.
II. Vulgar Fractions, wherein several
Things, not commonly met with, are
distinctly treated of, and laid down in
the most plain and easy manner.
III. Decimals, in which, among other
Things are considered the Extraction
of Roots; Interest both simple and compound; Annuities, Rebate, and Equation
of Payments.

IV. A large collection of Questions with
their Answers, serving to exercise the
foregoing Rules, together with a few
others both pleasant and diverting.
V. Duodecimals, commonly called Cross
Multiplication; wherein that sort of
Arithmetic is thoroughly considered,
and rendered very plain and easy, together with the Method of proving all
the foregoing Operations at once, by
Division of several Denominations,
without Reducing them into the lowest Terms mentioned.

The Whole being delivered in the most familiar way of Question
and Answer, is recommended by several eminent Mathematicians,
Accomptants, and Schoolmasters, as necessary to be used in Schools
by all Teachers, who would have their Scholars thoroughly understand, and make a quick progress in Arithmetic,

To which is Prefixt,

AN ESSAY
ON THE EDUCATION OF YOUTH;
Humbly offered to the consideration of

PARENTS.

By THOMAS DILWORTH,

AUTHOR OF THE NEW GUIDE TO THE ENGLISH TONGUE
YOUNG BOOK-KEEPER'S ASSISTANT, &c.

NEW-YORK:

PRINTED FOR THOMAS KIRK, NO. 48, MAIDEN-LANE.

1805.

Most popular American-published English arithmetic, 1805—note essay
on education addressed to parents.

The first seven arithmetic textbooks published in the Americas were in Spanish, four in Mexico and three in Lima, Peru. The first mathematics textbook was the *Sumario Compendioso* (1556) written by Juan Diez Freyle, and the first separate arithmetic was the *Arte Para Aprender Todo El Menor Del Arithmetica* by Pedro de Paz (1623), both published in Mexico. Incidentally, the first university in America was founded in Mexico in 1554, in which later the first lecturer in mathematics was Juan Negrete.

Apparently, most of the earliest arithmetic books used by the American colonists were reprints of English books. No copyright laws then applied. The first of these was William Bradford's *The Secretary's Guide* in 1705. It appeared in at least seven editions. Part II was "Arithmetick made easie." A similar but better book was George Fisher's *The Instructor: or, Young Man's Best Companion* (1748), which was rather fully based on an English text, and appeared here in about a dozen editions before 1800. Much of this book dealt with the practical applications of arithmetic. The last part of the book was entitled, "The Practical Gauger," which in part dealt with some elements of surveying. It has been claimed that George Washington made wide use of this book. In a sense this book was a forerunner of the *World Book of Knowledge*. However, the first arithmetic as a separate treatise was James Hodder's *Arithmetick: or, That Necessary Art Made Most Easy* (Boston, 1719), which was a reprint of the 25th English edition.

Thomas Dilworth. The text which was reprinted most often and which had by far the widest circulation here of any English authored arithmetic was Thomas Dilworth's *The Schoolmaster's Assistant; Being a Compendium of Arithmetic both Practical and Theoretical* (1773). Since arithmetics did not appear in graded series until about 1830, the early ones contained all phases of arithmetic in a single book. Thus Dilworth's text had five parts. Part I, Of Whole Numbers. Part II, Of Vulgar Fractions. Part III, Of Decimal Fractions. Part IV, Questions. Part V, Of Duodecimals.

Part I not only dealt with the simple fundamentals of arithmetic, but with such topics as interest, rebate, compound fellowship, weights and measures, double rule of three, alligation medial, and permutation. Part II dealt with vulgar or common fractions. Part III not only dealt with the fundamentals of decimal fractions, but also with square root, cube root, biquadrate root, sursolid root, second sursolid root, square biquadrate root, squared square cube root, and annuities and pensions. Part IV consisted mainly of 104 miscellaneous problems requiring solution. Many of these problems were stated in flowery rhetorical form; two even in poetic form. No. 87 follows:

> If one Pound Ten, and forty Groats
> Will buy a Load of Hay;
> How many Pounds with nineteen Crowns
> For twenty Loads will Pay? Answer L38 11s. 8d.

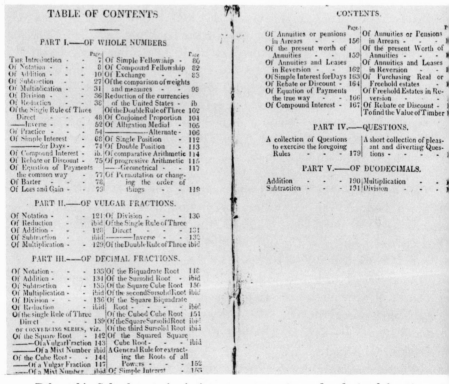

Dilworth's *Schoolmaster's Assistant*—note topics under decimal fractions.

The SCHOOLMASTER's Affiftant.

91. The computed Diftance between *London* and *York* is
Miles; now if a Man fet out from *London*, and walks every
towards *York* 20 Miles, and back again towards *London* 15
les; how long will it be before he gets to his journey's End?
w. 30 Days.

92. Bought 127 Pieces of Cloth, for which I delivered 3589
of Holland, at 7s. 11d. per Ell Englifh; what coft a Piece
that Cloth? *Anfw.* 11l. 3s. 8d. 2 qrs. ...

93. The Account of a certain School is as followeth; *viz.*
of the Boys learn Geometry, ¾ learn Grammar, ... learn
Arithmetic, ... learn to write, and 9 learn to read; I demand
Number of each? *Anfw.* 5 Geometers, 30 Grammarians, 24
Arithmeticians, ... Writers, and 9 Readers.

94. I have laid out for a Merchant 638l. 17s. 3d. he allows
2 ¼ per Cent. before that I owed him 184l. 17s. 9d. how
ch is he indebted to me? *Anfw.* 471l. 10s. 10d. 1 qr.

95. Bought a Tun of Wine for 75l. 17s. at what Price muft
ll it per Quart to gain 5l. 10s. by the Whole, when there
re 22 Gallons leaked out? *Anfw.* 22d. +

96. If out of 10s. per Week I lay up 4d. 2 qrs. per Day, Sun-
s excepted; and have faved 9l. 2s. 3d. how long was I in
ing it up; and how much have I fpent in that Time?

Anf. { 567 Days in laying up.
{ 3 ... 7s. 9d. fpent.

97. If I buy 1000 Ells Flemifh of Linen for 90l. what may
ll it per Ell in *London* to gain 10l. by the Whole? *Anf.*
4s. per Ell.

98. Bought threefcore Pieces of Holland for three Times
ny Pounds, and fold them again for four Times as much
t if they had coft me as much as I fold them for, what fhould
ave fold them for, to gain after the fame Rate? *Anfw.* 320l.

99. There are three Quantities of Silver, each of the fame
eight, but different in Value; the Weight of each Quantity
10 oz. the Value of the firft Sort is 4s. per oz. of the fecond
6l. per oz. and of the third 5s. per oz. I demand the Worth
an Ounce when they are all melted down together? *Anfw.*
6s. per Oz.

100. I have received Advice from my Factor, that he ha
buried upon my Account, the Sum of 4000 Guilders, 1
ivers; I demand what Sum I muft anfwer for that in Englif
ney. Exchange at Par; and alfo what his Commiffion come
at 2 per Cent.

Anfw. { 400l. 1s. 6d. Sterling.
{ 8l. 0s. 0d. 1qr. Commiffion. 101. A

The SCHOOLMASTER's Affiftant. 1

101. A Merchant bought a Parcel of Jewels for 220l. a
fold them again for 440l. payable at the End of 6 Months;
demand what the Gain was worth in ready Money, Rebate bein
made at 6 per Cent? *Anfw.* 213l. 11s. 10d. +

102. A Factor bought 4 Chefts of Sugar, the Mark a
Weight as follows;

	C.	qrs.	lb.
D	- -	10	3	14
E	- -	12	1	17
F	- -	13	1	19
G	- -	11	2	10

now fuppofe the Tare or Weight of every Cheft, when it
empty, to be 38 lb. I demand the neat Weight of the fai
Sugar; alfo I demand the prime Coft of the fame, fuppofing
it came to 18s. per C. including the Charges of Lighterage
Porterage, Ware-Houfe Room, Cuftom, &c. alfo I demand th
whole Gain, and the Gain per Cent. fuppofing the Chefts D an
E were fold afterwards at 28s. per C. and the other two Chef
viz. F and G, at 4d. per lb.

	l.	s.	d.
	Prime Coft - - -	42	4	8½
Anfw.	Whole Gain - -	34	16	4½
	Gain per Cent - -	82	8	9¼

103.
A Gentleman a Chaife did buy,
An Horfe and Harnefs too;
They coft the Sum of three Score Pounds,
Upon my Word 'tis true;
The Harnefs came to half th' Horfe
The Horfe twice of the Chaife;
And if you find the Price of them,
Take them and go your Ways.

Anfw. { Chaife - - - 15l.
{ Horfe - - 30
{ Harnefs - - 15

104. A Gentleman courted a young Lady; and as their Birt
Days happened together, they agreed to make that their Wed
ding-Day. On the Day of Marriage, it happened, that th
Gentleman's Age was juft double to that of the Lady's. that i
as 2 to 1. After they had lived together 30 Years, the Gen
leman obferved that his Lady's Age drew nearer to his, an
that his was only in fuch Proportion to hers as 2 to 1½. Thi
ty Years after this the fame Gentlemen found his and his Lady
ty Ages to be as near as 2 to 1¾: at which Time they both di
I demand their feveral Ages at the Day of their Marriage, an
of their Death? Alfo the Reafon why the Lady's Age, whic
was continually gaining upon her Hufband's, fhould, notwith
ftanding, be never able to overtake it?

Dilworth: problems—103 in verse.

Part V, in dealing with duodecimals, defined them as "Fractions of a Foot, or of an Inch, or any Part of an Inch, having 12 for their Denominator." The table of duodecimals was as follows:

Note, 12 Fourths make 1 Third.
12 Thirds make 1 Second.
12 Seconds make 1 Inch.
12 Inches make 1 Foot.

The explanatory contents throughout the book were presented in catechetical form. For example:

Q. What is the use of Addition?
A. Addition teacheth to bring several particular numbers into one total sum.
Q. How many sorts of Addition are there?
A. Two, viz. simple and compound.

After examining Dilworth's book one may wonder why it became so popular, yet in fact reprints of it continued to appear here for about fifty years. Furthermore, it influenced greatly the earliest American written arithmetics.

Following the first reprint of Dilworth's text here (1773), according to Karpinski,[1] a number of other English arithmetics were reprinted here. Among them were: Daniel Fenning's *Ready Reckoner, or, Traders Useful Assistant* (1774), which was really only a book of useful tables; Cocker's *Arithmetick* (1779); John Bonnycastle's *The Scholar's Guide to Arithmetic* (1786); Gough's *A Treatise of Arithmetic* (1788); and Daniel Fenning's *American Youth's Instructor* (1795).

CONTENT

It is believed generally that the contents of mathematics textbooks have changed less through the years than those in most other fields. This likely is true. Nevertheless some marked changes have taken place in American arithmetic textbooks. The findings of several studies are summarized in Table V. Burry's study includes an analysis of 65 arithmetics before 1810. The study by Smith and Eaton includes an analysis of a sampling of the arithmetics between 1820 and 1880. The sample does include an analysis of the more popular arithmetics, and thus reflects rather accurately what most pupils were taught in arithmetic. It may be noted that some rather marked changes took place between the textbooks before 1810 and those after 1820. The important topics that received most decreasing attention with time were: foreign exchange dropping from 8.7 per cent in the earliest books to 1.5 per cent in the last period; compound denominate numbers from 16 per cent to 9 per cent and treatment of federal

---

[1] Louis Charles Karpinski, *The History of Arithmetic.* (New York: Rand McNally & Company 1925), pp. 85-90.

money from 5 per cent to 2.4 per cent. Also, many topics that received at least noticeable attention in the earlier books virtually disappeared in the later ones. Among such topics were alligation; duodecimals; position, or rule of false; tare, tret, and cloff; barter; and permutations and combinations. In addition, some topics not listed in the table appear in the oldest arithmetics but seldom in the later ones, such as, bookkeeping, algebra, banking, and imports and exports. Also many tables that were included in at least some early arithmetics are no longer in more recent ones. Among them are tables related to fish, books, nautical measure, tret, English square measure, gunpowder, jeweller's weight, lead weight, paper and parchment, refiner's weight, wood and bark measure, bread, tare, Winchester measure, and measures of ale, beer, wool, wine, and cloth.

On the other hand, increased treatment has been given many topics. Treatment of the fundamental processes involving whole numbers increased from 9.3 per cent to 16.6 per cent to first rank; vulgar (common) fractions from 6.9 per cent to 11.9 per cent; partial payments from .9 per cent to 3.8 per cent; and numeration from 1.5 per cent to 3.1 per cent. It is clear that more topics have virtually disappeared or been totally dropped than have been added. In other words, the more recent authors of arithmetics aim to deal only with those topics most likely to be useful in post-school life.

Not only has there been considerable variation in emphasis on certain topics from period to period, great variation has appeared among in-

Pike, *Teacher's Assistant*, 1811, obsolete knowledge.

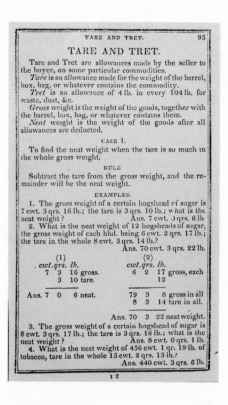

TARE AND TRET.

Tare and Tret are allowances made by the seller to the buyer, on some particular commodities.

Tare is an allowance made for the weight of the barrel, box, bag, or whatever contains the commodity.

Tret is an allowance of 4 lb. in every 104 lb. for waste, dust, &c.

Gross weight is the weight of the goods, together with the barrel, box, bag, or whatever contains them.

Neat weight is the weight of the goods after all allowances are deducted.

CASE 1.

To find the neat weight when the tare is so much in the whole gross weight.

RULE

Subtract the tare from the gross weight, and the remainder will be the neat weight.

EXAMPLES.

1. The gross weight of a certain hogshead of sugar is 7 cwt. 3 qrs. 16 lb.; the tare is 3 qrs. 10 lb.; what is the neat weight? Ans. 7 cwt. 0 qrs. 6 lb

2. What is the neat weight of 12 hogsheads of sugar, the gross weight of each hhd. being 6 cwt. 2 qrs. 17 lb.; the tare in the whole 8 cwt. 3 qrs. 14 lb.?

Ans. 70 cwt. 3 qrs. 22 lb.

(1)			(2)		
cwt.	qrs.	lb.	cwt.	qrs.	lb.
7	3	16 gross.	6	2	17 gross, each
	3	10 tare.			12
Ans. 7	0	6 neat.	79	3	8 gross in all
			8	3	14 tare in all.

Ans. 70 3 22 neat weight.

3. The gross weight of a certain hogshead of sugar is 8 cwt. 3 qrs. 17 lb.; the tare is 16 lb.; what is the neat weight? Ans. 8 cwt. 0 qrs. 1 lb.

4. What is the neat weight of 456 cwt. 1 qr. 19 lb. of tobacco, tare in the whole 15 cwt. 2 qrs. 13 lb.?

Ans. 440 cwt. 3 qrs. 6 lb.

I 2

TABLE V

PER CENT OF SPACE DEVOTED TO TOPICS BY PERIODS IN
AMERICAN ARITHMETICS, 1710–1880.

	Burry's[1] Study 65 Books Before 1810		Smith's[2] Study 13 books 1821–50		Smith's[2] Study 19 books 1851–80		
	Per Cent	Rank	Per Cent	Rank	Per Cent	Rank	
1. Compound denominate numbers	16	1	10.84	3	9.02	4	–7
2. Percentage	12.3	2	8.59	4	13.41	2	+
3. Fundamental processes (Whole numbers)	9.3	3	17.65	1	16.62	1	+7–
4. Foreign exchange	8.7	4	1.55	15	1.52	14	–7.2
5. Ratio and proportion	7.7	5	6.68	5	4.60	7	
6. Vulgar fractions	6.9	6	11.75	2	11.94	3	+5
7. Decimals	6.6	7	4.94	7	5.66	5	
8. Federal money	5	8	2.03	13	2.41	13	–
9. Powers and roots	5	9	5.83	6	4.12	8	
10. Practice	4.9	10	1.59	14	.46	19	–4.5
11. Miscellaneous problems	4.2	11	4.26	8	3.68	11	

12. Mensuration (geometric forms)	4.1	12	3.50	10	5.18	6	—
13. Progression	3.4	13	3.51	9	1.30	15	
14. Weights and measures	3.1	14	2.80	11	4.11	9	
15. Alligation	2.6	15	1.55	15	.97	16	—
16. Duodecimals	2.4	16	.84	19	.50	18	—
17. Partnership	2.3	17	1.21	18	.94	17	—
18. Position or rule of false	2.00	18	.59	20			
19. Tare, tret & cloff	1.9	19	.58	21	.09	20	—
20. Numeration	1.5	20	2.50	12	3.12	12	+
21. Barter	1.1	21	.49	22	.01	22	—
22. Partial payments	.9	22	1.27	17	3.76	10	+3
23. Permutations and combinations	.9	23	.33	23	.08	21	

[1] Harold E. Burry, "An Analysis of Early American Arithmetic Textbooks Through 1810." (Unpublished doctor's dissertation, University of Pittsburgh, 1958)

[2] H. L. Smith and M. T. Eaton, *An Analysis of Arithmetic Textbooks* (Second Period—1821 to 1850 and Third Period—1851 to 1880). Bloomington, Indiana: Bulletin of the School of Education, Vol. 18, No. 6, Indiana University, 1942.

dividual books of a period. For example Jones[2] analyzed the treatment of vulgar (common) fractions in 110 arithmetics before 1840. The mean amount of space given to fractions per book was 20.2 pages in the main section and 23.6 pages in the total treatment. However, the range was from 0.4 to 92.9 pages for the former phase, and from 0.6 to 117.7 for the latter. Likewise, there was variation in the relative placement of the two phases. The space division of the different aspects of fractions was as follows: introductory concepts, 11.9 per cent; reduction, 39.3 per cent; addition, 7.8 per cent; subtraction, 7.4 per cent; multiplication, 14.1 per cent; division, 9.6 per cent; Rule of Three, 5.4 per cent; and miscellaneous, 4.4 per cent. The rules and explanations dealing with fractions varied considerably.

CHARACTERISTICS

Graded series. In arithmetic, as in other subject fields, graded series were not common until about 1830. It is true that a number of authors of early arithmetics wrote more than one book, but generally the later books would be revisions or replacements of the earlier one. This was true of the popular arithmetics of Pike and Adams. One of the first attempts at grading was done by Colburn. In 1821 his *First Lessons in Arithmetic* appeared, followed in 1822 by a more difficult book, *Sequel to First Lessons.* In the *Sequel* he stated that it was not absolutely necessary to have studied the *First Lesson* before the *Sequel.* Even after graded series became common, the upper book or books very commonly would begin with the fundamentals and fractions nearly as though they had not been taught from a lower book. Too, in many cases the first book written by an author would be a "complete" book, then later a lower book would be written as an afterthought. For example, Davies wrote his *Common School Arithmetic* in 1833, but his *First Lessons* not until 1840.

The first well-planned graded series was by Emerson. In 1829

---

2 Emily K. Jones, "An Historical Survey of the Developmental Treatment of Vulgar Fractions in American Arithmetics from 1719 to 1839." (Unpublished doctor's dissertation. University of Pittsburgh, 1957).

he wrote the *North American Arithmetic, Part First*. In 1832 *Part Second*, and in 1834 *Part Third*. In 1837 Joseph Ray wrote the *Arithmetic, Part First; Part Second;* and *Part Third*. Thereafter nearly all popular arithmetics appeared in series, although the lowest book did not always appear first. However, all series did not consist of three books. Several series, counting the "Advanced" or "High School" arithmetics, were composed of four books. On the other hand, several series contained only two books. In fact, some authors eventually wrote two series, one of two and the other of three books. Apparently some parents and schools objected to buying three books, so the two-book series developed.

Mental arithmetic. Even before arithmetics appeared in well graded series, some authors emphasized the teaching of beginning arithmetic *mentally*. Both of Colburn's books stressed mental work. Thereafter at least one book of the series by Ray, Greenleaf, Thomson, Stoddard, Brooks, and Wentworth, contained either the word *mental* or *intellectual* in the title. However, the stress on mental arithmetic somewhat lessened the latter part of the nineteenth century. In fact, many of the books contained the statement that the exercises were first mental and then for the slate.

Methods and approaches. The contents of nearly all early arithmetics were so arranged as to imply the use of the deductive approach in teaching. A few did this by presenting the definitive matters of arithmetic like a catechism, by means of questions and prepared answers to be committed to memory. This was true of Dilworth's *Assistant*, Davies' *Practical and Mental* in 1829, and Thomson's *First Lessons*. However, by far the most commonly used deductive approach, especially in the advanced arithmetics, was first to present the definitions, tables, etc., to be committed, which later were to be applied to exercises or problems.

The first important author to use the inductive approach was Colburn. His *First Lessons in Arithmetic on the Plan of Pesta-*

lozzi was definitely inductive. Then in 1826 he had this book recopyrighted with the word *Inductive* in the title. In 1827 Adams' *Arithmetic* claimed to combine the advantages of both the "inductive and synthetic" approaches. In 1829 Smith published an arithmetic on the Pestalozzian plan. Numerous other authors prepared at least their lower arithmetics either partly or largely on the inductive approach. Naturally the mental arithmetics were largely inductive. An understanding of rules and combinations was to be developed by means of exercises rather than by memorization.

Then about 1850 many of the books claimed to follow the *analytic* or *analytic and synthetic* approaches. Several even included the word *Analytic* in the title. This was true at least of one or more of the arithmetics written by Davies, Ray, Greenleaf, Thomson, and Dean. In a sense these combined some of the features both of the inductive and deductive approaches.

Many authors attempted to help the teachers of arithmetic find the most effective method to use the books. A large fraction of the texts contained some such help. In many texts such help was presented in the preface. In others an additional special section, such as, "To Teachers," "Helps to Teachers," or "Suggestions to Teachers" was included. Usually these helps were in the beginning of the text, but some included a longer section in the back. In Brooks' *Normal Primary Arithmetic* (1858) ten pages of very fine print were devoted to a Preface, Suggestions to Teachers, and Remarks concerning the procedures to be followed. French's *Elementary Arithmetic* (1867) used four pages of fine print to explain the nature of the book in the Preface, and then in the back used twelve pages to present a Manual of Methods and Suggestions. Most of these suggestions were very specific in referring to particular problems and pages of the text.

Pictures and illustrations. The authors of arithmetic textbooks were slower to use pictures than those of spellers, readers, and geographies. One of the first to do so was Frederick Emerson in his *North American Arithmetic: Part First* (1829), which was the first book of the first well-graded arithmetic series. Pictures or counters were used on every page of the book except the pages of miscellaneous examples. The pictures evidently were wood cuts. However, *Part Second* and *Part Third* did not contain pictures. In 1830 Barnard's *A Treatise on Arithmetic* used numerous pictures. After 1850 many of the primary arithmetics contained pictures, especially the later editions of the most popular series. Among them were books by Ray, Fish, White, Goff, and Wentworth. One of the first upper or advanced books to include pictures was French's *Common School Arithmetic* in 1869. For more than two decades this practice became common. Evidently the Oswego Movement, which stressed the use of objects and pictures, contributed greatly to the use of objects and pictures in arithmetic textbooks.

Workbook and manuals. Many modern educators believe that the use of workbooks is of very recent origin. Though of different form, many old arithmetics contained or implied such use. One of the first arithmetics to do this was Samuel Temple's *An Arithmetical Primer* in 1809. Blank spaces were left for the solution of the problems. For example, a problem in subtraction was:

7854

5906

Diff. _____

Proof _____

Temple, *An Arithmetical Primer,* 1809, forerunner of the modern workbook.

This practice continued throughout the text. The earliest editions of Adams' *The Scholar's Arithmetic* even earlier had left blank spaces on some pages, but the later editions did not. However, it must be said that the practice was not common. A few books contained directions for work which in a sense resembled the features of a workbook. For example, the *First Steps in Number: A Primary Arithmetic* (1885) by Wentworth and Reed headed many lessons with directions, as "Copy and complete," "Copy and find the answers," etc.

Another type of book, which has often been classified as an arithmetic but really in a technical sense was not, was one like Daniel Fenning's *The Ready Reckoner; or Trader's Most Useful Assistant.* The first seven pages dealt with instructions regarding its use; the remaining pages of the rather large book consisted of detailed schemes and tables for calculating the price of things. This book was first printed in England and then reprinted in America. One edition was printed in Germantown, Pennsylvania, in 1774. Other similar books later appeared, but they should not be considered as regular school textbooks.

Answers and keys. Very early, most arithmetic textbooks included the answers to the problems. In most cases the answers immediately followed the problems, but in some books they appeared in the back. Some publishers printed two editions—one with and one without answers. Since teachers were very poorly prepared in those early times, apparently the demand soon arose for more help than merely the answers. So the practice developed to publish *Keys*, which would not only contain the answers but also the steps involved in the solution of the most difficult problems. In a few cases the *Key* would appear in fine print in the back of the book, as in Colburn's *First Lessons.* More often, however, the *Key* would be a separate book, apparently for use by teachers only. One of the first of this type was prepared by Frederic McKenny for Crukshank's *American Tutor's Assistant* in 1809. Later McKenny also prepared one for Pike's *Teacher's Assistant.* Armstrong published a *Key* for Stockton's *Western Calculator* in 1824. Later *Keys* were published for the popular arithmetics of Ray, Brooks, and others.

Unusual problems. Early arithmetics often contained very unusual, though interesting, problems. One which appeared in a
number of arithmetics, including Dilworth's, was:

> A Man driving his Geese to the Market, was met by another, who
> said, Good Morrow, Master with your Hundred Geese. Says he, I
> have not an Hundred; but if I have half as many as I now have, and
> two Geese and an half, beside the Number I have already, I should
> have an Hundred; How many had he? Answer 65

Dilworth's text also had numerous problems dealing with different kinds of liquor. For example:

> In 731 gro. bottles of wine, each 1 5/7 pint, how many hhds.?
> Answer 29 hhds. 52 gals. 5 pts. 5/7

Another problem that was found in a number of books, including
Pike's, was:

> How many combinations can be made of 6 letters out of the 24 letters
> of the alphabet? Answer 134596

A similar problem appeared in Thomson's, as follows:

> How many different ways may a class of 26 scholars be arranged?

Another in Thomson's was:

> A, B, and C, can trench a meadow in 12 days; B, C, and D, in 14
> days; and C, D, and A, in 15 days; and D, B, and A, in 18 days. In
> what time would it be done by all of them together, and by each of
> them singly?

Many clock problems appeared in old arithmetics. Stoddard's
American Philosophical Arithmetic contained this one:

> At what time between 2 and 3 o'clock will the hour and minute hand
> be together?

Another problem in Stoddard's was:

> A deer is 180 leaps before a hound, and takes 4 leaps to the hound's

9; and 5 of the deer's leaps are equal to 9 of the hound's. How many leaps must the hound take to catch the deer?

Ray's *Higher Arithmetic* was well known for its many puzzling problems. Here follow several:

How far does a man walk while planting a field of corn 285 ft. square, the rows being 3 ft. apart and 3 ft. from the fences?   5 mi. 6 rd. 6 ft.

A wooden wheel of uniform thickness, 4 ft. in diameter, stands in mud 1 ft. deep: what fraction of the wheel is out of the mud? .80449+ of it.

How many inch balls can be put in a box which measures, inside, 10 in. square, and is 5 in. deep?   568 balls

I have an inch board 5 ft. long, 17 in. wide at one end, and 7 in. at the other: how far from the larger end must it be cut straight across, so that the solidities of the two parts shall be equal?   2 ft.

EARLIEST AMERICAN WRITTEN ARITHMETICS

The first arithmetic written by a native of colonial America was the *Arithmetick, Vulgar and Decimal* (1729) by Isaac Greenwood, professor of mathematics at Harvard from 1727 to 1738. The second one written here was in Dutch. It was Pieter Venema's *Arithmetica of Cyffer Konst* (1730). More than fifty years later there appeared Dearborn's *The Pupil's Guide* (1782), and Alexander McDonald's *The Youth's Assistant* (1785). None of these attained wide circulation.

Nicholas Pike (1743-1819). The first American written arithmetic to become popular and to give Dilworth's *Assistant* keen competition was Nicholas Pike's *A New and Complete System of Arithmetic* (1788), "Composed for the use of the citizens of the United States." In fact, Pike had the manuscript for this book ready in 1785, but used three years to file copies with several states in order to secure royalties on it when published, and to secure endorsements from prominent persons. Recommendations from Benjamin West, President Ezra Stiles of Yale, Governor James Bowdoin of Massachusetts, and others, were in the book.

It contained 512 pages of rather fine print. The last 106 pages dealt with logarithms, geometry, trigonometry, mensuration, algebra, and conic sections. The content, in addition to dealing with the fundamentals of arithmetic, included treatment of such topics as duodecimals or cross multiplication, single rule of three, rule of three inverse, conjoined proportion, fellowship, tare and trett, involution, evolution, annuities, barter, brokerage, alligation, permutations and combinations, tables of various weights and measures, chronological problems such as finding the Julian Epact and finding the dates of Easter from the year 1753 to 4199, and many other topics. Among the tables not commonly found in present day arithmetics were those of English money, troy weight, apothecaries weight, cloth measure, wine measure, and ale or beer measure. The measures of beer consisted of pint, quart, gallon, firkin, kilderkin, barrel, hogshead, puncheon, and butt. Dutch and French money tables were also included. It must have been the first arithmetic to include a reprint of the Act of Congress of 1786 creating the U.S. Federal Money system of mills, cents, dimes, dollars, and eagles. However, none of the problems in the book involving money were based on the United States Federal money system, but rather on the English.

Although the extensive and far-fetched list of topics treated in Pike's book seems forbidding, the problems were always preceded by a rule and demonstrated by an example. To illustrate, the Rule of Three began as follows:

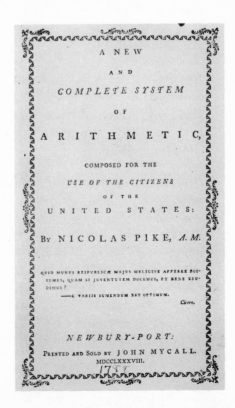

A NEW

AND

COMPLETE SYSTEM

OF

ARITHMETIC,

COMPOSED FOR THE

USE OF THE CITIZENS

OF THE

UNITED STATES:

By NICOLAS PIKE, A. M.

QUID MUNUS REIPUBLICÆ MAJUS MELIUSVE AFFERRE POSSUMUS, QUAM SI JUVENTUTEM DOCEMUS, ET BENE ERUDIMUS?
——E VARIIS SUMENDUM EST OPTIMUM.
Cicero.

NEWBURY-PORT:

PRINTED AND SOLD BY JOHN MYCALL.
MDCCLXXXVIII.
1788.

Title Page of early America's most popular arithmetic, 1788.

Rule

Having reduced your fractions to decimals, and stated your question as in whole numbers, multiply the second and third together; divide by the first, and the quotient will be the answer.

1. If 5/8 of a yard cost 7/12 of a pound; what will 9 2/3 yards come to?

5/8=, 625   7/12=, 583 + and 2/3=, 666 +

    Yd.   £

As, 625:   583:   :   9,666:   £9, os: 3 3/4 d Answer

This book was frequently reprinted with only slight revisions as late as the 1830's.

In 1793 Pike published an *Abridgement of the New and Complete System of Arithmetic*, which contained only 371 pages. The Preface claimed it suitable for public schools, and spoke of the larger book as, "That celebrated work, which is now used as a classical book in all the New England Universities." This book also appeared in numerous editions. The success of these books must have influenced other American written arithmetics. It is doubtful whether these difficult books were ever used in the elementary schools.

Benjamin Workman. In 1789 he published *The American Accountant; or, Schoolmasters' New Assistant.* This really was an abridged revision of Gough's *A Treatise of Arithmetic* published here in 1788. Workman's book contained 220 pages, while Gough's had 370.

Others. During the 1790's numerous other new arithmetics were published, but none gained much circulation. Most of these need mere mention; namely, books by: Consider and John Sterry (1790); John Vinall (1792); Erastus Root (1793); Thomas Sargeant (1793); Phinehas Merrill (1793); Todd, Jess, Waring, and Paul (1794); Donald Fraser (1796); Samuel Temple (1796); James Noyes (1797); David Kendall (*The Young Lady's Arithmetic*, 1797); William Milns (1797); F. Nichols (1747); Walkingame (1797); Chauncey Lee (*American Accomptant*, the first book to present monetary symbols and use

28 ·   T A B L E S.

BEER.

Cubic Inches.

$35\frac{1}{4} =$ 1 Pint.

$70\frac{1}{2} =$ 2 = 1 Quart.

282 = 8 = 4 = 1 Gallon.

2538 = 72 = 36 = 9 = 1 Firkin.

5076 = 144 = 72 = 18 = 2 = 1 Kilderkin.

10152 = 288 = 144 = 36 = 4 = 2 = 1 Barrel.

15228 = 432 = 216 = 54 = 6 = 3 = 1½ = 1 Hogshead.

20304 = 576 = 288 = 72 = 8 = 4 = 2 = 1 Puncheon.

30456 = 864 = 432 = 108 = 12 = 6 = 3 = 2 = 1 Butt.

ALE.

Cubic Inches.

$35\frac{1}{4} =$ 1 Pint.

$70\frac{1}{2} =$ 2 = 1 Quart.

282 = 8 = 4 = 1 Gallon.

2256 = 64 = 32 = 8 = 1 Firkin.

4512 = 128 = 64 = 16 = 2 = 1 Kilderkin.

9024 = 256 = 128 = 32 = 4 = 2 = 1 Barrel.

13536 = 384 = 192 = 48 = 6 = 3 = 1½ = 1 Hogshead.

13. D R Y M E A S U R E.*

2 Pints		Quart,	marked pts. qts.
2 Quarts		Pottle,	pot.
2 Pottles		Gallon,	gal.
2 Gallons		Peck,	pk.
4 Pecks		Bushel,	bu.
2 Bushels	make one	Strike,	ftr.
2 Strikes		Coom,	co.
2 Cooms		Quarter,	qr.
4 Quarters		Chaldron,	ch.
4½ Quarters		Chaldron in London.	
5 Quarters		Wey,	wey.
2 Weys		Laft,	laft.

Cubic Inches.

$268\frac{4}{7} =$ 1 Gallon.

$537\frac{3}{7} =$ 2 = 1 Peck.

$2150\frac{2}{7} =$ 8 = 4 = 1 Bushel.

$4300\frac{4}{7} =$ 16 = 8 = 2 = 1 Strike.

$8601\frac{1}{7} =$ 32 = 16 = 4 = 2 = 1 Coom.

$17203\frac{1}{7} =$ 64 = 32 = 8 = 4 = 2 = 1 Quarter.

86016 = 320 = 160 = 40 = 20 = 10 = 5 = 1 Wey.

172032 = 640 = 320 = 80 = 40 = 20 = 10 = 2 = 1 Laft.

COMPOUND

* This measure is applied to all dry goods, as Corn, Seed, Fruit, Roots, Salt, Sand. Oysters and Coals.

A Winchester bushel is 18½ inches diameter, and 8 inches deep.

Pike's Tables to be learned—probably not by elementary students.

DECIMAL TABLES OF COIN, WEIGHT and MEASURE.

TABLE I. COIN.
£1. the Integer.

Shil.	dec.	Shil.	dec.
19	,95	9	,45
18	,9	8	,4
17	,85	7	,35
16	,8	6	,3
15	,75	5	,25
14	,7	4	,2
13	,65	3	,15
12	,6	2	,1
11	,55	1	,05
10	,5		

Pence	Decimals
11	,045833
10	,041666
9	,0375
8	,033333
7	,029166
6	,025
5	,020833
4	,016666
3	,0125
2	,008333
1	,004166

Farthings	Decimals
3	,003125
2	,002083
1	,001041

TABLE II.
COIN & Long Meas. 1 Shill. & 1 Foot the Integer.

Pence & Inches.	Decimals.
11	,916666
10	,833333
9	,75
8	,666666
7	,583333
6	,5
5	,416666
4	,333333
3	,25
2	,166666
1	,083333

Farthings	Decimals
3	,0625
2	,041666
1	,020833

TABLE III.
TROY WEIGHT. 1lb. the Integer. Ounces the same as TABLE II.

Penny-weights.	Decimals.
10	,041666

Penny wt.	Decim.
9	,0375
8	,033333
7	,029166
6	,025
5	,020833
4	,016666
3	,0125
2	,008333
1	,004166

Grains.	Decimals.
12	,002083
11	,00191
10	,001736
9	,001502
8	,001389
7	,001215
6	,001042
5	,000868
4	,000694
3	,000521
2	,000347
1	,000173

1 Oz. the Integer. Pennyweights the same as Shillings in the first Table.

Grains.	Decimals.
12	,025
11	,022916
10	,020833
9	,01875
8	,016666
7	,014583
6	,0125
5	,010416
4	,008333
3	,00625
2	,004166
1	,002083

TABLE IV.
AVOIRDUPOIS WT. 112lb. the Integer.

Qrs.	Decimals.
3	,75
2	,5
1	,25

Pounds.	Decimals.
27	,241071
26	,232143
25	,223214
24	,214286
23	,205357
22	,196428
21	,1875
20	,178571
19	,169643
18	,160714
17	,151786
16	,142857
15	,133928

Pounds.	Decimals.
14	,125
13	,116071
12	,107143
11	,098214
10	,089286
9	,080357
8	,071428
7	,0625
6	,053571
5	,044643
4	,035714
3	,026786
2	,017857
1	,008928

Ounces.	Decimals.
15	,008370
14	,007812
13	,007254
12	,006696
11	,006138
10	,00558
9	,005022
8	,004464
7	,003906
6	,003348
5	,00279
4	,002232
3	,001674
2	,001116
1	,000558

qrs. of ozs.	Decim.
3	,000418
2	,000279
1	,000139

TABLE V.
AVOIRD. WEIGHT. 1lb. the Integer.

Ounces.	Decimals.
15	,9375
14	,875
13	,8125
12	,75
11	,6875
10	,625
9	,5625
8	,5
7	,4375
6	,375
5	,3125
4	,25
3	,1875
2	,125
1	,0625

Drams.	Decimals.
15	,059493
14	,055537
13	,051681
12	,047775
11	,043868
10	,039962
9	,036056
8	,03215
7	,027343
6	,023437
5	,019531
4	,015625
3	,011718
2	,007812
1	,003906

TABLE VI.
CLOTH MEASURE. 1 Yard the Integer.

Quarters.	Decimals.
3	,75
2	,5
1	,25

Nails.	Decimals.
3	,1875
2	,125
1	,0625

TABLE VII.
LONG MEASURE. 1 Mile the Integer.

Yards.	Decimals.
1000	,568182
900	,511364
800	,454545
700	,397727
600	,34
500	,284091
400	,227272
300	,170454
200	,113636
100	,056818
90	,051136
80	,045454
70	,039773
60	,034091
50	,028409
40	,022727
30	,017045
20	,011364
10	,005682
9	,005114
8	,004545
7	,003977
6	,003409
5	,002841
4	,002273
3	,001704
2	,001136
1	,000568

Feet.	Decimals.
2	,000379
1	,000189

Inches.	Decimals.
6	,000094
5	,000079
4	,000063
3	,000047
2	,000032
1	,000018

Pike's complexity of tables.

the $ sign, 1797); Peter Tharp (1798); Samuel Temple (2nd Edition, 1798); David Cook (1799 or 1800); Ezekiel Little (1798); and Zachariah Jess (1799).

ARITHMETICS, 1800-1820

Between 1800 and 1820 at least fifty different arithmetic text-books were published. Lack of space does not permit treatment, or even mention, of all of them. So only those that gained consider-able circulation will be discussed.

Nathan Daboll (1750-1818). In 1800 Daboll published his *Schoolmaster's Assistant*, an "Arithmetic adapted to the United

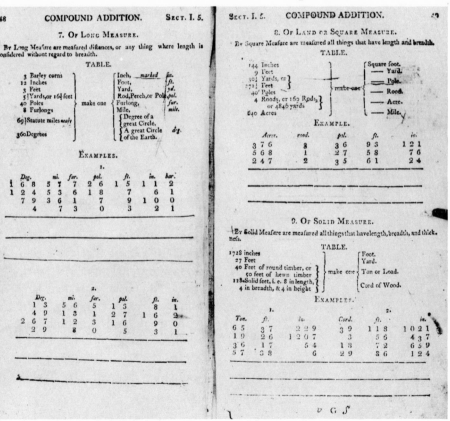

Adam's *Scholar's Arithmetic*, 1801—note tables and workbook.

States." It contained many recommendations, including one by Noah Webster. It was very plainly and attractively arranged and printed. Its monetary problems involved both the English and the American system, and it was the first book to make frequent use of the $ symbol. With minor revisions it continued to be published as late as the 1830's.

Daniel Adams (1773-1864). The author whose arithmetics gained the widest circulation of any before those by Joseph Ray was Adams. In 1801 he published *The Scholar's Arithmetic: or, Federal Accountant*. The contents were more clearly and simply presented than was done either in Dilworth's or Pike's books. The material was presented in sections, which were entitled as follows:

I Fundamentals of Arithmetic
II Rules Essentially necessary for Every Person to Fit and Qualify Them for the Transactions of Business
III Rules Occasionally Useful to Men in Particular Imploments of Life
IV Miscellaneous Questions
V Forms of Notes, etc.

One unusual feature was that space was left blank between the problems for their solution. In a sense this was a combination textbook and workbook. Too, he omitted such impractical matters as biquadrate root and sursolid root found in some other books.

In 1827 he published a radically revised *Arithmetic*,

Lee's *Accomptant*, for the bookkeeper.

"in which the principles of operating by numbers are analytically explained, and synthetically applied; thus combining the advantages to be derived both from the inductive and synthetic mode of instructing." This book contained more pages and many more problems than his earlier book. It contained no blank spaces for the solution of the problems. It was revised in 1848. Also in 1848 he published a *Primary Arithmetic or Mental Operations in Numbers*. All of these books appeared in numerous editions even as late as the 1860's.

The writer's collection contains twenty-seven copies of different titles or dates.

Joseph Crukshank. He was one of many successful printers of

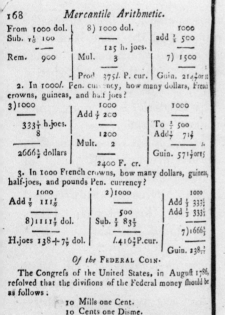

Workman's *American Accountant*, 1793—note table of U.S. coinage.

Philadelphia during the later colonial and early national period. It apparently was a common practice for printers to print books that were not bound by copyrights and sell them. This may be what Crukshank did with *The American Tutor's Assistant*, first published by Todd, Jess, Waring, and Paul in 1797. In 1809 Crukshank republished this book with certain revisions. In 1813 some further revisions were made. Later it continued through many reprintings. The full title became *The American Tutor's Assistant. Revised; or, A Compendious System of Practical Arithmetic*. All of the editions contained a statement on the title page that it was "Originally compiled by sundry Teachers in and near Philadelphia." In some respects it was similar to Adams' book, but nearly all the money problems were still based on the English system. It, like many other arithmetics of that period, contained a section on Bookkeeping.

Incidentally Zachariah Jess, whose name had been connected with the original 1797 edition, republished the same book with the same title in 1818, except that he used the American money system. It may be added that in 1809 Crukshank published a key for the *Assistant* prepared by Frederick M'Kenney. Since most teachers were poorly prepared in those days, keys were prepared for many of the popular arithmetics. In 1825 M'Kenney also prepared a key for Stephen Pike's *Teachers' Assistant*.

Joseph Stockton. In 1819 Stockton's *Western Calculator* was published in Pittsburgh. He claimed that it was "arranged, defined, and illustrated, in a plain and natural

American Tutor's Assistant, 1809 —note topics no longer in arithmetics.

order; adapted to the Use of Schools, throughout the Western Country and Present Commerce of the United States." Having a book published west of the mountains saved the trouble and expense of shipping eastern published books across the mountains, which was a cumbersome task then. He aimed to have this book fit the "age, capacity, and progress of the scholar." He further claimed for it "plainness and simplicity of style," "lucid arrangement," "clearness of definitions," and brevity. Apparently it filled a need in the "western country," for it appeared in numerous editions for more than two decades. At the time of the writing of this book he was president of Pittsburgh Academy, eventually to become the University of Pittsburgh. In 1824 John Armstrong published a Key to the *Western Calculator.*

ARITHMETICS, 1820-1850

None of the early arithmetics appeared in graded series. However, shortly after 1820 the authors of the more popular arithmetics began to publish books of varying difficulty. By that time textbook authors began to think in terms of children as well as of subject matter. So books changed radically from those by Dilworth and Pike. Again only those arithmetics that gained considerable usage will be discussed.

Warren Colburn (1793-1833). Colburn was the product of the common schools of Massachusetts and was graduated from Harvard in 1820. For some years he was a principal of a private school in Boston. In addition to being the author of popular arithmetics, he also wrote an algebra and readers.

In 1821 Colburn published his *First Lessons in Arithmetic on the Plan of Pestalozzi.* In 1826 he secured a new copyright on the same book, but with the title changed to *Intellectual Arithmetic Upon the Inductive Method of Instruction.* Without a change in the book new copyrights were secured in 1849 and in 1858. Again a new copyright was secured in 1863 with a few pages changed. These three copyrights were secured by his widow. In 1884 the book was considerably enlarged and changed with the copyright held by a daughter. A reprint of this ap-

T H E

American Accomptant;

B E I N G

A PLAIN, PRACTICAL AND SYSTEMATIC

C O M P E N D I U M

O F

FEDERAL ARITHMETIC;

I N T H R E E P A R T S:

DESIGNED FOR THE USE OF SCHOOLS,

AND SPECIALLY CALCULATED FOR THE

C O M M E R C I A L M E R I D I A N

O F

THE UNITED STATES OF AMERICA:

BY *CHAUNCEY LEE,* A. M.

L A N S I N G B U R G H:

PRINTED BY WILLIAM W. WANDS.
M,DCC,XCVII.

[*Published according to Act of Congress.*]

Title Page of first American book to use monetary symbols; 39 pages of bookkeeping, 1797.

Monetary symbols in Lee's *American Accomptant*, also 1797.

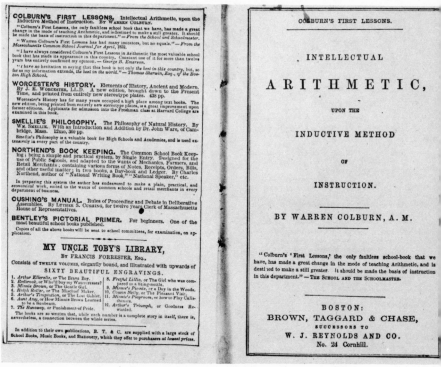

Colburn, 1826—note recommendations from schools.

peared as late as 1891. From these facts it can be seen that this arithmetic, with only a few changes in 1863, remained in print for 70 years. Next consideration should be given for the reasons of its longevity.

The Preface of the *First Lessons* used nine pages of fine print to present a "General View of the Plan." As mentioned on the title page, it was based on the Pestalozzian or inductive plan of teaching. Earlier American arithmetics were commonly planned on the deductive approach. This meant that the pupil was first to commit the rules and tables and then later apply them to problems. Colburn's book began with mental exercises from which an understanding of the principles of arithmetic was to develop. For example, the very first question or exercise was, "How many thumbs have you on your right hand? how many on your left? how many on both together?" Thus a mastery of the number combinations would be developed. Such exercises continued for 124 pages. Then on page 125 "Tables of Coins, Weights, and Measures" were presented, followed by exercises involving the facts of the tables. The last 32 pages constituted the Key with solutions of the more difficult problems. B. W. Tweed, Supervisor of Boston Schools, said of the plan:

> "Colburn's First Lessons" have undoubtedly done more to improve the methods of teaching, not only of numbers, but of language and other branches, than any other school-book published during the last half century.

Many other similar quotations could be given concerning the significance of Colburn's inductive plan.

In 1822 Colburn published his *Arithmetic; being a Sequel to First Lessons in Arithmetic*. This was a larger and more advanced book. He said: "It will be extremely useful, though not absolutely necessary, for pupils of every age, to study the 'First Lessons,' previous to commencing this treatise." The *Sequel* contained two parts. The first contained examples for the illustration and application of principles; the second contained the development of them. The examples of the first part consisted of questions. In 1826 the *Sequel* was considerably reduced in size. Apparently the *Sequel* never attained the popularity of the *First Lessons*, possibly because the schools or pupils were not yet ready to purchase two books in the same subject field.

Roswell Smith. In 1826 Smith wrote the *Practical and Mental Arithmetic*, "designed principally to accompany Daboll's System of Arithmetic." This was a small book of 107 pages, and written largely in the form of questions with the answers. Many monetary problems still involved the English system. In 1829 he wrote the *Practical and Mental Arithmetic On a New Plan*. This was largely a new book containing 268 pages. In it the United States money system was used. Like Colburn's books it more fully followed the Pestalozzian plan. It began with mental exercises, which were followed by "mental exercises combined with exercises for the slate." The tables of coinage and measures were taught in a catechetical question-and-answer method. The more unusual phases of arithmetic, such as alligation, involution, evolution, permutation, etc., appeared in the appendix. In the back there were ten pages of bookkeeping. This book was recopyrighted in 1835 and in 1859, with only minor changes.

In 1841 Smith produced an *Arithmetic on the Productive System*. This was a much larger book than the other two. He continued the practice of teaching by means of questions and answers. It contained several new features not found in previously discussed arithmetics. Numerous problems were illustrated with figure forms, and many pages contained elucidating footnotes and comments. This book, like the others, appeared in many reprintings.

It may be added that Smith was also the author of very popular grammars, and rather widely used geographies. They were also written on the inductive plan.

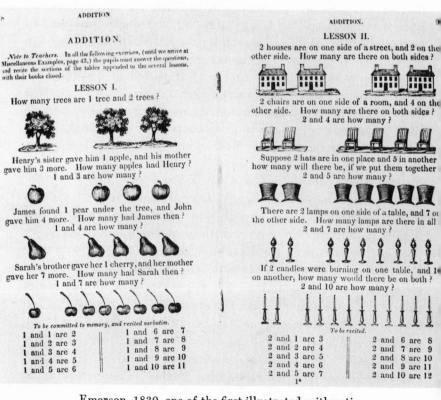

Emerson, 1830, one of the first illustrated arithmetics.

Frederick Emerson. Although a number of authors wrote more than one arithmetic before Emerson, none of them prepared as carefully a graded series as Emerson's *North American Arithmetic, Part First; Part Second;* and *Part Third.* In the Preface he bemoaned the fact that the teaching of arithmetic too often was postponed to nine or ten years. So *Part First,* first published in 1829, was prepared for children from five to eight years. "The plan of the lessons accords with the method of instruction practised in the school at Stanz, by the celebrated Pestalozzi." Ample cuts and unit marks illustrate the questions. Emerson was the first author to make frequent use of pictures and marks or counters. Forty-two of his 48 pages used such illustrations. The book was immediately adopted for use in the Boston school. In 1838 a slightly revised edition appeared.

In 1832 *Part Second* appeared in two editions—one in Boston of 190 pages, and one in Windsor of 215 pages. The first 180 pages were alike in the two editions. *Part Second* was intended for use by those who had been taught *Part First,* or who had already learned to add, subtract, and multiply numbers as high as ten, mentally. This book was much more difficult than *Part First,* and did not make use of illustrative pictures.

Part Third was published in 1834. It was a rather advanced book. Emerson stated that it was prepared for two classes; "those who are to prosecute a full course of mathematical studies, and those who are to embark in commerce." In addition to teaching the tables and measures that had been commonly found in most earlier arithmetics, it included not only many foreign coinage tables but also thirty tables of weights and measures of foreign countries and cities. Apparently these were included for those preparing for commerce. All three of these arithmetics appeared in many printings. In 1838 a Key for *Part Second* and *Part Third* was published. The 1854 edition of *Part First* contained a statement that these books were used in the cities of Boston, Salem, Portland, Providence, New York, Philadelphia, and Louisville. In several places it displaced Colburn's books.

Charles Davies (1798-1861). Davies was graduated from the United States Military Academy in 1815, after which he taught mathematics there for more than twenty years. Later he taught at several colleges, ending his teaching career at Columbia University. Undoubtedly he became one of the most prolific mathematics textbook writers in the United States. In addition to writing at least seven different arithmetic books, he wrote three popular algebras, three geometries, a calculus book, a combined geometry and trigonometry book, a general mathematics book, and one dealing with surveying and navigation.

He wrote the *Common School Arithmetic* in 1833. Its primary purpose was to prepare "young gentlemen . . . to enter the Military Academy at West Point." It was written in a very systematic manner. He began each section or topic with an example followed by a definition to be committed printed in italics. Then followed the rule or rules, review questions, and finally problems (applications) to be solved. This book was rather

10   FIRST LESSONS   IN ARITHMETIC.

LESSON VI.
In which One is added to each Number as far as Ten.

One and	one	are how many?
One and	two	are how many?
One and	three	are how many?
One and	four	are how many?
One and	five	are how many?
One and	six	are how many?
One and	seven	are how many?
One and	eight	are how many?
One and	nine	are how many?
One and	ten	are how many?

Commit the following Table to memory:—

1 and 1 are 2	1 and 6 are 7
1 and 2 are 3	1 and 7 are 8
1 and 3 are 4	1 and 8 are 9
1 and 4 are 5	1 and 9 are 10
1 and 5 are 6	1 and 10 are 11

LESSON VII.
In which Two is added to each Number as far as Ten.

Two and	one	are how many
Two and	two	are how man
Two and	three	are how man
Two and	four	are how man
Two and	five	are how man
Two and	six	are how man
Two and	seven	are how man
Two and	eight	are how mar.
Two and	nine	are how man
Two and	ten	are how man

Commit the following Table to memory:—

2 and 1 are 3	2 and 6 are 8
2 and 2 are 4	2 and 7 are 9
2 and 3 are 5	2 and 8 are 10
2 and 4 are 6	2 and 9 are 11
2 and 5 are 7	2 and 10 are 12

Davies, 1840, an early graded primary arithmetic.

thoroughly revised and enlarged in 1838. Its new title was
Arithmetic, "designed for Schools and Academies." The plan
was very similar to the earlier one, but the review questions appeared merely as footnotes and more problems of application
were introduced. A considerable number of mental exercises were
added. The book was again revised and enlarged in 1850, but in
1855 was reduced in size. The title was changed to *School Arithmetic: Analytical and Practical*. All of these appeared repeatedly.

After two editions of his earlier arithmetics, Davies awakened
to the fact that an easier book ought to precede them. So in 1840
he published his *First Lessons in Arithmetic*. This book, like his
others, was logically written, but was not nearly so attractive as
Emerson's *Part First*. It used some symbols, but no pictures. In
1855 it was made much smaller and the title changed to *Primary
Arithmetic and Table Book*. Neither of these seemed to have had
the popularity of his *Arithmetic*.

In 1850 Davies published an advanced book entitled *The
University Arithmetic*. Thus he had arithmetics for three levels,
but graded very differently from Emerson's series. The purpose
of the advanced book was to treat arithmetic as a science. Another purpose was "to adapt it to the business wants of the
country." About 90 pages were devoted to matters of business
and commerce. In 1864 it was revised and enlarged. It had many
printings.

In summation, it may be said that Davies was a mathematician, but not so fully a pedagogue. While he presented the material logically and much better than Dilworth and Pike, yet
not so simply and psychologically as Colburn, Smith, and
Emerson.

Joseph Ray (1807-1857). Ray was born on a farm not far from
Wheeling, when it was still a part of Virginia. This farm was
only a little more than ten miles from the one on which McGuffey
was born across the line in Pennsylvania. Since farming did not
appeal to him, he left home at 16 and went to Cincinnati, where
he began teaching school. Later he studied medicine, receiving
the M.D. degree when only 22. After several years of practice
he joined the faculty of Woodward High School as teacher of

mathematics. The remainder of his life was devoted to teaching and textbook writing. He, like Davies, became a prolific author of mathematics books. The Nietz Collection contains 38 copies of Ray's *Arithmetics* of different title, date, or publisher, and 17 algebras. However, some of these were published after Ray's death. It has been said that Ray "did for figures what McGuffey did for literature." The Ray's *Arithmetics* were published by the same company that produced the McGuffey *Readers*.

His first book was the *Eclectic Arithmetic* in 1834. Thus the term *Eclectic* was used here before McGuffey's first books were written in 1836. About 1837 a graded series appeared entitled Ray's *Arithmetic, Part First; Part Second;* and *Part Third. Part First* was intended for very young pupils, and contained simple lessons, illustrated with numerous counters. *Part Second* aimed to provide a "thorough course of mental arithmetic by induction and analysis." *Part Third* really was the *Eclectic Arithmetic* carefully revised. It was planned "on the inductive and analytic methods of instruction, designed for Common Schools, Academies, and High Schools." These three books were advertised to be "The Best and Cheapest Arithmetics ever Published." *Part First* sold for ten cents, *Part Second* for twenty cents, and *Part Third* for 35 cents. *Part Third* contained 264 pages of very fine print, and so was able to include "*twice* the usual quantity of matter contained in works of this class."

Apparently either Ray or his publishers became dissatisfied with the titles of the three *Parts*, so in 1853 *Part First* became *The Child's Arithmetic, Part Second* became the *Mental Arithmetic,* and *Part Third* became the *Practical Arithmetic.* These were enlarged revisions of the earlier books. Still not satisfied, in 1857 the titles of the first two were again changed. The first book became *Primary Lessons and Tables,* and the second became the *Intellectual Arithmetic.* The title of the third remained the *Practical Arithmetic.* It may be that the publishers rather than Ray made these changes and revisions, since some sources say that Ray died in 1855 rather than 1857.

The *Primary Lessons* was a book of 80 pages dealing only with the four fundamentals. Extreme care was claimed in making the lessons "gradually and almost imperceptibly progressive."

With some revisions it was republished in 1877 as the *New Primary Arithmetic*. In the meantime there apparently arose from those using these books objections to a series of three, so in 1879 the publishers produced a two-book series. The lower book was entitled *New Elementary Arithmetic*, which aimed to be sufficiently comprehensive as an introduction for the *New Practical Arithmetic*. The two formed the series. In 1903 both were revised and published under the title *Modern Elementary Arithmetic*.

Even before 1879 the publishers produced *The Rudiments of Arithmetic* (1866). Its purpose seemed to be to take the place of the two lower books. However, this edition did not become very popular.

The *Intellectual Arithmetic* (1857) was an enlarged revision of the *Mental Arithmetic* and contained 162 pages. It aimed to present the "Exercises on the primary principles and their applications, interspersed with appropriate models of analysis and frequent reviews." Less emphasis was placed on the mental work. The revised 1860 edition contained a statement on the title page that it was the One Thousandth Edition. In 1879 it was again revised into a somewhat simpler and briefer book.

In 1853 *Part Third* appeared under a supplementary title of *Practical Arithmetic*. In 1857 it was revised and printed in a more attractive form. This was its One Thousandth Edition. In 1877 it was again rather thoroughly revised and printed in even more attractive form. Too, the presentation of many top-

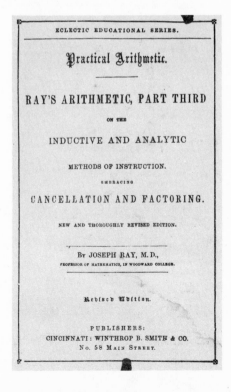

ECLECTIC EDUCATIONAL SERIES.

Practical Arithmetic.

RAY'S ARITHMETIC, PART THIRD

ON THE

INDUCTIVE AND ANALYTIC

METHODS OF INSTRUCTION.

EMBRACING

CANCELLATION AND FACTORING.

NEW AND THOROUGHLY REVISED EDITION.

By JOSEPH RAY, M.D.,

PROFESSOR OF MATHEMATICS, IN WOODWARD COLLEGE.

Revised Edition.

PUBLISHERS:
CINCINNATI: WINTHROP B. SMITH & CO.
No. 58 MAIN STREET.

Ray's *Practical Arithmetic,* probably the most popular arithmetic ever written in the U.S.

ics was rearranged, and several topics totally eliminated. Among those dropped were aliquots, alligation medial, duodecimals, permutation, and gauging. In 1903 still another revision was made and the title became Ray's *Modern Practical Arithmetic*. The revision provided for an enrichment of some topics, as practical measurements, bills and accounts, etc., and an abridgment of others of waning importance. Likely, more copies of the *Practical Arithmetic* were sold than of any American arithmetic before 1900.

In 1856 the publishers produced an advanced arithmetic with a double title; namely, Ray's *Higher Arithmetic*, and *Principles of Arithmetic*. This book was planned and begun by Ray, but due to illness he was unable to finish it. So the editor of the publishers, Charles E. Mathews, finished it in consultation with Ray. This became a well-known and widely used book for many

---

300   RAY'S PRACTICAL ARITHMETIC.

Rule for Permutation.—*Multiply together the numbers, 1, 2, 3, &c., from 1 to the given number; the last product will be the required result.*

1. In how many different ways may the digits 1, 2, 3, 4, and 5 be placed?   *Ans.* 120.

2. What number of changes may be rung on 12 bells?   *Ans.* 479001600.

3. What time will 8 persons require to seat themselves differently every day at dinner, allowing 365 days to the year?   *Ans.* 110 yr. 170 da.

4. Of how many variations do the 26 letters of the alphabet admit?   *Ans.* 403291461126605635584000000.

XXVIII. MENSURATION.

TO TEACHERS.—As this short article on Mensuration is intended for pupils who may not have an opportunity of studying a more extensive course, only the more useful parts are presented.

The definitions and illustrations are given in plain and familiar terms, not with a view to mathematical precision.

ART. 310. DEFINITIONS.

1. An ANGLE is the inclination of two straight lines meeting in a point, which is called the VERTEX. It is the *degree* of the opening of the lines.

2. When one straight line stands on another so that it makes with it two equal angles, each of these angles is a RIGHT ANGLE; and the straight line which stands on the other is said to be PERPENDICULAR to it, or at RIGHT ANGLES to it.

Right / Right angle / angle

3. An OBTUSE ANGLE is *greater* than a right angle; and an ACUTE ANGLE is *less* than a right angle.

Obtuse / Acute angle / angle

NOTE.—An angle is named by 3 letters, the middle one being placed at the vertex, and the other two on the lines which form the angle.

REVIEW.—308. What is Case 2? What the Rule? NOTE. What is the last term of a decreasing series of which the number of terms is infinite? 309. What is Permutation? What the Rule?

MENSURATION.

the angle. In the diagram the obtuse angle is called the angle A C B, and the acute angle, the angle A C D.

4. PARALLEL STRAIGHT LINES are everywhere equally distant from each other.

5. A SURFACE has length and breadth, without thickness.

6. A PLANE is a surface, in which, if any two points be taken, the straight line joining them will be wholly in the plane.

7. A FIGURE is a portion of surface inclosed by one or more boundaries.

8. If a figure has equal *sides*, it is E-QUI-LAT'-ER-AL; if it has equal *angles*, E-QUI-AN'-GU-LAR.

9. A TRIANGLE is a figure bounded by 3 straight lines. The side on which the triangle stands, is the BASE. The *perpendicular hight* is the shortest distance from the base to the opposite angle. Thus, A B C is a triangle; A C is the base, and B D the perpendicular hight.

10. A QUAD-RI-LAT'-ER-AL is bounded by 4 straight lines.

11. A POLYGON is bounded by more than 4 straight lines.

12. A PAR-AL-LEL'-O-GRAM is a quadrilateral whose opposite sides are parallel. Thus, M X O P is a *parallelogram*.

13. A RECT-AN-GLE is a quadrilateral whose opposite sides are parallel; its angles right angles. Thus, R E C T is a *rectangle*.

14. A SQUARE is a quadrilateral whose sides are equal to each other; its angles right angles. Thus, S Q U A is a *square*.

15. A RHOM'-BUS is a quadrilateral whose sides are equal to each other; its angles, *not* right angles. See Fig. Def.

16. A TRAP'-E-ZOID is a quadrilateral having only two sides parallel. Thus, Z O I D is a trapezoid; the sides Z D and O I being parallel.

17. A TRA-PE'-ZIUM is a quadrilateral having no two sides parallel to each other. Thus, T R A P is a *trapezium*.

Late edition of Ray's—note object pictures.

decades, popularly known as Ray's *Higher*. It was revised and made more attractive in 1880. Its list of 106 "Miscellaneous Exercises" at the end of the book constituted the challenge to anyone considered competent in arithmetic. In fact, some of the problems could not be solved without some understanding of certain principles of algebra and geometry.

The publishers of the Ray's *Arithmetics* deserve great credit for the frequent and well-planned revisions of these arithmetics, for many of these revisions were made long after Ray's decease. They did for these arithmetics exactly what they had done for the McGuffey *Readers* in revising them to meet the criticisms and the needs of the changing times. As a result the books enjoyed a wide usage for nearly a century. It has been claimed that about 120,000,000 copies have been sold.

Benjamin Greenleaf (1786-1864). He was a graduate from Dartmouth College, and later served as principal of several New England academies. While principal of Bradford Academy, he also conducted a teachers' seminary. In addition to being the author of numerous arithmetics, he also wrote several algebras. His first arithmetics were the *Introduction to the National Arithmetic*, and the *National Arithmetic* (1835).

Although the *Introduction* was the lower of the two books, it was a book of considerable size. This book was somewhat revised and recopyrighted in 1842, 1848, and 1856, and renewed in 1870. Interestingly, the covers of the later editions used the title *Common School Arithmetic*, but the title page continued to use *Introduction to the National Arithmetic*. Some of the claims for the book were the use of simple, precise, and accurate definitions; its practical character; reasons for the operations explained; and the abridging of the operations applicable to business transactions. Problems of alligation, permutation, involution, and evolution were still in the 1881 edition.

The *National Arithmetic* followed the "inductive system; combining the analytic and synthetic methods, in which the principles of arithmetic are explained in a perspicuous and familiar manner; containing also practical systems of mensuration, gauging, and bookkeeping; forming a complete mercantile arithmetic."

This description appeared on the title page. Each phase of arithmetic was introduced by several easy exercises and demonstrated by example, followed by the proper rule printed in italics. Progressive exercises followed. It was recopyrighted in 1836, 1847, 1857, and 1863. The last two editions were much larger than the earlier ones.

Apparently Greenleaf soon realized that the *Introduction* was too difficult as a beginning book, for in 1845 he published the *Primary Arithmetic.* This was the title on the outside cover. On the title page it was the *Mental Arithmetic, upon the Inductive Plan,* designed for primary and intermediate schools. It was revised in 1851. In 1857 it appeared as the *New Primary Arithmetic.* This same title appeared both on the outside cover and the title page. These primary books completed a series of three.

In 1851 Greenleaf added a fourth to the series, the *New Intellectual Arithmetic* to be used between the *Primary* and the *Common School Arithmetic.* It was revised and recopyrighted in 1857 and 1863.

After Greenleaf's death the publishers produced a new series of four; namely, the *New Primary, New Elementary, New Intellectual,* and *New Practical.* They suggested that the first two were excellent for ungraded schools. Other combinations were suggested for other types of schools. However, they were known as Greenleaf's *Arithmetics.*

James B. Thomson. In 1845 Thomson produced the *Practical Arithmetic.* He must have been very pedagogically conscious, for he used four pages to describe the characteristics of the book, and then presented a long list of suggestions on the teaching of arithmetic. The procedure followed in the book was first to present by analysis and solution a number of practical examples involving a rule. The operation was then defined and each principle analyzed. The general rule was then to be deduced, thus combining the inductive and synthetic modes of instruction. In the back of the book there were recommendations by 26 persons. The book was revised in 1853 and reprinted often thereafter until the 1870's.

In 1846 he published the *Mental Arithmetic, or First Lessons in Numbers.* The 1852 printing of this book was the 73rd edition. The definitive parts of the book were catechetical in form. In 1872 it was revised as the *New Mental Arithmetic.* In 1853 the *Rudiments of Arithmetic* was published as a supplementary book to the *Mental.* In 1872 it became the *New Rudiments.*

In 1847 the *Higher Arithmetic* appeared. This completed the series of three. The approach was the same as in the *Practical,* but it contained more difficult problems and more exercises relating to business matters. It went through numerous reprintings.

Much later a new two-book series was published. In 1878 *A Complete Intellectual Arithmetic,* and in 1882 the *Complete Graded Arithmetic* were published. Apparently this was done, as was common practice by publishers, to cash in on the established reputation of a well-known author of arithmetics.

John F. Stoddard (1825-1873). After graduating from the Albany State Normal School, he taught district schools in New York. Soon he gravitated to Pennsylvania, where he conducted private teacher training work. Later he was principal of a school in New York City.

He wrote the *Juvenile Mental Arithmetic* in 1849. This was an attractive little book of 71 pages. It taught the fundamentals by means of combination exercises, inductively, without the use of the tables in addition, subtraction, multiplication, and division. However, surprisingly for such a small book, it contained the tables of coinage, troy weight, apothecaries weight, avoirdupois weight, cloth measure, long measure, land measure, cubic measure, wine measure, table of time, table of paper, table of books, and the aliquot parts of the year.

Also in 1849 he wrote the *American Intellectual Arithmetic* to follow the *Juvenile.* It was more than twice the size of the *Juvenile.* Slight revisions were made in it in 1860 and 1866. In 1889 it became the *New Intellectual Arithmetic.* All of these editions contained a list of puzzle problems in the back. The publishers claimed in 1852 that the *Intellectual* was used in "many of the Public and Private Schools and Academies of New York, Pennsylvania, Ohio, Michigan, and Missouri, and is used extensively in the Schools of New England."

In 1852 the *Practical Arithmetic* was published. The preface said that "useless theories, or a long list of *arithmetical* curiosities" would be avoided. Rather the fundamental principles of the "Science of Numbers" would be presented, as employed in everyday business. It was a much larger and more difficult book than the other two. In 1865 it was enlarged and became the *New Practical Arithmetic*. It was again enlarged in 1868. At the end of the book many questions for examination and review were included. The 1868 edition still had a section on bookkeeping.

Also in 1852 Stoddard prepared the *Complete Arithmetic*. In the 1868 edition the first 303 pages were identical with those in the *New Practical*. The next 113 pages involved more difficult applications of the same types of problems of the earlier part, plus many new matters, such as circulating decimals, continued

---

60 .   MENTAL ARITHMETIC.

LESSON XIV.

MISCELLANEOUS TABLES.
AVOIRDUPOIS WEIGHT.

A gallon of train-oil weighs	7¼ lbs.
A stone of wire "	10½ "
A stone of iron, or horseman's weight, is	14 "
A peck of salt weighs	14 "
A bushel of salt "	56 "
A firkin of butter "	56 "
A quintal of fish "	100 "
A faggot of steel "	120 "
A barrel of flour "	196 "
A barrel of beef or pork "	200 "
A barrel of potash "	200 "
A fother of lead "	19 cwt. 2 qrs.

LONG MEASURE.

4	Inches make 1 Hand.	Used for meas. horses.
6	Feet " 1 Fathom.	⎰ Used by sailors for ⎱ meas. ropes, the depth ⎰ of water, &c.

7 92/100 Inches   " 1 Link of a surveyor's chain.
100   Links, or 66 feet, or 4 rods, make 1 Chain.
80   Chains, or 320 rods, or ⎱   " 1 Mile.
1760 yards, or 5280 feet ⎰

SOLID MEASURE.

231	Solid inches make 1 Wine gallon.
282	" " " 1 Beer "
2150 21/50	" " " 1 Bushel.

LIQUID MEASURE.

10 Gallons make 1 Anker.
18 "   " 1 Rundlet.
42 "   " 1 Tierce.
84 "   " 1 Puncheon.
9 "   " 1 Firkin of beer.
18 "   " 1 Kilderkin of beer.
36 "   " 1 Barrel of beer.
54 "   " 1 Hogshead of beer.
108 " or 2 hhd. 1 Butt.

MENTAL ARITHMETIC.   -   **61**

TABLE.

12 Single things make 1 Dozen,	marked	*doz.*
12 Dozen " 1 Gross,	"	*gro.*
12 Gross (144 doz.) " 1 Great Gross,	"	*g. gro.*
20 Single things " 1 Score,	"	*sco.*
5 Scores " 100.		

TABLE OF PAPER.

24 Sheets of paper make 1 Quire.
20 Quires   " 1 Ream.
2 Reams   " 1 Bundle.
10 Reams   " 1 Bale.

TABLE OF PARCHMENT.

12 Skins   make 1 Dozen.
5 Dozen, or 60 Skins   " 1 Roll.

TABLE OF BOOKS.

What a sheet of paper makes:
2 leaves, or 4 pages, the book is called a *folio*   size.

4	"	8	"	*quarto*	"
8	"	16	"	*octavo*	"
12	"	24 ·	"	*duodecimo*	"
18	"	36	"	*eighteenmo*	"

ARITHMETICAL SIGNS.

1. The symbol + is called *plus*, and is the sign of addition. Thus, 2 + 4 indicates the addition of 2 and 4.

2. The symbol — is called *minus*, and is the sign of subtraction. Thus, 5 — 2 indicates the subtraction of 2 from 5.

3. The symbol × is the sign of multiplication. Thus, 3 × 5 indicates that 3 is to be multiplied by 5, or 5 by 3.

4. The symbol ÷ is the sign of division. Thus, 8 ÷ 2 indicates the division of 8 by 2.

5. The symbol = is the sign of equality. Thus, 4 + 6 = 10.

Stoddard, *Mental Arithmetic;* many early arithmetics stressed mental work.

fractions, metric denominations, temperature, life insurance, and mariner's measure. The title *Complete* was apropos.

Ultimately, in 1853, he wrote the *American Philosophical Arithmetic*, designed for advanced classes. In it he attempted to "present clearly and concisely, all those important principles and properties of numbers, which are necessary to a full comprehension of the higher branches of Mathematics, and their application to practical business and scientific calculations." In the back 143 miscellaneous problems appeared. All of these books had numerous printings.

Others. Arithmetics by many authors were written between 1820 and 1850. The books of only eight of these authors have been discussed. Bare mention may be made of several others whose books did go through several printings. In 1825 Thomas Smiley wrote the *New Federal Calculator; or, Scholar's Assistant*, which appeared in a number of editions. In 1829 John Rose published *The Science of Arithmetic*, and later two other arithmetics. In 1844 George R. Perkins wrote a *Higher Arithmetic*, later *An Elementary Arithmetic*, and a *Practical Arithmetic*. In 1847 Horatio N. Robinson published *The American Arithmetic*, and later a series of *Progressive Arithmetics*. Later these were revised by Fish. None of these attained the wide usage of those by the eight authors discussed above.

ARITHMETICS, 1850-1900

Fewer authors will be discussed for these fifty years than for the previous thirty years. Although the writer's collection contains arithmetics written by sixty different authors during this period, only the books of about a half dozen gained much popularity, at least before 1900. Of course, it should be kept in mind in discussing the arithmetics of this period that the later editions, and even new editions by the authors of the 1820-1850 period continued to appear, some even to and after 1900, such as the books by Ray.

Edward Brooks (1831-?). Brooks was born in New York State, but soon moved to Pennsylvania. There he became associated with Millersville State Normal School, the first one in the state. From 1866 to 1883 he was its principal. From the time he first taught there, he began to write textbooks. Most of these were in the field of arithmetic, but he also wrote a geometry, an algebra, several methods books, and one on mental science (psychology). In the field of arithmetic his production was prolific. He began to publish the series of *Normal Arithmetics* in 1858. The writer's collection contains 30 copies of different dates under nine titles, one as late as 1908. It may be well to list these and then to discuss them in general. They were as follows:

Titles	Copyright and Revision Dates
Normal Primary Arithmetic	1858, 1878
Normal Mental Arithmetic	1858, 1863, 1873, 1908
Normal Elementary Arithmetic	1865, 1888
Normal Written Arithmetic	1863, 1877
Normal Higher Arithmetic	1877
Normal Union Arithmetic	1877
Normal Standard Arithmetic	1895
Key to Normal Mental Arithmetic	1860, 1873
Key to Normal Written Arithmetic	1863.

There may have been other editions not known to the writer. Nearly all of these went through numerous printings of different dates. The titles of the later editions were preceded by the word *New*. The first five books listed above apparently were meant to form a graded series. The other two were written later, each of which could be purchased as a book *Complete*, or in Part I, II, or III as a graded series.

Brooks was definitely pedagogically conscious when he wrote these books. For example, in the preface of the *Normal Primary* he carefully explained the features. Then followed eight pages in fine print of suggestions and directions for teaching it. Oral and written exercises were to be combined, and addition and subtraction were to be taught simultaneously—"the process of subtraction thus being derived as a result of addition." Only the four fundamental processes were included in this book.

The *Normal Mental* followed the *Primary*. It was a book of 188 pages of rather fine print consisting entirely of mental exercises. No tables were included. The process was by "analysis and induction." The purpose of the *Normal Elementary* was "to furnish young pupils with an introductory course of Written Arithmetic, realizing the necessity of such a course in connection with the *Mental Exercises.*" This book was more like other arithmetics, including tables of coinage, weight, and measures commonly taught in those days. However, it was not very large. The different editions varied from 185 to 215 pages.

The next book was the *Normal Written Arithmetic*, which was a much more advanced book. The 1863 edition had 328 pages, and the 1877 edition 421. This book followed the deductive approach. For example, the Reduction of U.S. Money was presented as follows: First, a statement defining reduction; next, the listing in italics of five rules or principles; and last, 18 examples for practice. A list of 135 miscellaneous problems appeared at the end of the book.

The last in the *Normal* series was the *Normal Higher* (1877). It was intended for use mainly in high schools, academies, and normal schools. As an advanced book its object was "to present a scientific treatise upon the science of numbers." It was further stated that formerly arithmetic was treated more as an art and a drill subject without developing conceptions of the "interesting relations of the science and the simplicity of its reasoning process." About 140 pages were devoted to varied and detailed problems involving percentage. One advanced section dealt with the "Properties of Numbers."

The *Normal Union* appearing in 1877 was nearly identical to the *Normal Written*, but could be bought as Part I, Part II, and Part III. Thus it really constituted an additional series, thus giving schools a choice of series. Then in 1895 the *Normal Standard* was copyrighted. About three-fourths of it was like the *Normal Union*. The last part of the book was rearranged. It could also be bought in Parts as a series.

It must be clear by now that Brooks attempted to have his books or series of books meet the needs of any kind of school or school system. A number of these contained statements on the inside covers concerning the adoptions of these arithmetics by various school districts. It is clear that their circulation continued for more than a half century.

Daniel W. Fish. The earliest arithmetics written, rather edited, by Fish constituted the Progressive Series. He apparently had some tie up with Horatio Robinson, who had become known as a leading mathematician and author of popular algebras, geometries, and an astronomy textbook. Most of Fish's books were acknowledged to belong to the Robinson's Mathematical Series.

The Progressive Series consisted of four books; the first three were first published in 1858. The first of these was the *Progressive Primary Arithmetic.* It was a very attractive little book containing a number of illustrative pictures. The first two pages were catechetical in form, followed by two pages of numbers in written form, printed figures, written numbers, and Roman letters. The remainder of the book consisted mostly of inductive exercises interspersed with complete analyses of model examples. Seven pages presented tables of coinage, weights, and measures. It was recopyrighted in 1863.

The second book was the *Progressive Intellectual Arithmetic.* It also was written on the inductive approach. It introduced the tables of coinage, weights, and measures on page 48. These were followed by 70 pages of problems involving them. Except for some miscellaneous problems at the end, the remainder of the book dealt rather extensively with percentage. It also was recopyrighted in 1863.

The third book was the *Progressive Practical Arithmetic.* It claimed to contain the "theory of numbers, in connection with concise analytic and synthetic methods of solution, and designed as a complete textbook." Like many other so-called complete arithmetics, it began with the fundamentals and ended with the difficult phases of arithmetic, such as the roots, difficult problems of percentage, and alligation. It was very similar to other arithmetics of the period. It went through numerous reprintings.

The fourth book was the *Progressive Higher Arithmetic.* This was the same title as one published by Robinson. In fact, they were virtually identical except the one edited by Fish contained many more problems dealing with mensuration. It was copyrighted in 1860, 1863, and 1875. The writer has not succeeded in determining the working and financial arrangement Fish had with Robinson in this series. Apparently Fish wrote the first three in consultation with Robinson and then merely added a little to Robinson's *Higher*.

Also in 1858 Fish published the *Rudiments of Written Arithmetic*, "containing slate and black-board exercises for beginners." This book was not a part of a graded series, but likely could have been used to serve in place both of the *Primary*, and the *Intellectual* of the above series. Its approach was not as inductive as the other two.

Then in 1874, after Robinson's decease, Fish published a new two-book series, a *First Book in Arithmetic*, including both oral and written exercises, and the *Complete Arithmetic*. Thus the work could be purchased in two parts or all in a single volume. The approach was *developmental*. Definitions, rules and explanations, and analyses accompanied or were interspersed with the problems. The *Complete* book went through numerous printings.

Ultimately, in 1883 Fish wrote a new two-book series; namely, Fish's *Arithmetic: Number One* and *Number Two*. *Number One* was prepared as the "first book in arithmetic for pupils commencing the third school year." Some "unique" features claimed for the book were: "Countings, Groupings, Signs, Drill Tables for abstract and Concrete work," etc. The first 140 pages dealt with the fundamentals, and the last thirty with measurements, percentage, and review. Although the next book was entitled *Number Two*, it really was a complete arithmetic, but not as large as the 1874 *Complete Arithmetic*. Too, its approach was more inductive than the 1874 edition. Fish, as was true of Brooks and others, apparently aimed to have arithmetic books suitable for the various kinds and systems of schools—graded, loosely graded, and ungraded.

Philotus Dean. Dean was connected with the public schools of Pittsburgh. Seeing the success of the locally printed Osgood *Readers*, apparently he thought there might be a market for some Pittsburgh printed arithmetics. His first one, in 1859, was the *Public School Arithmetic*. It really was a *complete* arithmetic, since it covered all of the commonly accepted aspects of the field. The next year he wrote the *Primary Arithmetic* as part of a series. It was well illustrated and largely inductive in approach.

It combined the mental with work for the slate and blackboard. It covered the four fundamentals, fractions, and twelve pages of problems in connection with certain tables.

The *Intellectual Arithmetic* was planned to follow the *Primary*. This book appeared in rather fine print and was much more difficult than the *Primary*. Analyses interspersed the problems. In 1865 he added the *Intermediate Arithmetic* to his list. This was very similar to his earlier *Public School Arithmetic*, and contained "all matter usually presented in a practical arithmetic, so simplified as to adapt it to beginners; with the most approved models and analyses." In 1868 he published the *Elementary Arithmetic* for schools having pupils dropping out when rather young. So in a simple way it presented nearly all of the more important aspects of arithmetic. Lastly in 1874 he wrote the *High School Arithmetic*, containing the matter commonly contained in higher arithmetics, of which there had been many written. It is doubtful whether these books attained very wide usage beyond the western Pennsylvania area.

John H. French. In 1867 a carefully graded series of four arithmetics written by French began to appear. The first one was a very simple book entitled *First Lessons in Numbers*, apparently to be used mostly for oral work with very young children. The second one was the *Elementary Arithmetic, For the Slate*. This book was designed for beginners in written arithmetic. It contained six chapters: Integers, Decimals, Compound Numbers, Fractions, Percentage, and Miscellaneous Review Problems. The title page contained the following statement in fine italic print: "If Principles are understood, Rules are useless." This meant that the book was arranged inductively. It contained many pictures which were carefully used to introduce or illustrate various types of arithmetical applications. The problems were of a very practical nature. The back of the book included a Manual of Methods and Suggestions of 12 pages in fine print. Most of it was devoted to suggestions regarding the work on specific pages in the book.

The third was the *Mental Arithmetic*. It referred to mental arithmetic as the "Logic of the Common School." It is not clear whether French meant this to be used after the *Elementary Arithmetic* or supplementary to it. In the Publishers' Notice it was listed as the third book, yet it was smaller and simpler than the *Elementary*. Evidence indicates that not as many copies and printings of this book were sold as of the others.

The fourth book entitled *Common School Arithmetic* appeared in 1869. The statement, "If the Understanding is thoroughly reached, the Memory will take care of itself," appeared on the title page. It was 116 pages larger than the elementary. More than two-thirds of the book was devoted to various kinds of tables, percentage, and mensuration, together with pictures, diagrams, and practical problems relating to these matters. All of these books were very attractively printed. The *Elementary* and the *Common School Arithmetics* appeared in numerous printings.

Emerson E. White (1829-1902). He was a leading mid-west educator during the latter half of the nineteenth century. He was one of the organizers of the National Educational Association and its president in 1872. The three most important positions held by him were Superintendent of schools at Cincinnati, state Superintendent of Public Instruction of Ohio, and President of Purdue University. He also was the author of a popular book on methods and one on school management.

The publication of White's graded series of three arithmetics began in 1868. These were published by the same company that published the McGuffey *Readers*. The first one was *A Primary Arithme-*

White, *Primary Arithmetic,* 1868 —note appeal to child's interest.

PRIMARY ARITHMETIC. 21

3. Two marbles and three marbles are how many marbles? Three marbles and three marbles? How many are 2 and 3? 3 and 3?

4. A man has five horses: if he sell three of them, how many will he have left? Three from 5 leaves how many? 3 from 6?

5. How many fawns are in these two groups? Five fawns and three fawns are how many fawns?

6. Four squirrels are running on a fence and three are on a tree. How many are four squirrels and three squirrels? Five squirrels and three squirrels? How many are 4 and 3? 5 and 3?

7. Six kittens and three kittens are how many kittens? 7 kittens and 3 kittens?

8. How many boys are six boys and three boys? Seven boys and three boys? How many are 6 and 3? 7 and 3?

9. Three kittens from nine kittens leave how many? Three kittens from ten kittens? Three from 9 leaves how many? 3 from 10?

10. How many pears are 7 pears and 3 pears? 6 pears and 3 pears? 5 pears and 3 pears? 4 pears and 3 pears? 3 pears and 3 pears?

tic, which united oral and written exercises in "a natural system of instruction." It covered only the four fundamentals of arithmetic, but contained none of their tables. The combinations were to be learned through exercises, which were profusely illustrated with many kinds of pictures.

The second book was *An Intermediate Arithmetic.* More than a third of the book was devoted to reviewing the fundamentals, after which it dealt with Properties of Numbers, Common Fractions, United States Money, Reduction of Denominate Numbers (dealing with the various tables of weights and measures), and Compound Numbers. Like the *Primary* book, it was attractively arranged and illustrated with some pictures and diagrams. The answers to the exercises were in the back of the book. It was slightly revised several times.

The third book was *A Complete Arithmetic.* In addition to dealing with the topics covered in the *Intermediate,* this book dealt with the metric system, ratio and proportion, involution and evolution, and in the Appendix with geometrical progression, alligation, and permutations. Much space was given to percentage, but very little to problems involving weights and measures. It was copyrighted in 1870, 1883, 1897, and 1901. Thus it was in use for more than three decades.

Later it became evident to White and to the publishers that many schools and parents objected to buying three arithmetics. So in 1883 he wrote *A New Elementary Arithmetic.* This included the material of both the *Primary* and the *Intermediate,* and with the *Complete* made a two book series. It is evident that White's books, together with the Ray's *Arithmetics,* went a long way to fill the arithmetic needs of the mid-west during the second half of the nineteenth century.

Milton B. Goff. At the time of the writing of his first arithmetics Goff was professor of mathematics at the Western University of Pennsylvania (now the University of Pittsburgh). Later he became its president, the only professor there ever to have become its head.

In 1876 there was published in Pittsburgh Goff's *First Book in Arithmetic.* It was a very attractive book of 144 pages profusely

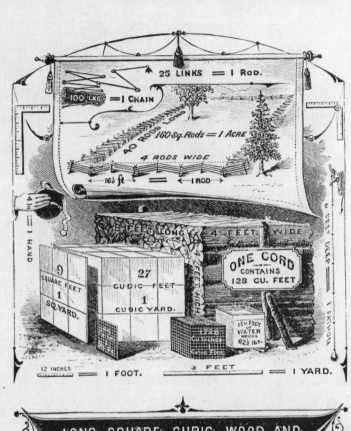

202. Long, or **Linear Measure,** is used in measuring distances, or anything that has length. The *Unit of Measure* may be 1 *mile,* 1 *rod,* 1 *yard,* &c. A **Line** has but *one* dimension—*length.*

Linear measure is so called because it may be taken with a line; it includes *Long Measure, Cloth Measure,* and *Surveyors' Linear Measure.*
186 .

Goff, 1876—note object lesson.

LESSON IV.

1. A hen has 12 chickens in groups of 3 each. How many groups are there?

Solution.—*3 chickens are contained in 12 chickens 4 times. Therefore, there are 4 groups.*

2. Sixteen horse-shoes are hanging in rows of 4 each. How many rows are there?

3. The black-smith uses 4 shoes in shoeing one horse. How many horses can be shod with 20 shoes?

4. How many groups of 3 each will 9 chickens make?

5. If 3 pears are put on each plate, how many plates will it take to hold 18 pears?

6. Four gills make 1 pint. How many pints in 36 gills?

7. How many books at 3 dollars each can Jennie buy for 15 dollars?

Goff, 1876, reflection of Object Lesson Movement in U.S.

illustrated. Evidently both Goff and White were cognizant of the influence of the Oswego Object Lesson movement, which emphasized the use of objects and pictures. Two-thirds of the book dealt with the four fundamentals, and the remainder dealt with fractions, and denominate numbers as related to the tables of coinage, weights, and measures. The fundamentals were taught in a sort of cycle method. First they were presented in a modified table form with very simple exercises, and then later with much more difficult exercises involving them. In the back of the book there were six pages in fine print of Suggestions to Teachers.

Also in 1876 *The Complete Arithmetic* was published in Pittsburgh, as well as in New York, Boston, and Omaha. This was a rather large book of 452 pages to follow the *First Book*. In defense Goff held that "too many books have been used and too much time has been spent in the study of Arithmetic." He believed that the sole use of a mental arithmetic was unnecessary. Mental work should have rather close connection with written arithmetic. The contents of the book were very similar to other complete arithmetics of that period. The approach was largely deductive rather than inductive as was true of some other competing arithmetics. In 1877 he published *A Book of Arithmetical Problems* designed for use by teachers and pupils as a drill book in connection with the *Complete Arithmetic*. It could also be used by pupils who desired to study advanced work. Answers accompanied the problems.

In 1888 the *First Book* was replaced by a considerably larger one entitled *Elementary Arithmetic*. Again the cycle plan was used to present the fundamentals. Apparently the first presentation of them was for one grade and the second for the next grade. The Second had fewer illustrations and was less attractive than the earlier book. In 1889 Goff's *Practical Arithmetic* replaced the *Complete* and was 50 pages smaller. The two chief changes were that fractions were omitted, since these were presented in the *Elementary* book, and treatment of the metric system was introduced.

G. A. Wentworth (1835-1906). The last series of arithmetics to be discussed in this chapter was written by Wentworth. After he was graduated from Harvard he taught mathematics at Phillips Exeter Academy for thirty years. Then he resigned to give full time to textbook writing. Previous to his authorship of an arithmetic he had written a very popular geometry. One of his algebras appeared the same year as his first arithmetic. One year later a trigonometry appeared. In all of these fields he wrote more than one text.

His first arithmetic was *A Practical Arithmetic* written in 1881 jointly with the Rev. Thomas Hill, ex-president of Harvard. It soon appeared in a number of printings, including one in 1893, when an identical printing was entitled *A High School Arithmetic*. Interestingly these books had an index and seven pages of definitions of mathematical terms in the beginning of each book. Its contents were very similar to other arithmetics commonly known as "complete," beginning with the fundamentals followed by the topics then generally taught. Undue attention seemingly was paid to metric measures in 36 pages of text, and fifteen pages to logarithms. Otherwise the problems seemed to be very practical. The book was considerably revised and recopyrighted in 1893 and again in 1897. Some topics were dropped, others rearranged, and the treatment of some enlarged. These editions appeared under Wentworth's authorship alone. In 1886 Wentworth and Hill also published an *Exercise Manual*.

In 1885 Wentworth and E. M. Reed wrote the *First Steps in Numbers: A Primary Arithmetic*. It contained no pictures and was unattractive. In some respects it took the form of a workbook, in that many of the lessons were headed by such directions as, "Copy and complete," "Copy and find the answers," "Copy and complete with figures," etc. In 1889 the same authors replaced it with the *Primary Arithmetic*. This book was very different. It contained many counters and pictures, and largely used the inductive or developmental approach. It soon appeared in several printings. In 1893 this book was replaced by *An Elementary Arithmetic* written by Wentworth alone. Thus two arithmetics which were co-authored originally were replaced by books written by Wentworth alone. In 1895 Wentworth wrote *A Mental Arithmetic* of 190 pages, apparently to be used in schools stressing mental exercises. However, it did not become popular. The popularity of the mental arithmetic approach had passed.

In 1889 *A Grammar School Arithmetic* appeared, which was a shortened revision of the *Practical* with the approach less deductive. Some of the sections resembled the work-book approach. The popular sale of these two books apparently paralleled each other, one taking a somewhat deductive and the other a more developmental approach. In 1898 Wentworth published *An Advanced Arithmetic* for high schools, normal schools, and academies. All of these appeared in numerous printings.

It is evident that Wentworth was the author of very widely used mathematics books at the turn of the century, not only in the field of arithmetic, but also in algebra, geometry, and trigonometry. Like the publishers of the Ray's books earlier, so the publishers of Wentworth's books aimed to have frequent revisions and reprintings.

COMMENTS

The basic treatment in this chapter has dealt only with the American arithmetics published before 1900. While the writer has made no detailed analysis of arithmetics published since 1900, certain comparative comments may be appropriate. Many of the changes are evidently due to a better understanding of children psychologically. In other words, the approaches are more psychological.

One of the most marked contrasts between the arithmetics before and after 1900 would be in the make-up of the book. The modern books are much larger; are printed with very much larger type; and contain many more pictures, which often are colored. The books are more appealing and attractive.

Modern arithmetics are graded much more finely. This is true in several respects. In some series there is a separate book for every grade. Then, also, the vocabulary and the concepts involved in these books are more carefully graded according to the maturity of the children.

Most current arithmetics are mathematically more meaningful and socially significant. More attention is given to the meaning and origin of numbers and the number system. Often the work is organized in units dealing with important aspects of life and society. The social and practical applications are given more attention.

In conclusion, it can be said that American arithmetic textbooks have markedly improved in appearance, grading and gradation, content, inclusion of learning and teaching aids, and their significance to the life and thinking of the children using them.

CHAPTER 6

GEOGRAPHIES

AN OLD STUDY

G EOGRAPHY is an old subject field. One of the first to systematize geography as a subject was Hecataeus of Miletus, who lived before 500 B.C., and is often called the Father of Geography. Other ancient writers of geography were Herodotus, Strabo, Polybius, Pliny, Ptolemy, Dionysius, and Pausanias; all wrote in Greek. As was true of other academic subjects, schools paid little attention to geography during the Middle Ages.

Geographical knowledge spread rapidly during the Renaissance, for two reasons. First, many of the ancient writings were rediscovered and the invention of the printing press made publication possible. Some of the old writings were translated even into the modern vernacular languages. Second, the invention of the compass and the astrolabe made it safe for mariners to go beyond sight of land in their travels and explorations. As a result, the Americas and new parts of the world were discovered and explored. Soon books and pamphlets were written about them, and the knowledge of geography and map making was greatly expanded.

It was inevitable with the Revival of Learning during the Renaissance and the expanding of knowledge, that the study of geography should become a school subject. From geography have come history, geology, and in part, some other sciences as school subjects of today. Geography is the mother of many other subjects.

AIMS OF EARLY GEOGRAPHY TEXTBOOKS

It has been the practice for textbook authors to state the aims which a study of their books should fulfill. These were usually in the preface, or sometimes in the introduction. All authors did not hold the same views regarding the aims of geography. An analysis of their aims shows that there seemed to be two reasons why the authors differed. First, the personal views of the authors would vary. Secondly, the aims themselves changed somewhat with the period or time.

Cultural aims. From the appearance of the earliest books to the present, the cultural values of the study of geography have been recognized. These values have been expressed in various ways.

1. Acquisition of Knowledge. Morse, in 1784, stated that the "more immediate aim is to facilitate the acquisition of geographical knowledge." John Smith's *A New Compend of Geography* (1816) began his Preface by saying, "The diffusion of knowledge, in republican forms of government, is of vital importance." Huntington's book (1835) stated that nobler achievements can be attained "if their minds were, in due reason, cultivated and enlarged by an acquaintance with the state of the world."

First geography written in U.S., 1784; 2 folding maps; "useful and agreeable science," Morse.

GEOGRAPHY
MADE EASY.
BEING A SHORT, BUT COMPREHENSIVE

Syſtem
Of THAT VERY USEFUL AND AGREEABLE SCIENCE.

E X H I B I T I N G

In an eaſy and conciſe View, the Figures, Motions, Diſtances, and Magnitudes of the heavenly Bodies:—A general deſcription of the Earth conſidered as a Planet; with its grand Diviſions into Land and Water, Continents, Oceans, Iſlands, &c.—The Situation, Boundaries and Extent of the ſeveral Empires, Kingdoms, and States, together with an Account of their Climate, Soil, Productions and commerce :—The Number, Genius, and general Character of the Inhabitants :—Their Religion, Government and Hiſtory :—The Latitude, Longitude, Diſtances, and Bearings of the principal Places from Philadelphia and London, and a Number of uſeful Geographical Tables.

Illuſtrated with two correct and elegant MAPS, one of the World, and the other of the United States, together with a Number of newly conſtructed Maps, adapted to the Capacities and Underſtanding of Children.

Calculated particularly for the Uſe and Improvement of SCHOOLS in the United States.

By JEDIDIAH MORSE, A. B.

" There is not a Son or a Daughter of Adam, but has " ſome concern in both Geography and Astronomy."
DR. WATTS.
" Among thoſe Studies which are uſually recommended to " young People, there can be few that might be improved to " better Uſes than Geography." *Eſſays on various Subjects.*

N E W - H A V E N :
Printed by Meigs, Bowen and Dana, in Chapel-Street.

1784

DIVISIONS OF WATER.   9

Straits.

A narrow passage, like a door or gate,
That leads into some sea, is called a *Strait*.

A passage of water that leads between two seas, or bodies of water, is called a Strait; as the Straits of Magellan, between South America and the Island of Terra del Fuego.

Channels.

A Channel is a strait that opens wide ;
As the *English Channel*, where proud navies ride.

A Channel is a wide strait ; as the English Channel.

Sounds.

A Strait so shallow that its depth is found,
By lead or anchor, oft is called a sound.

When a strait is so shallow that its depth can be measured by a lead and line, it is called a Sound.

Rivers.

Rivers are streams, by numerous branches formed,
That from the highlands to the seas are turned.

A River is a large stream of water, formed by numerous branches, that empties into some sea, gulf, lake or bay. The place where a river rises, is called its source ; the place where it empties is called its mouth. The small streams that empty into it are called its branches.

Firths.

A River wid'ning 'tween its banks of earth,
Towards its mouth, is called a *Frith or Firth.*

The widening of a river toward its mouth, is called a Frith or Firth ; as Solway Frith in Scotland ; the Firth of the River Forth.

Harbors or Havens.

A Harbor or a Haven, is a port,
Where ships in safety, from the storm resort.

A Harbor or Haven is a port where ships may run in and find shelter from the storm.

EXPLANATIONS NECESSARY TO THE USE OF MAPS.

Hemispheres.

The world's a Globe, the world we live on here ;
One half a globe is called a *Hemisphere.*

Eastern and *Western Hemispheres* are found
Upon the Map that shows, the world is round.
Northern and *Southern Hemispheres* beside,
One North, one South the Equator is espied.

The word *hemisphere* is formed from *hemi,* that sigfies half, and *sphere,* globe or ball ; so, half the earth is called a *hemisphere.*

The Western Hemisphere includes North and South America.

The Eastern Hemisphere includes Europe, Asia and Africa.

The Northern Hemisphere includes all that part of the earth North cf the Equator.

The Southern Hemisphere includes all South of the Equator.

The Poetical Geography, 1863, emphasizing the pleasure of learning.

One of the most popular series in geography was written by S. S. Cornell. In his *Primary Geography* in 1854 he said, in urging the adoption of the book, "First, that it will endow a pupil with a thorough and permanent knowledge of Geography." In Guyot's *Primary Geography* (1866) one finds a more modern statement in regard to acquiring knowledge: "The object of this little book is not so much to *impart* geographical knowledge, as to *prepare the pupil for its successive acquirement* in the future." And in a still later book, in Harper's *School Geography* in 1875, one finds an even broader purpose expressed in claiming that "The study of geography is now, much more than at any former period, an essential element in education. It is second in importance only to reading, writing, and rudimentary arithmetic." Thus, the acquisition of knowledge, both in its narrower as well as in its broader aspects, was certainly an aim in teaching geography.

2. Interest and Entertainment. Another cultural element claimed for geography was that it was interesting and enjoyable on a higher level. Huntington's text said that geography was "a source of mental diversion and entertainment," and that it "excites a continually increasing interest." This value of geography was mentioned in various ways by many authors, but the author who extended himself most by attempting to publish a book with this purpose foremost in mind was George Van Waters. In his *Poetical Geography*, in 1863, he wrote the entire text in poetical form. He claimed that he "spared neither time nor labor to make it useful and interesting." A few brief examples from the book may be of interest:

> The surface of the Earth, with all its tribes,
> Of sea and land, Geography describes.

> This Earth is but a mighty ball profound,
> Just five and twenty thousand miles around.

> In Mexico, high on table lands,
> In the interior of the province stands,
> Above the sea full seven thousand feet,
> Adorned with temples rich and structures great.

Civic aim. Another major aim mentioned by many authors was to

Morse, *Geography Made Easy*, folded map, 1817.

NORTH-AMERICA.

Boundaries, Situation, Extent. THIS division of the western continent includes all that part lying north of the Isthmus of Darien. It is bounded east by the Atlantic, and west by the North Pacific Ocean. Its southern boundary line is the parallel of 7 30 N.; whence it extends to the north pole; in length about 80 degrees, or 5200 miles. Its greatest extent, from west to east, is generally reckoned from the promontory of Alaska, in about 90° W. lon. to Cape Charles, the most easterly point of Labrador, in 50° E. lon. from Philadelphia; in breadth 4570 miles. If Greenland be considered as a part of North-America, to which it is probably united, its extreme eastern limit will extend nearly to 55° E. lon. Its average breadth is about 1500 miles.

Climate. In a region of such vast extent, as North-America, the climate must of course be various. It experiences every temperature of the atmosphere, from the burning heats of the torrid zone, to the intolerable colds of the polar regions. Almost every division of the continent has a climate of its own, which will be noticed in its proper place.

Seas. Baffin's Bay, is the largest and most northerly of any yet discovered. It lies beyond the 70th degree of N. lat. and opens into the Atlantic ocean through Davis's Straits, between the coasts of Labrador and Greenland. This bay has never been explored, except by its discoverer, William Baffin, in 1622, and many modern geographers doubt its existence; it however still occupies a place on maps. The strait, which connects it with the Atlantic, is as wide as the Baltic sea.

Hudson Bay, was discovered in 1610, by Henry Hudson, and lies between 53° and 65° N. lat. 900 leagues broad, communicating with the Atlantic ocean by Hudson's Strait. The gulf or sea, called Davis's Strait, may be considered as a part of Hudson Bay, and must probably joins the Arctic ocean. Hudson Bay abounds with the beluga, or white whale. Large sturgeons are also caught in some parts of it.

develop either nationalism or worldmindedness. These purposes were stressed more fully in the earlier books than in the later ones. This was because the early geographies contained content now classed as history and even civics. These early texts really constituted correlated social studies. Later, history and civics became separate subject fields.

A mild form of nationalistic spirit was expressed in the 1800 edition of Morse's *Geography Made Easy:* "our youth have been educated, rather as subjects of the British king, than as citizens of a free and independent Republic. But the scene is now changed . . . particularly to that of the Geography of our own country."

As history and civil government later became separate subject fields the civic aim continued for some time, but began to stress more fully the world view. Huntington in 1835 said, "of many parts of the world we are still extremely ignorant. They are yet to be explored," and as they are explored "new degrees of light are afforded." As late as 1872 Monteith in his *Comprehensive Geography* said, in justifying some history with geography, "One leading feature is that the student learns all about one country or state at one time." After 1880 geography books finally discontinued the use of history as one of their aims.

Relationships. The earlier authors rarely interpreted the facts presented in their books in relationship to each other. The content of most early geographies consisted of a body of unrelated facts concerning the world and its peoples. The correlation of facts was overlooked. The first one to begin showing such relationships in geography was Carl Ritter, a German geographer, although he did not carry the idea systematically to all aspects of the subject.

The first American geography author to develop this idea most fully in his books was Arnold Guyot. Although his texts were published in a number of editions, particularly his *Earth and Man* (1849 and later), yet they were not as popular as Mitchell's geographies during the same period, nor did other authors at that time commonly follow the practice of showing relationships. However, that is the common practice today. Guyot was ahead of his time.

The idea was to connect cause and effect. An attempt was

made to set up natural to natural, natural to cultural, and cultural to cultural relationships. Appleton's *Standard Higher Geography* (1881) favored developing relationships, so that "these facts will be readily remembered, if the reasons underlying them are properly comprehended." Intelligence as well as memory were to be developed. Items of location and occurrence were to be studied in relationship rather than as isolated parts.

Textbooks aims. In addition to the aims set forth for the study of geography, most authors also claimed certain aims for their particular texts in comparison with others.

1. Provision for individual differences. One of the first authors to try to adapt the content to the student's ability was Daniel Adams (1818). He divided his book into three parts for the different abilities of students. The next step in this development was to publish geographies in series. One of the first primary geographies was written by Emma Willard in 1826, entitled *Geography for Beginners.* Although a number of early authors wrote more than one textbook in geography, yet none wrote a graded series before 1850. One of the first graded series to be written by one author was by S. S. Cornell in 1854. On the title page of her *Primary Geography* appeared the following quotation: "First the blade, then the ear, after that the full corn in the ear." She proposed to give children "one thing at a time" and "to render this important branch as palpable to the understanding of pupils as some of the other branches of their education." No doubt she knew that in reading, spelling, arithmetic, and some other branches the books had appeared in graded series beginning in the early 1830's. After the Cornell series was published, most geographies appeared in series, some in a two-book series, and others in three. Other leading series were by Monteith, Mitchell, Guyot, Colton, Fitch, Goodrich, and Swinton.

2. Time-saving. Some authors wrote brief, concise books which they claimed would be time-saving. An illustration of such claim was found in Monteith's *Comprehensive Geography* (1872):

Owing to the limited time, which many scholars can give to the study of Geography, the author has endeavored to secure satisfactory results at the smallest possible expense in time and labor, both to the teacher and pupil.

Guyot (1875) stated that even though his book was small, it provided "a complete thorough and symmetrical summary of geographical knowledge." Other similar statements could be quoted.

3. Improvement of content. It is to be expected that many authors should claim, as their books were published, that the content of such books represented a great improvement over the other books on the market. For example, Augustus S. Mitchell, whose books later appeared in more editions than those of any other geography author, said in *A System of Modern Geography* (1840):

> Geography is, more than any other science, in its nature constantly progressive; and, hence, demands increasing diligence on the part of those whose attention is directed to the publication of works connected with it.

He added, "Several (authors) fail in representing various parts of the world," and "important misstatements have been also observed in some of the works alluded to." Roswell C. Smith in his *Introductory Geography* (1850) said, "if he did not think it (the book) better, he would certainly suppress it." Similar claims for their books continued to appear in the geographies of many authors.

PRESENTATION AND NATURE OF CONTENT

No common practice was developed by geography authors in regard to the organization and presentation of their content. Sahli[1] found that seven different plans of organization were followed in the geographies published before 1840; divisions, chapters, topics, sections, lessons, parts, and lectures. Some used two or more plans in the same book. Thirty-three of the 49 books analyzed divided the content into divisions and 39 used sections. Of these, three organized their content into divisions only, nine

[1] John R. Sahli, "An Analysis of Early American Geography Textbooks from 1784 to 1840." (Unpublished Ph.D. dissertation, University of Pittsburgh, 1941.)

GEOGRAPHY.

···•●◉●•···

☞ The "Interrogative system" of teaching, has now become very general in almost every branch of school education. The introduction may be traced to the Scholar's Arithmetic, in 1801, many years before the appearance of Goldsmith and of Guy in our country. A further improvement in this system is here attempted, and instead of printing the question at length, which necessarily swells the book, a character (ᵠ) is introduced, intimating both to the Instructer, and the pupil, that a question is required, and this character is invariably placed BE-FORE the word or words intended to ask the question, and to which the answer, FOUND BY READING THE SENTENCE, is to be a direct reply. For example, take the first sentence ; the character is placed before the words "certain knowledge ;" the question then is, Had the an-cients any certain knowledge of the figure of the earth ? The answer, from reading the sentence, is evident, No ; or, They had not.

Where the construction of the sentence suggests no particular form in which to put the question, it may be, What is said of, &c. ; as for instance, under the article " Agriculture," in Massachusetts, the char-acter is placed before the word " agriculture ;" the question then may be, What is said of the agriculture of Massachusetts ?

Let the class be directed to meditate answers to the questions to be asked on those subjects or words before which the character is placed. After reading, let those questions be put by the instructer, and answer-ed by the class in rotation. The exercise will be found both profitable and entertaining.

———

THE WORLD.

THE ancients had no ᵠcertain knowledge of the figure of the earth. But later discoveries, both by astronomy and navigation, demonstrate the world we inhabit to be a large opaque globe or ball, nearly eight thousand ᵠmiles in diam-eter. In proof of this it is only necessary to notice, that various navigators have actually sailed around it. Of these, the ᵠfirst was Sir Francis Drake, who in 1580 com-pleted the circumnavigation of the globe, after an absence of two years, ten months, and twenty days, from England, his native land.

About two thirds of the ᵠsurface of the earth are covered with water. In respect to its universal communication, the ocean may be regarded as one ; but, for geographical purposes, it has been found more convenient to consider it as distributed into portions or parts. The ᵠlargest of these

Adams, *Geography of the World,* 1830—note the use of *superior q* to direct student to questions teacher will ask.

into sections only, and 29 used a combination of divisions and sections. The divisions most commonly used and the average percentage of content devoted to each were as follows: general geography, 15.5 per cent; United States, 28.8 per cent; other North American countries, 9.4 per cent; South America, 6.4 per cent; Europe, 20.7 per cent; Asia, 10.9 per cent; Africa, 6.7 per cent; and Australia, 1.6 per cent. However, the percentage of space given to the different divisions varied greatly from book to book. For example, Jacob Willetts in *An Easy Grammar of Geography* (1826) devoted 44.7 per cent to general geography, and five of the 49 authors devoted none. Similar differences of emphases appear regarding the space devoted to the other six divisions.

Ned Culler,[2] who analyzed 97 geographies published between 1840 and 1890, found 10 different plans or combinations of plans followed in presenting the materials. Even by 1890 no common practice was followed. He, too, determined the average amount of content devoted to the different geographical content divisions. The averages varied considerably from those found by Sahli before 1840. Culler's averages were: general geography, 40.1 per cent; United States, 29.8 per cent; other North American countries, 6.2 per cent; South America, 4.5 per cent; Europe, 8.4 per cent; Asia, 5.5 per cent; Africa, 3.7 per cent; and Australia, 1.9 per cent. It should be observed that the books before 1840 devoted only 15.5 per cent of the space to general geography, while those from 1840 to 1890 averaged 40.1 per cent. The space given to the United States and to Australia remained rather constant. The space devoted to all of the other divisions was decreased, particularly European space dropped from 20.7 per cent to 8.4 per cent, and Asia from 10.9 per cent to 5.5 per cent.

SIZE OF BOOKS

No aspect or characteristic of geography books from the earlier

---

[2] Ned Culler, "The Development of American Geography Textbooks from 1840 to 1890." (Unpublished Ed.D. dissertation, University of Pittsburgh, 1945.)

to the later ones changed more than the size. The 49 books analyzed by Sahli (those before 1840) averaged 4.3 x 6.5 inches or 28.9 sq. in. On the other hand, Culler found that the average size of those published during the 1840's were 39 sq. in.; during the 1850's, 73.2 sq. in.; during the 1860's, 72.2 sq. in.; during the 1870's, 91.3 sq. in.; and during the 1880's, 98 sq. in. Thus the geographies of the 1880's were more than three times as large as those published before 1840. There were two rather definite reasons why these texts increased in size. First, the size of type in the earlier books was very small. The type in the first American written geography (Morse) was 8 point (pica), while most of the type in Harper's *School Geography* (1876) was 12

UNITED STATES.

emselves an Independent Nation, under the title of "The United States of America."

In 1783, Great Britain, after an immense loss of blood and treasure, acknowledged the independence of the United States. This separation of the colonies from the government of England, is called, "the American revolution."

In 1788, a government, embracing the general interests of all the states, was formed, and adopted by most of the states, and soon after by all of them. The articles of this confederation are called "the Constitution of the United States."

The government, which is *republican*, consists of a President, Vice President, Senate, and House of Representatives, all elected by the people; and when assembled, they compose what is called "the Congress of the United States."

The first President was Gen. George Washington, who was commander in chief of the American forces during the revolution.

The succession of the Presidents is as follows :—

		in office.
George Washington	from 1789 to 1797	8 years.
John Adams	from 1797 to 1801	4
Thomas Jefferson	from 1801 to 1809	8
James Madison	from 1809 to 1817	8
James Monroe	from 1817 to	

The United States, from the adoption of the Federal institution to 1808, increased in riches, power and population, more rapidly, than was ever before known in any nation. Their agriculture and commerce, the two principal occupations, were extensive and successful. They were respected by foreign nations, and, at home, enjoyed the blessings of peace, religion, and good government. In 1807, commerce became obstructed; after which war impediments were annually multiplied, till the 18th of June, 1812, when the United States declared war against Great Britain. This continued to the 17th February, 1815. when peace was again restored.

UNITED STATES. 41

Religion. There is no established religion in the United States. All sects are tolerated; but the most numerous are the *Congrega'tionalists,* sometimes called Independ'ents, and the Presbyte'rians.

In New England, religion is supported by a tax on the people, except in Rhode Island; in the other states, it is left to the liberality and voluntary exertions of individuals.

By the Constitution of the United States, all are eligible to offices of trust and profit, without regard to religion.

Population. The United States, in 1810, contained 7,230,514 inhabitants.

The following Table shows the respective number of slaves and free citizens in each state.

		Slaves.	Free Citizens.	Total.
Eastern States, or New England.	District of Maine		228,705	228,705
	New Hampshire -		214,460	214,460
	Vermont -		217,895	217,895
	Massachusetts -		472,040	472,040
	Rhode Island -	108	76,823	76,931
	Connecticut - -	310	261,632	261,942
Middle States.	New York - -	15,017	944,032	959,049
	New Jersey - -	10,851	234,711	245,562
	Delaware - -	4,177	68,497	72,674
	Pennsylvania - -	795	809,296	810,091
Western States and Territories.	Michigan Ter. - -	24	4,738	4,762
	Illinois Ter. - -	168	12,114	12,282
	Indiana - - - -	237	24,283	24,520
	Ohio - - - -		230,760	230,760
Southern States.	Kentucky - -	80,561	325,930	406,511
	Tennessee - -	44,535	217,192	261,727
	Maryland - -	111,502	269,044	380,546
	District of Columbia	5,395	18,628	24,023
	Virginia - - -	392,518	582,104	974,622
	North Carolina -	168,824	386,676	555,500
	South Carolina -	196,365	218,750	415,115
	Georgia - -	105,218	147,215	252,433
	Mississippi - -	17,088	23,264	40,352
Louisiana.	Orleans - - -	34,660	41,896	76.556
	Louisiana Territory	3,011	17,834	20,845
		1,185,223	6,045,291	7,230,514

4*

History, Civics, Geography in *Introduction to Ancient and Modern Geography,* J. A. Cummins, 1813.

point (pica). However, the principal reason for larger books was that maps became an integral part of all geographies. The earlier books either contained no maps or at most several folded maps. Of course, with frequent use the folded maps would soon tear. The use of folded maps was followed by the practice of having separate atlases to accompany the regular geography textbook. This was both inconvenient and expensive. Thus after 1840 the practice of including maps, and later maps in color, developed rapidly and maps were scaled in miles. After 1850 it became common to include map questions in the text. So the use of larger type and particularly the inclusion of maps resulted in the tripling of the size of geography textbooks.

Further to prove that the introduction of maps was the chief reason for the marked increase in the size as indicated by the fact that earlier books actually averaged more pages per book than the later ones: the six geographies published before 1800 averaged 358 pages, and the 24 published from 1800 to 1825, 254 pages; while those between 1850 and 1875, only 147 pages per book. The authors needed the large pages for the maps, not for the print.

TREATMENT OF CONTENT

The topics dealt with in the content of the geography textbooks did not differ too much on the average from the earliest (1784) to those of the latter part of the nineteenth century. However, during any particular period there were considerable differences among the authors. For example, in dealing with our Mother Country, England, Morse (1784) covered the following topics: boundaries and extent; air, soil, and productions; inhabitants and character; religion; government; and history. Dwight's *Geography of the World* (1795) asked 38 questions in catechetical fashion (with answers) about England. These dealt with many detailed matters not covered by Morse. Goldsmith in *An Easy Grammar of Geography* (1806) devoted most of the space on Great Britain to naming its various divisions and parts, naming the 40 counties of England, the 12 of Wales, the 33 of Scotland,

and the 32 of Ireland. Such treatment must have been very uninteresting to the students.

Apparently, it was soon discovered that the type of treatment followed by Morse was more satisfactory than the others just mentioned, so later authors soon began to model their treatment more fully on Morse. Parish in 1810 dealt with England under boundaries, climate, soil and products, rivers and mountains, bridges and canals, commerce, population and character, army and navy, literature, cities, political importance, curiosities, government, religion, and islands. Olney in 1830 covered England under boundaries, surface and soil, climate, minerals, character of the people, and towns.

Similar topics were treated in the following decades of the century. Cornell in 1859 dealt with geographical position, surface, soil, inhabitants, traveling facilities, manufacturing and exports, and cities. Harper's in 1876 dealt with a general description, occupations, mines, manufacturers, commerce, and government. In Mitchell's 1892 edition the topics were position and extent, natural features, products, population, chief towns, government, and religion. Thus the nature of the treatment of the content under the major divisions soon began to follow a general pattern which continued until the latter part of the nineteenth century.

QUALITY OF CONTENT

Modern authorities on the teaching of geography hold that geography should not consist of isolated details of heterogeneous material, but rather of an articulated body of geographic knowledge and principles. Such matters as temperature, rainfall, and topography should not be learned as isolated memory facts, but should be presented to show that man is what he is, at least partly, because of his surroundings. Relationships of cause and effect should be shown.

As stated in the aims three types of relationship are used in modern geography teaching: (1) cultural to cultural, (2) natural to natural, and (3) cultural to natural. The last one is considered to be the best. The cultural to cultural expresses the relationship between man and his cultural environment. The natural to natural shows the relation of natural facts. The cultural to natural shows how man and his culture either influence or are influenced by natural environment.

Since Great Britain has been covered in all regular geography textbooks, both Sahli and Culler carefully analyzed how the authors from 1784 to 1890 dealt with Britain as far as applying the above mentioned relationships was concerned. To illustrate how these relationships were applied to actual content, the following extracts are given. In discussing the characteristics of the English people, Mitchell's *Modern Geography* (1840) said: "Benevolence may be considered a striking feature in the national character; and in no country are there as many associations for charitable, benevolent, and religious purposes." The natural to natural was shown by Cummings (1818) in writing: "The weather is inconstant, and the frequency of fogs and clouds contributes much to the perpetual verdure of the country." The cultural to natural was shown in Adams' (1818) treatment of Ireland, as follows: "These fogs are a great obstruction both to travelling and to agriculture."

Next let us note how and to what extent the early authors applied these relationships to the content dealing with Great Britain. Two-thirds of the facts in the 49 geographies before 1840 were solely cultural, 20.2 per cent were solely natural, 4.7 per cent were cultural to cultural, 1.7 per cent natural to natural, and 6.8 per cent cultural to natural in relationship. Great variations of treatment appeared in the different texts. The greatest percentage of cultural to natural (21.7 per cent) appeared in *Rudiments of Geography* by William C. Woodbridge in 1835. On the other hand, in dealing with Britain none appeared in Joseph Scott's *Elements of Geography* in 1807.

These data show that the early authors dealt with geography mainly as a cultural subject centered around man and the activities of man. Elijah Parish (1810) defended his cultural treatment in saying: "While a pebble or a shell in some works commands a more lucid description than the inhabitants of the

country, here (in his text) *man* is the most distinguished object."
On an average the 97 geographies from 1840 to 1890, in dealing with Britain, devoted 71.8 per cent of the facts solely to the
cultural, 20.1 per cent solely to the natural, 3.4 per cent to the
cultural to cultural, .3 per cent to the natural to natural, and
4.3 per cent to the cultural to natural. Thus these later geographies devoted even a lower percentage of facts to the cultural
to natural, which is the modern emphasis. It seems evident that
memory work rather than a study of cause and effect relationships continued to be common in the geographies until 1890.

SUITABILITY OF SUBJECT MATTER

The early geographies were written before the field of child
psychology had developed. Little was known or recognized concerning the laws of learning or the stages of maturing. Consequently, the vocabulary used as well as many of the ideas presented violated both the laws of learning as well as principles of
good taste. Sahli analyzed the vocabularies of ten of the most
popularly used books before 1840. He applied the Yoakam[3]
Technique to three geographies by Morse, two by Goodrich, and
one each by Dwight, Adams, Olney, Smith, and Mitchell. The
lowest vocabulary grade placement of any of these books was that
by Olney (1830); namely, grade ten. Five had an eleventh grade
placement, one a twelfth, two a thirteenth, and one a fourteenth.
Thus all of these books should have been used only in the secondary school or junior college. Although Morse had written in
his *Elements of Geography* (1796) that it was "adapted to children from 8 to 14 years old," its vocabulary had an eleventh
grade placement. All of these books were commonly used in grades
much lower than their vocabulary difficulty warranted.

Culler found that the books published after 1840 were written
with much easier vocabularies. He, too, applied the Yoakam
Technique to determine the grade placement of the vocabularies
of fifteen geographies from 1840 to 1888. The five books published during the 1840's and 1850's which he analyzed all had a

---

[3] Yoakam, G. A. "Technique for Grading Books." Mimeographed form, University of Pittsburgh, Pittsburgh, Pa.

grade placement of 10 or a little above. After that the vocabularies became much easier, some as low as a sixth grade placement. Some of these, however, were lower grade geographies. Nevertheless, there was a marked improvement after 1850 in adapting the vocabularies to the maturation of the children in the books.

Another important way in which many of the early geographies were unsuited for the use of young children was the nature of the content and ideas in their descriptions and stories. Horror stories were all too common in some books. Peter Parley's *Geography* (1829) contained a thrilling narration of "rocks and stones crushing the inhabitants of the Notch in the White Mountains." In 1836 a teacher published the *Village School Geography*, which contained an apparent amplification of the Peter Parley story, as follows:

> A few years ago, at the foot of one of these mountains, at a place called the Notch, there lived a family, in which were three beautiful children. The house was many miles from any other. A storm came on, and it rained very hard for two days. A large quantity of earth and rocks, on the top of the mountain, above the house, was loosened. In the night the family was awakened by a great noise. They sprang from their beds and ran naked out of doors. They were overtaken instantly and covered with the earth, and trees, and stones and water, falling from the mountain.

Goodrich also portrayed a sea serpent "as large as the mast of a ship, has frequently been seen, along the shores of New England."

Olney (1840) in writing about the dangers of desert travel wrote, "In 1805, a caravan, consisting of 2,000 persons and 1,800 camels, not finding water at the usual resting place, died of thirst, both men and animals."

Tuthill in *My Little Geography* (1847) thrillingly narrated the terrible destruction caused by the eruption of Mt. Vesuvius. She followed her narration with a choice bit of poetry.

> A little child had gone to sleep
> Upon its mother's breast,
> And full of love she looked at it,

So peacefully at rest.

But soon a fearful sound she heard
She could not fly from death,
For burning lava filled the street,
And ashes stopped her breath.

For many years within their home
There was no light or air,
But in the ashes buried deep
In silence they were there.

The reading content often was not only morbid, but also frequently beyond the interests and understanding of the children. Too, sometimes it was ambiguous and inaccurate. For example, Scott's text in 1807 wrote that in North America, "The principal mountains are the Appalachian or Allegheny Mountains." Cummings in 1825 referred to "The boa, or serpent of the desert, is found" in the Barbary States of North Africa, which are "often 80 feet long." Olney's text in 1840 contained a similar reference. Olney also described the "Simoon of Nubia" . . . "The wind here moves the sand like the waves of the sea; and so rapidly that nothing can escape it. The Simoon, or poisonous blast from the desert blows here, and if received into the lungs, causes instant death." Nevertheless, he next refers to the climate as "dry and healthy." Later competing authors took apparent delight in referring to such fallacious statements as the above.

Another type of unsuitability was the confused manner in which certain authors explained things or processes. For example, Smith (1850) explained the cause of an earthquake as follows:

Earthquakes are sometimes supposed to be caused by electrical matter,* or inflammable air, pent up in the bowels of the earth, suddenly finding vent, and forcing its way through every obstacle.**

*Electrical matter, a thin fluid, of the nature of lightning.
**Just before the shock is felt, the sea often swells and roars tremendously; the water grows dark and muddy; birds and beasts are in consternation, and a rumbling noise, like distant thunder, is heard underground.

After 1850 fewer and fewer ambiguous, inaccurate, and confused statements appear in geography textbooks. Not only was the vocabulary better adapted to the maturity of the children, but the acquisition of more accurate knowledge of the geography of the world made the improvement of the content possible. Too, a greater understanding of the sensitive nature of children's minds led to the elimination of horror stories. The authors, whose books were in most common use after 1850, such as Colton, Guyot, Mitchell, and Swinton, did not commit many errors or resort to violations of good taste.

ATTITUDES REVEALED IN SUBJECT MATTER

Since geography textbooks dealt extensively with people and customs, the opportunity was great for authors to reveal their attitudes regarding the various peoples and their ways of living. In many geographies, especially in the earlier ones, the content revealed that the attitudes of the authors were often biased.

Religious Attitudes. The earliest geographies were written when our country was still dominantly Protestant and the academic leaders were either trained as ministers or at least deeply religious. Jedidiah Morse and Elijah Parish were both Congregational ministers. Not even all Protestant groups were equally respected. For example, in the first American written geography, Morse in 1784 referred to the Presbyterians and Lutherans as "numerous and respectable." Parish, in enumerating the religious groups, began with small letters the words Baptists, Methodists, Quakers, and Catholics, but began with capital letters Presbyterian, Congregationalists, and Lutherans.

Many of the early books particularly contained unfavorable comments about other religions than Protestants. Morse in his 1790 edition referred to Roman Catholicism in Spain as "of most bigoted, superstitious, and tyrannical character." Dwight (1806), Parish (1810), and Adams (1818) used the term "Popery" in referring to Roman Catholicism. Davies (1805) claimed that the priests in Ireland ruled with "blind superstition and ignorance." Many other early geographies contained similar statements.

Later several geography textbooks were written by Catholic

authors which were equally biased against Protestantism. Among these were texts by Pinnock (1853) and Sadlier (1880). The latter, in referring to religious conditions in Ireland, said:

> England abandoned the Catholic faith in the 16th century, and to this country belongs the ignoble distinction of having oppressed and persecuted the Irish nation with a barbarity unparalleled in the history of man's inhumanity to man.

Most Protestant authors referred to the Protestants in European countries with respect. Parish (1810) said, "The Scotch clergy are men of learning and piety." Woodbridge (1835) said, in referring to the Scots, "They are remarkable for knowledge and morality, produced by their numerous schools, and their attention to public worship."

In referring to non-Christian religions, likewise, uncomplimentary statements were often made. A number of authors referred to Mahomet as an "imposter." Morse (1800) wrote: "In a word, the contagion spread over Arabia, Syria, Egypt, and Persia; Mahomet, from a deceitful hypocrite, became the most powerful monarch in his time." Warren in 1872 referred to Mohammed as a "false prophet." Uncomplimentary statements were also made about the religions in Japan and India.

Reform Attitudes. The teaching of religion and morality was really the chief aim of education in early American schools. This aim was even dominant in geography textbooks. Thus many forms of behavior which the authors considered immoral were severely condemned.

Alcohol. Morse (1790) believed "in proportion as the use of beer increases, in the same proportion will the use of spiritous liquors decrease. This will be a happy exchange." Parish (1810) condemned the "numerous Taverns," and "grogshops." Several condemned the sale of liquors to Indians.

Tobacco. The use of tobacco was frowned on by Morse and Parish. Morse referred to a law enacted by Connecticut governing the use of tobacco. Parish said, "The culture of this weed produces wretchedness, and affords no sustenance to the labourers."

Sports and games. The moral teaching of these early books even related to sports and games. Morse (1790) in speaking of his own New Englanders, said:

> The gamester, the horse-jockey, and the knave, are equally despised, and their company is avoided by all who would sustain fair and irreproachable characters. The odious and inhuman practices of duelling, gouging, cock-fighting and horseracing, are scarcely known here.

In reference to moral habits in North Carolina, he wrote, "The time they waste in drinking, idling, and gambling, leaves them very little opportunity to improve their plantations or their minds." Davies (1805) added the vices of horseracing and cock-fighting to the list of bad habits of the North Carolinians. Most of the later geographies failed to comment on games and sports.

Slavery. A number of the earlier authors viewed slavery as one of the greatest of evils. Morse commented critically regarding it in several of his geographies. Davies (1805) said, "Here as well as in every other country where it has prevailed largely, slavery has produced its peculiar train of vices, pride, indolence, and cruelty." Dwight (1796), apparently in praise of New England wrote:

> Q. Are there any slaves?
> A. NONE.

Adams (1818) declared, "Slavery, that bane of morals, and reproach of free governments, is hardly known in New England."

By the 1830's the denunciations against slavery softened. For example, Goodrich explained what kind of persons were made slaves, in saying, "The slaves procured by these ships are generally obtained of the petty sovereigns along the coast, who sell criminals and captives taken in war." Huntington (1835) wrote, "Many of the slaves are treated by their owners with a good degree of kindness and humanity, and often contented and cheerful, though in a state of lamentable ignorance." No doubt, the desire by the authors to sell their books also in the South did much to change their treatment of slavery.

Attitudes Toward Sectionalism. Due partly to the lack of tolerance of the times and partly to the fact that most of the earliest authors were New Englanders, or at least Northerners, it could be expected that considerable bias of sectionalism entered the early geographies. Morse (1790) defended the New Englanders against the accusation that they were "knavish, artful, and dishonest," in saying of them, "there is as great a proportion of honest and industrious citizens, as in any of the United States." Olney (1830) said of the New Englanders, "The people of these states are intelligent, moral, industrious, and enterprising. They rank first in each of the learned professions, with the best mechanics, best farmers, and best seamen in the country."

In the main, a favorable attitude was expressed toward the Middle Atlantic States, particularly the Dutch in New York. Morse (1800) wrote:

> Hence it is that the neatness, parsimony and industry of the Dutch were early imitated by the first English settlers in the province, and until the revolution, formed a distinguishing trait in their provincial character.

This favorable attitude toward the Dutch may have been due partly to the fact that they were fellow Calvinists with the Calvinistic authors of New England. However, several books were critical of the Pennsylvania Germans. Morse (1790), who quoted Kalm, said, "They are very well known for their avarice and selfishness," and are guilty "of working themselves to death." He also said that they were superstitious, but acknowledged that even though "they possess less refinement than their Southern neighbors, who cultivate their lands with slaves, they possess more republican virtue." Both Morse and Davies praise the Pennsylvanians for opposing slavery.

It was the South that was most critically treated. Parish (1810), who was a New England minister, compared the sections of the U.S., as follows:

> We now proceed to examine another section of the country. A new

shade of character commences. We shall no longer describe a hardy race of industrious farmers, living together on terms of equality. Instead of the social villages of New England, and the Middle States, their highly cultivated farms, and numerous flocks, and herds, we shall discover thinly scattered farm houses, some of them miserable hovels, and a few miles distant, a lofty mansion, surrounded by 100 negro huts; some of these wretched inhabitants are in rags, and some naked; some of them black, and partly white; an index of their morals.

Morse described the Virginians as "indolent, easy and good natured; extremely fond of society, and much given to convivial pleasures." The young men were referred to as "gamblers, cock-fighters, and horse-jockies." Davies (1805), Dwight (1806), and Smith (1816) criticized the severe social stratification and lack of democracy in the South. By the 1830's these unfavorable characterizations of the South greatly softened. Their comparisons became more objective and analytical. After the 1830's the treatment of the South became even more unbiased.

Racial and nationality attitudes. The earlier authors, whenever they dealt with the different races at all, usually considered the Caucasian race superior to the others. A typical treatment in a very popular textbook was that by Mitchell (1840), as follows:

The European or Caucasian is the most noble of the five races of men. It excels all others in learning and the arts, and includes the most powerful nations of ancient and modern times. The most valuable institutions of society, and the most important and useful inventions, have originated with the people of this race.

The Negro race was referred to as "ignorant and degraded." Morgan described them as exhibiting "a degradation which usually attends an enslaved condition." The Mongolians were sometimes rated as civilized and possessing much intellectual power, but little enterprise.

The characterizations of peoples by nationality were much more extensive and complete than by race. So the treatment here will necessarily be a mere sampling by authors and peoples. It will be noted that most of the characterizations on the surface appear to be very biased. The question to be raised here, however, may be whether the authors themselves really were so biased or whether the limited sources from which they derived their information were the real cause.

American Indian. The American Indian was sometimes characterized as savage, barbarous, warlike, and rude; yet he was also defended by several authors. Morse (1790) criticized the Europeans "who first visited these shores, treating the natives as wild beasts of the forest, which have no property in the woods where they roam." Adams (1818) and Smith (1839) both mentioned the bad as well as the good characteristics of the Indians. Huntington respected their fighting qualities.

Latin Americans. The attitudes expressed by a number of the early authors would hardly have developed a "Good Neighbor Policy" toward Latin America. Morse (1790) said:

> The Creoles (Mexicans) have all the bad qualities of the Spaniards, from whom they are descended, without the courage, firmness and patience, which make the praiseworthy part of the Spanish character. . . . From idleness and constitution, their whole business is amour and intrigue; Their ladies of consequence are not distinguished for their chastity or domestic virtues.

A number of later authors continued to be equally critical of the Mexicans. Huntington (1835) referred even to their whites as "ignorant, superstitious, indolent and profligate." Goodrich (1839) said, "The whites are vicious, and lead indolent and luxurious lives."

The South Americans received similar treatment. Smith (1816) said, "A white person (in Paraguay) will rather starve than work. . . . They will beg, rob, or murder, rather than work." Huntington (1835), in describing the Brazilians, said, "The love of gold and diamonds, and the love of sloth, are paramount to the love of liberty, learning, industry and virtue."

Several authors, however, said only good things about the people of Chile. The Aricanians of Northern Chile were praised "for their love of liberty, bravery, and humanity," by Olney in 1830. Griffen (1839) said, "Chile is inhabited by a population that appears to be superior in industry, enterprise, and skill, to the other inhabitants of South America."

Europeans. In dealing with the Europeans it must be kept in mind there are involved many nationalities and that there were many authors who wrote about them, so only a sampling of comments can be presented here. Since the earlier geographies were written soon after the Revolution, a number of writers were critical of England. Morse (1796) said, "Her wealth and power have made her proud and haughty; and, in consequence, her fall, by many, is predicted to be not far distant." However, a change of attitude took place, due partly to the increased trade with her and, no doubt, partly to the fact that most authors had an English ancestry. Dwight (1806) referred to the English as being of "good stature, shape, and complexion; the women are handsome and graceful in their appearance, beyond that of almost any country." Adams (1818) said, "The English appear to possess a mien between the gravity of the German, and the liveliness of the French," and Griffen (1839) referred to them as "intelligent, brave and industrious."

The Scots received favorable treatment from most authors. A number of characterizations were similar to the one by Cummings (1818), who described them as, "temperate, industrious, hardy, and valiant." More attention was given the Irish by a number of authors, and generally the treatment was sympathetic, due, no doubt in part, to what was considered by many Americans, to unfair treatment of Ireland by England. Goodrich (1839) mentioned how the British trade restrictions affected Dublin, and accordingly said, "The crowds of ragged and miserable wretches, who appear in every part of the city, however, tell a melancholy story of poverty and distress which exist within and around it." Cummings (1818) characterized the Irish as, "generally well made, strong, active, haughty, careless of their lives, and greedy of glory; quick of apprehension, courteous of strangers, and often violent in their passions."

The characterizations of the German people were mixed, but more favorable than unfavorable. Davies (1805) wrote, "The Saxons are a lively and contented people; the Prussians dull and gloomy." Dwight (1806) said that they were "fond of show and parade in their dress." Woodbridge (1835) wrote, "The *people* are generally well instructed, industrious, and moral, except in some eastern provinces." Griffen (1839) prophetically said, "The Prussians are chiefly distinguished as a military nation."

The Austrians were described much like the Germans. A teacher (1836) said, "They resemble the Germans. They are patient, good natured, love to smoke, and make fine music." The Hungarians, the other people of the dual monarchy, received little praise. Mention by a number of authors referred to them as a strong and robust people, who, however, were rude, revengeful, and warlike.

The Swiss, most of them being Germanic in type, strongly Protestant and republican in spirit, received more universal praise than any European people. For example, Woodbridge (1835) said, "The Swiss are generally well educated, and are remarkable for their bravery, industry, and virtue."

Worcester (1822) described the Dutch as "industrious and honest but not beautiful." Goodrich (1839) said of them, "Smoking tobacco is practiced by both sexes at all hours; and as the Dutch are said to be ever ruminating on ways and means to get money, they are represented as very unsociable."

The Scandinavians, composed of the Swedes, Norwegians, and Danes, received mixed treatment, at first rather unfavorable and later mostly favorable. O'Neill (1816) said of the Danes, "Many of the peasantry continue in a state of vassalage; they are consequently idle, dirty, and dispirited." The Norwegians were described as honest, brave, and industrious. The Swedes received the most favorable treatment. Smith (1816) described them as "peaceable, seldom guilty of atrocious crimes, correct in their judgment, fond of convivial entertainments."

The Russian nation, in general, received the same treatment by the earlier authors as it is receiving today in the American press. Russia was condemned for defeating and taking territory from Sweden and partitioning Poland. Morse (1796) referred to the Russian government as "despotic, and the great body of the people are in a state of barbarism." Parish (1810) said, "The Russian husbands are unkind and cruel to a proverb," and Adams (1818) referred to the rule of the Czar as absolute.

The treatment of the peoples in the Romance nations was

mostly unfavorable. Of these, the French, no doubt partly due to their help during the American Revolution, received the best treatment, but not fully favorable. Certain extreme acts committed by them were condemned. Adams (1818) wrote, "Louis XVI was dethroned, and, contrary to every principle of humanity and injustice, in January, 1793, was beheaded," and Dwight (1806) referred to Napoleon as a "usurper." Most authors were more complimentary regarding the character of the French people than of their political actions. O'Neill (1816) wrote, "The French are polite, vivacious, and brave; but their levity has often led them into excesses which have proved ruinous to their national prosperity." Several other authors characterized them similarly.

The treatment given the Italians was mostly unfavorable in nature. Morse (1790) said, "They are amorous and addicted to criminal indulgences, revengeful, and masters of the art of dissimulation." Parish (1810) referred to the Sardinians as seizing "every opportunity to rob and murder." Olney, in 1830, offered a mixed characterization, in saying, "The Italians are affable and polite; and excel in music, painting, and sculpture; but they are effeminate, superstitious, slavish, and revengeful."

The treatment of Spaniards was mixed, but not very favorable. Morse (1796) said, "Spain might be one of the richest countries in Europe were it not that the inhabitants are indolent and unenterprising." In a later edition Morse (1800) said, "no deceit, no cruelty was too great to be made use of, to satisfy their avarice." On the other hand O'Neill (1816), even though admitting their cruelty at times, said "their treatment of prisoners of war has often been humane and generous." Other authors described them as brave and generous at times, but also haughty and bigoted.

Asiatics. Most of the Asiatics were given a more or less unfavorable characterization by a number of the early authors. Dwight (1806), who copied his description of the Turks from an English geography by William Guthrie (1792), said they were "indolent and superstitious, but commonly temperate. They are heavy, morose, treacherous, furiously passionate, unsocial, and unfriendly to people of other nations." Goodrich's treatment of them as late as 1839 was little better. Dwight was critical of the Arabs, in saying, "The word Arab signifies robber; and they answer perfectly to the name." However, Smith (1839) acknowledged, due to their belief in the Koran, that they were free from drunkenness and gaming.

The treatment of the Persians was mixed. Several early geographies contained tolerant treatment, but several later authors were quite critical. Woodbridge (1835) referred to them as "indolent, timid, and superstitious." Contrary to what one would find in a modern geography, the people of India received little attention in the early geographies. Different authors characterized the Chinese as being vain, artful, timid, jealous, and vindictive. However, Woodbridge (1835) was considerate enough to say that they were "ingenious and industrious."

*   *   *   *   *

On the whole, Sahli, who analyzed the American geographies before 1840, found that many of the authors expressed critical attitudes and characterizations of the peoples of many countries of the world. No doubt, such treatment was due to a number of reasons, among them nationalistic, racial, and religious biases held by the writers of these books. On the other hand, Culler, who analyzed the geographies from 1840 to 1890, found few such unfavorable attitudes expressed. No doubt, greater tolerance and objectivity on the part of the authors made for more favorable treatment.

TEACHING AND LEARNING AIDS

The first state teacher training and normal school established in the United States was at Lexington, Massachusetts, in 1839. Since forty-one of the geographies analyzed by Sahli were published before that date, it was not unexpected to have many of the authors present plans and suggestions as to how their texts should be taught. Cummings' (1818) book contained fourteen and one-half pages devoted to teaching methods. Woodbridge (1836) addressed a page to "Inexperienced Teachers," in which he enumerated ten specific steps for teaching geography.

Teaching methods. An analysis of geography textbooks reveals a variety of teaching methods, either definitely suggested by the authors or implied from the organization or presentation of the subject matter. The variety is due, no doubt, to the kind of method favored by the different authors personally, in part to the changing views on method with the passing of time, and to the acceptance of certain educational theories, for example, Pestalozzianism. The methods most commonly suggested or implied were the following:

Catechetical. Due to the strong influence of religion when the earlier books were written, many authors modeled their books on the catechetical part of the *New England Primer.* Among the early books which were written by the "question and answer" method, in whole or part, were those by Dwight, John Smith, Olney, Mitchell, Roswell Smith, and Goodrich. This was particularly true of primary geographies, after books were published in series. After 1840 this method decreased. Culler found that only 10 of the 97 geographies after 1840 used this method, and only one after 1860.

Correlation. Correlating the study of geography with the subject of reading, spelling, history, and numbers, was suggested by a number of early authors. Cummings (1818) said, "Whenever words occur in (geography) reading, whose signification is not perfectly well known, they should be marked with a lead pencil, or a pen, carefully looked up in a dictionary, and prepared to be given at recitation." The same author also said, "The history of any country without a knowledge of its geography, loses its reality, and to youth appears almost visionary." Mitchell, whose books were very popular, held similar views. Emma Willard correlated it with numbers, in suggesting:

> For example, the number 4 placed near a river, indicates that the river is 4 times the length of the Connecticut River. The length being reckoned at 400 miles, we have at once the real as well as the comparative length of the river.

After 1840 correlation was suggested by fewer authors.

Deductive method. The plan of beginning with general principles and then applying them to specifics was used only by a few of the early authors. However, it was used in many geographies after 1840, continuing until 1890. The plan was to study the continent as a whole first, then the countries, and next such details, as

> their boundaries, their extent, their rivers, lakes and mountains, their islands, civil divisions, and chief towns; and, to assist his memory, a uniform arrangement of these subjects has been carefully preserved: a short enumeration of natural productions, and of manufactures closes the geographical description of each country. (Bazeley, 1830).

Inductive method. This method reverses the procedure; namely, it goes from the particular to the general, from the known to the unknown. This was the plan strongly advocated by that great Swiss educator, Johann Pestalozzi (1746-1827). He referred to it as the "Home Geography" approach. His ideas began to be accepted by certain American geography writers during the 1820's. Woodbridge was the first to do so in 1822. Emma Willard (1826) said, "Instead of commencing the study of maps with the map of the world, which is the most difficult to understand, the pupil here begins, in the most simple manner imaginable, to draw the map of his own town." Olney (1830) said, "The learner must make himself master of simple things, before he can understand those which are complex." Other authors to use this approach, whose books were widely used, were Goodrich, Guyot, Fitch, and Hall.

Laboratory method. A later developed method used by several authors was to provide real experiences by having the pupils secure geographic information by direct observation or by doing things in relation to geography in the school. Guyot (1866) was the first to follow this approach. In the Preface there is stated, "The best possible plan will be to take them occasionally into the fields for a lesson." In Appleton's *Elementary Geography* (1880) there was suggested the making of relief maps with modeling sand. This teaching approach was a distinct departure from the most common earlier methods.

Use of visual aids and maps. In a subject like geography, where the need for eye training is great, it is important to determine to what extent visual aids are provided in the textbooks. Such aids may take the form of pictures, maps, drawings, graphs, and so on. An analysis of 146 geographies up to 1890 reveals that not nearly all contained visual aids. Only 25 of the 49 texts before 1840 contained maps, while every one but one contained them after 1860. Picture illustrations were in even fewer early books, in only 17 of the early 49 texts. Eighty-one of the 97 after 1840 contained illustrations. Graphs or diagrams were used in the same number of books as maps; namely 105 of the 146.

Questions. More books included questions than any other learning aid; namely, 126. In many of the earlier books these took the form of a catechism. However, later they were placed in the books in different ways, and related to different matters. Sahli found that 47.8 per cent were map questions, and 51.8 per cent related to reading matter, and a few to statistical data. Culler's study of the later geographies reveals that 74.9 per cent were map questions, 22 per cent related to reading content, and 2.9 per cent were about statistical matters. Sahli found that the words with which most questions began in order of frequency were: "What," "How," "Where," "Which," and "Describe." Culler found that the later books did not contain nearly so many questions, and the beginning words most commonly used in order of frequency were: "How," "Describe," "For," and "By." It should be noted that the nature of the questions must have changed radically.

Prefaces and introductions. Next to questions, prefaces appeared more frequently than any other aid; namely, in 125 of the 146 books. Prefatory content commonly dealt with reasons for writing the book, improvements in their books, criticism of other books, recognition of sources and materials, and, especially in the earlier books, suggestions for the more effective teaching or learning of the book. Fifty-nine books contained introductions. Nearly all books included either a preface or an introduction, and 47 had both. The introductions, too, were used for various purposes. One purpose was to motivate the study of geography by arousing an interest in it and acquaint the reader with the field and the purpose of the book. A few presented definitions in the introduction. In general, its purpose was to aid the teacher or the pupil or both in mastering the study of geography.

MOST POPULAR GEOGRAPHIES

Geography was given little attention in our colonial schools. Noah Webster, in a letter to Henry Barnard, wrote:

> When I was young, the books used were chiefly or wholly Dilworth's Spelling books, the Psalter, Testament and Bible. No geography was studied before the publication of Dr. Morse's small books on the subject.

Thus the treatment of geographies will begin with Morse. However, since the writer's collection contains approximately 350 geographies and atlases written by 113 different authors, it would be unwise to attempt to discuss all of them. Only those authors whose textbooks appeared in many editions will be discussed.

Reverend Jedidiah Morse (1761-1826). The first American author of a geography, as was true of many other early textbooks was a minister. The ministers were commonly the most highly educated persons in early American history. *Geography Made Easy* by Morse was published in New Haven in 1784. Apparently this text became rather popular, for it appeared in numerous editions. It was addressed:

> To the Young Gentlemen and Ladies, throughout the United States. This Compendious System of Geography, (a Science, no longer esteemed as a polite and agreeable accomplishment only, but as a necessary and important Part of Education)—is, with the most
> > Ardent wishes
> > for their improvement
> > dedicated and devoted
> > by their very
> > humble servant
> > The Author

Morse was graduated from Yale in 1783 and the following year

38   PENNSYLVANIA.

public, as well as private buildings. The bank of the United
States is doubtless the most chaste and elegant edifice in this

Scene in Philadelphia.

country. The Fair Mount water-works, by which the city is
supplied with water from the Schuylkill, is a most useful and ingenious construction. The daily expense of this establishment,
by which such prodigious quantities of water are raised from the
river, as to supply this great city, is very trifling. Philadelphia
contains 60 houses of public worship, several extensive and valuable public libraries, and many benevolent literary and scientific institutions. Population, 200,000.

View of Pittsburg.

Pittsburg, situated at the confluence of the Monongahela and
Alleghany, is the centre of an extensive trade, and is one of the

Mention some of its most remarkable public buildings and works. What is the population? How many houses of public worship in Philadelphia? What public institutions?
How is Pittsburg situated?

School Geography, 1831, Pennsylvania chapter.

published his geography. For more than thirty years he was the pastor of the First Church (Congregational), Charlestown, Massachusetts. Apparently his calling was the ministry, but his real interest was the writing of books in the fields of geography and history.

His *Geography Made Easy* had 214 pages 3½ by 6 inches in size, and included several folded uncolored maps. The small pages contained an average of 38 lines and ten words per line. The print was very small, 7 point type. The content was presented very factually, without the aid of pictures. However, the content was presented in an organized and systematized way. For example, the geography of the United States was divided by states, and then the facts about each state was treated under such headings as *divisions, counties, towns, rivers, climate, soil, produce, inhabitants and their character, government, religion, history,* and *curiosities.* However, it contained no specific table of contents, index, glossary, pictures, or questions. Under "curiosities" in Pennsylvania it described a mound of earth 100 miles below Pittsburgh 216 feet in height and 621 feet in circumference. This was inaccurate, for this mound was what is now Moundsville, West Virginia, but then was in Virginia.

Morse published *The American Universal Geography* in 1789; *Elements of Geography* in 1795; and *A New System of Modern Geography* in 1822, which was written jointly with his son Sidney Morse. These were larger than his first book.

Incidentally, Jedidiah Morse had three famous sons. Samuel F. B. Morse was a famous artist and the inventor of the first telegraph; Sidney E. Morse was a journalist, geographer, and inventor; and R. C. Morse, with Sidney, founded the *New York Observer* in 1823.

Nathaniel Dwight. In 1795 Dwight wrote *A Short but Comprehensive System of the Geography of the World.* This was a book of 216 pages in fine print. The last one-third of it dealt with the Americas. Throughout it was like a catechism consisting of questions and answers. It appeared in at least four editions. Under the "natural curiosities" of Pennsylvania it referred to *"Oil Creek,* on whose water floats an oil similar to the Barbados tar."

Minor Geographies: 1800-1820. During these twenty years geography textbooks were written by Benjamin Davies (1804), Joseph Scott (1807), John Hubbard (1807), Elijah Parish (1810), J. A. Cummins (1813), Benjamin Gleason (1814), Jacob Willetts (1814), John O'Neil (1816), John Smith (1816), Daniel Adams (1818), and J. E. Worcester (1819). Of these the textbooks by Parish, Cummins, Willetts, Adams, and Worcester appeared in more than one edition.

Jesse Olney (1798-1872). His educational career was largely spent in New York and Connecticut. He became a prolific textbook writer, writing readers, arithmetics, and histories, as well as geographies. His *Practical System of Modern Geography* first was published in 1828. The 1851 printing of this book was the sixty-third edition. Olney's was the first popular geography to follow the Morse books.

This book of nearly 300 pages was much more attractively prepared than most of its predecessors, containing many interesting pictures and many instructive tables. Its questions were arranged to check on the mastery of the content. The later editions were revisions of the first.

Peter Parley (S. G. Goodrich) (1793-1860). Goodrich wrote textbooks in reading, history, spelling, science, and geography. Of these his histories and geographies gained widest circulation. In 1831 he published the *Child's Book of American Geography* and *A System of School Geography.* Then in 1840 there appeared *A Pictorial Geography of the World,* and in 1844 *Peter Parley's Geography for Be-*

PARLEY'S

GEOGRAPHY FOR BEGINNERS.

Lesson I. .... What Geography means.

1. In this book I propose to tell you about *Geography;* but, before we proceed, please to look at a few pictures. Here you see a youth who has set forth upon a journey: for convenience, we will call him Thomas.

2. You will perceive that Thomas, as he goes along, sees a variety of objects, such as a carriage, a man on horseback, cattle in a field, trees, and houses   On the next page is another picture.

A pleasant illustrated children's geography, 1831.

ginners. All of these appeared in many editions. For example, the 1839 printing of his *System* was the twenty-seventh edition.

All of Peter Parley's textbooks were characterized by their attractiveness and the inclusion of numerous pictures. For example, the *Child's Book* contained 60 pictures and 18 maps. Up to that time no geographies were so well graded and illustrated. No wonder that they appealed to children.

Roswell Smith. In 1835 he published his *Geography on the Productive System.* This book, like Dwight's, was meant to be taught inductively. The first 100 pages are largely devoted to questions and answers. Then larger sections of content are presented factually and followed by questions at the end of sections. The book contains some pictures, but no maps. Separately he published an *Atlas.* Both books appeared in many editions. The 1857 book was the forty-first edition. He also published, in 1846, *An Introductory Geography.*

Minor Geographies, 1820-1840. Many geographies appeared during those twenty years. Books by the following authors appeared in more than one edition: Sidney Morse (1822), William Woodbridge (1823), J. L. Blake (1826), S. R. Hall (1828), Nathaniel Huntington (1833), Samuel Butler (1834), and probably others.

Augustus Mitchell. The geographies written by Mitchell apparently had the widest circulation of any appearing in the United States before 1900. The writer's collection contains 47 different copies under seven different titles. The first was *A System of Modern Geography* in 1839, and the lastest bears the date, 1895. Thus the period of their circulation covered more than 50 years. Of these seven different books the *System* apparently was the most popular, for the collection contains fifteen of them.

In make-up and size it was similar to Smith's *Productive System.* The first 50 pages were like a catechism of questions and answers. Then there were 25 pages of map questions in fine print. These were questions about the maps in the *Atlas.* The remainder of the book was descriptive geography about the different countries of the world, with questions at the end of each section. It contained more than 300 pages 4 by 6½ inches, and included many small pictures.

Next most popular were Mitchell's lower books; namely, his *Primary, New-Primary,* and *First Lessons in Geography.* His *Intermediate, Ancient,* and *School* geographies were less widely used. However, all of these went through several editions. His later books were larger in dimensions and contained colored maps. Mitchell apparently attempted to understand what kinds of geographies the schools wanted and then prepared them accordingly.

Arnold Guyot (1807-1884). Guyot was born and reared in Switzerland, where he was influenced by Karl Ritter's views about geography. After teaching physical geography there for ten years he came to America, where for six years he was employed by the Massachusetts State Board of Education as a lecturer on geography in their normal schools. It is claimed that he brought to America the rudiments of geography as a science.

In 1849 he published *The Earth and Man.* This book immediately gained wide acceptance. In it he attempted to relate the cultural elements of geography to the natural, which is the approach now followed in most modern geographies. Thus he was a forerunner in developing a new and meaningful approach in teaching geography. However, it contained no maps. It implied the use of an atlas. It was a rather advanced book.

Later Guyot wrote other texts to provide a graded series of geographies. In 1866 he published a *Primary,* and a *Common School Geography.* Still later he prepared an *Elementary,* an *Intermediate,* and a *Grammar School Geography.* His geographies continued to appear until the 1880's. His later books became very large, containing many pictures and maps to assist the pupils to relate the cultural elements to the natural.

S. S. Cornell. In 1854 she published her *Primary,* in 1855 an *Intermediate,* and in 1856 the *High School Geography.* These, she claimed, formed a "systematic series of school geographies." In the Preface of the *Primary Geography* she criticized other geographies for employing unexplained terms, "burying up of what, at present, only was attainable, by that which should be the very last learned," and "rendering maps, professedly intended to elucidate," as "Labyrinths of Perplexity." This book was very attractive, with many pictures, and a few simple colored maps. It was written on the inductive plan.

Most series of three did not specify the third part to be a *High School* book. It was different from the two lower books. Its outside dimensions were smaller and the number of pages greater. It contained 405 pages; the lower ones had fewer than 100 each. It contained many pictures but no maps. Questions appeared at the end of each section. All three went into many editions. Later Cornell wrote other geographies, but they failed to become popular.

James Monteith. In 1854 he published his *First Lessons in Geography.* This was a simple and attractive little book. It went through several revisions and editions until well after 1900. The later editions were planned on the "Object Teaching" approach, emphasizing an appeal to the eyes in addition to what may be derived from the reading material.

In 1856 the *Manual of Geography* appeared. This was a book of 112 pages, 7½ by 9 inches. It contained many pictures and maps. Throughout it was more or less in catechetical form. Later this book was enlarged, and in 1857 an *Introduction to the Manual* was published. Thus the series consisted of three books. These books also appeared in many editions.

Other Geographies. A number of other authors wrote geographies between 1850 and 1900 which gained considerable circulation. Francis McNally published *An Improved System of Geography* in 1855, which continued in different editions until the late 1870's.

In 1870 M. F. Maury published his *Manual of Geography.* He also wrote an *Elementary* and a *Physical Geography.* All of these want into several printings.

In 1875 Harper's *School Geography* was published. This was a large and attractive book with many pictures and colored maps. It was descriptive, with questions at the end of sections. Two years later Harper's published an *Introductory Geography* to precede the other. This was similar in nature and approach, but smaller. Both continued to have considerable circulation even through the 1880's.

Also in 1875 William Swinton published an *Elementary Course in Geography*. This was followed by the *Grammar-School Geography* in 1880. Apparently he soon realized that the *Elementary* was not well received, so he replaced it with the *Introductory Geography*. These geographies never became as popular as the textbooks by Swinton in other fields, such as reading and composition.

In 1880 the Appleton Series of geographies began to appear. The *Elementary* and the *Higher Geographies* appeared first. Then later the *Lessons in Geography for Little Learners* was published. The authorship of these, as well as of the Harper texts, was not identified. Each series was named after the publisher. Neither series became popular.

Beginning in 1887 geographies by Jacques Redway and R. Hinman appeared. These appeared under five different titles, several of which continued to appear even after 1900.

Many other geographies were written during the last half of the nineteenth century, but received few adoptions.

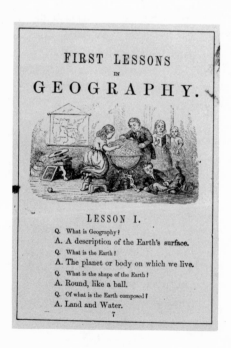

FIRST LESSONS
IN
GEOGRAPHY.

LESSON I.

Q. What is Geography?
A. A description of the Earth's surface.
Q. What is the Earth?
A. The planet or body on which we live.
Q. What is the shape of the Earth?
A. Round, like a ball.
Q. Of what is the Earth composed?
A. Land and Water.

7

CONCLUDING COMMENTS

The textbooks in no other field changed so in size from the earliest to the latest as geographies. For example, the pages of the 1796 of the *Elements of Geography* by Morse were 3⅛ by 5 inches, while in

Monteith, *First Lessons in Geography*, 1854—note question and answer format.

a late edition of Guyot's *Grammar School Geography* they were 10 by 12½ inches. Thus the latter was eight times the size of the former.

Another feature was that the catechetical approach was more common and continued longer than in the textbooks of any other field. Naturally the type of questions varied from author to author. Those questions which were rather factual evidently led to much memory learning. On the other hand, thoughtful questions of an inductive nature must have resulted in a meaningful understanding of geography.

Today we always expect a geography textbook to contain maps. Yet this was far from universally true in the past. Twenty-four of the 49 texts before 1840 analyzed by Sahli contained no maps. Even ten of the 97 analyzed by Culler between 1840 and 1890 had no maps. In most cases, however, the authors of these geographies had atlases to accompany their texts.

CHAPTER 7

———··❦··———

AMERICAN HISTORIES

A LATE ARRIVAL

AMERICAN history as a school subject seems to have been a laggard in entering the American school curriculum. Several reasons may be given. When such subjects as religion, reading, spelling, and geography were being introduced in the schools during the colonial period, there was no unity among the colonies, and hence no common American government. The interest of most early settlers was mostly only in their own colony. A common interest did not develop until the Revolution and later. Too, not a sufficient number of significant historical events were known or recognized in the area that now constitutes the United States to provide a common body of knowledge to compose such a school subject as American history.

While only eight or nine American history textbooks were published in our country before 1820, and apparently none had a wide circulation, this does not necessarily mean that children in our schools learned no American history. In fact they must have been exposed to considerable historical content, but mostly through their study of other kinds of textbooks. The two subjects through which historical content was most often presented were reading and geography. A number of the early readers contained many historical reading selections. This was particularly true of Noah

Webster's *An American Selection of Lessons in Reading and Speaking.* This was the Third Part of Webster's Grammatical Institute of the English Language. It went through a number of editions, each of which contained considerable historical content. About one-half of the third edition (1787) was historical, which content later became a part of McCulloch's textbook on history. Caleb Bingham's *Columbian Orator* (1806), which became even more popular than Webster's reader, contained many selections which were political and historical in character.

The other field in which the early textbooks presented much historical material was geography. In fact most of the early geographies were a combination of geography, history, and what is now known as civics. This continued to be true from Morse's first book in 1784 until the 1820's, when separate textbooks of history became more or less common. Thereafter the content in the geographies became generally only geography.

THE FIRST AMERICAN HISTORY TEXTBOOK

The first book written to be used to teach United States history was published in 1795 by John M'Culloch, a printer who had come from Scotland to Philadelphia in 1774. He first published an *Introduction to the History of America*, in 1787, but its contents consisted, as he said, mainly of "a collection of public papers, a short sketch of the war, and a few other detached articles," and apparently was

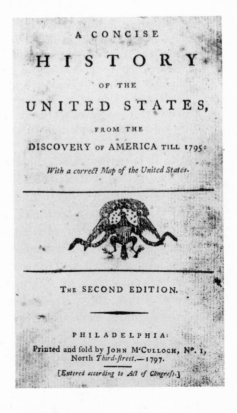

Second Edition, first American history textbook (1492-1795).

not intended as a textbook. The 1795 book was entitled *A Concise History of the U.S. from the Discovery of America till 1795.* It was this edition which apparently was compiled to be used as a textbook. At least, in the preface of the slightly enlarged second edition of 1797 its use was suggested "especially for schools, and to such as had not time to peruse larger works." The book appeared under the same title, but slightly enlarged, as a third edition in 1807 and a fourth edition in 1813.

Since no author's name appeared on the title pages of these editions, but only the printer's name, John M'Culloch, it prompted the question of the authorship of the content of these books. This question has been answered in a dissertation written by Alice W. Spieseke,[1] in which she shows that it appears as though M'Culloch copied all or nearly all of the content from other printed sources. Such practice was more or less common during that period, due to the absence of copyright laws. Miss Spieseke, in her conclusion states:

> Considering M'Culloch's lack of training, it is remarkable that he used as good sources of information as he did. The writer is inclined to believe that this was a matter of chance, rather than the result of research. He used what was at hand, which happened to be Barlow, Webster, Ramsay, Gordon, and Carver, public papers of various kinds, and almanacs. Of the writers, three of them—Ramsay, Gordon and Carver—were accepted as reliable historians in their day, at least by most of the people. (p. 104.)

Yet it is rather remarkable that M'Culloch was able to piece together so many borrowed selections from varied sources and produce a rather orderly and balanced treatment of American history suitable as a textbook. In fact, it appears that the four editions of his *Concise History* set a pattern for later American history textbooks. They included treatment of eight of the nine topics under which the contents of American history textbooks have been analyzed, as shown later in a table appearing in this chapter. Too, the percentages of the content devoted to the different topics correspond rather closely to the average per-

---

[1] *The First Textbooks in American History and Their Compiler, John M'Culloch.* (N.Y. Bureau of Publications. Columbia University. 1938.)

centages for 54 texts before 1886. The chief deviation was a lesser treatment on colonial history and more on governmental matters.

AIMS OF AMERICAN HISTORY TEXTBOOKS

Most old textbooks contained a preface in which the author stated why the text was written and what he expected the study or use of it to accomplish. In explaining why it was written the author usually mentioned something about the nature of the content, how it was arranged, and how it was to be used or taught. Such explanations constituted more a justification for the writing of another textbook than for the study of American history, and so may be called textbook aims.

Textbook aims. A lucid example of a textbook aim may be quoted from Peter Parley's *First Book of History of the United States* (1848), as follows:

> The common method is to begin at the earliest date, and follow down the train of events to the present time. The author of this work has partially reversed this method. He begins with the individual states of our country, and first exhibits their present condition. He then notices a few recent events, and having fixed the attention of the reader upon the subject, proceeds to detail its history.

The same author, whose real name was S. G. Goodrich, in a later and more advanced book entitled, *Pictorial History of the United States* (1850), said:

> Two plans have been adopted: one called the ethnographic, which presents each colony or settlement separately; and one called chronographic, which blends the several subjects in one general view, and carries them all forward with the advance of years.

He then proceeded to explain that his text used "a combination of the two systems, so far as to secure the advantages of both."

Other authors mentioned other matters about the merits of their books, such as the arrangement of the material into epochs; presenting the events of history with clearness, accuracy, and truthfulness; conciseness; use of maps, charts, and illustrations; the use of side notes for the reader's convenience; the use of questions; the correlation of geography and history; the omission of minor details; and its adaption for purposeful instruction. Thus each new appearing history textbook claimed some merit to increase its sale.

Historical aims. Many purposes for the teaching of history have been mentioned in the prefaces of American history textbooks. These purposes were somewhat different in the earlier books, where their usefulness for arousing proper attitudes in youth was stressed. A few brief quotations will illustrate the more emphasized virtues.

1. Character training. The earlier books more so than the later ones stressed the training of character. Emma Willard in her *Abridged History of the United States* (1846), said:

> We have, indeed, been desirous to cultivate the memory, the intellect, and the taste. But much more anxious have we been to sow the seeds of virtue, by showing the good in such amiable lights, that the youthful heart shall kindle into desires of imitation.

Peter Parley's *First Book of History* (1848) said history "relates to us what has been done by mankind, . . . (and) acquaints us with the existence of good, and shows us how to attain it." A much more recent book stated this aim somewhat differently. Guitteau, in his *Our United States, A History* (1924), said:

> History is the lamp by whose light we see human nature in action; and we can understand causes. The significance, the results of events in proportion to our comprehension of the character of men or natures conceived.

In fact, the purpose mentioned most frequently in various ways was to present clearly those deeds which may properly be imitated.

2. Patriotism and good citizenship. One of the earliest books to have considerable circulation was Hale's *History of the United States* (1835) in which he said:

> It is the purpose of this work to exhibit, in a strong light, the princi-

ples of political and religious freedom which our forefathers professed, and for which they fought and conquered; to record the numerous examples of fortitude, courage, and patriotism which have rendered them illustrious.

C. A. Goodrich (1828) said that the end of all reading, particularly history, is to make "good men and citizens." Similar comments were made by many authors. A much later book: namely, Hamm, Bourne, and Benton's *A Unit History of the United States* claimed "the chief justification of American history in the curriculum is to stimulate the growing citizens of the nation to think honestly and efficiently about the problems of modern life."

3. Improvement of memory and thinking. A considerable number of authors, particularly the earlier ones, commented how the study of history would help improve the memory, especially by committing important dates and events. On the other hand, the later authors stress more often the development of thinking and recognition of causes and effects. For example, Mace's *American History* (1925) said:

> One of the fundamental ideas in history is continuity. In every series of historical facts the student must look not only for connection between the individual events of the series but for the connection which this series has with some other series.

Freeland's *America's Progress in Civilization* (1936) said the chief purpose is "to make a citizen better equipped to face realities, (and) to see their relationships to everything that surrounds them."

Many other aims have been mentioned by one or more authors, but the above mentioned purposes were those most frequently mentioned.

ORGANIZATION OF AMERICAN HISTORY TEXTBOOKS

C. D. Jacobs,[2] who analyzed 54 American history textbooks

---

2 "The Development of School Textbooks in United States History from 1795 to 1885." (Unpublished Doctor's Dissertation, University of Pittsburgh, 1939.)

published before 1886, found that these books were organized in various ways in presenting the subject matter. Thirty-nine books presented the content by chapters, 16 by periods, 12 in parts, 7 in sections, 2 by epochs, and 1 by lessons. Thus some authors used more than one plan. The most common combination was to divide the book into parts and then to divide the parts into chapters. There was great variation how minutely the material was divided. For example, one of Goodrich's books (1850) contained 200 chapters, and another of his books (1831) contained 453 sections.

James Rial,[3] who analyzed 64 books after 1885, likewise found great variation. Forty-six presented the content by chapters, 16 by units, 14 by parts, 9 by sections, 2 by divisions, 2 by epochs, 2 by topics, and 1 by problems. A number of those divided into parts were further divided either into chapters or sections. West's text (1918) contained 70 chapters and 912 sections. These data show very clearly that there has been no common practice in the plan of organizing the content of American history textbooks.

NATURE OF CONTENT

Jacobs analyzed 54 textbooks published before 1886 under the following nine headings: aboriginal history; exploration and discovery; colonial history; war content; travel and transportation; industrial progress and inventions; government and political content; social, recreation, religion, and education; territorial and westward expansion; and slavery. Rial used the same nine headings and added the treatment of world relations as a tenth. The average per cents of subject matter devoted to the different topics by periods are presented in Table VI.

An examination of the percentages in this table reveals a number of interesting facts, changes, and trends. There is marked variation in the amount of average space given to the different topics. For example, Jacobs found that before 1886, the texts devoted nearly 45 per cent to war and over 19 per cent to government and politics. On the other hand, less than two per cent of the space was given to each of four other topics. The 6.4 per cent

---

3 Unpublished materials.

given to exploration and discovery was third highest. However, Rial found that for 41 textbooks during the 1926-1942 period only 18.8 per cent of the space was devoted to war. The percentage dealing with government and politics rose to 35.4 during the 1906-1925 period. The later books devoted less space to aboriginal history and more to transportation, industrial development, social and educational matters, territorial expansion, slavery, and world relations.

In addition to the studies by Jacobs and by Rial, which dealt primarily only with elementary school American history textbooks, Caputo[4] analyzed 87 American history textbooks most commonly used in junior high schools. Although the primary purpose of the present book is to deal only with old textbooks used in the common or elementary schools, the lower grades of the junior high school traditionally belonged to the elementary level, so it may be pertinent to present a summary of his findings about their content.

Caputo reported the findings under twenty headings rather than under eleven used by Rial. According to Caputo on the average the following per cents of space were devoted to the twenty topics: Aborigines, 1.2; European backgrounds, 1.3; discovery and exploration, 6.3; colonial history, 18.5; government and politics, 13.8; foreign relations, 5.0; travel and transportation, 3.0; industrial progress, 5.2; inventions, 1.4; economics, 4.2; territorial expansion, 5.3; war, 20.1; slavery, 3.4; immigration, 1.0; social aspects, 2.1; religion, 0.1; education, 0.9; recreation, 0.2; world peace, 0.8; and miscellaneous, 6.0. At a glance, it can be seen that these texts devoted much less space to war and politics and more to industrial progress and economics, and particularly more to social and cultural matters than in Jacobs' study.

ABORIGINAL HISTORY

More than two-thirds of the books before 1886 devoted some

---

[4] Frank R. Caputo, "Development of Junior High School American History Textbooks from 1886 to 1954." (Unpublished doctoral dissertation, University of Pittsburgh, 1956.)

space to aboriginal history, while only 41 per cent of those after 1886 did so. One of Noah Webster's books (1835) devoted 18.5 per cent to it. The nature of the treatment by those who included it varied. Some claimed the original American inhabitants were of a different race than those of the old world. Others thought the American Indians descended from the Antedeluvians who survived the deluge. Still others thought they may have come from Asia via the Bering Straits. Mention was even made that some earlier people inhabited America before the Indians. Various evidences, such as paintings and engravings in caves, mounds, and earth works, and so on, possibly attest to their superiority to the Indians. All such discussion, however, was speculative.

The attention given the Indians was often detailed. Many books specifically named the more important tribes, particularly of the eastern part of the country. Reference was frequently made to their characteristics, manners and customs, government, and

TABLE VI

AVERAGE PER CENT OF SUBJECT MATTER OF AMERICAN HISTORY TEXTBOOKS
BY PERIODS DEVOTED TO EACH TOPIC.[1]

Periods	Number of Books	Aboriginal History	Exploration and Discovery	Colonial History	War Content	Travel and Transportation	Inventions and Industry	Government and Politics	Cultural	Territorial Expansion	Slavery	World Relations
		1	2	3	4	5	6	7	8	9	10	11
1797-1825	5	4.3	4.2	18	53.8	0		.3	15	1.6	2.7	0
1826-1845	11	2.7	3.5	21	49.4	.2		.9	18.2	2.	1.8	.3
1846-1865	15	2.9	7.1	26.7	40.1	.07	1.4	16.3	1.2	3.3	.5	
1866-1885	23	3.5	7.7	18.9	43.9	.05	.8	22.2	1.	1.4	1.4	
1886-1905	10	2.6	4.8	15.3	26.8	1.2	2.	29.	7.1	5.4	4.7	1.1
1906-1925	13	.8	3.7	17.5	20.4	1.7	3.5	35.4	5.4	4.3	5.5	2.
1926-1942	41	.8	5.2	12.1	18.8	3.	8.9	26.	9.6	5.2	4.6	5.6

[1] Above data derived from studies by Jacobs and Rial.

religion. They were frequently characterized as "wild," "treacherous," "brutal," "cruel," "barbarous," "uncivilized," "lazy,"
and as leaving a trail of "fire and blood." Mention was made that
they would fight not only the white men, but would enter an
Indian village of another tribe, while the men were away hunting,
and massacre the old men, women, and children, or make prisoners of those useful to their nation.

Under manners and customs mention was made of their wig-
wams, dress, social customs, and habits of work. Goodrich in
1831 wrote:

> The employments of the men were principally hunting, fishing, and
> war. The women dressed the food; took charge of the domestic con-
> cerns; tilled the narrow scanty fields; and performed almost all the
> drudgery connected with their household affairs.

Even though the later books either omitted treatment of the
Indians or were less derogatory of them, yet the Barnes histories,
which were very popular from the first edition in 1871 to as late
as the 1920's, were rather critical of the Indians. The Barnes
texts were really written by Joel D. Steele and his wife Esther
Baker Steele, but published by the A. S. Barnes Co. After describing the Indians as "brave and alert," they referred to them
as "cruel and revengeful," "lazy and improvident," "grave and
haughty," preferring "cunning to open battle," delighting in
"finery and trinkets," decking his unclean body with "paint and
feathers," and bearing the "most horrible tortures without a
sign of suffering."

Noah Webster (1825) described their government as follows:

> The tribes of Indians were under a government somewhat like a
> monarchy, with a mixture of aristocracy. Their chiefs, called saga-
> mores, sachems, or cazekes, possessed the powers of government; but
> they usually consulted the old men of the tribe on all important
> questions.

Many other authors described their government in a similar
manner, except that several referred to the chief as consulting
with "counsellors."

Their religion was described in various ways. Reference was

often made that they believed in one "Supreme Being" or "Great Spirit," but also that their religion was idolatrous. For example, Webster (1835) said:

> Their religion was idolatry, for they worshipped the sun, the moon, the earth, fire, images, and the like. They had an idea of the Supreme Being, whom they called the Great Spirit; and they believed in an evil spirit. They had priests, called pow-wows, who pretended to arts of conjuration and who acted as their physician.

Others refer to the Indians' "dream of a Heaven of happy hunting grounds or of a gay feast where his dog should join in the dance."

DISCOVERY AND EXPLORATION

All except two of the books analyzed by Jacobs and all analyzed by Rial dealt with discovery or exploration, or both. Emma Willard's book of 1859 devoted 27.2 per cent of the space to this topic. Those authors dealing with discovery usually began with the discovery of America by Columbus, although several dealt with the voyages to America by the Norsemen. M'Culloch's *Concise History* referred to the discovery of America as the "most important event in the history of the world. It brought one half of the globe into connexion with the other, and caused great changes in the commerce and politics of the world." Butler's book in 1827 said the discovery of America would "ultimately be productive of the greatest consequences to the world."

Most of the authors in dealing with this topic did so by devoting the treatment to the discoveries and explorations of the Spanish, French, English, and Portuguese.

Spanish. Not all early explorers sailed under the flag of their own countries. Several of the greatest explorers were Italians who sailed for Spain and England. The explorers most frequently mentioned as sailing for Spain were Columbus, Ponce de Leon, Balboa, Cortez, Magellan, Pizarro, and Cabrillo. Many authors played up the great wealth of the Montezumas and the Incas. Barnes' *Brief History of the United States* (1873) said, "Men of the highest rank and culture, warriors, adventurers, all flocked to the new world." Mention was often made that these Spanish adventurers were "cruel" and "harsh" in the treatment of the natives, preying on their wealth and leaving a trail of blood and bitterness.

Not all of the cruelty of the Spaniards was spent on American natives. Sometimes they ruthlessly attacked the settlements established by peoples from other European countries. One of the bloodiest narrations was in Ridpath's book (1880), describing how the French Hugenots who had settled on the St. John River in Florida were butchered by the Spanish under Melendez.

Other books relate how DeSoto tried to enslave the Indians, and when they refused to serve the Spanish their hands were cut off and other forms of cruelty imposed. Even the textbooks published after 1885 continued to use such phrases, as "barbarous cruelty," "blood-stained conquerors," "terrorism rather than justice," "ruthless plunderers," in describing the explorations of the Spanish. However, the books do acknowledge that the Spanish did colonize South America and part of North America, and even founded colleges long before Harvard was founded.

French. France did not produce many explorers of note, but nevertheless profited by the discovery of America. The French explorers most frequently mentioned were Verrazzani, Cartier, DeMonts, Ribaut, Laudonniere, Marquette, Champlain, and La-Salle. The French were pictured in a rather favorable light by most authors. This may in part have been true because of the help given the English colonies during the Revolution.

Even more recent textbooks included thrilling stories of the fur trader, Joliet, and the Jesuit missionary, Father Marquette. Although the French staked out magnificent claims to much of the northern and central part of North America, they were unable to hold most of them after the French and Indian War. The reasons given in a number of books were: they established mostly only fur trading posts rather than well populated settlements; and the French traders, trappers, and soldiers were not the type to sink deep roots in a new country. French farmers did establish a substantial community in Quebec, but their officials prevented the freedom of the press and of thought, which in turn prevented the community from growing strong and self-reliant.

English. England's interest in the new world was activated when Henry VII commissioned John Cabot in 1496 to make new discoveries in the Atlantic and Indian Oceans. However, little was done about them for three-quarters of a century, until Queen Elizabeth's reign when new endeavors followed. Then the exploits of Drake, Gilbert, Frobisher, and others were filled with stories of adventure. The early textbooks vary in their treatment of these adventures. Some referred to the English as more humane and good than the Spanish, while others tell of the cruel exploits of the English pirates.

Later authors even more glowingly wrote of the exploits of Drake, and how he circumnavigated the globe, returning with Spanish gold, silver, and jewels. Although Queen Elizabeth died (1603) before any permanent English settlement was established in the new world, the writers point out that it was England's unified hope to eclipse Spain and colonize in the new world.

The books also vary in their treatment of the relations between the English and the Indians. Some seem to defend the English while others present incidents of cruelties. For example, Ridpath (1880) critically wrote:

> Hostilities soon broke out between the English and the Indians. Wingina, the King, and several of the chiefs were lured into the power of the English and murdered. Hatred and gloom followed.

Portuguese. Little attention was given to the Portuguese explorers by the early textbook authors. No doubt, this was largely due to the fact that they never established a foothold in what is now the United States. However, several books mention the explorations of Prince Henry, called "The Navigator."

COLONIAL HISTORY

All 118 American history textbooks analyzed by Jacobs and Rial devoted some space to colonial history. The two earlier books devoting most space were Keene's (1822) 43.2 per cent, and Peter Parley's (1848) 70.2 per cent. The later books more evenly devoted space to this topic, the highest being Eggleston's 30.3 per cent in 1888.

Little attention was given to the fact that the two oldest settlements in what is now United States territory were settled by the Spanish, St. Augustine in 1565 and Santa Fe in 1582. Reference was made that the Spanish and French came here for riches and trade, while the English finally came to establish homes.

Most authors made much of the first permanent English settlement at Jamestown, Virginia, in 1607. Attention was given to difficulties of those earlier settlers caused by vice, laziness, recklessness, famine, and disease, and how Captain John Smith helped them improve their conditions.

Most authors devoted even more space to the settling of New England by the Puritans. Several reasons may be given for this. One was the fact that the Puritans came here with their families with the definite resolve to remain here, which was not always true in early Virginia. Another reason possibly was because most of the earlier textbooks were written by New Englanders, who were more interested in and knew more about their own section.

Reference was generally made of the religious persecutions of the Puritans in England, and also to the fact that they did not permit religious freedom to those of other faiths in New England. However, the treatment varied in the different books on the latter matter. Certain authors made much of the witchcraft trials, while others belittled them. Even prominent members of society were affected by the puzzling powers of imaginations and witchcraft. The nature of evidence brought against the accused bordered on hallucinations. Stories of how the Devil tried to carry them off were common. Grimshaw's text (1843) said:

> Bricks, sticks, and stones, were often, by some invisible hand, thrown at the house, and so were many pieces of wood; a cat was thrown at a woman of the house, and a long staff danced up and down the chimney; and afterwards the same long staff was hanged by a line, and swung to and fro; and, when two persons laid it on the fire to burn it, it was as much as they were able to do, with their joint strength, to hold it there.

Ridpath, in referring to the most active period of witchcraft activity in 1692, said:

> Between June and September, twenty victims were hurried to their

doom. Fifty-five others were tortured into the confession of false-
hoods. A hundred and fifty lay in prison awaiting their fate. Two
hundred were accused or suspected, and ruin seemed to impend over
New England.

Further mention was made that the Rev. Mather expressed his
"thankfulness" *that so many witches had met their just doom.*

Social practices. In general, the earlier textbooks did not over-
glorify the early settlers. Their peculiarities and weaknesses, their
selfishness, and the strict standards that were set up, were all
depicted. No early author was so generous in treatment of the
Puritans as Fish in his *History of America* (1925), in saying:

> There has seldom been a gentler and kinder group of people than the
> Pilgrims. They appear to have had good will toward all men, even
> toward the cruel king from whom they had fled and towards the
> savages of the forest. They valued so highly the freedom to worship
> God in their own way that they would not refuse the same freedom
> to others.

The earlier writers not only commonly mentioned the witchcraft practices, but also how the New Englanders mistreated the
Indians by firing on them without just cause, cheating them, and
stirring up hatred rather than a friendly spirit from the Indians.

The social life of the northern settlers, these histories said, was
more equalitarian than was true in Virginia, where early marked
social cleavages developed. Too, the northern settlers were more
stable, having come by families, while many of the earlier southern
settlers were single men, not sure about remaining in America. As
a consequence, the moral habits were looser than in New England.

The earlier textbooks mentioned little about such matters as
colonial amusements or culture. However, Rial found that textbooks after 1885 devoted some space to them. Recreation, hunting, house-raising and husking bees were mentioned. In the South,
dancing, music, and horseracing were common. Mention was
often made of the scarcity of books in the colonial period. The
Bible, the *New England Primer*, and an almanac constituted the
library of many colonial homes. The first newspaper, the *Boston
News Letter*, appeared in 1704.

War content. Jacobs found that 44.6 per cent of the content of the American history textbooks published before 1886 was devoted to war. Interestingly the earliest texts, dealing only with the French and Indian and the Revolutionary wars, gave even more space to war. The highest per cent in any text, 79.6, was in Cooper's in 1800. The lowest in the older books was in Peter Parley's *First Book of History*, 19.8 per cent.

The later textbooks, as found by Rial, devoted considerably less space to war. The average for 41 texts in the period of 1925-1941 was 18.8 per cent. Although Adams and Trent's *History of the United States* in 1903 contained 38.3 per cent pertaining to war, yet Faulkner, Kepner, and Bartlett's *The American Way of Life* contained only 6.1 per cent. Thus the textbooks have changed in their treatment of war.

The oldest texts, having to deal only with the earlier wars, devoted considerable space to the wars between England and France, particularly as they concerned the thirteen colonies. It was not uncommon for the authors to deal with the terrible brutalities involved. For example, Hale's *History of the United States* (1835) described the Indian attack of Schenectady in part as follows:

Opening their doors, they (the inhabitants) met the savages, with uplifted tomahawks. . . . In a few minutes, the buildings were on fire. Women were butchered, and children thrown alive into the flames. The Indians, frantic from slaughter, ran, with fatal haste, through the village, massacring many, who, in their attempt to escape, were betrayed by the light of their own houses.

Such descriptions were not unusual. However, after 1850 the tone was somewhat different. The authors would deal more with facts, causes, men involved, and effects of war, rather than horrid incidents.

The Revolutionary War was given considerable attention in most books. The chief difference found between the earlier and later books in dealing with it has been in the nature of its treatment. The earlier books dealt mostly only with the war and not much with its causes and results, while the later ones dealt more with the causes and outcomes. The narration of battles between the poorly-armed and ill-clad colonial soldiers and the well-armed and trained "Red Coats" of England was common. The authors glorified the colonials in their victory over the English. The heroic figures most often mentioned were Paul Revere and Washington as soldiers, and John Hancock and Patrick Henry as patriots.

The War of 1812 was termed by a number of authors as the "Second War for Independence." The content pertaining to this war was usually a brief discussion of the battles fought, the number of men engaged and killed, and laudations of the Americans.

The treatment of the Mexican War varied more than of any of the wars. Several books dealt very critically of United States' part in it. Guernsey in 1885 referred to it as impolitic, if not unjust.

Thirty of the 54 books analyzed by Jacobs were published before 1860, and so contained nothing on the Civil War. Those after 1860 contained much on it. For example, the popular Barnes' history (1873) devoted 65 pages to the Civil War. The subject-matter pertained chiefly to military campaigns, details of important battles, number of men engaged and lost, and the results.

Just why the earlier authors of American history textbooks devoted so much attention to war cannot exactly be proven. However, certain possible reasons may be considered. First, the source materials regarding wars were more abundant. Since battles are sensational they are written about more fully than such matters as religion and education, even though most will admit the latter more important. Second, the earlier books were written when our nation was young, and so the patriotic and nationalistic sentiments of our young nation found fuller expression in the treatment of war than peace. Third, the authors likely attempted to instill in the youth of America the glory of the heroic. This can be easily done by dealing with the heroes of war.

TRAVEL AND TRANSPORTATION

Only five of the textbooks before 1885 dealt with travel and transportation as a topic. Less average space was devoted to this category than any of the ten categories; namely, less than one-

tenth of one per cent. The books after 1885 allotted more space
to it; namely, two and one-half per cent. All except three of the
64 books after 1885 recognized it as a distinct topic. In fact,
Lawson and Lawson in 1938 devoted 12.3 per cent of their content
to it, and McGuire and Portwood 12.4 per cent in 1942.

Several reasons can be given for this marked change in attention. Many of the oldest textbooks were written before the modern
means of travel developed, when people travelled afoot, on horseback, and by canoe or sailing vessel. Footpaths, streams, trails,
lakes, and oceans provided the highways for travel and transportation. As roads were developed, stage coaches and light vehicles
came into use. Later canals were dug to provide new ways particularly after the invention of the steam boat. Then the railroad
gradually replaced the canal, and in more recent times the auto-
mobile and airplane supplement the others.

INDUSTRIAL PROGRESS AND INVENTIONS

The treatment in early American history textbooks of these
matters was very meager. The average page space devoted to
these factors in the textbooks published before 1885 was less than
one per cent. No doubt, this meager treatment was due to the
fact that the period of invention was in its infancy and, consequently, so was technology and industrial progress. However, the
textbooks after 1885 contained fuller treatment of industrial
development, especially after 1925. The textbooks from 1885 to
1942 inclusive devoted an average of 6.8 per cent to these matters,
and those after 1925 nearly 9 per cent. Of the 54 textbooks before 1885, 30 gave them no regular topical treatment, while only
two of the 64 texts after 1885 failed to do so. Beard and Beard's
book of 1937, *The Making of American Civilization*, devoted 20.5
per cent to technological influences.

1. Agriculture. The ancient occupation of agriculture employed most of the early settlers and has continued to employ
millions to this day. According to the treatment in the early
textbooks the crops consisted both of native American plants,
such as Indian corn, tobacco, and potatoes, as well as imported
grains like hemp, flax, wheat, peas, and beans. Since much of the

soil settled by the colonists was very fertile, agriculture became a source of livelihood and even of wealth. However, according to Butler:

> The expense of labor was high, and the labor of clearing their lands arduous and difficult; and above all the numerous Indian wars, to which they were often harassed, distressing beyond expression; still the rich luxuriant soil yielded them abundance for their support, in peace and war, and a good supply for the purpose of commerce.

Farming became easier and also more productive after the invention of the mower, reaper, cotton gin, and other later labor saving implements.

2. Fishing. Noah Webster's text stated that fishing began at Cape Ann in 1639 and that this trade developed rapidly thereafter. It was said that in 1641 more than 300,000 codfish were sent to market.

3. Shipbuilding. Commerce and fishing could not develop commercially without ships. New Englanders especially were anxious to build ships, but were greatly handicapped by a lack of ship carpenters. So house carpenters were enlisted to build ships, which were small at first. Later this became an important industry.

4. Arts and manufacture. Reference was made in the early texts to the restrictive laws enacted by England preventing or limiting manufacturing in America. Since most colonists were too poor to buy many manufactured products from England, they felt compelled to make or manufacture their own salt, paper, glass, shoes, hats, gun powder, and some farm tools. A loom was to be found in many homes.

5. Inventions. Apparently the authors of history textbooks, if they dealt with this topic at all, enjoyed mentioning the products of American inventors. It was said that Thomas Godfrey invented a quadrant to aid navigators. Franklin invented the lightning rod. In South Carolina a machine for hulling rice was developed. Many authors referred to Eli Whitney's cotton gin, and Robert Fulton's steam boat. In addition to Cyrus McCormick's reaper and mower, the threshing machine and improved plows were invented. The invention of the sewing machine by

Elias Howe, and the telegraph by Morse also received mention. The history textbooks after 1885 listed numerous newer inventions and then treated much more extensively the development of industry and technology and what these have meant to the rapidly growing power and importance of the United States, which is now the most important manufacturing country in the world.

POLITICS AND GOVERNMENT

American history textbook writers devoted more page space to this topic than to any except to war. However, the emphasis in treatment from the earliest to the latest books developed in reverse to the treatment on war. The earliest textbooks devoted more than half of the space to war, while the books for the 1926-42 period used only 18.8 per cent for war. On the other hand, the earliest books devoted only 15 per cent of the space to political matters, while the books published from 1906 to 1926 devoted 35.4 per cent to the topic. Abbott's text (1877) devoted 42 per cent of its pages to political matters, which means that from 1795, when the first United States history textbook was published, to 1942, the textbooks on an average devoted from 50 to 70 per cent of the page space to the two topics of war and politics.

The treatment of political matters by the various authors usually was under one or more of the following headings: The constitution, establishing the new government, political parties, international relations, and domestic matters.

1. The constitution. A number of the authors referred to the constitution as the greatest political document ever developed by man. Yet Cooper's text (1800) did not mention it, and Mrs. Thayer's book (1823) devoted only 115 words to it, which read in part:

> By this constitution, the blessings of civil and religious liberty are guaranteed to the people, and one of its chief excellencies is, that it contains a provision for future amendments, as the exigencies of the states shall require. One legislative and judicial power pervades the whole union. The executive power is vested in a President and Vice President, and the legislative in a Senate and House of Repre-

sentatives, all chosen by the people. The ratification of the Constitution was celebrated with great joy.

Several authors referred to the explanatory essays concerning the constitution written by Alexander Hamilton, John Jay, and James Madison.

2. The new government. With the inauguration of George Washington as president, the new government began to function. Emma Willard (1859) wrote as follows concerning the inauguration:

> The ceremony of his inauguration was witnessed with inexpressable joy. He made an address to Congress, in which he offered his "fervent supplications to the Almighty Being, whose providential aid can supply every human defect, that his benediction would consecrate to the liberties and happiness of the people of U.S., a government instituted by themselves; and would enable every officer to execute with success, the functions allotted to his charge."

Many authors of history referred to the problems and confusion facing the new government, especially the economic. They referred to the financial practices and principles developed by Hamilton, and how the establishment of the credit system helped strengthen the federal government and the rapid economic development of the United States.

3. Political parties. Most textbooks devoted considerable space to the part the different political parties played in American political history. Of course, the earliest books dealt only with the Federalists and the Anti-Federalists or Republicans. Since the Federalists more strongly favored the adoption of the Constitution, Noah Webster's (1835) book stated:

> To that party, the United States are indebted for the adoption of the Constitution, and for the organization of its government, and particularly for the funding system which has extinguished the public debts . . . these great measures being opposed by the anti-federalist party, with earnestness and persevering zeal.

The wrangles between the parties led Mrs. Willard in her text (1846) to say, "The conduct pursued by both parties in Congress, on this occasion, manifests how little party spirit cares for the public good." Nevertheless, the Republican Party grew sufficiently strong to elect Jefferson as our third president. This party remained in power for many years. Later the Whig Party arose and elected Harrison and later Taylor as presidents. In the meantime, beginning with Jackson, the Republican Party became known as the Democratic Party, continuing this title until the present. Then in 1860 Lincoln was the first president to be elected by what is now known as the Republican Party.

Some authors also mentioned the activities of certain political parties which never succeeded in electing a president. Among these were the Know Nothing or American Party, which arose to resist the influence of foreigners under the motto of "America for Americans"; the Anti-Masonic Party, organized to counteract suspected secret power of the Masonic Order; and later the Progressive Party. However, one fact seemed to be apparent in all the history textbooks; namely, that regardless of the names of the political parties, only two major parties seemed to have been strong at any one time.

4. Domestic relations. Nearly all early American history textbooks contained considerable content presented under the respective presidential administrations, which could be identified as Domestic Affairs. These were concerned with such matters as financial plans for raising revenue, internal improvements, admission of new states, states' rights, Indian affairs, the tariff question, and slavery. Generally only meager discussion accompanied the presentation of these matters. They really enumerated facts of history to be memorized rather than to be understood.

5. International relations. Our country from its beginning has had to be concerned with international matters. Nearly all texts relate how we won the aid of France to win our independence. Yet George Washington, the first president, declared a policy of isolation. Eliot's text (1856) quoted him as having said on April 22, 1793, "that the duty and interest of the United States require that they should with sincerity and good faith, adopt and pursue a conduct friendly and impartial towards the belligerent powers." Many authors commented favorably on this policy.

Another policy, which in part changed the isolation policy, given favorable comment in many books was the Monroe Doctrine, although the texts by Grimshaw, Willard, Guernsey, and a few others failed to mention it.

The following were the international events or incidents receiving attention in many of the early books: (1) Washington's Proclamation of Neutrality during the French Revolution, leading to the expulsion of Citizen Genet; (2) trade relations with England resulting in Jay's Treaty in 1795; (3) Algerian pirates plundering American trading vessels; (4) boundary negotiations with Spain concerning Florida and Louisiana; (5) differences with France resulting in the oft quoted declaration by Pinckney, "millions for defense, not one cent for tribute"; and (6) the controversies with Britain concerning our north-west boundary, resulting in the Webster-Ashburton Treaty in 1846.

CULTURAL MATTERS

Great variation existed among the authors regarding the amount of space devoted to matters that could be called cultural, such as those pertaining to religion, recreation, social conditions and customs, and education. Of the fifty-four books written before 1885, twenty-six failed to give any topical attention to any of these matters. However, Goodrich's text of 1852 devoted nearly 10 per cent of the pages to them. Only an average of 1.3 per cent of the space was allotted to these matters. On the other hand, the texts written after 1885 devoted 8.4 per cent of the space to them, and no book failed to give topical attention to one or more of these matters. Lawson and Lawson's *Our America: Today and Yesterday* (1938) allotted nearly 30 per cent of its space to cultural matters.

Apparently the chief reason for the meager attention given to these matters in the earlier textbooks was that American society in those days was much less complex. Travel was difficult and towns were small, so contacts in large numbers were few. Too, earning a livelihood required so much time on the part of most people that little time was left for cultural pursuits, except attention to religion. However, after 1885 life in the United States became more and more complex, and so as the authors of American history textbooks began to give less space to war they gave more to cultural factors.

1. Religion. Of the cultural factors, religion received the most attention in the earlier textbooks. This was due, no doubt, to the fact that many of the earliest settlers came here for religious reasons, particularly in early New England and in several of the middle colonies. For example, M'Culloch's text (1797) said:

> America was settled by persons of various religious denominations . . . to New England . . . Congregationalists (Puritans),— to New York and New Jersey, Presbyterians,—to Pennsylvania, Quakers,—to Maryland, Catholics,—to Virginia and Carolina, Episcopalians. The Independents of New England, and the Episcopalians of Virginia and Carolina, fought to give ascendency to those of their own religious tenets. Discord, and a degree of persecution, was the consequence.

Too, since M'Culloch's book was published shortly after the adoption of the U.S. Constitution and its first amendment separating church and state, it contained an interesting statement concerning the significance of such separation, in saying:

> But each party (denomination) is left to support itself, and must stand on its own foundation. Protection is equally enjoyed by all. —From this new state of things, the world will be able to determine, whether genuine Christianity is diminished by the want of civil, or national establishments;—or whether these have not been an hindrance to the spreading of the truth, and detrimental to morality as well as to religion.

The meaning of this statement becomes clearer when it is recognized that the countries of Western Europe from which the settlers had come had state religions. So this was an experiment in church-state relations.

Religion apparently was a major factor in the regulation of the behavior, customs, and life of the colonists. Butler's *A History of the United States of America* (1827) stated:

> Our ancestors combined a practical religion with the most scrupulous morals, which laid the foundation for a set of customs and habits, that operated upon society more forcibly, if possible, than the laws, and gave a peculiar force and energy to their civil codes. Under such a system, industry and frugality, patience and perseverance, magnanimity and valor, with a practical display of all the moral virtues,

formed the characters of the first settlers of New England.

The deep religious scruples of certain colonists led them to question the propriety of referring to the names of the days of the week by the names derived from pagan gods. The same was true of certain of the months of the year. So reference was made that some colonists referred to the days and weeks by number rather than by pagan name.

Many histories referred to how early settlers depended on divine guidance by observing days for fasting at times of drought, famine, or pestilence, as well as days of thanksgiving for good crops and health. Thanksgiving thus became a national holiday.

A number of the early books referred to the Quakers as the lovers of peace, even keeping on peaceful terms with the Indians and allowing settlers of other religions to settle in Pennsylvania. Not much attention was given to the religion of the southern colonies. And finally, later history textbooks devoted much less space to religion.

2. Customs. With the lessening of the strong influence of religion on the lives of people during the latter part of the colonial period the manners and customs gradually changed. The change was greatly hastened by the Revolution. In regard to this Butler (1827) stated:

> The licentiousness and corruptions of the armies, both British and American, sowed the seeds of dissipation; the French army sowed the seeds of infidelity, and the fluctuating state of the paper money sowed the seeds of speculation and fraud; all which combined, greatly lessened the force of moral virtue, and weakened the moral character of the nation.

Other books mentioned the widening breach between social classes, and how some became richer and others poorer. Too, how the growth of cities changed urban life, and how certain inventions and the development of industries affected the lives and customs of people.

The textbooks published between 1850 and 1885 said very little, if anything, about the manners and customs of the people of the United States. However, they did devote much space to war and governmental matters.

3. Education. M'Culloch's book, the first United States history textbook, devoted more than four pages to educational matters. It begins its treatment by saying:

> Knowledge is necessary to the preservation of liberty. When people are instructed in the nature of their rights, they will neither be led aside by artful demagogues, nor suffer their rulers to oppress them. It is also a source of happiness to the mind; elevates man above the beast; and gives civilized nations a superiority over the savage.

It then continues by listing the dates of the founding of many educational institutions in the United States, and by listing charitable institutions, institutions for promoting science, national societies, mutual benefit societies, health offices, insurance companies, and certain American scientific discoveries, such as those by Franklin, Rittenhouse, Godfrey, and Fitch.

Other authors referred to the strong early attention given to education by the New England colonists, next only to the attention given to religion. For example, Butler's textbook (1827) stated:

> The colonists instituted primary, or district schools in all their towns, and obliged by law every county or town to maintain a grammar school, where youth could be fitted for college. They also made such provision for the support of these schools, that they were free to all classes of people, and the children of the poor had equally the advantage of early education, with those of the rich. All classes could read and write, and understand common arithmetic.

It must be said, however, that Butler overstated the case for the status of education in early American history. The above educational conditions were obtained only in New England, and even there the schools were not all free and it is doubtful whether even all there learned to read and write.

Goodrich's text (1831) said:

> Scarcely had the American colonists opened the forests, and constructed habitations, before they directed their attention to the object of education.

Hale (1835) mentioned the Law of 1647 in Massachusetts,

which required every town of more than fifty householders to maintain a reading and writing school, and the fact that "the same system was adopted by the other colonies of New England" (except Rhode Island). He continued in saying:

> The effect of this system has been to render the great body of the people of these states the most enlightened in the world. All can read and write, and rarely can one be found not qualified, by education, to transact the common concerns of life.

Hale, like Butler, apparently was unmindful that this was more true as a wish than a fact.

A number of the early textbooks seemed to take pride in listing the colleges that had been founded in the United States, possibly because soon there were more colleges here than in England, the mother country.

One of Goodrich's texts (1852) said:

> At the opening of the present century, the colleges of the United States were twenty-five; now one hundred and twenty. Of theological institutions, there are thirty-two; law schools, twelve; medical schools, thirty-seven.

He further mentioned that schools for the blind, insane, and idiots had been founded.

The textbooks between 1850 and 1885 devoted much less space to education.

TERRITORIAL AND WESTWARD EXPANSION

The authors of the early American history textbooks apparently were little interested in territorial expansion. Much space was devoted to the various wars involving England, France, and Spain in their struggles for the control of North America, but little pertaining to the expansion of United States territory following the treaty with England ending the Revolutionary War. Jacobs in his analysis of the textbooks before 1885 found that only an average of 2.2 per cent of the space dealt with expansion. Rial found that the textbooks after 1885 devoted 4.8 per cent of the space to it.

Apparently the earlier authors were more concerned with set-tling and developing what the United States had than in acquiring more territory. For example, the Congress under the Articles of Confederation enacted the ordinances of 1785 and 1787 provid-ing for the survey and government of the Northwest Territory, which consisted in part of lands claimed by various states. Then attention was paid to the admission of new states to the Union. However, many of the early textbooks gave no regular topical treatment to the Louisiana Purchase, the acquisition of the Flor-ida territory, or the annexation of Texas, but usually devoted considerable space to the Mexican War.

Charles Goodrich's *History of the United States* (1823) de-voted 16 pages to Jefferson's administration, but failed to mention the Louisiana Purchase. However, he discussed at length the war with Tripoli and the quarrel between Aaron Burr and Hamilton, which occurred during that administration. Marcius Willson, in his rather popular *American History* (1846), devoted just one brief paragraph to the Louisiana Purchase. Egbert Guernsey, in his *History of the United States of America* (1847), used only a paragraph to deal with the admission of Ohio as a state and the Louisiana Purchase. Apparently, the early authors of American history textbooks considered the Purchase very unimportant, ex-cept that it opened up the trade route on the Mississippi River for the U.S.A. Even the books that gave it definite treatment failed to deal with its territorial significance.

The books even differed regarding the facts involved in the Purchase. For example, Butler's text of 1827 stated:

> Spain ceded this country to France, and France to the United States
> for 15,000,000 dollars. Eleven millions of the purchase money were
> to be applied to the demands of the citizens of the United States, by
> way of indemnification for the spoliations of France upon American
> commerce.

Other authors cited different amounts as indemnity payment. Grimshaw stated the indemnity to be two and one-half millions, Quackenbos three millions, and Ridpath three and three-fourths millions.

In contrast, modern authors either do not mention the indemnity at all or make mere mention of it. On the other hand, they deal with the Purchase at considerable length and make much of its territorial significance. Muzzey's text of 1936 includes a picture of the signing of the Purchase Treaty, a two-page territorial map, and a sub-topic entitled, "The Significance of the Purchase." The Woodburn, Moran, and Hill text (1930) also includes a map, and specifically enumerated the acres and its population in 1930. The Faulkner, Kepner, and Bartlett text (1941) mentions that 15 states, in whole or in part, were created from it. They then quote Henry Adams in saying that it ranked "next to the Declaration of Independence and the adoption of the Constitution, events of which it was the logical outcome; but as a matter of diplomacy it was unparalleled because it cost almost nothing."

Strange as it may seem, many of the early authors gave more attention to the acquisition of Florida in 1819 than to the Louisiana Purchase. A possible reason for this was because the Florida Purchase was preceded by a virtual war led by Jackson. Although the treaty involved a five million dollar purchase price, yet this money was not paid to Spain. It was apportioned to American citizens, whose property had been seized in Spanish ports. More attention was paid to Jackson and the war than to the significance of the acquisition.

Most history textbooks published soon after 1848 devoted much more space to what involved the annexation of Texas territory than to any of the other acquisitions. This was apparently true because the authors seemed bent upon treating at length the struggles and heroism of war. Thus the Mexican War was given considerable space. Guernsey's 1855 edition of his *History of the United States of America* contained 29 pages dealing with the Texas-Mexican affair, mostly on the war. No question was raised regarding the justice of it, and the treatment concluded by saying:

> Thus, the United States have gained a vast amount of territory, stretching from the Gulf of Mexico westward to the ocean, embracing New Mexico and a large portion of California.

Willson's *American History* (1856) also devoted much space

to the Mexican War, ending his treatment of the War, saying:

> Such was the conclusion of the Mexican War,—a war opposed as
> impolitic and unjust by one portion of the American people, and as
> cordially approved by the other, but admitted by all to have estab-
> lished for our nation, by the unbroken series of brilliant victories
> won by our army, a character for martial heroism which knows no
> superior in the annals of history, and fears no rival in the pathway
> of military glory. (p. 497.)

However, according to Willson's treatment of the whole affair,
the opposition to the Mexican War was not so much on its injustice as on the fact that it would add much slave territory,
which led to the northern opposition.

Some of the later authors dealt briefly with the Oregon territory, the Gadsden Purchase, and the Purchase of Alaska. However, the majority of the writers of American history textbooks
seemingly merely aimed to state the facts regarding the various
territorial acquisitions. The meaning and significance of these
acquisitions were left to the readers to interpret.

SLAVERY

Historically speaking, slavery has been one of America's most
serious problems. It engendered bitter domestic controversy, even
helping to cause the Civil War. Yet slavery received little treatment in the history textbooks before 1860, other than the acts
passed by Congress pertaining to its regulation. The early writers
apparently did not grasp the moral, social, and economic significance and meaning of slavery. In the books before 1860 less than
one-half of one per cent of the space was devoted to it.

In the main, about the only treatment given slavery was that
relating to its introduction into the colonies. Too, the books
differed widely regarding the data of its introduction. The date
of 1619 was mentioned by the following authors: S. G. Goodrich,
Venable, Eliot, Doyle, Eggleston, Berard, and Thalheimer. The
following gave 1620 as the date: Frost, Guernsey, Anderson,
Scott, Lossing, and Holmes. Some failed to mention the date.

Other than the content dealing with the Civil War in the books
after 1865, most of the other content pertaining to slavery con-

cerned itself with brief treatment of such matters as the Missouri
Compromise, Fugitive Slave Law, Kansas-Nebraska Act, Dred
Scott Case, and Omnibus Bill. Although nearly all of the textbooks were written by Northern authors, yet most of them, even
those written in the South, dealt with slavery objectively.

MOST POPULAR AMERICAN HISTORIES

Early Histories: 1795-1825. The next textbooks dealing with
American history after M'Culloch's, heretofore discussed, were
written by Noah Webster. In 1802 he published his *Elements of
Useful Knowledge,* Vol. I. The subtitle was "Historical and Geographical Account of the U.S. for the Use in Schools." This
dealt largely with the colonial period. In the back was a "Chronological Table of Most Remarkable Events Respecting America."
It consisted of fourteen double-column pages of detailed historical
events. Vol. II, published in 1804, dealt with the history of the
U.S. from the beginning of the Revolution to the completion of
the organization of the government in 1789. It ended with "Wash-

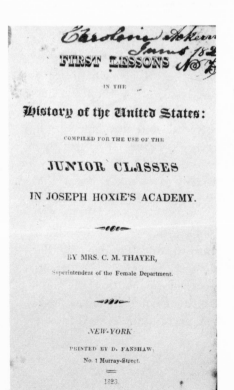

ington's Farewell Address."
These volumes went through
many editions. The 1812 edition of Vol. I was the fifth.
Soon after Webster completed
his *American Dictionary,* in
1828, he published his *History
of the United States.* Its 1835
printing was the sixth edition.

Several other American history textbooks soon appeared
after those by Webster, but
none became popular until the
appearance of Hale's *History
of the United States* in 1815.
This book, 322 pages of very

An early primary history, 1823.

fine print, dealt individually with the history of each of the original thirteen states, the Revolution, adoption of the Constitution, the administrations of the first four presidents, and the War of 1812. In the back were 24 pages of questions relating to the content of the XXV chapters. It appeared in many editions even into the 1840's. Charles Wiley's name was connected with some of the later editions.

Another to attain popularity was Reverend C. A. Goodrich's (1790-1860) *A History of the United States* in 1822. He was a son-in-law of Noah Webster and taught at Yale for many years. This was a larger book than those by Webster and Hale, having 432 pages. It presented the content under eleven periods, ending with Monroe's administration and contained many interesting wood-cut pictures. A chronological table and an index were in the back which was kept up-to-date in later printings. Few textbooks of that period contained an index. The 1834 printing was the 64th edition. Thus it was the most popular early American history textbook. After Goodrich died the publishers produced *The Child's History of the United States* under his name, one edition as late as 1884.

American Histories: 1825-1850. One of the first American histories written during this period was the *Republic of America* (really an American history) by Emma Willard (1787-1870). She was one of the first women authors of successful school textbooks, in geography, world history, and American history. She became famous as an advocate of more educational opportunities for girls. As head of Troy Female Seminary she made it an outstanding school for girls. Later the title of her book became *Abridged History of the United States*, which appeared in many editions to as late as 1869. This book was larger than many of the contemporary histories.

In 1832 William Grimshaw published a *History of the United States*, which appeared in several editions for more than ten years; and in 1833 Bishop Davenport's *History of the United States* was published. It likewise continued to appear for a decade.

About 1835 Peter Parley (S. G. Goodrich), author of popular

textbooks in several other fields, began to write a graded series of American histories, entitled, *The First Book of History for Children and Youth*, and *The Second Book of History*. These were very attractive little texts with many stories and pictures. In 1843 he published *A Pictorial History of the United States*, which became very popular and appeared long after his death. Like all of his other textbooks, it was illustrated with many pictures and several maps.

In 1837 John Frost published *A History of the United States*, which continued to appear for about two decades. One interesting feature was an extensive appendix of 27 pages of fine print, which included the Declaration of Independence, the Constitution, population data, and several chronological tables.

Other American history textbooks to appear in more than one edition during this period were written by C. B. Taylor (1830), J. Olney (1836), Marcius Willson (1845), and Egbert Guernsey (1847). And there probably were others.

American Histories: 1850-1875. In 1854 Benson Lossing pub-

Goodrich, *Child's First Book of History,* 1835—note questions relating pictures to text.

lished *A Pictorial History of the United States*. This was a well organized and attractive looking book with many pictures and portraits. One objection to it may have been its small print. The body of text was in 7 point type and the footnotes in 4 point. It was one of the first histories to include extensive and interesting footnotes. In 1858 Lossing published *A Primary History*, in 1864 *A Common School History*, and in 1875 *An Outline History of the United States*. These books were used widely into the 1870's.

Another author whose histories became popular was George P. Quackenbos (1826-1881). His first history was an *Illustrated School History of the United States* in 1857. This was widely used to the late 1870's. In 1860 he wrote a *Primary* and an *Elementary*, and later in 1877 an *American History*.

In 1869 John Anderson published *A Grammar School History of the United States*. As late as 1887 it appeared as the *New Grammar School History*. In 1871 he wrote the *Pictorial School History*, and in 1874 an attractive *Junior Class History* with many pictures.

William Swinton wrote *A Condensed School History* in 1871, which received a number of reprintings. He also wrote the *First Lessons in Our Country's History*. However, these never became as popular as some of his textbooks in other fields.

The American history books first written during this period which enjoyed the longest extended popularity were written by Joel Dorman Steele (1836-1886) and Esther Baker, later his wife. Their *A Brief History of the United States* was first published in 1871. With time it became

The famous Barnes history actually written by Steele and Baker, dramatic and appealing.

BURIAL OF DE SOTO.

of their wanderings (1541), they emerged upon the bank of the Mississippi. After another year of fruitless explorations, De Soto died. At the dead of night, his followers sunk his body in the river, and the sullen waters buried his hopes and his ambition. "He had crossed a large part of the continent," says Bancroft, "and found nothing so remarkable as his burial-place." De Soto had been the soul of the company. When he died, the other adventurers were

tives, preferring starvation to slavery, died on the voyage. History tells us that in 1525, when De Ayllon went back with the intention of settling the country, the Indians practiced upon him the lesson of cruelty he had taught them. His men were lured into the interior. Their entertainers, falling upon them at night, slew the larger part, and De Ayllon was only too glad to escape with his life.

more popularly known as the *Barnes History*, named after the publishing company, the A. S. Barnes Company. It continued in popularity in some areas as late as the 1930's. It happened that Steele earlier had written very popular books in several fields of science. Evidently the history was largely written by Miss Baker, who was a teacher of history, with the help of Steele. When Steele, a scientist, was criticized for writing a history, the Company began to call the histories the *Barnes Histories*. The *Brief History* was characterized by its logical organization, human interest pictures, its blackboard outlines, large type, and human interest footnotes. In 1885 the Steeles wrote *Primary History of the United States*, but it never became as popular as the *Brief History*.

Other authors whose histories appeared in more than one edition in this period were A. B. Berard (1855), David B. Scott (1860), George F. Holmes (1870), L. J. Campbell (1870) and possibly others.

American Histories: 1875-1900. Most of the popular histories first written in the previous period continued in circulation in this period, at least for some time. One of the first to become popular written in this period was by John C. Ridpath. His *Popular History of the United States* was published in 1876. Then he wrote the *History of the United States*, which was a grammar school edition, which received numerous reprintings. It contained many maps, some of which were colored; several colored historical charts; and many portraits of prominent Americans. In the back five double columned pages presented the pronunciation of hundreds of proper names.

In 1888 Edward Eggleston published *A History of the United States and Its People*, and the next year *A First Book of History*. These books appeared in several editions.

Beginning in 1889 Mara L. Pratt began publishing a series of *American History Stories* in at least four volumes. They dealt largely with early American history; Vol. IV was on later colonial history.

The last history originally written during this period to become rather popular was D. H. Montgomery's *The Leading Facts of American History* in 1890. This book continued to appear in edition after edition for years, and provided the Barnes *Histories* very keen competition. It was a little larger than the earlier editions of Barnes. It contained its "Leading Dates" in the beginning of the book rather than in the back and it had an appendix of 96 pages. In 1892 Montgomery wrote *The Beginner's American History*, which apparently became more popular than the Barnes' lower book. Then after 1900 he wrote *An Elementary American History*.

No doubt several other histories first written in this period attained considerable circulation after 1900, but no attempt has been made by the writer to determine which ones. John McMaster's *A School History of the United States* (1897), for instance, evidently was one.

CONCLUDING COMMENTS

The study of American history largely evolved out of the geography textbooks. The earliest geographies contained considerable historical content. It seems that the interest in the study of history was stimulated by American wars. The first interest seemed to have come with our second war with England (War of 1812). Many history textbooks soon appeared thereafter. A second great impetus followed the Civil War. There was a great flux of American history textbooks during the late 1860's and the early 1870's.

The use of pictures in history textbooks was more extensive, except in the earliest ones, than in most other subject fields except in geographies. Portrait pictures were very common, particularly of war heroes. It was not until after the 1880's that the texts began to decrease their overly extensive treatment of wars and their heroes. Little treatment of cultural matters was given in American histories until after 1900.

CHAPTER 8

CIVIL GOVERNMENT TEXTS

MOST of the common subjects in the American school curriculum had their origin in Europe, particularly in England. Not only did America borrow the practice of teaching the subjects commonly taught there, but even many of the early textbooks used here were brought from England. Such subjects as reading, arithmetic, writing, spelling, grammar, geography, and European history, as well as the textbooks from which they were taught, had European antecedents. However, the teaching of civil government (civics) and of American history originated here after our independence from England and the formation of a republican form of government. It was only natural that a better understanding of the principles and practices of our new government should be taught in the schools. Civil government was not commonly taught in European schools.

FALSE IMPRESSIONS[1]

Although numerous studies and references have been made touching the evolution of the teaching of the different subjects

---

[1] Part of the material of this chapter previously appeared as two articles written by John A. Nietz and Wayne Mason for *Social Education* in October, 1949 and May, 1950.

270

included under social studies, certain errors concerning their early development have persisted. The chief misconception concerning civil government seems to have been that it entered the curriculum of our schools about the middle of the nineteenth century. Wayne E. Mason[2] found and analyzed twenty-six separately authored textbooks, exclusive of duplicate editions, that were published prior to 1850 and apparently used in the American schools. This refutes the frequently expressed opinion that the early schools provided only incidental instruction concerning political institutions, patriotism, and citizenship.

Burke Hinsdale, whose book *How to Study and Teach History* (1894) contained a chapter on "Teaching Civics," stated that there was very little pedagogical literature relating to civil government. The oldest textbook to which he referred was Andrew's "Manual of the Constitution" (1874). He further stated that "For a decade and more increasing attention has been paid in our schools to teaching the branch of study called Civics and Civil Government."

Henry Bourne, in a similar book in 1903, allotted to civil government only two of the twenty chapters, and stated that "Civics, like history, has only within recent years got beyond the stage of utter neglect or perfunctory attention." The 1926 edition of Monroe's *Encyclopedia of Education* referred to the subject matter of civics not having been taught in the schools until after the middle of the nineteenth century. Similar statements were made in certain writings of Charles H. Judd and Howard C. Hill regarding the introduction of civil government in the curriculum. Even Edgar Dawson, an outstanding authority on early social studies textbooks, listed only seven civics books published before 1850. Likewise certain writings of Earle Rugg and of Clyde B. Moore greatly understated the number of early civil government textbooks published in the United States. The latter referred to the appearance of five before 1860 and a dozen more by 1892.

What was the true picture of the publication of civil government textbooks before 1890? Mason discovered and analyzed

2 "Analysis of Early American Civil Government Textbooks." (Unpublished doctor's dissertation, University of Pittsburgh, 1944.)

seventy published in the United States before 1890, all of which bore separate titles, and thus he did not count the many editions in which these books appeared. Chronologically, two were published before 1800, two more before 1825, twenty-two during the 1825-1849 period, eighteen during 1850-1874, and twenty-six during the 1875-1890 period.

Certainly there must have been a sale and use for textbooks in civil government, else not so many books would have been published in the field. Further light is thrown on their possible use by statements appearing either in the prefaces or on the title pages. Thirty-five title pages specify "For Use in Schools."

Evidence concerning the rather wide usage of books in this field can be gathered from an examination of their republication. The books of the following authors, arranged in chronological order, were published in many editions: William Sullivan, Andrew Young, John Burleigh, Furman Sheppard, Joseph Alden, and D. W. Andrews. The Nietz Collection of Old Textbooks contains eleven civil government textbooks under five titles, without a duplicate, written by Andrew Young, his *Introduction to the Science of Government* first appearing in 1835. The 1854 edition of this book states that it is the 24th thousand.

EARLIEST TEXTBOOKS

The introduction of civil government as a separate school subject probably began in 1793, when Nathaniel Chipman published a book entitled *Sketches of the Principles of Government* (Rut-

The earliest text well-balanced in content for the teaching of Civics.

THE

POLITICAL CLASS BOOK;

INTENDED

TO INSTRUCT THE HIGHER CLASSES IN SCHOOLS

IN THE

ORIGIN, NATURE, AND USE

OF

POLITICAL POWER.

"Government is instituted for the common good ; for the protection, safety, prosperity, and happiness of the people ;—and not for the profit, honor, or private interest of any one man, family, or class of men." *Mass. Bill of Rights.*
"Ignorantia legum neminem excusat ; omnes enim praesumuntur eas nôsse, quibus omnes consentiunt."

BY WILLIAM SULLIVAN,
COUNSELLOR AT LAW.

WITH AN APPENDIX
UPON STUDIES FOR PRACTICAL MEN;
WITH NOTICES OF BOOKS SUITED TO THEIR USE.

BY GEORGE B. EMERSON.

New Edition,
WITH AMENDMENTS AND ADDITIONS.

BOSTON:
RICHARDSON, LORD AND HOLBROOK,
133 Washington Street.
1831.

land, Vt.). It is not certain that this book was used as a school textbook. Its organization and contents, however, follow a textbook pattern. In a later textbook in 1833 Chipman referred to the fact that his earlier work had been "well received at the time." This may mean that his earlier book of 1793 marked the beginning of the formal teaching of civil government in 'some United States schools.

The textbook which heretofore has been recognized as the first in the field was Elhanan Winchester's *A Plain Political Catechism Intended for the Use of Schools in The U.S. of America: Wherein the Great Principles of Liberty, and of the Federal Government are Laid Down and Explained by Way of Question and Answer*, which was published in 1796. This evidently attained some popularity, for a second edition was published in 1802.

Even if these two books were used in some schools as civil government textbooks, they did not present a well balanced civics content. Both books dealt only with two of the six topics with which nearly all later books dealt: (1) the origin and background of American governmental institutions, and (2) the federal government in operation. No treatment was given to state government, local government, common and statutory law, or international law. The first book to give a more balanced treatment to all six topics was William Sullivan's *The Political Classbook* in 1831.

Even though these two books appeared early in our national history, their use must have been confined to a mere fraction of the schools in our country. Most pupils attending school must have gained their political education elsewhere or not at all. An analysis of early textbooks reveals that considerable content which can be classified as related to civil government appeared in books of other fields, particularly geographies, histories, and readers. The earliest American geography, Jedidiah Morse's *Geography Made Easy*, published first in 1784, briefly described the operation of the government of the several states. In 1798 Noah Webster's *The Little Reader's Assistant* contained a chapter on "A Federal Catechism or a Short and Easy Exposition of the Constitution of the United States." His *Elements of Useful Knowledge* in 1804 presented a somewhat detailed description of the operation of the executive, legislative, and judicial departments of the federal government, and of several state governments.

To the field of American history, however, the study of civil government owes its greatest debt. For example, John McCulloch's *A Concise History of the United States* (1797) devoted 35.5 per cent of the pages to governmental matters. C. D. Jacobs, in an analysis of 54 early American history books published before 1886, found an average of 19 per cent of the content devoted to political and governmental matters. From such humble beginnings the study of civil government gained impetus and a place in the American school curriculum.

CIVIL GOVERNMENT AIMS

The aims for the teaching of civil government were usually mentioned in the prefaces or introductions of the textbooks, but sometimes they were left to be inferred from the content, the manner in which it was presented, or the distribution of emphasis given the different topics. Since there were no professional organizations then in existence to help determine the purposes and emphases in this field, each author was on his own in determining the aims and the content of his book.

An analysis of the title pages reveals that most of the authors were of the legal and educational profession. Several were ministers, and a few were public office holders. Only S. G. Goodrich and Andrew W. Young seemed to have been professional textbook writers. Thus most of them apparently wrote these books as a public service.

Patriotism. The teaching of patriotism, expressed or implied, was an aim of nearly every author. One of the most emphatic appeals for the teaching of patriotism was in Judge Joseph Story's *The Constitutional Classbook* (1834). This was written while he was a professor of law at Harvard. In part, he wrote:

> If this work shall but inspire the rising generation with a more ardent love of their country, an unquenchable thirst for liberty, and a profound reverence for the Constitution and the Union, then it will have accomplished all that its author ought to desire.

S. G. Goodrich, who was better known by his pen name of "Peter Parley," wrote in his book, *The Young American* (1834):

> I have therefore sought to set forth the necessity of honesty in politics; hoping to do something to restore to favor that good old word, "so weary, stale, and unprofitable" to hack politicians— patriotism.

Andrew W. Young, the most prolific writer in this field, having written six separate and distinct textbooks aggregating an enormous number of editions, wrote in his popular *The Government Class Book* (1859):

> To preserve and transmit the blessings of constitutional liberty, we need a healthy patriotism. It has been one of the objects of the writer to bring to view the excellencies of our system of government, and thus to lay, in the minds of youth, the basis of an enlightened patriotism.

Other authors writing strong statements for the teaching of patriotism were Edward Mansfield (1839), Judge Story in his second book (1840), Andrew Young in his 1845 book, Furman Sheppard (1855), and Will Hart (1889).

Preparation for Citizenship. Another frequently mentioned aim was to prepare the youth regarding the rights and duties of citizenship. Sullivan, in his *Political Class Book* (1831) said:

> Every citizen of a state is also a citizen of the United States. Being entitled to all

Young, a popular Civil Government text, for schools and general reading.

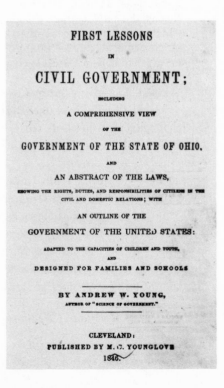

FIRST LESSONS

IN

CIVIL GOVERNMENT;

INCLUDING

A COMPREHENSIVE VIEW

OF THE

GOVERNMENT OF THE STATE OF OHIO,

AND

AN ABSTRACT OF THE LAWS,

SHOWING THE RIGHTS, DUTIES, AND RESPONSIBILITIES OF CITIZENS IN THE
CIVIL AND DOMESTIC RELATIONS; WITH

AN OUTLINE OF THE

GOVERNMENT OF THE UNITED STATES:

ADAPTED TO THE CAPACITIES OF CHILDREN AND YOUTH,
AND

DESIGNED FOR FAMILIES AND SCHOOLS

BY ANDREW W. YOUNG,

AUTHOR OF "SCIENCE OF GOVERNMENT."

CLEVELAND:

PUBLISHED BY M. C. YOUNGLOVE

1846.

the rights of national citizenship, and held to the performance of all its duties, he must be presumed to know what these are.

Salter S. Clark, in his revision of Young's *Government Class Book* in 1885, stated:

The aim of this book, in supplying a want believed to exist, is to present, in such form as to be used chiefly as a textbook for schools, a broad and comprehensive view of the principles of government and law in the United States (which are substantially the same throughout the country), and thus to teach the young the varied rights and duties of a citizen in relation to his government and his fellow citizens.

Principles of Government. As may naturally be expected, the teaching of the principles of government was the most frequently stated aim in the civil government textbooks. The very first book, namely, Chipman's *Sketches of the Principles of Government* (1793) contained the following interesting statement:

I do not know that any writer, ancient or modern, has attempted to analyze the social nature of man, and from the relations thence resulting, to derive the principles, which ought to be pursued in civil institutions. It will, I believe, however, be readily perceived, that this is the only certain ground of investigation, the only mode in which any general, consistent, practicable principles in the science of government can be established. This mode of investigation has been attempted in the following sketches.

Almost a century later (1887), William Mowry stated in his *Studies in Civil Government* that his purpose was to "set forth with great plainness of words and becoming brevity the history, the principles, and the essential facts of our peculiar government, local, state and nation."

It may be noted from these two quotations that both authors strongly believed in the teaching of the principles of government, as was true of most authors writing textbooks between 1793 and 1887, yet their approaches were quite different. Chipman attempted to derive these principles philosophically, while Mowry approached them through a study of the functions and organization of our government after a century of operation.

Moral and Religious Teachings. Fewer authors mentioned the teaching of morals as an aim. However, several of the earlier authors referred to this as a specific purpose. Chipman (1793) wrote that he would "pursue truth wherever it led, uninfluenced by the weight on the one hand, or a spirit of opposition on the other." Winchester (1796) apparently attempted to counteract the infiltration of European religious doctrines, particularly the anti-religious feelings from France, by writing:

> . . . let Americans beware of infidelity, which is the most danger-
> ous enemy that she has to contend with at present, and the only foe
> that she has reason to be afraid of; as it aims at the entire destruc-
> tion of all that is valuable and dear to us.

Maitland's *Political Instructor* (1833) contains the rhetorical question, "O, American citizens! Do you know, do you consider, the value of the civil and religious privileges which you enjoy, and are secured to you by our most excellent political institutions?" Goodrich in his *The Young American* (1844) aimed to teach the importance of keeping politics clean and moral by stating:

> The conviction is a very general one, that, morality and politics
> are in a state of divorce among a large portion of our political
> leaders. . . . If something need be done, to remedy this great evil,
> how can it be better done than by beginning in that universal semi-
> nary—the common school.

Thus some of the earlier authors of civil government textbooks included the teaching of morals as one of their aims.

Miscellaneous Purposes. Several authors, particularly those authors whose textbooks went through several or numerous editions, mentioned the *non-controversial* features of their books. Some explanations advanced were: (1) a criticism of other textbooks that appeared to be biased, (2) a defense for the objective or scientific treatment in their own books, (3) an attempt to allay the political tensions between sections of the country, and (4) an argument for the greater sale of their own books. For example, in his *Introduction to the Science of Government* (24th ed. 1854), Young stated:

It is to be remembered that this work is, as its title denotes, an "introduction" to political science being intended to teach ELE-MENTARY PRINCIPLES, rather than to settle questions on which the most eminent statesmen and economists are divided. Most of these controverted questions have therefore been avoided.

Goodrich's popular book, "sought not to write a line or sentence, with a view to party effects." In Sheppard's *Constitutional Text-book* (1855) appears a statement that "there is no attempt . . . to deal with disputed points in the manner of a controversialist or a partisan."

Lastly, among the purposes stated by many authors were the use or uses of the book. Townsend's *Analysis of Civil Government* (1868) is designed as a "Class-Book for the Use of Grammar, Normal, and High Schools, Academies, Seminaries, Colleges,

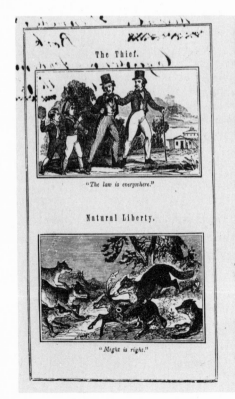

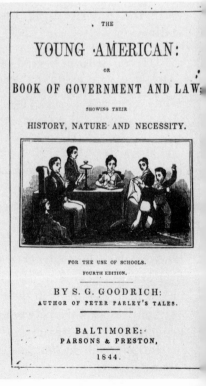

Goodrich, 1844, one of the few Civil Government texts with pictures.

Universities, and Other Institutions of Learning." The terms "elementary school" and "secondary school" did not appear in the textbooks analyzed. However, such terms as "common school" and "grammar school" were common. Many authors also mentioned the use for general readers, libraries, families, citizens, members of the bar, and anyone engaged in business transactions.

CIVIL GOVERNMENT CONTENT

The following treatment is based upon an analysis of seventy civil government textbooks published in the United States before 1890. Although many of these books appeared in more than one edition, each title was counted only once unless the content was materially revised.

For analytical purposes the total time span has been divided into four twenty-five year periods, and the texts published within these periods have been grouped and subjected to comparative and diagnostic analyses. The over-all analysis, a summary of which appears in Table VII, indicates that nearly all of the content can

TABLE VII

AVERAGE PAGE AND PERCENTAGE DISTRIBUTION OF SUBJECT MATTER
CONTENT IN CIVIL GOVERNMENT TEXTBOOKS, 1790-1890.

Periods	1790-1814		1815-1839		1840-1864		1865-1889		Average 1790-1889	
Number of Books (70)	3		10		20		37			
Origin and background of American governmental institutions	*	**	*	**	*	**	*	**	*	**
	131	75	41	25	42	19	32	14	40	19
Federal government in operation	36	21	86	51	118	54	145	66	124	59
State government matters	7	4	34	20	36	17	31	14	32	15
Local government matters	0	0	2	1	5	2	8	3	6	3
Common and statutory law	0	0	3	2	14	7	3	2	6	3
International law	0	0	1	1	3	1	1	1	2	1

* Average number of pages devoted to each category of subject matter by periods.
** Average Percent for each category by periods.

be classified under six major headings. A close examination of the data presented will also reveal some clear trends in the content of the books.

Treatment of the Origin and Background of American Government. To provide a clear picture of the content classified under this heading, the material was found to relate to five sub-topics. The one receiving most attention during the first period related to concepts, moral and ethical, which may affect society. During the subsequent periods gradually these concepts received decreasing treatment.

The second aspect with which the authors were concerned was the theory, type, and history of law and government. This topic received slightly increasing attention through the four periods. Chase, whose *Civil Government in Theory and Practice* (1885) compared and contrasted the government of the United States with that of other existing governments, allotted over 81 per cent of his book to this topic. More than half of the authors defined or described the more prevalent forms or types of government.

A third sub-topic was the settlement of America, including a description of colonial life and government, although treatment usually was brief. In only four books did the space allotted to this exceed 10 per cent of the entire text. The textbooks of the last period devoted much more space to it than the earlier ones.

The fourth sub-topic related to the work of The Continental Congresses and the

THE

CONSTITUTIONAL TEXT-BOOK:

A

PRACTICAL AND FAMILIAR EXPOSITION

OF THE

Constitution of the United States,

AND

OF PORTIONS OF THE PUBLIC AND ADMINISTRATIVE LAW OF THE
FEDERAL GOVERNMENT

By FURMAN SHEPPARD.

" It is of infinite moment that you should properly estimate the immense value of your National Union to your collective and individual happiness: that you should cherish a cordial, habitual, and immovable attachment to it: accustoming yourselves to think and speak of it as of the palladium of your political safety and prosperity."
WASHINGTON'S *Farewell Address to the People of the United States.*

PHILADELPHIA:
CHILDS & PETERSON, 124 ARCH ST.
1856.

A popular Civil Government text of a century ago.

Annapolis Convention. The fifth dealt with the convention for and adoption of the United States Constitution. Surprisingly, twenty books failed to give even as much as a full page to this sub-topic. The other fifty authors devoted from one to twenty-one pages to it.

As the data in Table VII indicate, three or more times as much space per book was devoted to background material during the first period as in any other. It is apparent that much of the subject matter of five of the sub-topics was not definitely considered civil government material by later authors. Much of it was rather historical and highly theoretical in nature. However, it was not uncommon in other subject matter fields for the textbooks to contain mixed materials. For example, Webster's famous "blue-backed" *Speller* included reading and other materials, and the early geographies usually contained considerable history and government.

Treatment of the Federal Government. The subject matter relating to the federal government and its operation received more over-all attention than the other five categories combined; namely, 59 per cent. In contrast to the attention paid to background material, which steadily decreased during the nineteenth century, the treatment of the federal government received increasing emphasis. The percentages of book space devoted to it during the four periods were 21, 51, 54, and 66 respectively.

The matter of the federal government receiving by far the most attention in the books related to the powers and duties of the Congress, averaging 35.3 per cent of the space. Some authors devoted as much as 50 per cent of the space to these powers and duties. Apparently they were keenly conscious of the legislative body of our national government and how it functions or should function as a democratic government.

The sub-topic receiving next most attention related to the powers and duties of the president or the executive branch of our federal government, averaging 15.5 per cent of the space devoted to the federal government. It happens that the Constitution itself devotes 25 per cent to this branch. In general, the later books devoted more space to this than the earlier ones. No doubt, the period following the Civil War, with a growing population, increasing foreign and domestic commerce, changing social and economic matters, all demanding the creation of new agencies, bureaus, commissions, and other administrative units, helped create a greater need for more executive or administrative duties.

Naturally, the judicial department received third most attention, averaging 8.1 per cent of the federal government space. This is the same per cent devoted to it in the Constitution itself as written by its framers. Sixty-four of the eighty texts gave this department space. Story's book (1834) used 54 pages to discuss judicial matters. Being a judge, he was highly qualified to elaborate on the judiciary.

On an average, 5.8 per cent of federal governmental space was devoted to the printing of the Constitution and its amendments. Fifty texts included the Constitution, fourteen placing it in the body of the texts and seventeen in both the body and the appendix. In these cases, apparently the Constitution was considered as formal subject matter and was to be analyzed as such.

A discussion of the nature of the Constitution, and of the government set up under it, involved 4.6 per cent of the space. Fifty-two texts dealt with the peculiarities of it and the federal government. This was done in various ways, by such means as contrast and comparison, or by definitions or explanations. Nordhoff, in his *Politics for Young Americans* (1867), devoted 34 pages to this category. Too, no treatment of this category usually preceded the foregoing topics as an introduction to the details of the Constitution and its provisions.

About 70 per cent of the space concerning the federal government was devoted to the five above mentioned topics. The remaining space dealt briefly with one or more of the following matters: relation of the states to the federal government; amending the Constitution; and the rights, duties, and responsibilities of the citizen.

State Government. Only 15 per cent of the space in all of the textbooks was devoted to matters involving state governments. The average percentage space during the four periods was 4, 20, 17, and 14. It was during the second period (1815-1839), a period of western expansion, that the greatest attention was given to this topic. Despite the fact that the operation of state government is nearer to the people than that of the federal government (and this was certainly true during the nineteenth century), more than one fourth of the authors omitted this subject from their books. Calvin Townsend even vehemently opposed dealing with it, saying in the preface to *A Shorter Course in Civil Government* (1875):

> To learn the duties of town, city and county officers has nothing whatever to do with the grand and noble subject of civil government. Such books on state governments have no place in the school room. They would be nothing but a pile of rubbish. To attempt class drill on petty town and county officers would be simply burlesque of the whole subject.

This remark sounds strange indeed to twentieth-century ears.

Not only did 49 of the 70 textbooks include some material on state governments, but the later books even presented the matters of state government before those of federal. The first author to use this approach was Elisha Howe in his *The Young Citizen's Catechism* in 1860. Jesse Macy, in his *Our Government* (1886), defended this approach by saying:

> The order of topics here presented is such that institutions nearest, and naturally most familiar, shall receive special attention first.

This became the more commonly followed approach, which was in harmony with the developing pedagogical ideas.

The subject matter in these books relating to state governments dealt with state constitutions, resumé of existing state governments, legislative functions, executive duties, judicial functions, education, taxation, election matters, public institutions, and public improvements. No one book dealt with all ten matters, but three authors dealt with nine of the ten; namely, Young in his books of 1846, 1848, and 1864; McKinney in 1856; and Fitch in 1889.

More treatment was given to state constitutions than to any other sub-topic. Sixteen books presented one or more state constitutions in the appendices, and twelve others placed them in the body of the texts with accompanying discussion and treatment. Pardou Davis's text, *The Principles of the Government of the United States* (1823), devoted 83.2 per cent of the book to the treatment and discussion of the state constitutions of nine middle states.

Next most space involved presenting a resumé of interesting and comparative material about state governments. The data usually included the date of admission to statehood, the state mottoes, term of state officers, and other miscellaneous information.

Next in order of space emphasis attention was given to the legislative, the executive, and judicial departments of state governments. On an average one-third of the state government space was devoted to these three departments.

Only one-fifth of the space was given education, taxation, elections, public institutions, and public improvements combined. Even though education is fundamentally a matter of state concern in the United States, since the federal constitution does not mention education, yet only 19 of the 70 textbooks allotted from one to 12 pages to a treatment of the educational provisions of the states. Only 15 of the books dealt, and then only meagerly, with the problems of state taxation. The only book dealing extensively with taxation was Thatcher's *Outline Lessons in Civil Government* (1889) in 20 pages.

Although 20 books mentioned state elections, the treatment was commonly very meager. However, Thorpe's *Government of the People of The United States* (1889) spent eleven pages on the topic. Public institutions were mentioned in only nine books, and public improvements in eight. In other words, the technical matters of state governments were given much more attention than matters that concerned the cultural development of the people in the states.

Local Government. Although agencies of local government have sometimes been referred to as the "cradle" or "backbone" of American democracy, only 27 of the 70 textbooks dealt with them. Only two books during the first two periods did so. In all, only three per cent of the page space of all books dealt with this topic. Those including a treatment did so under one or more of the following matters: Village or borough government, municipal or city government, and rural (township, county, or town, as in New England) government.

The first two sub-topics received only meager attention, except in the later books. In discussing the municipal or city governments major consideration was given the "mayor-council" or "mayor-aldermanic" type.

Rural government was given more attention than the other two forms. Treatment of the town, the county, and the county-township were all classified under rural government. The town type of government prevailed throughout New England, the county type was most common in the South, and the township type existed largely in the middle and mid-western states. Most of the books dealing with this subject largely confined their explanation to some one type of rural government. No doubt this was a concession to the area where the author lived or where the text was published. Two authors devoted considerable space to this subject, which may be inferred from the titles of their texts; namely, Rosenberger's *Civil Government of Iowa and the United States* (1886), and Hart's *Civil Government of The United States, and The State of Kentucky* (1889). It may be said that some publishers printed supplements dealing with particular states to accompany the more general civil government textbooks.

Common and Statutory Law. Only 17 of the 70 textbooks devoted space to this topic, but in a number of these the treatment was rather extensive. The first author to deal with it was Sullivan in *The Political Class Book* in 1831. He was an attorney, which fact at least partially explains why he would emphasize an understanding of law. More than one-sixth of the book discussed wills, contracts, deeds, mortgages, and even domestic relations as pertaining to the obligations the child owes the father and the wife the husband.

The author, whose books went through more editions and who wrote under more titles than any other writer in the field, was Andrew W. Young. All of his texts, except one for beginners, devoted considerable space to law. In his 1864 edition of *The Government Classbook* he defined common and statutory laws:

> Statute laws are those which are enacted by the legislature, and recorded in writing, and are usually collected and published in books. . . . The common law is not a code of written laws enacted by a legislature, but consists of rules of action which have become binding from long usage and established custom.

A number of other writers of civil government believed that the legal fundamentals of business should be taught in the schools. Others enumerated and defined the chief forms of crime, misdemeanors, and their punishments as established by statutory regulations.

International Law. Eleven textbooks dealt with international law or the laws of nations. Only two authors dealt with it before 1849; namely, Sullivan (1831) with eleven pages, and Mason with four pages. The two authors devoting most space to it were: Burleigh (1849) with seventeen pages; and Young with 24 pages in 1854, 18 pages in 1864, and 19 pages in his 1885 text. It seems quite evident that the textbook writers in the field of civil government before 1890 were not very conscious of the importance of understanding international matters.

MISCELLANEOUS CHARACTERISTICS

An examination of old school textbooks reveals many characteristics not common among modern ones. One of these relates to the nature of the titles of old texts. Commonly titles were rather long and very descriptive. A good example of this was Andrew W. Young's popular text of 1845. Its title follows:

First Lessons
in
Civil Government
A Comprehensive View
of the
Government of the State of Ohio
and
An Abstract of The Laws,

Showing The Rights, Duties, and Responsibilities of Citizens in The
Civil and Domestic Relations; with
An Outline of The
Government of The United States:
Adapted to The Capacities of Children and Youth,
and
Designed for Families and Schools

By Andrew W. Young

Cleveland
Published by M. C. Younglove

Some title pages even included quotations; for example, excerpts
from Washington's Farewell Address.

A second peculiar characteristic often was to include endorsements, testimonials, and advertisements. For example, *The Constitutional Text-Book* (1856) by Furman Sheppard contained
22 pages of testimonials in very fine print, which preceded the
title page. These were written by superintendents of schools,
judges, governors, bishops, college presidents, legal writers,
attorney generals, senators, and secretaries of state.

Fourteen textbooks contained such material. Some of these
inserted a copy of a letter from United States Secretary of State
attesting to the correctness of the reproduction of the U.S.
Constitution as presented in the books. Others were testimonials
from persons who had used the earlier editions of the books. Still
others were endorsements by very distinguished men who had read
a copy of the book. Several of the latter type follow:

Monticello, Sep 26, 1823

It can not be doubted that it is advisable to make our young
people acquainted with the principles of our government *as early as
possible.*

Th. Jefferson
Ex-president of the U.S.

This was quoted in Pardou Davis's *The Principles of the Government of The United States* (1823).

In Joseph Burleigh's *The American Manual* (1854) the
following endorsement was quoted:

Department of State
Washington, Oct. 1, 1850

This is to certify, that Joseph Bartlett Burleigh's Script Edition of the U.S. Constitution with the amendments, has been carefully collated with the originals in the Archives of this Department, and proved to be accurate in the CAPITALS, ORTHOGRAPHY, TEXT, and PUNCTUATION.

David Webster
Secretary of State
W. G. Derrick
Chief Clerk

Nine textbooks contained dedicatory pages. These often reflected the idealistic sentiments which pervaded the early part of our national existence. The authors evidently expected these ideals to influence those who would use the books. An outstanding example of this is in Alexander Maitland's *The Political Instructor* (1833), which in part follows:

To JAMES MADISON

To you, Sir, as the surviving member of the august assembly that framed the Constitution, and of that illustrious triumvirate who, in vindicating it from the objections of its first assailants, succeeded in recommending it to the adoption of their country; to you, . . .

In addition to including endorsements and testimonials, many of the earlier books contained advertisements. Fourteen textbooks contained advertisements either preceding the title page or at the end of the book. Commonly these

THE

AMERICAN MANUAL;

CONTAINING

A BRIEF OUTLINE OF THE ORIGIN AND PROGRESS OF POLITICAL POWER, AND THE LAWS OF NATIONS;

A COMMENTARY ON THE CONSTITUTION

OF

THE UNITED STATES OF NORTH AMERICA,

AND

A LUCID EXPOSITION OF THE DUTIES AND RESPONSIBILITIES OF VOTERS, JURORS, AND CIVIL MAGISTRATES;

WITH

QUESTIONS, DEFINITIONS, AND MARGINAL EXERCISES;

DESIGNED TO DEVELOPE AND STRENGTHEN THE MORAL AND INTELLECTUAL POWERS OF YOUTH, AND IMPART AN ACCURATE KNOWLEDGE OF THE NATURE AND NECESSITY OF POLITICAL WISDOM.

ADAPTED TO THE USE OF

SCHOOLS, ACADEMIES, AND THE PUBLIC:

BY

JOSEPH BARTLETT BURLEIGH, A.M.
A Member of the Baltimore Bar, and President of Newton University.

"REGNANT POPULI."

PHILADELPHIA:
GRIGG, ELLIOT & CO.
No. 14 NORTH FOURTH STREET.
1848.

A very complete and well-received text, attested for accuracy by the Secretary of State.

would list, and often describe, the books printed by the publisher of the text. For example, Burleigh's *The American Manual* (1849) listed (and described some) 54 books published by the Grigg, Elliot & Co., Philadelphia.

TEACHING AND LEARNING AIDS

In some respects the development in the use of teaching and learning aids in textbooks in the various subject fields has had a similar evolution. However, in the use of some types of aids considerable differences appear according to the subject field. For example, only 16 civil government textbooks include illustrative material, such as maps or charts, while nearly all old geographies use them.

No one teaching aid was used in all of the 70 civil government textbooks. In general, the use of teaching aids increased after the first period. Of the 70 books analyzed, 66 contained prefaces, 57 tables of contents, 51 appendices, 47 indexes, 44 questions, 32 notes, 18 introductions, 16 answers, 16 illustrative material, 10 outlines, 10 references, 6 glossaries, and 4 summaries.

CHAPTER 9

———···⟨∞⟩···———

PHYSIOLOGIES

EARLIEST HISTORY

THE urge for self preservation has made man throughout
history cognizant of the laws of physiology and hygiene,
consciously or unconsciously. Hieroglyphic inscriptions of the
ancient Egyptians evidenced standards for personal and public
hygiene. Later the famous Hellenic library at Alexandria contained writings dealing with anatomy, physiology, and hygiene.

The Romans, in contrast to the Greek emphasis on individual
bodily development, paid more attention to public sanitation, for
example, the water supply. Asceticism as developed under medieval Christianity greatly lessened the attention to bodily health.
Thus the study of the principles of physiology and hygiene was
sadly neglected. Only the few who studied medicine in the medieval universities gave the field much attention. Among the masses
occultism and superstition were too commonly followed. Physiology failed to be among the "Seven Liberal Arts," which largely
constituted the curriculum of medieval higher learning.

In the field of physiology and health, as in several other fields,
a gradual change took place during the Renaissance. Many of the
famous Court schools of Italy introduced physical training and
play. Some of these schools spent as much as two hours and even
more to such exercises. Among the outdoor games were "ball

play," and running and jumping. Soon other games and exercises were developed. There is no evidence, however, that textbooks in the field were used.

One of the earliest significant textbooks of anatomy was the *Fabrica Humani Corporis* (Structure of the Human Body) written by Andreas Vesalius (1514-1564) and published in 1543. This book marked the beginning of an epoch in the history of anatomy, and so also of physiology and medicine. This represented a great improvement over the writings of Galan and other earlier writers. Other scientists soon began to be interested not only in the structure of the human body, but also in its functioning. One significant aspect of this was to deal with the circulation of the blood. While a number of men concerned themselves with this problem, the man generally recognized as making the greatest contributions about it was William Harvey (1578-1657). In 1628 he daringly published his significant findings concerning the circulation of the blood in his *Exercitatio de Cordia Moto*. Nearly all of these early works were published in Latin and were not intended as textbooks to be used in lower schools.

One of the first, if not the first, popular textbook to contain considerable content on anatomy and physiology was the *Orbis Pictus* by Jan Comenius (1592-1671). This book was first published in 1658, and continued to be used in western Europe for more than a century. It consisted of 154 short lessons, each illustrated with a picture. More than 20 lessons dealt with animals, birds, and fish. Nine illustrated lessons dealt with man, under such titles as *Homo* (man), *Membra Hominus Externa* (outward parts of man), *Caput et Manus* (head and hand), *Caro et Viscera* (flesh and bowels), *Canales et Ossa* (flesh and bones), *Sensus Externi et Interni* (outward and inward senses), and so on.

Some of the vernacular schools during the period of Realism taught some science. Franke (1663-1727) taught anatomy in his Pëdagogium, and about animal life in his lower school. Basedow (1723-1790) treated elements of anatomy and physiology in his *Elementarwerk*. Later Salzmann (1744-1811) taught about animals in his school, and also introduced sports and gymnastics. Thus the teaching of some science was introduced in the lower school levels. However, apparently no regular textbooks of physiology and anatomy were then written for use in elementary schools.

The earliest textbooks of spelling, grammar, arithmetic, and geography to be used in American common schools were brought here from Europe, and many were reprinted here, but this was not true of textbooks of physiology and anatomy. Although several European written textbooks were republished here, they were chiefly suitable for use in professional and medical schools.

AIMS OF AMERICAN PHYSIOLOGY TEXTBOOKS[1]

About seventy-five per cent of the nineteenth century textbooks in this field were written by medical doctors. On the other hand, during the twentieth century only about one-third were written by them. The other texts were written by scientists, professors, and others.

It is interesting to note the uses of the texts suggested by the authors on the title pages or in the prefaces. Of course, since the authors sought as wide a usage as possible, most books mentioned more than one use. Most frequently they suggested use for schools, homes, higher education, and academies.

The following were the most frequently mentioned aims or objectives the books were to fulfill:

Popular Interest. Brigham in an early book (1833) stated:

> He would again express the hope that his countrymen, and particu-
> larly those who have the care of youth, would give more attention
> than they have hitherto, to the study of anatomy and physiology.

Cutter in a very popular text (1847) stated:

> The design of the following pages, is to diffuse in the community,
> especially among youth, a knowledge of Human Anatomy, Physi-
> ology, and the Laws of Health.

---

[1] Most of the objective data presented in this chapter were taken from Helen Barton's unpublished doctoral dissertation, University of Pittsburgh (1942), entitled, "A Study of the Development of Textbooks in Physiology and Hygiene in the U.S." She analyzed 62 textbooks published before and 19 after 1900.

Many other books contained statements concerning the general value of learning more about this field of study. Lambert's *Practical Anatomy, Physiology and Pathology* (1851) contained the following interesting statement:

> The study you are commencing has become a very fashionable one, so to speak. A few years ago some sentimental young lady would occasionally be found, who thought it was hardly proper for her to study the condition of the lungs and blood vessels, as if she had not any.

Correlation with Natural Sciences. Hooker, in his popular *Human Physiology* (1855), said:

> The relations, then, of Physiology to some of the common branches taught in the higher classes in schools, are of the most intimate character. . . . The analogies that exist between the human body and all other living things, in relation to structure and growth, are so numerous and striking.

Other similar statements appeared in other textbooks in the field.

Laboratory Work. During the second half of the nineteenth century some authors began to suggest activities and projects for the students. In one of his later texts (1872) Cutter suggested:

> As the study of objects is more simple and impressive than mere words, and as illustrations are more instructive, particularly to children, than written sentences, this work has been so arranged as to be used advantageously with OBJECT study and TOPICAL instruction, especially with Outline Anatomical Charts, both human and comparative.

Steele (1884) strongly advocated the use of the microscope, and gave directions in his texts for experimental activities. Smith (1885) even suggested the "dissection of a cat or dog or rabbit, illustrating the lessons," to make the "text clear, and fix the essential facts in mind."

Prejudices. Superstitions and prejudices were common regarding many matters involving physiology and hygiene. So numerous authors mentioned the overcoming of prejudices as an objective for teaching physiology. In his *Guide to Health* (1845) Colby said:

> Let us strip our profession of everything that looks like mystery and imposition, and clothe medical knowledge in a dress so simple and intelligible, that it may become a part of academical education.

In his *Human Physiology* (1856) Draper wrote:

> It was chiefly, indeed, for the sake of aiding in the removal of the mysticism which has pervaded the science that the author was induced to print this book. Alone, of all the departments of knowledge, Physiology still retains the metaphysical conceptions of the Middle Ages.

A number of the authors mentioned the overcoming of mystery regarding the human body as an aim.

The Effects of Alcohol. More authors mentioned this as one of the purposes to be fulfilled than any other aim. This was particularly true of the textbooks of the latter part of the nineteenth century. It was then that the Women's Christian Temperance Union became very active in securing many state legislatures to enact laws requiring the teaching of the evil effects of alcohol and tobacco through the textbooks of physiology and health. Thus authors, in order to secure adoptions in the various states, would claim that their books met the legal requirements. Thus the *Child's Health Primer* (1885) stated:

> As this little book goes to press, Massachusetts, by an act of its legislature, is made the fourteenth state in this country that requires the pupils in the primary as well as in the higher grades of public schools, to be taught the effects of alcoholics and other narcotics upon the human system, in connection with other facts of physiology and hygiene.

Some authors prepared different editions for different states according to legal requirements.

In many books each chapter would have a section dealing with the evil effects of alcohol. For example, Cutter's popular *Comprehension Anatomy, Physiology, and Hygiene* (1884) closed the following chapters with a section on alcohol: Living Properties, The Framework and Its Coverings, Contractile and Irritable Tissues, Vascular System and the Circulation, Respiration Apparatus, Foods, Digestive Organs, Nutrition, Nervous System, Special Senses, and the Larynx and Voice. Nineteen of the twenty-four texts between 1880 and 1895 dealt with this topic.

CONTENT

The content of the early physiology textbooks evidently was greatly influenced by the interests and whims of the authors. Since many of the earlier books were written by medical doctors, it can be understood easily why their books often were very technical and difficult for the average common school student to understand. Consequently in a number of respects the textbooks written before 1900 were different in content than those after 1900.

An examination of Table VIII shows that the percentage of space devoted to certain topics greatly increased while that of others decreased. The stress given the more technical topics generally decreased, while that given matters of health and hygiene greatly increased. The attention given to the structural matters of the human body, such as the muscular system, the nervous system, and the skeletal system markedly decreased. On the other hand, the percentage of space devoted to functional matters, as disease, exercise and fatigue, food and nutrition, emergency and accidents, and growth and development increased.

Nervous System. The topic receiving most attention in the books before 1900, and next most after 1900, was the nervous system. Likely one reason for such marked attention was because the nervous system has been recognized as the master of the other systems. However, no prescribed pattern for studying the topic was followed. The older books more or less commonly dealt with a detailed analysis of the nerves, in some cases nine nerves, and with an analysis of the sense organs. Often cross section pictures showing the nerves or the parts of the brain were included. In fact one-fifth of the pictures presented in all the books dealt with

TABLE VIII

PERCENTAGE OF SPACE DEVOTED TO THE VARIOUS TOPICS IN AMERICAN
PHYSIOLOGY TEXTBOOKS BEFORE AND AFTER 1900.

	62 Books Before 1900	19 Books After 1900
	Percentage of Space	Percentage of Space
1. Alcohol, Narcotics, Stimulants	7.34	4.80
2. Alimentary System	9.23	7.75
3. Animal Heat	1.67	0.81
4. Circulatory System	8.05	5.20
5. Excretory System	0.77	1.03
6. Exercise, Fatigue, Rest	2.34	5.90
7. Food and Nutrition	4.19	9.03
8. Glandular System	0.64	0.30
9. Muscular System	7.33	3.62
10. Nervous System	22.15	11.82
11. Respiratory System	8.77	7.90
12. Skeletal System	9.54	3.70
13. Skin and Membranes	4.89	6.30
14. Directions for Nurses and Sick	0.19	0.10
15. Disease	1.74	13.00
16. Emergency and Accident	0.78	6.61
17. Growth and Development	1.72	5.30
18. Moral Education	0.60	1.25
19. Reproductive System	0.12	0.00
20. Sex Education	0.00	0.30
21. Miscellaneous	7.94	5.28

some aspects of the nervous system. Only one textbook failed to consider the nervous system.

The textbooks of the 1880's and several decades following dealt rather extensively with the effects of alcohol, stimulants, and narcotics on the nervous system. For example, Palmer's *Hygiene for Young People* (1884) said:

More alcohol goes to the brain of the drinking man, than to any other organ except the liver; its effect on the nerve-substance is deadening—paralyzing—as you have learned.

In Cutter's *Anatomy, Physiology, and Hygiene* (1884) a rather lengthy statement appeared. In part it said:

Alcohol taken into the system effects rapid changes in the working of the nerve-centres. When taken continuously, it impairs the nutrition of these centres. . . . Impaired cell-nutrition induces imperfect, abnormal, or perverted action,—mental, organic, muscular.

Other textbooks made similar and even stronger claims concerning such effects on the nervous system.

Alimentary System. The topic receiving second most attention was the alimentary system. However, the textbooks varied greatly in the amount of space devoted to it. Dunglison's *An Elementary Physiology* (1885) devoted thirty per cent of its pages to it. On the other hand, four gave it no treatment. Apparently an accident in Michigan in 1822 resulted in a stimulation of interest in its functioning. Alexis St. Martin suffered a severe wound in his stomach. He was treated by Dr. William Beaumont, who began to observe the processes of digestion through the aperture. Too, he experimented by having Martin eat a variety of foods, recording the results of his observations. In 1833 Dr. Beaumont published the results. Many textbooks thereafter used these findings.

The study of the alimentary system commonly dealt with mastication, the canal structure, peristalsis, digestive fluids and their reactions, absorptions, and defecation. Later books included the effects of alcohol, state of mind and food selection, and the effects of exercise, varying with the interests of the author. Some of the more recent books began to deal with the diet. Richie's *Human Physiology* (1911) included a chapter on dietetics.

Respiratory System. This topic received a more constant and undeviating attention throughout the years than any other topic. There was roughly little more than one per cent variation in space treatment during the fourteen decades. Nearly all described the process of respiration. Hooker's *Human Physiology* (1859) described it as follows:

> You can see that, if all the muscular fibres in the diaphragm contract, the arch will be flattened, and thus the room in the chest will be enlarged. To occupy this room thus made, the air rushes in through the windpipe. This is inspiration. In expiration, the reverse movement takes place—the arch of the diaphragm rises, and, compressing the lungs, forces the air out of them through the trachea.

Nearly identical descriptions appeared in books about sixty-five years later.

Gaseous exchange within the cells of the lungs and the protection provided the lungs by the ribs were subdivisions receiving treatment in many books. Other matters discussed were residual air, carbonic acid intoxication, dizziness, and swooning. Some authors also discussed artificial respiration.

Circulatory System. Much more extensive consideration was given this topic during the nineteenth than the twentieth century. The invention of the stethoscope by Laënnec in 1816 sharpened the attention of the earlier writers upon the circulatory system. The treatment of the topic became rather standardized in the texts. The circulation of the blood through the heart and its control of the valves, and the arterial, venous, capillary, and pulmonic circulation were subdivisions receiving attention in most texts of both centuries. Some authors discussed the connection of the digestive and circulatory system with cellular nutrition. As early as 1847 Cutter's *Anatomy and Physiology* discussed this process as follows:

> It is through the medium of the capillaries that the operations of nutrition and secretion are performed. They are remarkable for the uniformity of diameter, and for the constant divisions and communications which take place between them. They inosculate on the one with the terminal extremity of the arteries, and on the other with the commencement of the veins.

The more modern texts often dealt with the chemical composition of blood. After the 1880's some texts mentioned the vasodilation of the peripheral vessels after consuming alcoholic drinks.

Skeletal Structure. The earlier physiology textbooks gave much more attention to this topic than the later ones. Twenty of the sixty-two texts of the nineteenth century dealt with it as Chapter I. While the human framework has always been of interest to man, it was not until Vesalius made a detailed study of a skeleton procured from a hangman's scaffold that a better understanding of it developed. Later others began to discuss the marvels of the healing processes which they had observed in fractured appendages.

Early authors frequently discussed in detail the anatomy of the bones, including such matters as ossification, chemical structure, descriptions of the ligaments, and the microscopic details of the canals of the bones. Evidently the detailed discussions in many books were too difficult, and generally uninteresting for the students. The following is an example from the *Elementary Anatomy and Physiology* (1861) by Hitchcock and Hitchcock:

> Of Synarthrosis there are four varieties: first, Sutura, the articulation between the bones of the skull by ragged interlocking edges; second, Harmonia, that between the two upper maxillaries, where the bones with comparatively straight edges are simply placed edge to edge; third, Schindylesis, or the joint between the vomer and sphenoid, where the expanded edge of one bone is fitted into a corresponding groove in the other; fourth, Gomphosis, the articulation of the teeth with the jaws, and so named since it resembles the manner in which a common nail is driven into a plank.

This is an example of the poor grading of the content in early school textbooks. Writers too often thought only in terms of content rather than in terms of the children who were to learn it.

Other authors began to think of the hygiene and function of bones. Cutter as early as 1854 said:

> If the bench is so high as not to permit the feet to rest upon the floor, the weight of the limbs below the knee may cause the flexible bone of the thigh to become curved.

Jarvis (1848) discussed rickets, and several authors pointed out the relationship between the bones of the body and the physical laws pertaining to levers of the first, second, and third class. The texts after 1900 placed more stress upon the function of bones rather than their structure.

Skin and Membranes. This topic received little or no attention by the earliest authors of physiology textbooks. In fact, four of the five oldest books analyzed gave it no treatment. However, an exception was Combe. In his *Principles of Physiology* (1841) one-sixth of the book dealt with it. He bemoaned the neglect of it by other authors. He raised a question relating to the scarf skin (epidermis) and its uses in saying:

> Being homogeneous in structure, it is supposed by many to be merely an exudation of albuminous mucus; and although depressions are obvious on its surface, and exhalation and absorption are proved to be carried on through its substance, it is still in dispute whether it be actually porous or not.

He was concerned with the whole question of epidermal penetrability by external substances.

Soon other authors gave this subject attention. The aspects most commonly receiving treatment pertained to the protective peripheral covering, the functional properties of sweat and oil production, the appearance of the skin, and its ability to assist in temperature regulation. Several even warned against the excessive use of cosmetics as injurious to the skin.

This was the first of the major topics under discussion to receive more attention in the physiology textbooks after 1900 than before. It may be that the discoveries relating to bacteria by such scientists as Koch, Pasteur, Welch, and Lister influenced textbooks authors. Dangers of infectious diseases received attention. For example, Blaisdell's *Our Bodies and How We Live* (1910) said in part:

> The outer skin helps protect the true skin from poisons . . . if there is a scratch or sore, so that the true skin is exposed, the poisons may be absorbed into the blood with great rapidity.

Muscular System. Eighty-nine per cent of the nineteenth century physiology textbooks dealt with this subject. In all, four properties of muscles were discussed by some authors; namely, contractility, extensibility, elasticity, and tonicity. Of these the contractile power of muscular fibers received most attention. As early as 1848 Cutter explained its importance as follows:

> It is by their contraction that we are enabled to pursue different employments. By their action the farmer cultivates his field, the mechanic wields his tools, the author his pen, the sportsman pursues his game, the orator gives utterance to his thoughts, the lady sweeps the keys of the piano, and the young are whirled in the mazy dance.

Extensibility and elasticity were illustrated by Conn (1906) as follows:

> If we stretch a rubber band, it becomes longer and thinner; when we let go of the ends, it shortens and becomes as thick as before. In somewhat the same way the muscles of the body are shortened, the muscle growing thicker as it contracts.

Tonicity was not discussed until the more recent books appeared. Fatigue and the effects of alcohol and narcotics also were given fuller treatment in the later books. The earlier books had dealt more fully with the structure and location of muscles, while the later ones discussed the hygiene of the muscular system and its functioning during work and physical exercises.

Food and Nutrition. This topic was given more than twice the percentage of space in the texts after 1900 than before. More than one-fourth of the texts before 1900 omitted it. Since such a large fraction of the population before 1900 lived either on farms or in small towns where it was common to have gardens, the supply of food, and its quality, were not so critical as after 1900, when urbanization required the masses to buy their food. Consequently the nutritional value of the various types of food, and their relative costs, became a matter of serious concern, especially of urban dwellers. Thus charts of food values, calorie content, and balanced diets appeared. Even refrigeration of foods received attention.

Alcohol, Narcotics, and Stimulants. This was the last topic to have received more than an average of four per cent attention in the texts before 1900. However, most of this attention was given during the last two decades. Twenty-eight of the thirty-nine texts before 1883 failed to discuss this general subject. On the other hand, only four of the twenty-three between 1883 and 1900 omitted it. Nine of the twenty-three devoted more than twenty per cent of their space to it. This was largely due to the efforts of the W.C.T.U. in securing the enactment of state laws requiring the teaching of the harmful effects of alcohol and narcotics. Two books devoted more than forty per cent of space to these effects. While only one text after 1900 omitted the topic, only one gave it more than nine per cent space.

Other Topics. The following topics were given less than two per cent average space in the texts before 1900: Animal heat, disease, growth and development, excretory system, glandular system, emergencies, moral education, directions for nurses, reproductive system, and sex education. Exercise and fatigue were given 2.34 per cent space.

CHANGES IN TEXTBOOKS

Marked changes took place in the physiology textbooks after 1900 in their lessened attention to certain topics and their greatly increased attention to others. The topics receiving lessened attention in the later books were the muscular system, the nervous system, and the skeletal system. These were treated rather factually and technically in most of the earlier textbooks. More early attention was given to structural matters rather than how these systems functioned. Many of the technical facts apparently were to be committed to memory by the students.

On the other hand, at least five topics received markedly increased attention in the texts after 1900. Treatment of exercise, fatigue, and rest increased from 2.34 per cent to 5.9 per cent in average space; food and nutrition from 4.19 per cent to 9.03 per cent; disease from 1.74 per cent to 13.00 per cent; emergency and accident from 0.78 per cent to 6.61 per cent; and growth and development from 1.72 per cent to 5.3 per cent. It may be noted that these topics dealt more with functions and care relating to health and well being of children rather than structural matters. The later writers thought more in terms of the physical needs of boys and girls rather than the mastery of technical subject matter.

PHYSIOLOGIES BEFORE 1860

Physiology did not become a common subject for study in what is now the public school level at a very early date. In fact, it was one of the last content subjects to gain acceptance in the common schools. The earliest physiology textbooks seem to have been used largely only in medical schools. Apparently it was not until after Horace Mann, while head of the public schools in Massachusetts, began in the 1840's to advocate strongly the study of physiology and hygiene that it gradually was added to the school curriculum. As evidence of its lesser popularity, the writer's collection contains about 900 readers published before 1900, but only a few over 100 physiologies. These were written by 56 different authors. Even many of these were intended for use in higher education.

The oldest of these was a *Manual of the Physiology of Man* by Ph. Hutin, originally in French, translated into English by Joseph Togno, and reprinted in Philadelphia in 1828. This was intended for use in medical schools. The organization of its contents was very interesting. After an introductory chapter of 34 pages of definitions and explanations, the other parts were:

FIRST CLASS
Life of the Individual
FIRST ORDER
Functions of Secretion

FIRST CLASS
SECOND ORDER
Functions of Relation
Functions which are subservient to the preservation of the species.

SECOND CLASS

It contained much technical material. The last part contained material of an intimate nature which certainly could not have been taught to children. The book was bound in leather.

One of the first, if not the first, physiology written for children in America was W. A. Alcott's *The House I Live In* (1834). Apparently this book gained little acceptance as a textbook.

J. L. Comstock. The first physiology school textbook to gain considerable usage was written by Comstock. He already was the author of textbooks in mineralogy, natural philosophy (physics),

chemistry, botany, and geology. He was America's first prolific
textbook writer in the sciences. In 1836 his *Outlines of Physiology*
appeared. It was intended for "Use in Schools and Heads of
Families." In justification for this book he quoted a Dr. Dick as
follows:

> It is somewhat unaccountable, and not a little inconsistent, that
> while we direct the young to look abroad over the surface of the
> earth, and survey its mountains, rivers, . . . that we should never
> teach them *to look into themselves,* to consider their own corporeal
> structures, the numerous parts of which they are composed; . . . and
> the lessons of practical instruction which may be derived from
> such contemplations.

Comstock aimed to fulfill these purposes by "adapting his language and manner to the understanding of youth." He particularly wanted the text to be useful, "especially that of females, to
the preservation of their forms and their health, by avoiding
habits and fashions, which at once deform their persons and ruin
their constitutions."

This book consisted of 310
pages, which included many
pictures. The contents consisted of six parts: I. Me-
chanical Functions; II, Verte-
brated Animals; III, Animal
Functions; IV, Circulation of
the Blood; V, Sensorial Functions; and VI, Mental and
Physical Exercise. The topic
titles under the first three
parts reveal that half of the
book was really general biology, and only the second half

308   APPENDIX.

The fact that the female form has undergone a very
material change within the last 20 years, and that this
change has been caused by the pressure of stays on parts
of the system which are of the utmost importance to the
nutrition, and consequent growth, and health of our species, cannot, and will not, be denied by any competent
witness. And that we shall become a stinted, puny, and
short lived race, in consequence, it requires no more inspiration to predict, than it does to foretell that starvation
will produce dwarfs in infancy, and emaciation in adults.
The effects, indeed, are already visible in the number
of pale, dwarfish, and crooked children, which may be
seen in the schools and streets of all our cities, and many
of our smaller towns and villages. And whoever, having been interested in the welfare of the rising genera-
tion, will contrast, so far as she can recollect, the aspect
of a school composed of both sexes, at the present day,
with the appearance of the same number and ages, 15
or 20 years ago, cannot, we think, but be convinced, that
that there has been a great deterioration in our youth,
both in respect to form, size, and healthy looks.
And who, we enquire, would not expect to see such a
change in our race, when they behold such a metamor-

Fig. 136.   Fig. 137.

Venus de Medicis.   *A Modern Lady.*
phosis in the better half of our species, as to have produced from a stock like that represented by Fig. 136, a

Comstock, 1836, "to be useful to
youth, and especially to females
. . . by avoiding fashions which
deform and ruin."

of the book dealt with human physiology. This book appeared in several editions. An appendix of 40 pages dealt with the "Description of the Attitudes" (Posture), which discussed the proper bodily positions in standing, walking, and sitting, as well as the effects of tight lacing, and other similar matters.

The above book was recopyrighted in 1847 with the title changed to *Physiology Both Comparative and Human.* However, its contents were identical with the 1836 edition, except that five pages were added dealing with the "predisposition to consumption" and exercise of the lungs. This edition also appeared in several reprintings.

Physiologies of the 1840's. The success of Comstock's text, plus the advocacy of the teaching of physiology by Horace Mann, apparently aroused a number of authors to write physiology textbooks during the 1840's. Books written by Combe (1840), Colby (1844), Griscom (1845), Cutter (1846), Nichols (1846), Jarvis (1847), and Hamilton (1849) appeared. However, only the books by Cutter gained wide circulation. So only a few words need be said about some characteristic features of several of them.

Combe's *Principles of Physiology* was first written in Scotland and then reprinted in New York in 1840. This book was the first to devote extensive attention to the structure and functions of the skin. Colby's *Guide to Health* dealt more fully with matters pertaining to health and disease rather than the technical and structural matters of the body. Griscom's *First Lessons in Human Physiology* was a very elementary and attractive little book. It went through several reprintings. Jarvis published a *Practical Physiology* in 1847, and a *Primary Physiology* in 1848. The former was a rather large book of 400 pages of fine print, while the latter was a small and rather attractive book with numerous pictures. In 1849 Hamilton's *Elements of Vegetable and Animal Physiology*, originally printed in Edinburgh, Scotland (1844), was reprinted in New York. This was a rather technical book of biology, dealing only in part with man.

Calvin Cutter. Cutter's physiology textbooks apparently became the most widely used of any written before 1900. The writer's collection contains fourteen different books under six titles. The first one was published in 1846 and the latest in 1888. He served as a professor of physiology in several universities.

His first text was an *Anatomy and Physiology* (1846). It was "designed for Academies and Families." He too quoted the same Dr. Dick as Comstock as the reason for writing it. Its purpose was to "diffuse in the community, especially among youth, a knowledge of Human Anatomy, Physiology, and the Laws of Health." He presented the structure of organs, their functions, and matters of hygiene and health. It contained more than 200 engravings. It also had a glossary in the back. This book went through several printings.

In 1852 he published his *Treatise on Anatomy, Physiology, and Hygiene,* "designed for Colleges, Academies, and Families." It was much larger than his 1846 text, and contained 150 engravings. It appeared in numerous printings. Several hundred thousand copies of these were sold. In 1854 a small text, entitled *Human and Comparative Anatomy, Physiology, and Hygiene,* by Mrs. Eunice P. Cutter appeared. She was Calvin's wife, and the book was printed by the same publisher as Calvin's 1852 book. It was an attractive and simple one with 100 engravings. It definitely was an elementary physiology. Evidently it had considerable circulation.

To satisfy his publishers, in 1870 Cutter thoroughly revised and remodeled his 1852 text. The new title became *New Analytic Anatomy, Physiology and Hygiene.* By this late date he was not merely concerned with the contents of such a work, but also how it should be taught. On a page addressed "To Teachers," he suggested that the method be "Analytical, with Synthetical Reviews," and so on. He aimed to make the anatomy and physiology more concise and definite, the hygiene plain and practical, and to introduce comparative anatomy. The glossary was enlarged.

In 1871-1872 Cutter decided to publish a two-book series, so he prepared a *First Book on Analytical Anatomy, Physiology and Hygiene* for "Common and Grammar Schools and for Families," and a *Second Book* for "Academies, Grammar Schools and Families." The organization and table of contents were nearly identical except that the *Second* contained chapters on General

Histology and General Chemistry not included in the *First*. The *Second Book* was more than 100 pages larger.

Apparently to continue to profit from the reputation of Calvin Cutter as a physiology textbook author, the son, John C. Cutter, wrote the *Comprehensive Anatomy, Physiology, and Hygiene* in 1884. This was intended for the upper grades and secondary schools. The next year he published *Lessons in Hygiene*, an "Elementary Textbook on the Maintenance of Health." On the title pages of both books reference was made to "Lessons on the Action of Stimulants and Sedatives." The earlier Cutter books did not contain such lessons. Beginning in the 1880's such lessons were required in some states.

It may be asked why the Cutter physiologies continued to be so popular. One reason may be because one revision followed the other to keep them up-to-date. However, other reasons were that they kept a balanced presentation among the content relating to the structure of the organs of the body, the functioning of them, and lastly their care so as to maintain health. Also each of these books contained a hundred or more pictures and illustrations. Then, too, the pupils and teachers were guided by the inclusion of questions. In the earlier books the questions were at the bottom of every page. In the *Analytic* text 60 pages in the back of the book were devoted to an "Analytic Examination," chapter by chapter. Cutter made his books teachable and learnable.

Worthington Hooker (1806-1867) The most successful physiology to appear first in the 1850's was Hooker's *Human Physiology* in 1854. After receiving a medical degree from Harvard in 1829, he devoted much time to writing medical books. He also wrote textbooks in natural history, chemistry, physics, geology, and nature study.

His *Human Physiology* was designed for colleges and the higher classes in schools. It was reprinted many times through the 50's and 60's. The style was that of a lecturer. He claimed to have thought of the readers of this book as his audience, and thus was lecturing to them. The appendix of 34 pages dealt with directions to teachers and included questions. Nearly 200 engravings were included.

In 1874 his book was revised by J. A. Sewall as Hooker's *New Physiology*. This book was smaller, less technical, and organized better pedagogically. It could well have been used at a lower level than the earlier one. It also went through reprintings.

OTHER PHYSIOLOGIES OF THE *1850'S*

In 1850 the *Practical Anatomy, Physiology, and Pathology; Hygiene and Therapeutics* by T. S. Lambert was published. He classified the bodily organs into First and Second Class. Under the First Class were the organs of thought, feeling, voluntary motion, and sensation. Under the Second Class were those of digestion, circulation, respiration, temperature control, and ex-

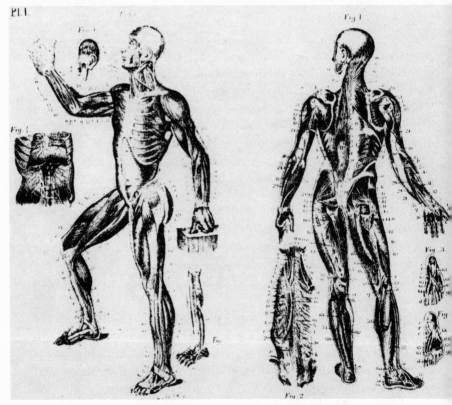

Colored plates from Lambert's *Practical Anatomy, Physiology, Pathology; Hygiene and Therapeutics,* 1850.

cretion. It included many pictures, five being colored. This was the first physiology to use colored plates. Lambert also wrote the *Pictorial Physiology*, a small book for young children of 96 pages and sold for 37½ cents; and a large text entitled *Popular Anatomy and Physiology*. Also in 1850 Fowle's *Human Physiology* was published. This was a treatise of 180 pages explaining Fowle's "Series of Eight Diagrams," prepared for use by parents and teachers illustrating parts of the body.

Hollick's *American Class-Book of Anatomy and Physiology* was published in 1853. It was a rather small book printed in large type and contained ninety engravings. Questions followed each of the rather small chapters. In 1856 Draper's *Human Physiology, Statistical and Dynamical* appeared. This was a large book of 649 pages. It was based on the Lectures on Physiology he had been giving in the University of New York.

In 1854 Comings published his *Class-Book of Physiology*. This was a well illustrated and carefully organized book, intended "for the major portion of our schools." It contained a glossary and index of 18 pages. It was intended to precede his *Principles of Physiology*, which was a larger and more difficult book and adapted to more advanced institutions.

In 1859 the *Illustrated Self-Instructor in Phrenology and Physiology* by O. S. and L. S. Fowler was published. A "Character Chart" began the book. A picture of the cranium showed the cranial seat or location of 37 character traits. Likely this book was not used as a regular physiology textbook in the schools, except possibly as a reference work by some teachers.

PHYSIOLOGIES, 1860-1880

J. C. Dalton. The first physiology textbook to attain considerable circulation during this period was Dalton's *A Treatise on Physiology and Hygiene* in 1868. In the Introduction he stated:

> Physiology is a science which teaches us the natural actions of the living body, and the manner in which they are performed. It is very important for us to know what these actions are.

This statement indicated that he was more interested in the functioning of the bodily organs than in their structure. The titles of the chapters further proved this. After introducing structure in the first chapter, the titles of the remaining chapters were: Food and Its Ingredients, Different Kinds of Food and Their Preparation, Digestion, Absorption, Liver and Its Functions, Blood, Respiration, Circulation, Animal Heat, Nutrition, Nervous System, Spinal Nerves and Cord, Cranial Nerves, the Brain, Sympathetic System, Special Senses, and Development. This edition went through numerous printings. Then in 1875 it was re-copyrighted with no changes except that a chapter on the Anatomy of the Human Body was added, and the Glossary enlarged. Each chapter was followed by a long list of questions. This edition also appeared in several printings.

Joseph C. Hutchinson. Another popular physiology textbook of this period was Hutchinson's *A Treatise on Physiology and Hygiene* (1870). Although he was a medical doctor, he claimed to use "Familiar language . . . rather than that of a technical character." He like Dalton also emphasized the functions of bodily organs. Although he did not favor dissections or experiments on animals in the classroom, he did include a chapter on the use of the microscope in the study of physiology. Meaningful questions were included at the bottom of each page, and review questions at the end of each chapter. The appendix listed the more common poisons and their antidotes. The Glossary not only defined the technical words, but indicated their

NUMBERING AND DEFINITION OF THE ORGANS.

O. S. and L. N. Fowler, *Illustrated Self Instruction in Phrenology and Physiology,* 1859.

pronunciation and root origin. This edition was recopyrighted in 1875, but no changes were made. In 1884 it was again recopyrighted, but enlarged by 52 pages. Some of these additional pages were devoted to such matters as drowning, care of a sick room, disinfection, and emergencies. In all this *Treatise* appeared in many printings for two decades.

Hutchinson eventually sensed that the *Treatise* was too difficult for most public schools, so in 1884 he published *The Laws of Health*. This was intended for the grammar grades. The plan of this book was very similar to the *Treatise*, but contained 100 pages less content. Then in 1886 he wrote his *First Lessons in Physiology*. This was intended for the elementary grades. Its plan was also similar, but contained 60 pages fewer than *The Laws of Health*. Thus Hutchinson's texts constituted a graded series of three books.

J. Dorman Steele. Next to Hutchinson's physiologies those by Steele apparently were the most widely used during this period. In 1872 Steele published his *Fourteen Weeks in Human Physiology*. Other texts by him in the Fourteen-Weeks Series were in natural philosophy (physics), chemistry, geology, and astronomy. Like all of Steele's textbooks, his *Human Physiology* was organized and written to make it very teachable. An analysis of it reveals that it really was a practical combination of anatomy (structure), physiology (function), and hygiene (laws of health). It contained many interesting and informing footnotes, practical questions, as well as illustrations and charts.

J. Dorman Steele, author of popular physiologies, 1872, 1884.

In 1884 he published his *Hygienic Physiology*, which was more than 150 pages larger than his earlier one. The titles of the chapters were the same in both, but the latter was more complete and added a chapter on Health and Disease. Much more attention was given to hygiene. In the Preface he stated:

> To the description of each organ is appended an account of its most common diseases, accidents, etc., and, when practicable, their mode of treatment.

As a special feature it contained nearly 90 pages of Selected Readings to illustrate and supplement the text. Like most texts of the 1880's it listed antidotes to poisons, contained a glossary, and dealt with alcoholic drinks and narcotics. This book continued to appear even after 1900.

R. T. Brown. He was Professor of Physiology at the University of Indiana. In 1872 Brown wrote the *Elements of Physiology and Hygiene* in response to a resolution of the Indiana State Teachers' Association asking for such a text. It was a book of 286 pages, which were divided into fifty lessons. A lesson was to be covered each day. It was adapted to the "common division of the school year into terms of about twelve weeks each. If five lessons are recited each week, the work can be completed in a term, and ten recitations left for review."

Apparently to sell books beyond the confines of Indiana, in 1884 Brown wrote the *Eclectic Physiology*. It was published by the same company that produced the McGuffey *Eclectic Readers*. It was divided into seventeen chapters rather than lessons. The book contained 179 pages of rather simply and clearly written content. In 1887 Brown wrote even a smaller and simpler book entitled, *The House I Live In.* The content of this text consisted rather largely of matters of hygiene. Some of the lesson titles were: Good Kinds of Food and Drink, The Poison Appetite, How To Make Muscles Strong, How We Should Take Exercise, How To Bathe, and so on. It was endorsed by the Woman's Christian Temperance Union for the primary grades, as was the *Eclectic* for the more advanced grades.

Less popular physiologies. In addition to the above discussed physiology textbooks several others appeared during the 1860-1880 period, but which did not gain wide circulation. One was Martindale's *Human Anatomy, Physiology, and Hygiene* in 1872. Although he held an M.D. degree, he was Principal of Madison Grammar School in Philadelphia. Likely one reason why this text failed to gain popularity was because it wAs too similar to several other physiology textbooks which already had wide adoptions. Too, it placed more emphasis on anatomy than was true of some of the more popular texts.

In 1889 a book entitled *How To Get Strong and How To Stay So* by William Blaikie appeared. This was not a regular physiology textbook, but it may be mentioned here because of its marked attention to physical hygiene. The first half of the book dealt with the background factors and matters regarding health and strength, and then the second half with specific exercises for given muscles and for different ages.

PHYSIOLOGIES, 1880-1900

The physiology textbooks of this period were written by a greater number of authors than in the other two periods. The writer's collection contains texts by 32 different authors. Certainly one reason was because by the 1880's physiology was taught in more schools than earlier. This was particularly true on the elementary level. In fact many of the texts heretofore discussed in this chapter were used chiefly in academies, and even in colleges. Evidently the passage of laws in many states requiring the teaching of the evil effects of alcohol and narcotics, due to agitation by the W.C.T.U., virtually required the teaching of physiology in all schools. Many of the physiology textbooks of this period contained an endorsement of approval by the national headquarters of the W.C.T.U.

While many different authors wrote texts during this period, no one writer's physiology gained very wide circulation. This was not so true of the textbooks of any other field for this period. However, a goodly number of the physiologies of this period were published by one publishing company; namely, what is now the American Book Company and its affiliates, such as A. S. Barnes

& Company, and the Ivison, Blakeman & Company, and others.

A. B. C. physiologies. This company published several graded series of physiologies during this period. One was known as the *Pathfinders Series.* It consisted of No. 1—*Child's Health Primer* for primary classes; No. 2—*Hygiene for Young People* for intermediate classes; and No. 3—*Hygienic Physiology* for advanced pupils. They were copyrighted in 1884, and recopyrighted in 1885 and 1888. They were well illustrated, not only with pictures of the structure of organs, but also with pictures illustrating health and sanitation. They were not very technical. Hygiene rather than anatomy was emphasized.

Another was the Eclectic Series. It consisted of *The House I Live In* for primary schools; *The Youth's Temperance Manual* for intermediate schools; and *The Eclectic Physiology*, or *Guide to Health* (1884) for advanced classes. The name of Eli F. Brown appeared on the title page of the earlier editions, but omitted in the 1886 edition of the *Guide to Health.*

A series begun in 1884 was written by William T. Smith. It consisted of the *Primer of Physiology and Hygiene*, and *The Human Body and Its Health.*

The so-called Authorized Physiology Series, also begun in 1884, consisted of No. I—*Health for Little Folks;* No. II—*Lessons in Hygiene* by Johonnet and Barton; and No. III—*Anatomy, Physiology, and Hygiene* by Roger Tracy.

In 1897 the same company published the Frank Overton texts: *Applied Physiology, Intermediate Grade;* and the *Applied Physiology, Advanced Grade.* These books evidenced great improvement over the other series in appearance, quality of pictures, arrangement, and careful explanations. They continued in circulation after the turn of the century.

If we add the texts written by Steele, heretofore discussed, it can be seen that the American Book Company, successor to the Antwerp, Bragg & Company, and their affiliates, published six series of physiologies during the last quarter of the nineteenth century. The only popular physiologies during this period not only published by A. B. C. and affiliates were those by Blaisdell published by Ginn & Company. A. B. C. in 1890 also took over some textbook publishing rights from Harper's and Appleton's.

Albert F. Blaisdell. In 1891 he began a series of three physiologies. The first was *The Child's Book of Health.* This was a simple book with very limited content. Each brief chapter was followed with a rather long list of questions. It left the impression that the content was virtually to be committed. Soon thereafter *How to Keep Well* appeared for the intermediate grades. This book was followed in 1892 by *Our Bodies and How We Live,* which was meant for the upper elementary grades. It was more than three times the size of the *Child's Book.* In 1897 *A Practical Physiology* for secondary schools appeared. This was only a little larger than *Our Bodies.* Then in 1902 he published his *Life and Health,* which was meant for those secondary schools teaching physiology only one semester. These books went through several printings.

Less popular physiologies. In 1882 Charles K. Mills published his *First Lessons in Physiology and Hygiene.* This was a book of 250 pages, which appeared to be more difficult and larger than most beginning books. He apparently meant it to be for elementary schools using only one physiology book. It appeared in several printings.

Beginning in 1883 H. Newell Martin, Professor of Biology at Johns Hopkins, wrote a series of three texts entitled *The Human Body—Elementary Course* of 261 pages, *Briefer Course* of 364

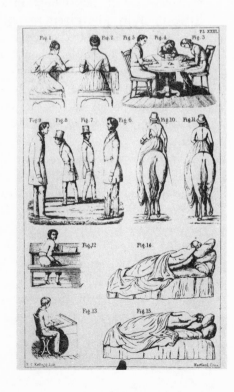

Comings, 1854, position and posture for health, *Class Book of Physiology.*

pages, and *Advanced Course* of 655 pages. The beginner's text
was larger and more technical than most other lowest level texts.
In contrast to other physiologies of that period, they contained
no glossary. These books appeared in at least three editions.

In 1891 the following two texts by Oliver P. Jenkins appeared:
Primary Lessons in Human Physiology, and *Advanced Lessons
in Human Physiology.* Although the latter title used the word,
advanced, it was meant for the upper elementary grades. These
books constituted the Indiana State Series. They were well illustrated, but included no glossary. Both appeared in several
editions.

CONCLUDING COMMENTS

Physiology was a late entry into the American common school
curriculum. When physiology textbooks did appear, most of
them were written by medical doctors. These men knew little
about teaching methods or the gradation of materials according
to the age of learners. Except for Horace Mann's influence urging
the teaching of physiology in the common schools, apparently
little thought was given to teaching it at the lower levels. So
most of the earlier texts were meant to be used in academies and
colleges. For example, when the Yoakam Vocabulary Formula
was applied to Cutter's popular *Anatomy and Physiology* (1846)
it was found that the vocabulary difficulty placement was at the
14th grade level, and that even Mrs. Cutter's *First Book on
Anatomy, Physiology, and Hygiene* had an 11.7th grade placement.

Not only was physiology a late entry in the curriculum, the
authors were very slow in producing texts for this field in graded
series. In most other subject fields graded series became common
in the 1830's and even earlier. The Cutters were the first to write
physiologies for different levels in the 1850's. In fact, physiology
graded series did not become common until the 1880's, when certain state laws required the evil effects of alcohol and narcotics
to be taught at all levels.

Since so many of the texts were written by medical doctors,
who likely had been trained in medical schools, there was a tend-

ency for a considerable time to make the texts rather technical in treatment, placing the emphasis on the structure of the bodily organs. Even the pictures in the books largely dealt with structure. More than 85 per cent of the pictures in the nineteenth century books related to the alimentary, circulatory, muscular, nervous, respiratory, and skeletal systems. After 1873 many books contained some pictures in color, particularly showing the circulatory and the muscular systems. Only one book contained colored pictures before 1873; namely, Lambert's text in 1851. While the emphasis on the structural features gradually decreased, considerable attention to them continued until after 1900.

The first texts to emphasize the functions and the hygiene of the bodily organs were those by Dalton (1868), and Hutchinson (1870). Thereafter most authors gave these features considerable attention. Foods and their values received increasing attention, as well as prevention and treatment of diseases. After 1900 even public hygiene received attention. The treatment of matters relating to personal hygiene increased from an average of 4 per cent of the space in the texts before 1900 to 11 per cent in those after 1900. The increase in matters of public hygiene was even greater; namely, from an average of 1 per cent to 15 per cent.

Virtually no suggestions for pupil activities entered the texts until after 1850. In the 62 texts before 1900 only 16 suggested observing the characteristics of lower animals, 11 reciting about the charts and plates in the text, 25 reciting about the topical outlines, and 26 answering the questions of the text. Three of these four activities certainly were not very creative. The suggested pupil activities most frequently mentioned in the nineteen texts after 1900 were very different and more thought provoking and creative. Nine suggested reporting on home experiences, 11 on community activities, 11 on habit forming activities, 8 studying microscopic slides, 10 writing on suggested topics, and 11 working on construction work.

Another marked distinction between earlier textbooks and those more recent was the absence of learning and teaching aids. The five most commonly appearing aids in the 62 books before 1900 were tables of contents in 61, prefaces in 59, illustrations in 57, notes in 52, and questions in 50. On the other hand, only 15 included summaries, 22 suggestions for teachers, 23 tables or charts, 23 introductions, 25 appendices, 26 references, and 38 indexes. Thus textbooks in physiology not only greatly improved in content after 1900 but even more so in their teachability.

CHAPTER 10

PENMANSHIP, ART, AND MUSIC

SKILLS AND TASTE

I N the preceding chapters one entire chapter has been devoted to each of the eight subjects most commonly taught in the elementary schools of America before 1900. Since penmanship, art, and music were usually not considered content subjects, and since the latter two were not even commonly taught in the schools before 1900, the three will be treated in the same chapter. All three involve mainly the development of skills and taste.

PART I. PENMANSHIP

Of these three subjects, penmanship has been taught longest. In fact, it was taught with reading in the earliest New England Reading and Writing Schools. However, pupils did not have a textbook from which to learn to write; sometimes they had a Copy-book. Copy-books were either like a bound and lined tablet with covers, or merely a bound tablet with empty lines and printed model script at the top of each page. In some instances the inside page of the cover would contain instructions how to write well. Many local printers throughout the United States very early printed copy books for local sale. The Nietz Collection contains many of these.

As soon as teachers began to give handwriting careful and analytical attention, there began to develop penmanship systems. And handwriting manuals were prepared to guide teachers in more effective penmanship instruction. Throughout the years many such manuals have appeared. Just how many handwriting systems have been developed in the United States is difficult to say. The purpose in this section is to deal with some of the writing systems most popular before 1900.

PENMANSHIP SYSTEMS

The Jenkins' System. Certainly one of the earliest systems was developed by John Jenkins. The Collection has a copy of a handwriting manual by Jenkins entitled *The Art of Writing, Book I,* published in 1813. The text consists of 68 rather large pages. In addition 52 pages are devoted to a long preface and recommendations for use. It is an unusual book to have been written so early in American textbook history. A page of dedication reads as follows:

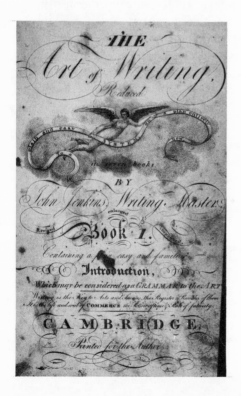

To Gentlemen and Ladies, Instructors of Youth, and to the Young Masters and Misses Throughout the United States, the following New and Easy System of Penmanship is Dedicated.

The Preface states that this work or system had been used by Jenkins since 1781 in ten states of the Union. He bemoans the poor methods of his day, so "To remedy this deficiency, he has, with much

First well-organized manual for *penmanship,* 1813.

study, indefatigable labor, and great expense of time and money, composed the following System." He had already published a simpler and earlier manual in 1791. So the 1813 *Manual* represents his improved System.

Jenkins must have spent considerable time to gather the enormous number of endorsements and recommendations included in the book. By actual count it contained endorsements by 220 persons and recommendations by 109. Among these appeared the names of such famous personages as John Adams, Elbridge Gerry, Manasseh Cutter, Jonathan Edwards, Esq., Benjamin Rush, George Clinton, Benjamin West, Robert Morris, and many others of note. Among them also appeared the names of authors of textbooks in other subject fields, Nicholas Pike, Noah Webster, Chauncey Goodrich, Albert Picket, and Jedidiah Morse. The presidents of Harvard, Yale, and Columbia also endorsed it.

A few words ought to be mentioned regarding some of the comments contained in some of the recommendations. Several mentioned that the other writing masters of that period were Dean, Wrifford, Leonard, Farrar, Towne, and Mills. Dean was mentioned as the author of an *Analytical Guide* (to writing), and Wrifford of a copy book. However, several of the recommenders stated that all of these masters really had taken their systems about writing from Jenkins' 1791 *Manual*.

Jenkins' 1813 book was plainly and interestingly written. He began by presenting the six principal strokes from which all letters, in part or whole, can be made. The strokes were: 1. Direct, 2. in-

Art of Writing, Jenkins, 1813— note systematic instructions.

ART OF WRITING.   15

7. All the stems and body parts of the letters are to be drawn down slanting from right to left, an angle of not more than fifty-five degrees, and the hair strokes after the turns are formed; ascend from left to right, at an angle of about forty-five degrees.

8. *Q.* How is the Art of Writing acquired?

A. By learning to draw and combine six principal strokes.

9. *Q.* Is it needful to know what these strokes are?

A. Yes; for unless we get a perfect idea of each separately we can never write handsomely.

10. *Q.* Why should the principles first be attended to?

A. Because it is much easier to proceed from the single parts to a whole letter than to form a whole letter accurately at once.

11. *Q.* How many principal strokes are there?

A. Six.

12. *Q.* What are they named?

A. 1st, The direct *l.* 2d, The inverted *l,* 3d, the curved *l.* 4th, The *j.* 5th, The *o.* 6th, The stem.

13. *Q.* What is the use of these six strokes?

A. They serve to make twenty-five small letters, and several of the capitals.

14. *Q.* Which of the small letters are made by the help of them?

A. All, except the little *s* and *z.*

15. *Q.* Which are the capitals?

A. The *O, U, Y,* and one kind of *V.*

verted, 3. curved, 4. j, 5. 0, and 6. stem. Then he showed how the different letters can be made from their use. He presented a "Dialogue on Writing." Other sections dealt with the position for sitting to write, directions for holding the pen, exercise of the pen, proportion of the letters, joining the létters, formation of capitals, and use of the pen both wet and dry. Near the end of the book he presented exercises of sentences and verse for writing. A page and a half was devoted to the making of quill pens. Apparently steel pens had not yet been invented. The directions throughout the book were very explicit. From the foregoing it is evident that the first thorough system of handwriting was presented in Jenkins' *The Art of Writing* in 1813.

Old Copy-books. The writer has a number of copy-books which were said to have been used during the 1830's and 1840's. Some have wood-cut pictures on the cover, which indicates their age. In several of them the capitals and even some small letters were strongly shaded. In all of them the letters were slanted.

Geo. J. Becker. On the back cover of Comly's *New Spelling Book* (1842) an entire page was given to an advertisement of Becker's *Writing Books.* The ad stated:

> This Series of Copy Books, consisting of Ten Numbers, recommends itself . . . to the attainment of a clear and elegant style of writing; by the beauty of the designs and the elegance of their execution.

These books were lined with model forms of writing at the top of each page. This ad further stated that a work on *Ornamental Penmanship* was in preparation. Becker was professor of Writing, Drawing, and Bookkeeping in Girard College.

Payson, Dunton, and Scribner. After 1860 more writing manuals appeared. One of these in 1862 was the *Theory and Art of Penmanship* by Payson, Dunton, and Scribner. This had 152 pages of detailed analyses and instructions for better handwriting. In Part I such matters as requisites, difference between script and print, line and angles, positions and movements, elements and principles, scale of lengths, analysis and combination of letters, and drill and counting were discussed. Part II presented lessons and exercises to execute the above matters. Drill was given considerable attention. These authors also published the *National Series of Copy Books*, which consisted of a *School Series*, *Business Series*, *Ladies' Series*, *Primary Tracing Books*, *Primary Short Course*, and the *Pencil Series*.

S. A. Potter. In 1866 appeared his *Penmanship Explained; or the Principles of Writing Reduced to an Exact Science*. It really was a teacher's manual explaining the use of copy-books by Potter and Hammond. In "Hints to Teachers" Potter condemned the use of quill pens, and suggested that the teachers "procure a uniform and suitable pen for the whole class." In discussing the movements while writing, he analyzed the movement of the finger, the forearm, and the whole arm. The finger movement "gives nice touches of beauty," "the fore-arm gives freedom to the style," and the whole arm accomplishes "such strokes with the pen as a skilful painter might make with a brush in tracing a bold sketch." He added that the *"combination* of the *finger* with the *fore-arm* and *whole-arm movement* is adapted to any sized handwriting."

In the latter part of the book nineteen pages are devoted to explaining Potter and Hammond's *Synthetical, Analytical, and Progressive System of Business Penmanship for Public and Private Schools*. These *copy-books* appeared in three series:

Theory and Art of Penmanship, 1862.

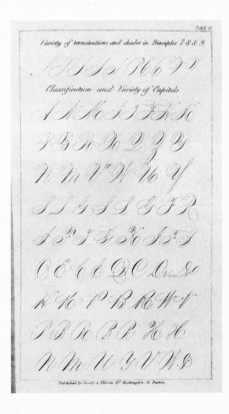

1. The School Series—Nos. 1 to 9 inclusive.
2. The Ladies' Series—Nos. 10 to 12 inclusive.
3. The Mercantile and Ornamental Series—Nos. 13 to 15 inclusive.

The authors also published corresponding Charts.

Other Series of Copy-Books in the 1870's. In the back of Appleton's *Third Reader* of 1877 one publishing company advertised the sale of six different systems of copy-books. 1. Appleton's *Standard Copy-Books* by Lyman D. Smith, four series. 2. Barnes's *National System of Penmanship*, three series. 3. The above mentioned series by Payson, Dunton, Scribner. 4. The *Eclectic Copy-Books*, three series. 5. The Harper's *New Graded Copy-Books* by H. W. Shaylor, three series. 6. *Spencerian Penmanship*, four series. The prices of these various copy-books were listed. Most of these books sold for 72, 75, or 96 cents per dozen.

Spencerian System. The writing system that became most popular during the latter part of the nineteenth century was the *Spencerian System of Penmanship* beginning in 1873. The outside cover of these copy-books contained the names of five Spencers and three others as authors. These books were 8½ inches wide and 7 inches high. The inside of both the front and back covers plus the outside of the back cover contained detailed explanation in fine print of the Spencer system. Seven basic principles were listed, as follows: The first principle was a straight line on the main slant of 52°; the second was a right curve usually on a connective slant of 30°; the third was a left curve, usually on the connective slant; the fourth was a loop upon the main slant; the

Detail chart, *Penmanship*, Potter, 1866.

fifth was a direct oval or capital O; the sixth was a reversed oval upon the main slant; and the seventh was the capital stem. At the top of each page appeared either words or sentences printed in model script. Below this was a heavy red separating line. Parallel blue lines were for the student's writing.

In 1874 a teacher's manual appeared explaining more fully, together with some pictures, the system, which was entitled *Theory of Spencerian Penmanship*. It was a sort of catechism of questions and answers concerning the system. The slant in the Spencerian system was more marked than most earlier systems. Shading was given considerable attention.

Eclectic System. Also in 1873 L. S. Thompson, O. H. Bowler, and N. E. D. Bowler published the *Eclectic System of Penmanship*. Like the Spencerian copy-books, their system was explained and illustrated on the back of the front cover and on the inside of the back cover. It used only blue lines and was not as attractive as the *Spencerian Copy-Books*. The slant was as marked as the Spencerian, and shading was emphasized. The back of the back cover advertised the nine copy-books of the series, the writing-cards, an exercise book, a key, and even Eclectic Pens. It claimed to be the "most easily taught of any system published."

Vertical Script. Until about 1875, nearly universally, all writing systems used the slant, many were 38° from the vertical. At about that time certain French and German medical men discovered numerous cases of spinal curvature and eye trouble among children. They

Theory of Spencerian Penmanship, 1874.

MOVEMENTS.

Remarks.—The venerable PLATT R. SPENCER, originator of the Spencerian System of Writing, said: "Our intention has been to present to the public a system,

"Plain to the eye, and gracefully combined,
To train the muscle and inform the mind."

The training of the muscles of the arm and hand, by appropriate movement exercises, *must* be attended to. For, however distinctly a letter may be pictured in the mind, the execution of it on paper at all times depends on the control the writer may have over the muscles of the arm and hand. The *will* communicates its directing power through the numerous little telegraphic nerves, which descend from the brain—the direct organ of the mind.

In first attempts at writing, the muscles may not properly perform what the mind directs, but by frequent and careful practice they are rendered supple and obedient in the execution of every variety of form.

4. How many different movements may be employed in writing?

Four: Finger Movement, Fore-arm Movement, Combined Movement, and Whole-arm Movement.

FINGER MOVEMENT.

5. Will you assume the writing position, describe the Finger Movement, and make it?

The Finger Movement consists in the action of the first and second fingers and thumb, and is used chiefly in making the upward and downward strokes.

EXAMPLES.

NOTE.—This movement should at first be made with the dry pen, as indicated in the cut; at the same time deliberately naming the strokes: Upward, Down-

blamed the slanted writing systems for these troubles. For example, many who followed the Spencerian system directed the children to sit with the right side toward the desk, the right elbow resting on it, and the left arm hanging from the shoulder, except that the hand rested on the paper. This meant that the right shoulder would be raised higher than the left and the head inclined to the left. This could cause a lateral curvature of the spine in the back and neck. Too, the left eye would be farther from the writing than the right. Unequal accommodation and eye strain could result.

In 1879 the Society of Public Medicine of France recommended certain remedies: (1) The shoulders should parallel the desk while writing; (2) the right elbow should not rest on the desk; (3) the paper should be held with the left hand; and (4) the vertical form of writing should be adopted. Later it was also argued that vertical writing was more legible than the slant. On the other hand, those that favored the slant argued that it could be done with greater ease and rapidity. As a consequence of these

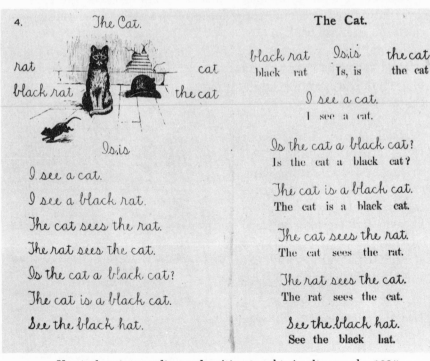

Vertical script, reading and writing taught simultaneously, 1895.

Position illustration number 2. Read page 7 for instructions.

The Palmer Method, 1901.

arguments conflicting systems of writing soon appeared. Also considerable experimentation resulted.

In 1898 Potter and Putnam published *The New Vertical Script Primer*. The earliest lessons were printed in vertical script. Further in the book the lessons were alternately printed script and Roman print. The purpose was to present written letters vertically as were the printed letters. At the turn of the century many schools taught the vertical script.

The Palmer Method. Although in the analysis of textbooks in other subject fields the terminal date has been roughly 1900, here for evident reasons limited treatment will be given past that date. During the confusion concerning the best system of writing A. N. Palmer in 1901 published *The Palmer Method of Business Writing*. This manual had the shape of a copy-book 9 inches wide and nearly 6 inches high, but contained no pages for copy practice. Rather it was a manual of 96 pages, consisting of 146 lessons with writing instructions. On the title page appeared the following statement:

A Series of Self-teaching Lessons in Rapid, Plain, Unshaded, Coarse-pen, Muscular Movement Writing for Use in All Schools, Public or Private, Where an Easy and Legible Handwriting is the Object Sought; Also for the Home Learner.

In the Preface Palmer claimed that his system had "nothing in common with copy-books which have been so largely used in public schools for more than half a century." If they were right, his book was wrong. His aim was not to develop one's skill as a pen artist, but good practical legible writing ability. He opposed fancy shaded writings. He further claimed that the use of copy-books killed individuality and made freedom of movement impossible. His lessons should result in a "handwriting that embodies these four essentials—legibility, rapidity, ease, and endurance." His manual appeared for several decades in many editions after 1901. Palmer was also the editor of the *American Penman*.

More Recent Handwriting Systems. Apparently the confusion regarding the merits of the best system of handwriting continued long after 1900. Many city and state school systems had developed their own handwriting manuals to be followed. In addition many authors and commercial publishing houses continued to produce manuals for particular handwriting systems. It may be in order to mention some of them. In 1912 *The Healey System of Freearm Movement Writing* appeared. Then in 1914 Zaner published the *Short Cut to Plain Writing*. Since then the Zaner-Bloser Company has published a number of handwriting manuals, including several co-authored by Frank N. Freeman. *The Hausam System of Plain Penmanship* was published in 1923. In 1927 Ellen C. Nystrom produced the *Self-Corrective Handwriting Charts*. F. O. Putnam wrote *Helpful Suggestions for Teaching the Practical Handwriting Course* in 1935. Also in 1935 H. M. Hill published the *Handwriting Made Easy* manual. The next year John G. Kirk and F. N. Freeman published a manual on *Functional Handwriting*. The *New Laurel Handwriting* by Almack, Billington,

Staffelbach, and Powers was published in 1937. The same year Lucretia Cavanah and Alonzo Myers wrote a manual for *Handwriting for Expression*. In 1938 *The Rice System of Business Penmanship* appeared. Max Rosenhaus later published several manuals (1938, 1953, 1959). J. A. Savage published a manual for *Manuscript Writing—Print Writing—Made Easy* in 1938. In 1954 Dorothy Emerson published the *Help Yourself to Better Handwriting*.

Several handwriting manuals of a special nature were also published. In 1929 Alonzo Myers and Nellie Slye wrote a manual on *Remedial Handwriting*. In 1938, Luella Cole published the *Cole Diagnostic Exercises in Handwriting* and in 1939 wrote an article on "Instruction in Penmanship for the Left-Handed Child." Then Warren Gardner wrote the *Left Handed Writing Instruction* manual in 1945, and Mildred Plunkett her *Writing Manual for Teaching the Left-handed* in 1954. It can be seen that eventually writing exercises were developed to meet special needs.

In the meantime, surveys, experiments, and studies relating to handwriting have been made. Commonly Thorndike's *Handwriting Scale* (1910) or *Ayres Scale* was used to measure the quality of handwriting. Freeman worked on developing acceptable standards for both quality and speed. Generally the slant was ignored in measuring quality. In other words the slant has not been standardized. In the *Third Yearbook* (1925) of the Department of Superintendence a minimum standard of 50 in quality on the *Ayres Scale* and a speed of 70 letters per minute was recommended.

PART II. ART

Attempts to find expression and communication in visual art were made even by the primitives. So art is as old as mankind, and has been practiced by nearly all peoples throughout history. However, its purposes and forms have differed greatly among the different peoples and times. Among the ancients, the Greeks developed it more highly than any other peoples. Since then the part played by the quality of expressions in art has varied considerably. The purpose here, however, is not to present a history of art, but rather to present the evolution of the use of manuals or textbooks of art in American schools.

The sources of information regarding the beginnings of the teaching of art in American schools seem to be limited. It appears evident that the teaching of art was emphasized in certain schools in the continental countries of Europe before it received much attention in England and the United States. Much of the emphasis in the early teaching of art was on its relation to industry and commerce. Tradesmen were often taught to draw in relation to their work. Hence it was natural that its appearance both in English and American schools would be in industrial centers. Much of England's pioneer work in teaching art related to drawing and design. Exhibitions at the London World's Fair in 1851 revealed clearly how art and science applied to trade and industry. Both Englishmen and Americans were stimulated by these exhibits. Parliament soon took several actions to further the teaching of art in England.

In the United States no concerted action toward the teaching of art was taken very early. However, certain schools and cities did attempt to introduce art. Most of the earliest schools to do so were not regular public schools. For example, in Philadelphia three special schools rather early began to teach certain aspects of art. In 1806 the Philadelphia Academy of Fine Arts introduced instruction in drawing and clay modelling. Beginning in 1824 the Franklin Institute began to teach several types of drawing. In 1847 a School of Design was opened for women. Soon similar special schools for teaching different forms of art were opened in other cities, New York, Baltimore, Boston, Cincinnati, and Pittsburgh.

The first introduction of art in a public school likely was when in 1812 William Fowle, headmaster of a Boston public school, required its study. Soon thereafter he translated for use a French book of drawing geometric figures. In 1827 art was made optional in the English High School in Boston. However, no special teacher of art was appointed in Boston until 1853. Even earlier, Philadelphia appointed a leading artist, Rembrandt Peale, to

supervise graphic art in the public schools in 1842. The Nietz
Collection has a pamphlet, apparently written by Peale entitled
"Graphics, The Art of Accurate Delineation, A Department of
School Exercise, For the Education of the Eye, and the Training
of the Hand, as Auxiliary to Writing, Geography, Geometry
and Drawing." The pamphlet contains a lengthy testimonial enumerating seven values of the teaching of graphics signed by ten
principals and teachers in the Philadelphia schools. It further
quotes Pestalozzi and Horace Mann as favoring the teaching of
art in the schools. Pestalozzi said, "The art of writing, to be
taught consistently with nature, ought to be treated as *subordinate*
to that of drawing. . . . Writing itself is a sort of linear drawing." So he suggested that drawing be taught before writing.

Later agitation in Boston led the legislature of Massachusetts
in 1860 to permit drawing to be listed as an optional school
subject. In 1864 Boston made it a required subject in the upper
grades, and in 1868, in all grades and in the normal school. Then
in 1870 the Massachusetts legislature enacted a law which read
in part:

> Sec. 1. . . . to include Drawing among the branches of learning
> which are by said section required to be taught in the public schools.
> Sec. 2. Any city or town may, and every city and town having more
> than 10,000 inhabitants shall, annually make provision for giving
> free instruction in industrial and mechanical drawing to persons over
> fifteen years of age, either in day or evening schools.

In the same year Walter Smith, a headmaster of an art school in
England, was brought here to become the State Director of Art
in Massachusetts, and to teach art in the Boston Normal School.
He remained here thirteen years.

The Centennial Exposition in Philadelphia in 1876 further
quickened interest among educators through its art exhibits, many
of which had been sent here from European countries. Between
1870 and 1907 drawing was made a required subject by twelve
state legislatures. Many cities and town school systems in thirty-
one other states required it. Many cities published their own
courses of study in art. In some cities it was taught only in the
upper grades and high school.

ART MANUALS AND TEXTBOOKS

Some of the earliest textbooks in what may be termed as art, in a sense at least, were books dealing with certain specialized aspects of art. This likely was true because art was mostly taught at first in specialized schools rather than in general public schools. Hence books appeared dealing with graphics, geometrical figures, perspective, and so on. The lack of including the teaching of art in regular academic schools, until rather recently, certainly did not reflect the place of art among nearly all peoples of all ages. In other words, formal academic curriculums have not always reflected the interests and appreciations of peoples.

Lambert's Hand-book. One of these early specialized books was Miss Lambert's *Hand-book of Needlework* published in 1842. The book contained twenty-two chapters dealing with the different types of needlework. Of course, it dealt with the development of skills involved in the use of the needle in these types of work, yet also much emphasis was given to producing artful needlework. Certain chapters dealt with tapestry, braid, embroidery, canvas work, crochet, knitting, netting, and bead work. The book was attractively printed and contained numerous pictures and designs.

One very interesting feature of the book was that each chapter opened with one or more poetic quotations referring to the use of the needle, usually as an instrument of art. Many of these quotations were written by John Taylor, the water poet. In the 1600's he wrote a book entitled *The Needle's Excellency—A Booke wherein are diuers Admirable Workes Wrought with the Needle.* One extract read:

> Thus is a needle prov'd an instrument Of profit, pleasure, and of ornament, Which mighty queenes have grac'd in hand to take.

Miss Lambert's *Hand-book* ends with a long poem by Taylor. It referred to the needle both as an instrument of utility and of art or ornament. Certain extracts follow:

> A Needle (though it be but small and slender)

Yet it is both a maker and mender:

. . . .

And thus without the needle we may see
We should without our Bibs and Biggins bee;
No shirts or Smockes, our nakedness to hide,
No garments gay, to make us magnifide:
No shadowes, Shapparoones, Caules, Bands, Ruffs, Kuffs,

. . . .

No Table-cloathes, for Parlours or for Halls,

. . . .

Nor any Garment man or woman weares.

. . . .

That as their Daughters Daughters up did grow,
The Needle's Art, they to their children show.

George Childs. One of the earliest drawing books for use in regular schools was Childs' *Drawing Book of Objects: Studies*

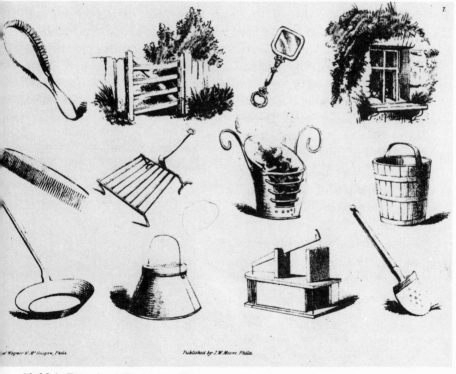

Childs' *Drawing Book of Objects,* 1846, one of the earliest used in schools.

from Still Life. The writer's copy is a third edition published in 1846. Childs was born in Baltimore in 1829 and when fourteen moved to Philadelphia. There he soon became a clerk in a bookstore. After four years he opened a store of his own. In due time, he became a publisher of books. In 1864 he became the owner of the Philadelphia *Public Ledger.* He later contributed liberally to benevolent causes.

This book contained 23 pages 10½ inches wide and 7 inches high each with pictures of twelve rather common objects. Thus it contained 276 pictures of objects as models for drawing, and also apparently for coloring; for many pictures in the writer's copy have been colored. The first page had pictures of a key, scissors, cap, teapot, compass, spoon, kettle, etc. The title page stated the book to be "for young pupils and drawing classes in schools." No directions or instructions were given for drawing. The book contained only the pictures of objects.

J. G. Chapman. One of the first, if not the first, real drawing manual to include instructions was *The American Drawing-Book* by Chapman in 1847. The title page stated it to be "A manual for the Amateur, and basis of study for the professional artist: especially adapted to the use of public and private schools, as well as home instruction." It consisted of 168 large pages 12 inches high and 9 inches wide. It contained 12 testimonials from "gentlemen distinguished in the Fine Arts, Literature, and the promotion of Education." One was written by Samuel F. B. Morse.

The Introduction began by saying, "Anyone who can learn to write can learn to draw and, as writing is not

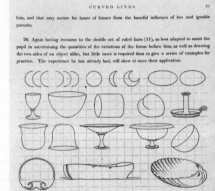

Chapman, *American Drawing-Book,* 1847—the circular movement.

taught to those only who are destined to become authors, . . . so is drawing equally important to others besides professional artists." He then presented careful instruction for the development of drawing skills: first, only straight lines, then simple designs made by straight lines, and next rather complicated designs of straight lines. On page 19 exercises began involving curved lines, resulting in the construction of artistic designs. Chapter II dealt with rudiments of drawing the human head. The chapter ended with a drawn head of George Washington in curved lines. Then Chapter III dealt with the rudiments of drawing the human figure. Other chapters dealt with the elements of geometry, perspective, and the "art of writing in connexion with drawing." One gets the impression that this manual was more to develop technical skills in drawing rather than to develop an appreciation of art. Nevertheless it was a pioneer school drawing text.

Mayo and Sheldon. In 1863 E. A. Sheldon published a 407 page book entitled *Lessons on Objects.* This was a revised and rearranged edition of a book which was first written in England by Elizabeth Mayo, a Pestalozzian devotee, in 1831. Actually it was mostly a methods and nature study book, but it contained certain elements that were related to art. In fact, the first chapter was entitled, "Hints on Sketch Writing." This book helped spread the so-called Oswego Movement in American education. The development of drawing as a school subject became closely related to that movement, for many drawing books soon appeared on the market.

W. N. Bartholomew. One of the first graded series in drawing was written by Bartholomew in the late 1860's. This series contained four books, accompanied by a *Teacher's Guide* for each. The *Guide to Drawing, Book No. 4* appeared in 1870. In the Introductory Remarks Bartholomew criticized learning to draw by copying pictures. Thus the drawing produced, he said, became an end, not a means to an end. He held drawing to be a language, and thus to be learned, step by step. "The eye should first be disciplined to see, the mind to recognize, and the hand to draw,

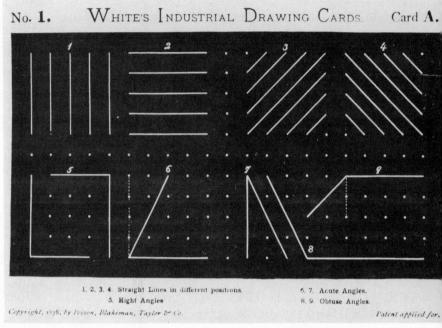

1, 2, 3, 4. Straight Lines in different positions.   6, 7. Acute Angles.
5. Right Angles   8, 9. Obtuse Angles.

Copyright, 1878, by Ivison, Blakeman, Taylor & Co.   Patent applied for.

Dictation Lessons in Drawing was accompanied by the *Drawing Cards,* 1878.

lines of any length, in any required position, and bearing any given relation to each other." This was only the first step.

Each *Guide* contained specific directions for teaching twelve lessons. These lessons were rather long and detailed. Evidently more than one day would be devoted to a lesson. He recommended that the teacher always should use the blackboard. Each movement or step should be illustrated and thoroughly directed and explained. These books appeared in several editions.

S. F. Buckelew and C. A. Halstead. In 1878 the Misses Buckelew and Halstead published the *Dictation Lessons in Drawing* for use in the primary grades to accompany White's *Primary School Drawing Cards.* This is a manual of 92 pages giving detailed directions for teaching drawing in six grades. The numbering of the grades was in reverse order; namely, the beginning work was to be given in the Sixth Grade (actually First Grade), and the most advanced work in the latter part of the book in the First

Grade (Sixth Grade). Such reverse numbering of grades was common in some European schools. The first nine pages were devoted to general directions and definitions of the different kinds of lines, rectilinear figures, and curvilinear figures.

The steps suggested were first, draw the guide lines; second, sketch the design very lightly; and third, erase all mistakes and untidy marks. Reproduced plates of twenty-four of White's *Industrial Drawing Cards* appeared with the directions for the various lessons or exercises in the book. Although some of the plates represent such concrete objects as houses and barns, they are shown only in two dimensional form. Nevertheless, this book appeared in several editions.

The Prang Art Textbooks. In 1886 the Prang Educational Company published *The Use of Models* by Mary D. Hicks and John S. Clark. Evidently Prang engaged these writers to prepare it. Its sub-title was "A Teacher's Assistant in the use of the Prang Models for Form Study and Drawing in Primary Schools." They claimed this to be the first work of its kind. Its claim was based on "a course of exercises in Form Study and Drawing which has in view mental development through the combined use of the hand and the eye." It was true that most previous art books aimed largely at the development of skills only, but this system aimed at mental development as well. Very early in the book the exercises involved three dimensional drawing. It contained 183 attractive pages of directions, exercises, and picture models. In the back, 14 pages were devoted to listing and describing Prang's art materials available for school use. The 1887 edition of this manual already listed 64 cities using the Prang Method.

Prang, *The Use of Models,* 1887.

L'ENVOI.   181

Miss Lucy Fitch, whose delightful drawings have done so much to make this work interesting, offers this closing sketch as an illustration of how children, accustomed to express their thoughts by making, by drawing, by reading, and by writing, may be expected to use these aquirements.

It is hardly necessary to say that these children can READ, can WRITE, can MAKE, can DRAW.

In 1888 the *Teacher's Manual for Prang's Shorter Course in Form Study and Drawing* was published. It was prepared by the above two authors and Walter S. Perry. This *Manual* presented "not Form Study alone, not Drawing alone, but Form Study and Drawing as complementing each other." Its work and exercises were presented in Books I, II, III, IV, and V. The exercises involved a wide range of objects and interesting subjects, ending in an introduction to manual training.

In 1893 *The Prang Primary Course in Art Education* by Mary D. Hicks and Josephine C. Locke was published. It represented a further development of the previous two manuals. It added to the use of Form Study and Drawing the use of Color. Lessons for thirty-six weeks of work were concretely presented for each year. Even a casual examination of these books will impress one that the Prang art manuals were the best to appear up to that time.

Jacobs and Brower. In 1887 a *Hand-Book to Accompany the Graphic System of Object Drawing* by Hobart B. Jacobs and Augusta L. Brower was published. This was a rather small and unattractive book of 59 pages. It included only two pictures. It primarily aimed only to help the student to develop skills in graphic drawing. It evidently failed to gain wide usage.

Art Books after 1900. Although the primary purpose of this book has been to discuss only those old textbooks that were published before 1900, yet in several chapters brief treatment has been given to certain textbook developments after that date. So only a few art books after 1900 will be mentioned.

Among the first art books to appear after 1900 were the *Text Books of Art Education* published by the Prang Company. Book V was written in 1904 by Hugo B. Froehlich and Bonnie E. Snow. Mention was made that these books were planned in a series of conferences and consultations with leading educators and teachers of art, so they would reflect not only the latest ideas about art education, but also that the educational principles involved would accord with the latest accepted psychological laws of child development. The lessons in the books were divided into three groups to be known as The "Observational or Objective

Group, in which the study of things is the aim; the Subjective Group, in which the study of principles or laws of beauty is the aim; and the Creative Group, in which the application of accumulative knowledge and ability is the aim." In the primary grades the work was largely objective. In the intermediate grades the children were introduced to principles involving balance, rhythm, and harmony. Book V explained the subjective and creative aspects. The first topic was "Selecting a Picture," such as views from a car window, from a window at home, and so on. Many of the model pictures in this book were in beautiful colors. These Books show great developmental progress in the teaching of art since Child's *Drawing Book* of the 1840's.

In 1809 Fred H. Daniels published the *School Drawing, A Real Correlation*. It contained example pictures relating to history, literature, geography, animal life, the seasons, and city and country life, accompanied by explanations and descriptions of the pictures. Certainly it could have been of no more value than as a supplementary drawing book.

In 1929 Bridgman's *Handbook of Drawing* appeared. He was both the author and publisher of this and other books and materials related to art. He also published art books and materials written by other authors. The particular purpose of his *Handbook* was to make drawing appeal to children. This was in harmony with the growing Dewey philosophy of Progressive Education. He further mentioned that the "way to interest a child in anything is by telling a story, drawing therefore is only a medium employed. The first thing to do is to create interest." The *Handbook* then consisted of 62 pages of curiously interesting pictures with comments explaining their meanings and suggested drawing activities. In the back of the book a long list of Bridgman art educational books were advertised for sale.

CONCLUDING COMMENTS

From the foregoing presentation it can be seen that art had great difficulty in gaining admission to the common school curriculum. It was taught in specialized schools long before it was admitted to public schools. Thus most of the earliest books dealing with art were of a specialized or technical nature; for example, books dealing with graphics, perspective, and needlework.

Eventually when art textbooks for public schools began to appear, they were very different from the art books of today. One of the first was by Childs, and consisted merely of pictures to be copied or drawn. Chapman's manual was one of the first to include instructions for drawing. In the 1860's Bartholomew developed a graded series of drawing books. However, they dealt only with two dimensional drawing. In the late 1880's the Prang Company employed a number of art teachers to help develop a more advanced system of art teaching, which aimed at the development of the mind as well as of skills. The later Prang manuals included the use of color and original child activities. In 1926 Bridgman based his system considerably on the interests of children. Thus there was a gradual and progressive development in the teaching of art which is reflected in the textbooks dealing with art.

PART III. MUSIC

Music in some form or other is about as old as mankind. Even the primitives made much of music; sometimes they would sing when they worked. Since primitive times music has gone through numerous developmental changes. It is, however, beyond the scope of this chapter to give an extensive history of music.

In general, the earliest most extensive use of music was related to religious exercises or worship. The primitives used both vocal and crude instrumental music in connection with religious rites. Often these rites would also contain some tribal and patriotic significance. With the development of civilization the forms and instruments of music changed, but the purposes largely continued to be either religious or national or a combination of both. In the Western World both Catholics and Protestants have made wide use of music in churches. Likewise, with the development of nationalism, music has been used for patriotic, military, and political purposes.

Early New England settlers brought psalm singing with them. The *Bay Psalm Book* (1640) became one of America's earliest printed books. Later, when hymn writers, such as Charles Weslay and Isaac Watts, multiplied the availability of good hymns, an even wider use of music in churches became common. But how and where would the people learn to follow the tunes properly? In many European churches choir boys would be taught how to sing. But in early American churches this was not so common. Hence the development of good church music was slow here.

One development in America helped to remedy this weakness. Beginning about 1720 singing-schools sprang up. Two early music instruction books made their appearance for use in such schools. One was by Reverend John Tufts in 1721, and another by Reverend Thomas Walter also in 1721. The latter book was one of the first to contain printed music. These books thus provided the tool for teaching music. As a consequence, singing-schools soon spread throughout the colonies. At first apparently mainly only religious songs were taught, but later these schools served wider purposes, such as social and patriotic.

Other music books soon made their appearance. Among them were some using a very different musical notation. One type used shaped or buckwheat notes. This type was presented in *The Easy Instructor* by William Little and William Smith, written in 1798 and later appearing in many editions. The notes were shaped in triangles, squares, rounds, and diamonds, representing the musical syllables of fa, sol, la, and mi. A number of song books using these notes appeared during the nineteenth century. However, by the time music was introduced in the public schools, the European type of musical notation became common. Nevertheless singing-schools using the two types of musical notation continued for some time. The singing-school was nearly the sole means of musical instruction in a popular sense until music began to be taught in the public schools.

BEGINNINGS OF PUBLIC SCHOOL MUSIC

The introduction of music in the public schools was largely due to the efforts of Lowell Mason (1792-1872), who has often been called the "father of public school music in the United States." He was born and reared in Massachusetts, taught district schools there, taught music and conducted choirs and singing societies in

Georgia, returned north to help organize the Boston Academy of Music, and went to Switzerland to study Pestalozzianism and Swiss and German schoolbooks containing music and songs.

On his return he directed his efforts to expanding the opportunities for learning music. After failing at first to induce Boston to include music in the public schools, he organized classes for children on Wednesday and Saturday afternoons. Hundreds attended these classes, resulting in the presentation of juvenile concerts. In the meantime he also wrote the *Juvenile Psalmist*, (1829), a music book for Sunday schools, and later the *American Tune Book* for choirs and singing societies. In 1834 he wrote Mason's *Manual of Instruction*, the first formulation of modern principles of teaching music in the United States.

In 1837 Boston adopted a resolution "to try the experiment of introducing vocal music, . . . in the public schools of the city." Music was introduced at first only in the Hawes School. Its success led the School Committee to contract a teacher of vocal music for all the schools in 1838. This action has been referred to as "The Magna Charta of musical education in this country." Mason was placed in full charge of the music in the Boston schools, including the music training program in the normal school.

Although a few individual schools, where the principal favored the teaching of music, had introduced music before 1838, the real spread of teaching music in public schools came after that date. Soon some other cities followed Boston in teaching music in their schools: Buffalo, 1843; Pittsburgh, 1844; Cincinnati, 1845; Chicago, 1848; Cleveland, 1851; San Francisco, 1851; and St. Louis, 1852. The U.S. Commissioner of Education, John Eaton, reported in 1886 that less than 250 school systems were regularly teaching music. Thus the spread of teaching music was not universal, especially not in the rural schools, but its popularity was increasing.

THE AIMS AND CONTENT OF MUSIC BOOKS

In 1954 Walter Jones[1] made an analysis of 96 public school

---

[1] Walter R. Jones, "An Analysis of Public School Music Textbooks Before 1900." (Unpublished doctor's dissertation, University of Pittsburgh, 1954.)

music books published in the United States before 1900. The data presented in this section are largely based on his findings.

Music Aims. The three most frequently mentioned aims for teaching music were to teach the rudiments of music, serve religious purposes, and provide pleasure. The first aim was mentioned in 58 books, the second in 38, and the third in 29. The percentage of books mentioning the development of music skills in the different decades remained rather constant, but those mentioning religion declined after 1870. Other aims were less frequently mentioned.

Content of Music Textbooks. Since the books varied greatly both in regard to the size of the pages as well as in the number of pages, it was thought best to determine the content of them in terms of the number of songs dealing with the different content themes. So the number of songs were counted in each book, and then the percentage relating to the different themes determined. The findings by decades are presented in Table IX.

Little and Smith, *The Easy Instructor,* 1798—note the "buckwheat" note system.

TABLE IX

AVERAGE PERCENTAGE DISTRIBUTION OF SONG CONTENT
of MUSIC TEXTBOOKS PUBLISHED BEFORE 1900 BY DECADES.

Decades	Number of Books	Average Percentage of Song Content by Decades												
		1 Religious	2 Moral	3 Nature	4 Patriotic	5 Seasonal	6 School	7 Home	8 Occupational	9 Baby and Childhood	10 Sports	11 Lament	12 Friendship	13 Miscellaneous
1830–1839	3	16.3	8.3	43.7	4.1	12.4	4.9	3.7	3.4	2.0	1.7			3.2
1840–1849	11	24.0	21.7	18.1	9.2	7.8	3.0	3.0	4.5	1.5	.2	.6	.5	7.7
1850–1859	16	18.9	12.5	24.0	6.5	7.5	10.4	4.6	4.4	1.1	.5	.7	.8	7.1
1860–1869	11	22.8	10.0	22.7	15.0	4.9	4.8	5.7	4.4	.7	1.6	.8	1.3	5.6
1870–1879	14	24.9	17.2	20.3	4.4	8.7	5.0	5.2	4.0	2.1	1.8	.6	.7	4.9
1880–1889	22	33.7	10.4	20.1	4.9	7.8	5.8	3.2	5.9	2.6	1.0	.4	.3	7.5
1890–1899	19	17.7	7.9	27.5	6.9	13.2	5.7	2.8	4.4	3.6	2.1	.8	.3	6.6
Average		22.9	8.0	25.2	7.3	8.9	4.4	4.0	4.4	1.9	1.2	.6	.6	6.1

It can be seen that although the religious aim was not mentioned in the prefaces very often after 1870, yet the percentage of religious songs was still very high in the 1880's, but dropped in the 1890's. When the religious and moral songs were added together for the entire period, nearly one-third of all songs were of this nature. The next highest frequency, one-fourth of the songs, dealt with such things of nature as birds, animals, trees, and so on. When the songs related to the seasons are added to those of nature, they represent more than one-third. Of the other themes, only the patriotic songs represented as much as seven per cent. Nevertheless, it can be seen that the themes of the songs dealt with many thoughts and sentiments.

MUSIC TEXTBOOKS

The Nietz Collection contains many very old song books, five with buckwheat notes, including a copy of *The Easy Instructor* by Little and Smith, which began that system. Most of these apparently were not intended for public school use. Some were plainly hymn books with no notes included, and others with notes intended for use in singing-schools as well as churches. So it is very difficult to say which one was first used in the common schools. Probably the safest approach on this matter is to depend upon the statements in the books themselves regarding their intended use.

Augustus Peabody. The Child's Song Book for "the use of Schools and Families" edited and compiled by Peabody was published in Boston in 1830. In the preface it was stated that the "leading object in compiling this little book has been to aid Teachers of Infant Schools." The songs were mostly in one-part music. The songs were such as to appeal to children. Just how widely this book was used is now uncertain, since the teachng of music in public schools had not started.

Lowell Mason. The second school music textbook was written by Lowell Mason, who previously had written music books for religious use. This one was the *Juvenile Lyre*, which was submitted

THE

CHILD'S SONG BOOK,

FOR THE USE OF

SCHOOLS AND FAMILIES;

BEING A SELECTION OF

FAVOURITE AIRS,

WITH

HYMNS AND MORAL SONGS,

SUITABLE FOR

INFANT INSTRUCTION.

Augustus Peabody Esq Editor Hampshire

" We will our little voices raise,
" To sing our Father's love ;
" And bow in pure and fervent praise,
" To him who rules above."

Boston :

PUBLISHED BY RICHARDSON, LORD & HOLBROOK.

No. 133, Washington Street.

1830.

Child's Song Book, first music book published in U.S. for juvenile use.

for copyright in 1831, but published in 1832. It was intended for "use in primary and common schools." A third music textbook, *The Juvenile Singing School*, was also written by Mason. It was published in 1839, which was one year after Boston introduced music in the public schools. Evidently this book was intended for Boston use.

Later Mason wrote numerous other music textbooks. Among them were: *Boston School Song Book* (1843) ; *Song-Book of the School-Room* (1847) ; *The Singing School* (1854) ; and the *Normal Singer* (1856). Several of these books continued to be republished even after his death. E. Ives assisted in writing the *Juvenile Lyre*, and G. J. Webb the *Song-Book of the School-Room*. The later books included mostly songs in four parts.

Mason held that the three chief reasons for teaching music were (1) to promote devotional feeling; (2) to promote health; and (3) to improve the heart. He always believed that many more can learn to sing than do. From all the foregoing data it is clearly evident that Mason exerted greater influence on the beginnings and later development of the teaching of music in the public schools than any other author.

Asa Fitz. In the early 1840's Fitz wrote *The American School Song Book*. It opened with seven pages of fine print dealing with the elements of music. Most of the songs were in two part music. Since it was for young children, it omitted the bass notes. It was bound with limp paper covers.

William B. Bradbury. After Lowell Mason the next early important writer of music textbooks was Bradbury. In 1842 he with Charles W. Sanders wrote *The Young Choir*. Then in 1852 he alone wrote *Musical Gems for School and Home*. The first 37 pages dealt in detail with the elements of music. Thus the book was more technical than some of the other music textbooks then extant. Songs in two part, three part, and four part music were included. The last 22 pages presented a selection of metrical tunes and other sacred pieces. It was intended to be "a complete musical manual for teachers and students." He also wrote *The Key-Note*

JUVENILE LYRE:

OR

HYMNS AND SONGS,

RELIGIOUS, MORAL, AND CHEERFUL,

SET TO APPROPRIATE MUSIC.

FOR THE USE OF PRIMARY AND COMMON SCHOOLS

by
Lowell Mason

BOSTON:
RICHARDSON, LORD AND HOLBROOK.
HARTFORD:
H. & F. J. HUNTINGTON.

1832.

Lowell Mason, "for use of primary and common schools," 1832.

(1863) for churches and singing-schools, and *The Victory* for miscellaneous purposes.

I. B. Woodbury. In 1847 Woodbury published the *Youth's Song Book.* This book was for "schools, classes, and the social circle." It devoted eight pages to the elements of music. An examination of this book reveals that it was better adapted to singing societies than for common schools. He earlier had written other books on music, such as the *Choral,* and *New England Glee Book;* and later *The Dulcimer, Lute of Zion, Liber Musicus,* and *The Cythara.* The latter was a comprehensive work.

Song Books in the 1850's. In 1852 J. W. Greene published his *School Melodies.* This was a small but rather appealing song book written expressly for the use in schools. It was much less technical than most other song books of that period. The first selection was "The Scholars' Pledge." It began as follows: "Never the *Drunkard's* drink Our lips shall stain; Ne'er shall the *Swearer's* words Our tongues profane." The second selection was "Fair

THE

SONG-BOOK OF THE SCHOOL-ROOM:

CONSISTING OF A GREAT VARIETY OF

SONGS, HYMNS,

AND SCRIPTURAL SELECTIONS WITH APPROPRIATE MUSIC,

ARRANGED TO BE SUNG IN ONE, TWO, OR THREE PARTS:

CONTAINING, ALSO,

THE ELEMENTARY PRINCIPLES OF VOCAL MUSIC,

PREPARED WITH REFERENCE TO THE INDUCTIVE, OR PESTALOZZIAN
METHOD OF TEACHING: DESIGNED AS A COMPLETE MUSIC
MANUAL FOR COMMON, OR GRAMMAR SCHOOLS.

BY LOWELL MASON & GEORGE JAMES WEBB.

BOSTON:

WILKINS, CARTER, & CO.

1847.

Song-Book of the School-Room, 1847, Mason and Webb—one of the most popular.

Freedom" to be sung to the tune of "Cheer up, my lively lads."

Also in 1852 Joseph and Horace Bird published their *Singing School Companion*. This, like many other similar music books during that period, was not written primarily for common schools. In fact, the title page stated that it was designed for "singing and common schools, social assemblies, choir practice, and for religious worship." It was a rather large and difficult book. So likely its use in the public schools was limited.

In 1855 E. H. Bascom wrote *The School Harp*. This was an attractive book. The author stated that "a large proportion of the Songs in this Work are original, and have been expressly written for it." Thus the songs were rather simple and no doubt appealed to children. The first selections in it were entitled: "Morning Hymn," "Little Things," "Hope On, Hope Ever," "Diligence," and "We'll Study On." It contained one-, two-, three-, and four-part songs.

Other authors who wrote song books during the 1850's were Edward Chester, George Root, Schuyler Clark, Elias Mason, William Tarbutton, A. S. Cleaveland, L. O. Emerson, and T. Bissell. Later editions by previously mentioned authors also were published.

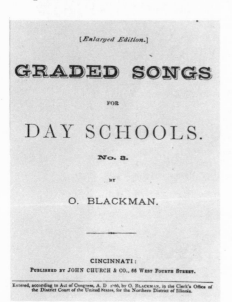

[*Enlarged Edition.*]

GRADED SONGS

FOR

DAY SCHOOLS.

No. 3.

BY

O. BLACKMAN.

CINCINNATI:
PUBLISHED BY JOHN CHURCH & CO., 66 WEST FOURTH STREET.

Entered, according to Act of Congress, A. D. 1866, by O. BLACKMAN, in the Clerk's Office of the District Court of the United States, for the Northern District of Illinois.

Song Books in the 1860's. As in the 1850's, a number of school song books were published in the 1860's. Among them were books by John Bower, W. O. and H. S. Perkins, Horace Waters, J. W. Dodum, Charles Butler, O. B. Brown, and O. Blackman.

Up to this time most of the music books were adapted primarily for the upper grades and high school, and the books

One of the earliest graded song-books, 1866.

were not prepared in series. However, O. Blackman in the 1860's prepared a series of *Graded Songs for Day Schools*. The prices were: No. 1, 10 cents; No. 2, 15 cents; No. 3, 25 cents; No. 4, 50 cents. The fact that these were prepared in graded series is evidence that he was conscious of the varying ability of children to learn music according to their ages and interests. Even in No. 3 the songs were only in one-part and two-part music. It will be seen that these books were the forerunners of the song books of the next decade, when grading and method would receive marked attention.

Luther W. Mason (1821-1896). Luther Mason, who belonged to a distant branch of the family of Lowell Mason, and who studied under him, made nearly as great a contribution to public school music as did Lowell. In 1864, after building up a musical reputation in Kentucky and Ohio, he was called to Boston to organize the instruction in music for the primary grades. Before this little had been done in the primary level.

In 1870 he wrote the *Primary or First Music Reader*, and the *Second Music Reader*. In 1871 the *Third Music Reader* was published. At times these books were referred to as constituting *The National Music Course*. He also prepared *National Music Charts* to precede the *Readers*, and *The National Music Teacher*, as a practical guide in teaching vocal music and sight-singing to "even the youngest pupils." The historian of public school music, Birge,[2] referred to him as the "founder of school music methodology," and added that the *National Music Course* was the first planned music course to receive national recognition. Too, these books were translated into German for use in Europe. Even Japan borrowed its methods for use there.

The *First* book was planned to review and then follow the *Charts*. Thus the work in the first part of the *First* book was presented for the fourth time as follows: (1) Chiefly by rote, (2) step by step from the blackboard, (3) practiced daily from the charts, and (4) from the book. All the songs in it were in one-part music.

2 Edward B. Birge, *History of Public School Music in the United States*. Boston: Oliver Ditson Company, 1928.

In the *Second Music Reader* two-part music was introduced. Mason claimed that most people do some singing, in Sunday School, church, or elsewhere, but most of it was haphazard singing. The purpose of this course was to start with a regular course of instruction in rote singing. In this the pupils were expected to be aided by their knowledge of the notes, so as to learn two-part singing by sight. This book was followed by the *Third Music Reader*, in which three-part singing was introduced, "as based upon the Triads of the Major and Minor Scales."

In 1886 Mason prepared *The New Third Music Reader*. It was much larger than the earlier *Third*. This revised edition was based largely upon a system developed by C. H. Hohmann, "showing the harmonic relation of sounds." Too, it contained fewer three-part songs than the earlier edition. All of Luther Mason's music readers were published in numerous editions, particularly after they became known as the *National Music Course*.

George B. Loomis. When he began to teach music in the Indianapolis schools in 1866 few suitable books were available, so he began to prepare a series of music books in 1870. The first one was the *First Steps in Music*. In 1875 he revised it with the title, *First Book of Progressive Music Lessons*. It was a carefully graded book intended for the beginning of music instruction in the lower grades. Only one-part singing was used.

Soon the series included five books. In all, the series aimed to guide in the teaching of music from its first principles to "full chorus and glee singing." The advance in part singing was not as rapid as in Mason's *National* series. For example, the *Third Book* did not include any three-part music. However, the *Fourth Book* introduced three-part songs in the latter half of the book. The prices of the books were as follows: No. 1, 18 cents; No. 2, 20 cents; No. 3, 30 cents; No. 4, 55 cents; and No. 5, $1.00. These books gained a wide circulation in the midwest, where they were originally published.

H. R. Palmer. In 1871 *The Song King* by H. R. Palmer was published. It was intended for singing classes, day schools, conventions, etc. This was a rather advanced book, which, if at all used in public schools, must have been used only in the upper grades. In 1891 he published the *Graded Series* "in the Art of Reading Music at Sight." It included lessons presented in sections entitled Junior Grade, Senior Grade, Day School and Institute Department, Temperance Department, and Miscellaneous. In addition he wrote many other music books for Sunday schools, churches, institutes, conventions, glee clubs, and singing classes.

Other Music Books in the 1870's. The 1870's constituted a fruitful decade for the publication of school music books. In addition to the books by Mason, Loomis, and Palmer, a number of others first were published then.

In 1873 N. Coe Stewart wrote the *Merry Voices*. This book, like many other music books, was intended for multiple use in schools, seminaries, and juvenile classes. It began with theory, definitions, and signs, followed by sight exercises, and songs involving one-, two-, three-, and four-part singing. It certainly was not well adapted for the lower grades.

The New Favorite by W. T. Giffe was published in 1875. Although day schools were also mentioned for its use, it was primarily suited for use in "singing schools, conventions, choirs, musical societies, and musical academies." It contained "musical notation, exercises, glees, solos, duets, trios, quartets, hymn tunes, anthems, choruses, etc."

Music books were also written by H. S. Perkins, N. C. Burnap and W. J. Wetmore, J. C. Bechel, George F. Root, and Hottie S. Russell.

Music Books during the 1880's. Apparently no important series of music books was first written in the 1880's, although later editions and revisions of the popular books by Mason and Loomis continued to appear. One of the first to appear in that decade was the *National Kindergarten Songs and Plays* by Mrs. Louise Pollock in 1880. All except 20 pages consisted of songs presumed to be suitable for kindergarten children. Mrs. Pollock was the principal of the Kindergarten Normal Institute in Washington, D.C. No attempt was made in the book to teach the elements of music. The method of teaching music by ear was suggested.

In 1883 *The Normal Music Course* by John W. Tufts and

H. E. Holt was published. This book was to supplement the *Charts* by the same authors. The *First Reader* was divided into three parts: (1) exercises and short songs, (2) introduction of two part music and longer songs, and (3) a few rote songs to which "pianoforte accompaniment" was added. Interesting pictures appeared beside many of the songs. For example, a picture of sheep appeared with the song of "Little Bo-Peep." Many of the songs related to things of nature, such as birds, animals, and flowers. The *Normal Course* appeared in numerous editions and revisions.

Also in 1883 (C. E.) Leslie's *Challenge* appeared. No claim for public school use was made by this book, yet the nature of the earlier songs in it appeared suitable for children. Many related to nature. Later he wrote the *New Silver Carols* (co-authored with W. A. Ogden) in 1884, *The Cyclone of Song* in 1888, and *The Ensign* in 1897.

In 1886 *The Royal Proclamation*, "Hear the Royal Proclamation, Do, Ray, Mi, Sol, La, Si, Do," by Aldine S. Kieffer and William B. Blake was published. The book opened with twelve pages of Theoretical Statements prepared by B. C. Unseld, Principal Virginia Normal Music School. Throughout the book shaped or "buckwheat" notes were used. Likely its chief use was in singing schools rather than public schools.

In 1887 James R. Murray's *Dainty Songs for Little Lads and Lassies* was published. The first selection was entitled "Dainty Songs." Its first verse was:

> Dainty songs for little lads,
> Dainty songs for lasses;
> Sing them with the happy birds,
> 'Mid the flow'rs and grasses.

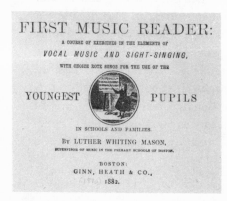

A first music reader.

The next five selections were: "Sweet Little Bird," "Storm and Sunshine," "In the Snowing," "Happy Children," and "Room at the Top." While the titles of most songs were appealing, the music was nearly all in three and four parts. It contained 155 pages.

Music Textbooks during the 1890's. In 1894 Frank Damrosch's *Popular Method of Sight Singing* appeared. The place for its intended use was not made clear. It appeared too technical for very young children, yet its lessons were developed step by step. Fewer than half of the selections or exercises included words. Apparently they were to be sung by note. It may well have been used as a supplementary music book.

In 1895 Samuel W. Cole prepared *The Child's First Studies in Music*. This was a very attractive and well bound book with a light blue cover. It did not begin with technical lessons. The teacher was instructed to teach the children these songs by a suggested procedure. The first song was "Come, Little Children, and Sing." All the songs appeared to be appealing to children. The same author had also prepared a series of twenty charts for supplementary use.

Also in 1895 J. D. Luse began a graded series of *The Wreath Music Course*. In that year *The Juvenile Wreath* was published. It contained 144 pages of one and two part songs for primary children, with a course of rudiments suited to the lower grades. In 1896 *The Ideal Wreath* appeared as a second book. It was for the grammar grades and ungraded schools. It contained one-, two-, three-, and four-part songs, with a more thorough treatment of the rudiments. Later *The Royal Wreath* for high schools, and in 1899 *The Imperial Wreath* for more advanced groups, appeared. These were published by the author himself.

In 1896 B. C. Unseld's *The Choral Standard* was published. It claimed to comprise "a Complete Course of Instruction and a Graded Collection of Music for Singing Schools, Day Schools, Choirs and Conventions." The same year he, together with J. H. Fillmore, published the *School Singer*. It consisted of a graded course of exercises for sight singing and a choice collection of songs. Most of the songs were in four-part music.

School song books were also written in the 1890's by M. M. Appleberry, D. Wilson, Harry Deems, J. F. Kinsey, Emma Thomas, John H. Haaren and W. Mattfield, and Lydie A. Coonley. Then, too, later editions by Showalter, Tufts and Holt, Mason, Roberts, and Perkins appeared in that decade.

After 1900. The writer has made no careful attempt to deal with the textbooks published after 1900, yet he does have music books of *The New Educational Music Course* (1905) by James M. McLaughlin and W. W. Gilchrist; the *Laurel Songs* (1914) by M. Teresa Armitage; and *The Progressive Music Series* (1915) by Parker, McConathy, Birge, and Miessner.

Concluding Comments. It is clear that music was a tardy entrant in the American public school curriculum. However, singing schools, apparently mostly taught in the evenings, began to develop in the later colonial period and continued to thrive for more than a century. Thus adults rather than children were the first to be taught music in America.

The first city formally to provide for the teaching of music in the public schools was Boston, in 1838. This was done largely through the efforts of Lowell Mason, the father of public school music in the United States. He was the author of many music books for various purposes.

Most earlier music books were adapted chiefly for the upper grades and the secondary schools. Then in the late 1860's and 1870's graded series of music textbooks appeared. The person who wrote the first well-recognized series was Luther Mason. Other rather popular series before 1900 were written by Loomis, Tufts and Holt, and Luse.

Today most public schools teach not only vocal music, but also many types of instrumental music. Most large high schools sponsor bands, orchestras, and glee clubs. Hence the greatest development of music in the public schools has really been since 1900.

INDEX

Since the exact titles of most old textbooks are very long, only the general title of the subject field concerned (e.g. arithmetic) will be used whenever a title reference is made.

357